ENDURE AND CONQUER

endure and conquer

dr. sam sheppard

THE WORLD PUBLISHING COMPANY
CLEVELAND AND NEW YORK

Published by The World Publishing Company
2231 West 110th Street, Cleveland, Ohio 44102

Published simultaneously in Canada by
Nelson, Foster & Scott Ltd.

Library of Congress Catalog Card Number: 66-29489

First Edition

Printed in the United States of America

ACKNOWLEDGMENTS

More years ago than I care to remember, one of my many loyal supporters, the late Mrs. Dorkas Wright, bequeathed to me a handsome gold ring with an onyx setting, to be worn as a symbol of courage and hope during my ordeal. Simply inscribed on the ring, which had belonged to her husband before he died, were the Latin words *"Vincit Qui Patitur,"* which in English mean "He who endures, conquers." The phrase quickly became the watchword of the Sheppard family and close friends. Virtually all corrrespondence between family and friends and this writer included a simple reminder of this expression—the initials V.Q.P. From that phrase the title of this book—when it could finally be written—was derived.

What you are about to read is my story, as I have lived it. It is written for one purpose only—so that my son, Sam, and daughter, Iris, can learn the true facts of this case, and, therefore, it is dedicated expressly to them. However, in a larger sense it is also dedicated to all those who over the years have expressed implicit faith in me and have toiled unselfishly so that this story could someday be related in my own words. They include my late parents, Dr. and Mrs. R. A. Sheppard; my brothers, Richard and Stephen, and their wives, Dorothy and Betty; Rev. Alan Davis; Mary and Bud Brown; Drs. Arthur Miller and Theodore Classen; my lovely wife, Ariane, and her parents; F. Lee Bailey, Russell Sherman and Ben Clark, giants on my legal team; and many others too numerous to mention.

To them go my eternal thanks.

This is a story that was started on a faded legal pad more than a dozen years ago. Through the years the raw material grew to include dozens of legal pads with handwritten personal observations, millions of words of courtroom oratory and testimony, a stack of legal documents too heavy for one man to carry, hundreds of thousands of words on tape and uncounted numbers of letters, telegrams and cards.

I would like to thank William V. Levy, who served as editorial consultant on this book for The World Publishing Company and whose able assistance was invaluable in helping to crystallize this material and commit it to final form.

Endure and Conquer was written with the fervent hope that as a result of my ordeal no one in the future will have occasion to write a book of this kind.

S.H.S.

FOREWORD

It was a bitter cold day in November, 1961, when I walked from the state prison in Marion, Ohio, after my first meeting with Dr. Sam Sheppard. But the feeling of numbness did not come principally from the temperature; I have always liked the cold. It came from a very deep emotion that our meeting had spawned, an almost instinctive feeling that the man I had left behind the bars was innocent and the victim of an outrage, and, more shocking, that what had happened to him could as easily have happened to me, or to any of us. I resolved then and there to somehow get him out and clear him. It took just five years to do it.

To many who have followed with interest and even fascination the agonizing developments of the Sheppard case for the past twelve years, Sam has been the image at the spearhead of a great cause, a tragic image that achieved almost legendary status long ago. But behind the image is a man, a remarkable man, who was somehow chosen to suffer twelve years of society's worst abuse in order to demonstrate that our system of justice is badly flawed.

Now, finally, society can get acquainted with its victim, through the pages of this book. And each American citizen who too complacently believes that American justice is too grand to need improvement ought to read this book, and subject his complacency to a badly needed jolt.

There is no experience quite so depressing as "pulling hard time" in a penitentiary—that is, being locked in a cage for a crime one did not commit. The convicts know who the "hard-timers" are, and that is why when Sam was freed in 1964 and again when he was acquitted a week ago there came a deep and resounding cheer from those left behind the bars. A few lawyers know who the "hard-timers" are, for they represent them as I did Sam; and a few families know, for they must suffer along with the injustice. But society seldom has an opportunity to learn just what hard time is, or what it can do to a man. Sam is one of the few who can tell with authority what hard time is, and that is why this book had to be written.

It is difficult to conjure up in the imagination a more extreme example than Sam Sheppard. A brilliant neurosurgeon at thirty years of age, Sam was healthy, popular, happily married, easygoing, and on his way up the ladder of personal success. Suddenly, and without warning, his attractive young wife was taken from him, butchered in her own home. This would have been enough to crumple many men, but for Sam it was only the threshold of a horror chamber. He was given no respite in which to grieve over his loss. Jealous little men charged in and multiplied that grief by compounding it with embarrassment and shame; they pointed reckless fingers and accused him of being the butcher that had robbed his son of a mother.

Like a giant snowball rolling down a mountainside, the oppression of Sam Sheppard gathered momentum. Officials of little dignity and less mettle scampered before the roar of callous news media, and flew in the face of plain facts to prosecute Sam while the real murderers walked freely in the streets. The snowball became an avalanche, and crushed before it each of the checks and safeguards that are supposed to protect a citizen against persecution. One court after another let him down, and a mistake that need never have occurred became encrusted with one rubber-stamped approval on top of another. The machinery of the law failed, and failed worse than it has ever failed before. The State of Ohio protected its miscarriage as zealously as it guarded its great seal.

The Sheppard case has been very good to me. Although it took countless hours of nerve-wracking work, it came along when I was young enough to spend those hours freely. And it introduced into my life some of the finest people I will ever meet.

First there was Paul Holmes, who wrote a book about Sam and captured the outrage of the case in what he wrote; were it not for that book, Sam would still be languishing behind prison walls. Next there was Dr. Steve, Sam's brother, whose stainless steel backbone could never be snapped even though he was told by all and sundry to quite fighting. There were Ben Clark and Russ Sherman, two lawyers of whom Ohio can justly be proud, who went on tirelessly without fees to join me in a cause they knew had to be kept alive. There was Judge Carl Weinman of the federal court, who had the courage of a lion, and used it to tell Ohio and the world that Sam Sheppard had been raped by the law.

And then there was Ariane, who left a life of comfort and ease because she got an idea, a feeling that she had to pledge herself to a cause, and the man within that cause. Had I not known her when she first came, and known her through all of the dog days when we

could win nothing but ridicule and abuse, I might not believe that
she is real. But she is, and she has behind her that same stubborn
quality found in each of the people who battled for Sam when his
case was thought hopeless.

There is young Sam Sheppard, probably the finest young man
I have ever met in my life. Stolen from him were both of his parents,
and he walked alone through his youth bearing a name that pro-
moted smirks and whispers of derision whenever it was mentioned.
From this experience he has emerged with more wisdom, humility
and unwavering loyalty than most men will ever know.

And there are countless others, all found within the covers of
this important book. At the center, of course, is Sam himself. I
know Sam far too well to appraise him objectively, and I have come
to like him far too much to be a proper critic. But I am certain
that he is a proper man to explain to his fellow citizens what most
of them will never know or learn. And I am also certain that as he
has endured for more than a decade, and now finally conquered, he
has somehow survived and emerged as a whole man, more philo-
sophical than embittered, anxious to ensure that what he has gone
through need not be repeated upon some other hapless soul.

Now that Sam is free for all time, and the world is beginning to
blink and realize that his case was more macabre joke than due
process of law, I can turn to other men in other places whose freedom is in jeopardy or lost. The tremendous relief that has flooded
my system since this case went to final judgment is accompanied
by an equally tremendous fatigue, and I am almost as glad as Sam
that it is over.

There are still loose ends. Justice has corrected itself only on
the first plateau. There still remains the question of who will pay
for those cruel, wasted years, and perhaps before it is answered we
will write yet another chapter into American law. Meanwhile, perhaps some public good will come from this grotesque miscarriage.

The strength of our justice lies not only in the lawyers and the
courts and lawyers, but in the people. In Sam's case the people were
not only uninformed, but deliberately misled. So deep were the
roots of prejudice driven that there will always be a hard core of
petty, shrill, citizens who with little knowledge of the true facts

will cling to a fervent belief in Sam's guilt as long as they cling to life.

But these are the minority. It is tough medicine to swallow, but honest men will gradually accept the fact that Sam is innocent, and that they have failed him. When the next Sam Sheppard comes along, the rolling snowball will somehow be smashed before it is large enough to snow the people. The next Sam Sheppard will not be victimized by foolish little officials who care not for justice or by large newspaper editors who cannot show some conscience for their power. The next Sam Sheppard, if he is convicted because the system misfires, will not have to wait twelve long years for justice to complete its cycle.

There need never be another Sam Sheppard if enough people come to know and understand this one, and understand what happened to him, how it happened, and why it was all so unnecessary. One of the ways to understand is to read this book carefully.

F. Lee Bailey
Boston, Massachusetts
November 21, 1966

PROLOGUE

There was nothing that happened during the first thirty years of my life to indicate that some day my name would—unfortunately—become a household word in the United States and better known throughout the world than those of many of this country's leaders. Mine was a life not untypical of hundreds of thousands of upper-middle-class young men who set their sights on a professional career and then set about to achieve it.

I was the youngest of three sons born to Dr. Richard A. Sheppard and Elizabeth Sheppard, his wife. My father, a tall, handsome man, was a successful general surgeon, who practiced osteopathic medicine. My mother was a beautiful woman, who taught school before her marriage. Mom, Dad, my two older brothers, Richard and Stephen, and I lived in a modest red-brick home on a tree-shaded street in Cleveland Heights.

As an osteopathic surgeon, Dad practiced in a field that represented a relatively new addition to medicine. Osteopathy functioned on the theory that most ailments resulted from pressure of displaced bones and nerves and were curable by manipulation. The larger group of doctors, called medical doctors, practiced allopathy, which called for treatment of most disease by drugs. Medical doctors were continually making it rough on my father and his professional colleagues.

When I was about ten years old, Dad founded a small osteopathic hospital in a three-story building near downtown Cleveland. The task of running the hospital and his busy surgical practice kept him on the go countless hours during the day and night. His strength was seemingly endless, and he never neglected his family.

Since medicine and surgery were Dad's life, he hoped fervently that his three sons would become doctors. Richard and Steve committed themselves rather early in life to following in his footsteps. But I had another love that was greatly stimulated by my father—athletics. As a boy I dreamed of a career as a professional athlete and I could hardly wait until I entered junior high school to compete in interscholastic sports.

Athletics were a major part of my life at Roosevelt Junior High School and at Cleveland Heights High School. At the latter, where I was elected president of my class all three years, I was a regular on the track, basketball and football teams, and my performance earned for me in the senior year an award as the school's most outstanding athlete. But by that time, I, too, had decided that a career in medicine would be far more rewarding and stimulating than one in athletics.

I met the love of my life at Roosevelt Junior High School. Her name was Marilyn Reese. She was a pretty, vivacious girl with long, dark-blond hair and sparkling hazel-green eyes. Marilyn was a very athletic girl, with an outgoing personality and a knack for making friends easily. Life had not been all pleasant for her. Marilyn's mother died in 1929 while trying to give birth to her second child, a boy, who also died. Marilyn was only six at the time and her father, Tom Reese, a successful inventor and manufacturer, sent Marilyn to live with her mother's sister, Mary Brown, and her grandparents, in East Cleveland. After Tom Reese remarried, Marilyn went to live with him and her stepmother in University Heights.

However, even after moving to University Heights, she frequently spent weekends with one or the other of her grandparents, Mr. and Mrs. C. K. Reese and Mr. and Mrs. Blake, or her aunt, Mary Brown, in East Cleveland. She developed a deep affection for her grandmothers and Aunt Mary, who were really more like parents to Marilyn than Tom Reese's second wife was.

But, if Marilyn's life was deficient in parental love, it was not at all lacking in material things. Her father gave her virtually everything she wanted. I believe he loved her very much, but for some reason they were unable to attain the deep and sustaining father-daughter relationship that often develops when a man has lost his wife.

Like most teen-age romances, ours had its ups and down. Marilyn was a year and a half ahead of me in school, and our romance faltered slightly between the time she graduated from junior high school and when I joined her at Cleveland Heights High School. But once we were both in high school together, we were virtually inseparable.

During the summer of 1940, Marilyn and I established a relationship that we never lost. We came to understand one another and began discussing seriously a future together. Marilyn had originally been scheduled to graduate in January, 1941; eventually, it worked out so that she finished only one year ahead of me in school. She spent the next year at Skidmore College in Saratoga, New York, and I completed my high school career.

World War II was raging when I graduated from high school and my first inclination was to enlist in the armed forces and worry about college later. However, my father convinced me I could do a lot more for my country as a doctor than I could as a soldier in the field. I decided to enroll as a preosteopathic student at Hanover College, a small Presbyterian school in Hanover, Indiana.

Later, the matter was taken out of my hands. Selective Service handed down a "freeze" order and all people in "A" vocations had to remain at their present status, unless a change was okayed by the draft board. Premedical and preosteopathic students were in this category. Those in premedical school were issued uniforms and given the pay of an Army private. Because of pressure from regular medical organizations, the osteopathic students were discriminated against, however. Preosteopathic medical students were frozen but were given no uniforms and no pay, even though they were studying the same basic curriculum as regular premedical students.

Though I still had a nagging feeling I should be in service, I realized the only way to accomplish this was to flunk out of school. I decided against that as it would prevent any later medical training and would reflect badly on my father.

Because of the war, the preosteopathic course was accelerated. By attending class at Western Reserve University in Cleveland during the summer of 1943, I was able to complete the course in two years and enroll at the Osteopathic School of Physicians and Surgeons in Los Angeles in the summer of 1944. I was the third of the Sheppard boys to reach Los Angeles. Richard had been there first, had completed his medical training and was back in Cleveland. Steve had been graduated from medical school and was about to begin his one-year internship.

I had become accustomed to a heavy study load at Hanover, but it was nothing compared to the rigorous program in medical school. There were classes during the day and study sessions from six to midnight every night, and for forty-eight hours at a stretch when it came time for exams.

As we had done while I was at Hanover, Marilyn and I continued our romance by mail. At least while at Hanover, we could see each other during vacation or holiday periods. The distance between Cleveland and Los Angeles made that impossible. The separation was extremely difficult and only the daily letters from her helped me to exist without her.

In the fall of 1945, when I was in the second year of medical school, I could no longer stand the lengthy separation. I asked Marilyn to come to Los Angeles to marry me. She agreed and we were married in November at the First Hollywood Methodist Church. We moved into an apartment on Sitchell Street. My father paid the medical school tuition and helped with the finances and Marilyn's father also made a monthly contribution so that we could eat regularly.

Marilyn seemed to enjoy my intensive training. Besides doing the routine household chores, she pitched in and helped in many ways. She took a job as a secretary for one of the professors. This helped to keep our heads above water as far as money was concerned. She corrected, typed and retyped my medical and surgical papers and quizzed me on examination material. Marilyn often knew phases of my work as well as I did. Many of the quiz sessions took place as she washed and I dried the dishes.

My wife became pregnant in the spring of 1946, and for the most part her pregnancy was uneventful. The delivery was another story. The period of labor was prolonged and painful owing to complications. Surgery was contemplated but was averted by the skill and dexterity of the obstetrician. When it was all over, she gave birth to a son, whom we named Sam. The entire experience was very rugged psychologically for Marilyn. For several years, it affected her sexual drive and her desire to have additional children.

By 1948, I had completed medical school and my internship. I applied for and was granted a residency in neurosurgery. During my residency, I became associated with Dr. Randall Chapman, a brilliant neurosurgeon, and worked closely with him for more than two years. He had a way of instilling confidence in me. When I displayed quick reflexes and the ability to grasp a situation rapidly, he turned over most of the surgery to me and stood by to counsel.

Los Angeles County Hospital is said to be the largest civilian hospital in the world and it provides a surgeon with a wide variety of cases. Normally, a resident in a specialty such as neurosurgery is not allowed to go beyond his chosen field. There are exceptions, of course. Hospital officials would loosen the reins and allow a young surgeon-in-training to work in other fields if he displayed competence in his own specialty.

The hospital was crowded, and because of the war there still was a shortage of qualified residents in many fields. Fortunately, I was doing well in neurosurgery and with the help of Dr. Chapman and Dr. K. G. Bailey was able to work out a schedule which permitted me to work in general surgery and heart and blood surgery.

Dr. Chapman and Dr. Bailey took a liking to Marilyn and me and introduced us into a social atmosphere we had never known existed. We were frequently invited to Dr. Chapman's ranch near Monterey. As the months rolled by, he began asking me to take part in cases he handled privately as well as at County Hospital. This worked out to our mutual advantage. It enabled me to get a great deal of experience I wouldn't ordinarily have received. When Dr. Chapman went to his ranch in Northern California, he left the patients in my care. If there were complications, there was someone he trusted to handle them, sparing him a return trip to Los Angeles.

Near the end of my residency in mid-1951, Dr. Chapman urged us to remain in Los Angeles, suggesting that I become his associate. Marilyn and I loved Southern California and were tempted to accept his offer. However, we both felt that I had a duty to return to Cleveland to join my father and brothers at Bay View Hospital, a new hospital Dad had founded in 1948 in suburban Bay Village. It had approximately eighty beds, twenty bassinettes and incubators, a well-equipped surgical suite and other modern facilities.

So, with hesitation and a wish we could stay, we packed our things and returned to Cleveland in the summer of 1951. I immediately went in with my father in general surgery and started taking cases in neurosurgery and traumatic surgery. The latter involved accident cases. I was appointed chief surgeon in charge of the emergency room. We had a great number of accident cases every day, but weekends were frantic. There are several major, heavily traveled roads in the areas, and we treated our share of traffic accident victims. There were times when I spent the entire weekend in the hospital.

About six weeks after we returned from California, Marilyn and I purchased a home on the north side of Lake Road in Bay Village, about three miles west of the hospital. I was just starting in practice and had almost no money, but Dad helped to swing the deal. It was an old white, frame, four-bedroom house that had been modernized. It was set on a large, tree-studded lot that stretched back from Lake

Road until it banked steeply to the Lake Erie beach. The bank leading to the beach was covered with vines and thick brush, over which a long stairway led down to the sand and a beach house. It wasn't perfect, but it was ours and we loved it.

We had very little furniture of our own and very little money. We furnished the house mainly with hand-me-downs from other members of the family. The wine-colored carpeting was left over from the previous owners.

There were advantages to stepping right into an established family surgical practice. After years of existing on handouts from my father and Marilyn's dad, we began to gain some affluence of our own. My neurosurgical practice grew quickly and I was soon accepting cases in cities throughout Ohio and other nearby states. My income zoomed into five figures. We bought appliances for the kitchen and basement and Marilyn treated herself to some new clothes. We bought a second-hand car for her.

We became caught up in the swirl of suburban life. We enjoyed our home and the social life together. Marilyn joined the local dance club, took part in potluck groups and other informal gatherings. She became president of the Women's Osteopathic Auxiliary, a member of the Bay Village Women's Club, and was active in church work. She also handled much of my professional paper work, typing letters and other written material, and the Sheppard Clinic paid her for this.

I was appointed the police surgeon of Bay Village and neighboring Westlake and as such became friendly with many of the officials in the community, including part-time Bay Village Mayor Spencer Houk, a butcher, who lived three doors down Lake Road from our house. In 1952, Houk and I purchased a fourteen-foot aluminum boat. Marilyn and I bought a twenty-five-horsepower outboard motor for the craft. At first we used the boat primarily for fishing and pleasure boating on the lake. Then Marilyn and I began water skiing and became ardent enthusiasts.

We taught youngsters and adults in the neighborhood how to water ski. Among our more eager students were Don and Nancy Ahern, a couple that lived on the other side of a small cemetery which separated their home from the Houk house.

Marilyn loved sports of all kinds. When she wasn't skiing, she bowled, played tennis or golf. Athletics always had been a part of my life, and together we encouraged youngsters in the neighborhood to participate. We put a basketball hoop on the garage, and the driveway back of our home was constantly filled with teen-aged boys. We turned two rooms above the garage over to the boys as a clubroom and got some barbells for them.

By July, 1954, exactly three years after our return from California, you might say I had everything a man could ask for. I was working in our Sheppard Clinic in Fairview Park, had an office at East 32nd and Euclid Avenue in Cleveland, and, of course, was performing surgery at Bay View and other hospitals. My average monthly earnings were about $2,500 and we had just gotten our noses above water financially. We had paid off the major portion of the mortgage on the Lake Road house and had repaid virtually all the money lent to me by Dad for the down payment.

Our son, Chip, as he was nicknamed, was almost seven, and was growing into a fine, rugged, well-adjusted boy. We had a nice home, a pleasant social life and a warm family relationship. What's more important, Marilyn's fear of pregnancy and her sexual coldness, which dated back to the birth of Chip, had abated. We were expecting our second child and we were both thrilled. Our marriage, like most, had its ups and downs, but now as we approached our ninth anniversary we were as happy as a couple of newlyweds.

However, in one horrifying moment, it would all change, shattering the tidy world of Marilyn and myself and those we loved and setting the stage for a long and bizarre story that would be heard around the world.

1

The incessant clatter of the alarm clock shattered a deep sleep at seven in the morning on Saturday, July 3rd. I turned off the alarm and lay in bed an extra few moments, soothed by the sound of the waves breaking on the beach below. Finally I got up, walked to the guest room and tried to arouse an old classmate from Los Angeles, Dr. Lester Hoverston. Les, a tall, prematurely bald fellow who at one time had worked at Bay View Hospital and then left there to practice in Dayton, was returning to the West Coast. Over Marilyn's objections, I had asked him to spend a few days with us before returning to California. She disliked him and disapproved of our friendship.

Les knew about the operation I was going to perform that morning and had asked if he could assist. I agreed. But, when I told him I was getting ready to leave, he said he wanted to stay in bed a little longer and would meet me at the hospital. I turned and left the room, shaved, dressed and gave Marilyn a kiss, telling her I would try to be home as early as possible to start the Fourth of July weekend.

I walked down the stairs, patted our dog, Koko, on the head and went out the Lake Road door. It was a perfect, warm July morning. Our Jaguar was parked in the garage. In a moment, the car was turned around and I was heading out of the driveway and down Lake Road to Bay View Hospital. Surgery was not normally scheduled on Saturdays at Bay View, unless, of course, there was an emergency.

However, I had scheduled an operation for an old gentleman of whom I was very fond. During a previous operation, for a cancerous growth, I had removed ninety per cent of his stomach. Now he had another problem, a blood clot on his hand. I felt that corrective action should be taken as soon as possible.

There was very little traffic on Lake Road that morning and the drive to the hospital took less than five minutes. I turned left into the parking lot, drove behind the road entrance to the building and parked in the space reserved for me. I entered the hospital, greeted a handful of nurses and doctors who were on the floor and went to the cafeteria for breakfast. Then I went to the surgical suite, scrubbed, put on a green gown and began the operation. A few moments later, Les Hoverston arrived. The operation was performed without complications.

A short time after I left surgery, a man rushed into the hospital carrying a little boy. At first glance, the child appeared dead. He was not breathing or showing any evidence of life. The youngster had been run over by a telephone company truck and had nasty-looking, reddish-blue tire marks across his chest and throat.

We rushed the youngster into the major surgical suite and tried to revive him. I grabbed a scalpel, opened his chest and began to massage his heart. For a few moments, he seemed to be responding to the massage. His little heart began beating slowly, then it stopped. We didn't give up. I continued to massage the heart until my hand was numb, then other doctors took over. It was no use.

It was especially difficult to have to tell the father that his boy was dead because the youngster was about the age of Chip. There is little one can say that would comfort a man in a situation like that. I merely told him we had done our best. He shook my hand, thanked me and then in a flurry of anger said he was going after the truck driver and punish him for what he had done to his son. I didn't restrain the man physically, but grasped his hand firmly and tried to give him a little insight into how this tragedy could have happened. The telephone company would be the first to investigate the accident, I assured him, and urged him to leave the matter in the hands of the company and the police. He calmed down a little.

By the time I left the hospital, it was late afternoon, and there were still some errands. The first stop was a garage for minor adjustments on the Jaguar. Later, I stopped at a beverage store, to purchase a couple of cases of beer, and then stopped at the home of my parents for a chat. I stayed there for about a half hour before driving the three miles to my home.

Marilyn, dressed in white shorts, a gaily colored blouse and moccasins, greeted me in the driveway. She had had a busy day, too, but looked radiant. She had spent most of the day cleaning the house and shopping for food for the party we planned for Sunday. The guests were to be the graduated interns from Bay View and their wives. Marilyn had also typed a paper for a talk I was to give later in the month at the American Osteopathic Association meeting in Toronto, Canada.

Don and Nancy Ahern, our neighbors, and their two children were coming for dinner that evening, and Marilyn had cooked most of the meal and baked my favorite dessert, blueberry pie. When I stepped out of the car, she told me that we were to have cocktails at the Aherns then return to our home for dinner.

We went into the wood-paneled den for a few moments to do some paper work connected with my practice, then drove several hundred feet up the street to the Ahern house. Chip had been playing with the two Ahern children, Michael, nine, and Leslie, seven. Don and Nancy were working in the yard and we told them not to stop for us but to wind up what they were doing. When they completed their work, we went into the house for cocktails.

I was just finishing a second Martini, when the phone rang. It was a doctor at the hospital calling me, about a boy who had fractured his thigh bone in an auto accident. The physician on duty had some question as to the best method of treatment and whether the patient could be transferred to a hospital near his home in Youngstown, Ohio, about seventy miles from Bay Village. I put some cloves into my mouth to take away whatever odor might persist from the gin and vermouth and returned to the hospital, examined the boy and X-rays of the injury and recommended that he be put in traction for a few days.

I drove back on Lake Road toward my home. The Aherns' car wasn't in our driveway, so I went back to their home, and found everyone there. We remained for a short time and then all went to our house. The girls finished preparing dinner, fed the three children in the kitchen, and then called Don and me to dine on the porch, overlooking the lake.

A brisk wind was blowing in from the lake. We all wore jackets or sweaters. I was wearing blue cord pants and a white T-shirt and put on a brown corduroy jacket. We ate cottage ham, tossed salad, string beans, apple sauce and, of course, the blueberry pie Marilyn had baked earlier in the day. We dined in a leisurely mood. It was dark by the time we were finished.

After dinner, Marilyn and Nancy cleaned up the kitchen. Don Ahern took their two children home, put them to bed, and returned. Marilyn put Chip to bed. The four of us then gathered in the living room. Don was huddled in a chair in the northwest corner of the living room, listening to the Cleveland Indians-Chicago White Sox game on a portable radio. The girls were engrossed in a television movie called *Strange Holiday*. I sat in a chair near the television set, half-watching television and half-listening to the ball game. Soon Marilyn came over, sat on my lap and put her arms around me. Don, who had been giving us periodic reports on the baseball game, turned off the radio and joined us. Nancy, sort of mocking Marilyn and me, sat in Don's lap for a few moments. It wasn't long before Marilyn complained of a cramp in her back and moved to another chair. So did Nancy.

We continued to watch television for a while. However, I was bushed from the strenuous day at the hospital, got up from the chair and lay down on the couch. I don't recall whether I took my corduroy jacket off or not. I lay on the couch with my head toward the television set and watched the movie, and, eventually, dozed off.

The Aherns apparently stayed for some time after I fell asleep. Nancy said later it was twelve-thirty a.m. when they departed from the Lake Road door after watching Marilyn lock the door facing the lake. Nancy said she did not know whether my wife bolted the Lake Road door behind them. It was frequently left unlocked, mainly to provide access for hospital personnel who came to my home at all hours of the night for consultations on accident cases, or for the maid, who came to work early in the morning. Les Hoverston had gone to Kent that afternoon and had left his clothes and money in the house.

I believe Marilyn made an attempt to arouse me while I was sleeping on the couch and indicated she was going to bed and urged me to come up. Evidently, I was not aroused very much and went back to sleep.

The next thing I knew, Marilyn was screaming or moaning my name. It was not exactly a scream. I really can't explain it. I jumped off the couch and headed up the stairs. My subconscious reaction was that she was having a convulsive seizure similar to those she had during her first pregnancy. I rushed into the room and several things happened almost simultaneously. I thought I could see a white form—an individual. I heard Marilyn moaning loudly and then some other noises. Then I felt I was struck down from behind, but can't say for sure.

Sometime after that (I have no way of knowing how long), I came to in a sitting position, facing the doorway of the bedroom. I saw a glimmer or reflection and recognized the police badge on my wallet, which was lying on the floor. As I picked it up, I felt an excruciating pain in my neck and I knew I had been injured.

I was fearful for my wife. I got up from the floor, went over to the twin bed, where Marilyn was lying, looked at her and felt her pulse. Everything was hazy and it was difficult to see clearly, but I felt that she was dead. I believe I then rushed into my son Chip's room, adjacent to ours. I wanted to find out if anything had happened to him. I don't know how I determined it, but after seeing him came to the conclusion that he was not harmed.

As I came out of Chip's room, I thought I heard a noise downstairs and ran down the stairs as rapidly as I could. It seemed to me that this noise was coming from the front part of the house—the part toward the lake. I turned down on the north section of the stairway and rounded the L-portion of the living room and went toward the dining room table. At that point, I spotted a figure between the front door of the house and the front door of the porch or slightly beyond that point, perhaps, slightly toward the yard.

I gave chase, but lost sight of this intruder on the stairs heading down to the beach. By the time I got to the landing where the beach house was located, the figure was on the beach. I bolted down the remaining stairs, and tackled this individual from behind. It seemed to me he had a rather large head. Then, I felt as if I had been twisted or choked. That's all I remember.

The next thing I can remember with any clarity at all was returning to consciousness on the water's edge, at the beach. My head was facing toward the bank and my feet were in the water. I had the impression I was being wallowed back and forth by the waves. I slowly dragged myself onto the beach and came to some sort of sensibility. Somehow, I made it up the stairs.

The time element is hard to estimate. I went back up the stairs to the bedroom where Marilyn was. I looked at her and felt for her pulse on her neck. When I touched her, I thought she was gone. It's hard to explain my reaction. I guess I thought I would wake up and find out it was all a horrible, fantastic dream. I'm not sure what I did in the next few moments. I may have gone into other rooms. I may have walked around upstairs. I may have gone back into the room where Marilyn was and looked at her again.

All I know is that eventually I somehow realized that this was, at least momentarily, real. I went downstairs, searching my numbed mind for what to do, where to turn.

2 ⁊

"For God's sake, Spen, get over here quick. I think they've killed Marilyn." Those were my words to Mayor Spencer Houk when he sleepily answered his bedroom telephone at approximately five forty-five on the morning of July 4th. He said he would be right over.

Although we had not been nearly as socially friendly with Houk and his wife as we once had, I still saw quite a bit of him in my official capacity as police surgeon for the community. As mayor, he was also safety director. Together we frequently rode in police cruisers, studying police habits, how officers dealt with accidents or other emergency situations. We felt that this type of information would help in establishing procedures for dealing with accidents and also help me to become a better police surgeon. This relationship and the fact that he was the top police official in the community and lived only a few hundred feet from our home apparently played on my subconscious. My immediate reaction was to call him, rather than the police department.

As I waited for him to arrive, it seemed like an eternity, I guess I felt that Houk would be there in seconds—less than a minute. But he waited for his wife to get dressed. Why, I'll never know. It took them five to ten minutes to arrive at my home. They entered from the Lake Road door. Houk sent his wife upstairs, if you can imagine such a thing, and came into the den, where—bare to the waist—I was half-slumped in a chair. Drawers were pulled from my desk and contents of my medical bag were strewn on the floor. My face was badly beaten and my neck and head ached. He asked me what had happened and I told him what I knew.

What he saw was nothing compared with what confronted Esther Houk when she reached the bedroom, which contained two twin beds, a night stand, a dresser, and a rocking chair. Marilyn was sprawled on her bed in a pool of blood. There was blood everywhere, on the bed, on the wall, on the floor. Her head and face were badly lacerated. My wife's pajama tops were rolled up around her neck. The lower part of her body, except for the lower part of her legs, was covered. (Marilyn was a modest woman and somehow in the confusion of the situation I had the presence of mind to cover the lower part of her body when I went upstairs after the assault on the beach.)

Esther ran down the stairs and shouted for her husband to call the police and an ambulance. Police records show that Houk reached Patrolman Fred Drenkhan at five fifty-eight a.m. Drenkhan called for an ambulance, alerted other police officials and rushed to the home. Meanwhile, Houk, who never went upstairs to the murder room while I was in the house, telephoned my brother, Dr. Richard Sheppard, who lived nearby. Esther Houk remained at my side. She offered me a drink of whisky, but I declined. Officer Drenkhan, whom I had known for almost three years, was the first policeman to arrive, followed quickly by other Bay Village officers and firemen, who manned the ambulance. Richard arrived at six ten a.m. Mrs. Houk met him on the front lawn and told him that Marilyn was dead.

Richard rushed into the kitchen, grabbed a knife and went upstairs to the bedroom at the head of the stairs. It was obvious to him that the situation was hopeless, but he put a stethoscope to her chest and listened for any faint sound of heartbeat. There was none. He told me later he had taken the knife upstairs for use in case he felt revival was possible by cardiac massage. When he saw that Marilyn was beyond help, Richard came down the steps, walked into the den, and said softly, "She's gone, Sam." I'm not sure what he said after that, but the gist of it was that I should try to bring my thoughts to some sort of conclusion, get myself together, and remember what happened. "This is serious," he said. "Marilyn is dead!"

(Mayor Houk said later that Richard had asked me pointedly: "Did you do this, Sam?" I'll admit I was in a fog, but don't remember him asking that. Richard said that he had never put that question to me. There might have been some misinterpretation, but I don't think so.)

Patrolman Drenkhan conferred with Mayor Houk and the two apparently came to the conclusion that the murder of my wife was too big for Bay Village to handle alone. Drenkhan called the Coroner's Office, a standard procedure, and the Homicide Unit of the Cleveland Police Department. By this time, my brother Steve and his wife, Betty, arrived, spoke briefly with Richard and then came to the den to examine me. Richard had given me a cursory examination and later with Steve was more thorough. They told police officials that I was badly injured and should be taken immediately to the hospital. As I understand it, the police did not object and I have a hazy recollection they offered to take me in an ambulance.

Steve had his green Mercury station wagon there and suggested we travel to the hospital in it. I guess I wanted to assert myself as best I could and struggled to my feet and with the help of my brothers and Betty walked to the station wagon. Steve and Betty drove me to the hospital. Betty cushioned my head and neck in her hands to ease the pain. Meanwhile, Dorothy, Richard's wife, had arrived and she and Richard carried Chip out of the house without waking him and took him to their home.

It was later charged that I had been "spirited away" to Bay View Hospital by my brothers. That's ridiculous. The police were there and saw me get into the station wagon. The point I am trying to make is that there was no hidden situation at all, as some charged. Everything was done with police approval. Hindsight is great, but if I had to do it all over again, I would have gone in their ambulance and let them carry me into the hospital in a stretcher. If this had happened there would have been far less innuendoes.

Those who first saw me at the hospital when I arrived said my face was badly swollen and I was shaking. My mouth was cut and there was a considerable amount of blood on my teeth. They said my neck was obviously painful, that my body was cold and clammy, and my feet were shriveled up as if they had been in water for a long period of time.

Several doctors and a nurse removed my wet clothing—trousers, shoes, and socks. Mrs. Anne Franz, a registered nurse for more than a quarter of a century, put a thermometer into my mouth. It was below 94° and didn't register, a sign of shock. Following shots for shock, I was wheeled into the X-ray room. Despite the fact that several hot water bottles and blankets were placed on me, I was still shivering and cold. I still had the feeling that the horrible experience was a bizarre, grotesque nightmare and somehow couldn't believe what had happened to Marilyn and me.

After X-rays were taken, I was wheeled into a private room. Steve entered and began giving me a thorough examination. He found a swelling and discoloration on the right side of my face and that I was only able to open my mouth about half way. He noticed several bleeding lacerations and cuts inside of the cheek and this accounted for the blood on the teeth.

In his initial report, Steve also noted that the teeth in my upper right jaw were loose and could easily have been removed, and two teeth in the same area appeared to have been broken or chipped. His examination of the reflex of the right eye revealed it was sluggish. On the back of the neck he found a severely bruised area approximately three inches long and about an inch and a half wide, extending from the base of the skull toward the left. He noticed a muscle spasm on the back of the neck, which I couldn't control.

On the left side, at the root of the neck, he found superficial discoloration. I felt no pain at that spot. My brother said he found an absence of the left abdominal reflex, the cremasteric reflexes, and bicep and tricep reflexes on the left hand. The lack of these reflexes, he said, indicated to him a brain injury and certainly a concussion.

While I was being examined and treated at the hospital, Dr. Samuel Gerber, the Cuyahoga County Coroner, arrived at my home three miles away. He made a brief examination of Marilyn, conferred with other police officials and came directly to the hospital to talk with me and examine me. When he arrived, he asked to see my clothing. My father had put my clothing aside in a hospital receptacle. He immediately turned it over to the coroner, without question.

Gerber, a gray-haired man who spoke in a monotone, questioned me about the events at my home that morning. I related as best I could what happened. He examined me, paying special attention to my external parts. He was looking for blood. He looked in my hair and there was no blood. He checked my fingernails most carefully and examined my wrist, eyes, ears, and eyebrows. He found no blood. I understand he carefully checked my trousers and belt, especially the belt, because leather picks up blood and retains it. He found only a smudge of blood on the left knee, which must have gotten there when I knelt on the bed to take Marilyn's pulse. Then he went back to my home.

When he got there, Detectives Patrick Gareau and Robert Schottke and fingerprint specialist Michael Grabowski from the Cleveland Police Department were inspecting the house. I received all of this information second hand, but was told that Grabowksi made a two-hour check of the house. All he found, he said, was a partial palm print of my son, Chip, on the living room desk. The detectives found much of the downstairs in disarray. In addition to the contents of my medical bag dumped on the floor and drawers pulled out of the desk in the den, they found smashed athletic trophies and Marilyn's blood-stained watch on the floor. A writing desk in the living room also had been rifled.

Schottke and Gareau checked windows in the house for signs of forcible entry and couldn't find any. This was not surprising to me. On most nights one of our doors was open and could well have been on that night, allowing the killer free access to the house without forcing a window or door.

Later in the morning, Schottke, Gareau, and Police Chief John Eaton of Bay Village drove to Bay View Hospital and were admitted to my room to talk with me. I was under sedation and am not sure how long they spent with me. I was later told their visit lasted about twenty minutes. As I had done with Dr. Gerber, I again told them what had happened in the house and on the beach. I answered all their questions.

In that first visit, they asked me whether Marilyn had any affairs with other men. I told them to my knowledge she had not. They questioned me about Les Hoverston, who had spent the night in Kent, and asked whether I had heard rumors that he was infatuated with my wife. My answer was that I had heard about the rumors, but hadn't paid any attention to them. The detectives wanted to know if I had been chasing around with other women. The answer was "no."

It was during this first questioning period that I was asked about submitting to a lie detector test and indicated I would be willing as long as it was administered by objective persons. "Well, you know, a lie detector never misses," one of the detectives said. "It's always right." I guess I looked at them rather quizzically. I thought to myself, "Who do they think they are talking to, some kind of a dope?" I was no big brain, but I did graduate fourth in my class of over one hundred in medical school and had plenty of practical experience. I knew what a lie detector, or polygraph, was and while unfamiliar with the technical aspects, I knew one thing—it wasn't foolproof. That's why evidence gained from the use of a lie detector is generally not admissible in court.

The three men left my room and returned to the house. Chief Eaton enlisted the aid of some of the youngsters in the area to comb through the brush in my yard to see if they could find a murder weapon or other clues. Some time after noon, Larry Houk, the mayor's teen-aged son, found a green motor boat tool bag in the brush on the slope leading to the lake. Inside the bag was my wrist watch, which had some moisture inside the crystal and blood on the face and the rim; my key chain and keys; and a fraternity ring from Hanover College. The watch had stopped at four fifteen a.m.

Whoever had bludgeoned Marilyn and attacked me had apparently removed these items from me, put them in the small green bag and tossed it away while he was fleeing. But Schottke and Gareau read something else into the finding of the bag. They came to the conclusion that I had killed my wife and had faked a robbery to cover up the crime. They decided to confront me immediately, accuse me of the murder and try to get a quick confession. I suppose that is what the average policeman or detective is taught to do, but I don't think they are taught to disregard other clues, too.

They came back to the hospital and again were admitted to my room, despite the fact I was heavily sedated with demerol and morphine. Schottke, a thin, wiry man, started asking questions in an intense manner. Gareau was a little smoother—a "good-guy" type. That's the way they operate, I guess.

I don't remember the exact line of questioning, but Schottke said later, he questioned me about the moisture in the watch and that I responded about being caught in a downpour a few days before. I must have forgotten to mention at the time that I had also gone into the lake to help my brothers free the boat two nights before. The detective said I told him the blood on the watch probably resulted from feeling my wife's pulse.

Schottke also said he had interrogated me about my corduroy jacket, which he said had been found lying neatly folded across a pillow at the head of the couch in the living room. The homicide specialist related that I told him of faintly remembering getting too warm during the night, taking off the jacket, and putting it on the floor or couch. He explained that he had told me during that questioning session that had I put the jacket on the floor it would stillI have been there when they checked the house and had I put it on the couch it would have been wrinkled from my sleeping on it. Schottke also said that during that session I had denied keeping company with a former technician at the hospital and visiting her in California.

There was only one part of that confrontation I recall vividly. I was lying in the bed, slightly propped up. Because of my condition, hospital attendants had put rails on the side of the bed to keep me from falling off. Gareau was standing near the foot of the bed. Schottke was standing to my immediate right, leaning on the rail. After several minutes of interrogation by Schottke, Gareau again brought up the matter of the lie detector test. He mentioned how it was always right and how no one could fool it.

"I don't want to fool it or you or anybody," I said. "I want to find out who killed Marilyn. Why don't you go look around, get some clues and find out who did it. You're detectives and you're sure wasting a lot of time here."

Schottke leaned closer to me on the rail and said, "Why should we look for any clues when we have everything we need right here?"

"What do you mean?" I countered.

"What do you think I mean," he said. "I don't know what my partner thinks, but I think you killed your wife."

"Don't be ridiculous," I answered. At that moment, it seemed that all the sedation wore off in an instant. I became indignant, as any man would. I was infuriated that anyone would suggest such a thing! It hadn't crossed my mind that I would be considered a suspect. I told them that if they were proceeding on that premise, they were way off base. I immediately pushed the call button. A nurse came into the room and I instructed her to get my father.

When Dad entered the room, I told him that the two detectives had accused me of killing Marilyn. "Get the hell out," he shouted without hesitation. He told them that he and my brothers had been good enough to permit questioning of me alone, even while I was under sedation. If and when I regained my health, I could throw both of the detectives out of the room by myself, Dad said.

Gareau stepped back and said: "Well, I don't know about that."

"Well, I do," Dad answered. "Now, get out!" He meant business. He was sixty-four years old, but he didn't take a back seat to anyone. He was all man, all spunk, all doctor, and all surgeon. In ordering the two cops out of the room, he did what he felt was right. Infuriated, Schottke and Gareau turned and went out the door, determined, I believe, to nail me, one way or another.

3 &

Police singled me out as the Number One suspect and then set about to build a case against me, almost to the exclusion of considering any other clues or suspects. Late in the day, Dr. Gerber sent Dr. E. Richard Hexter, a general practitioner from Bay Village, to the hospital to examine me. He was a medical doctor and we, of course, were osteopathic physicians and surgeons. Despite the basic difference in philosophy and the long standing conflict between the two schools of medicine, I readily submitted to his examination. When he completed the check ordered by the coroner, he reported to Dr. Gerber that in his opinion my injuries were only superficial.

Meanwhile, at the request of Dr. Gerber, who had assumed charge of the investigation, a twenty-four-hour guard was established outside my room by Bay Village police. My father did the only natural thing. He called our attorney, Arthur Petersilge, a rather robust, red-haired man whose primary practice dealt with general law matters. He handled most of the hospital's legal work.

Petersilge telephoned William Corrigan, a prominent Cleveland criminal attorney. The average man thinks a criminal attorney defends only criminals—of course that's not true. The innocent man has to be defended, too. Before all this happened, I always had the impression that a criminal attorney was sort of a shady guy who tries to protect criminals. That had been my opinion so I can't criticize other people.

Corrigan, a short, white-haired man with a flair for the dramatic came to see me that evening. By this time, the newsmen in Cleveland were out in force, cluttering the lobby of the hospital and poking around the neighborhood. Whether he meant it or not, Corrigan put on quite a show that first night during the visit. He made it apparent he was there and lingered long enough to get his picture taken.

Another visitor that night was Otto Graham, the great quarterback of the Cleveland Browns and a friend. Otto just came and went without fanfare. A reporter asked him whether he felt I had anything to do with my wife's murder. He answered that if I had anything to do with it, he would lose faith in human nature. I just couldn't help but compare the two men. Otto didn't sneak around but he wasn't the kind of guy that went around posing for pictures.

Perhaps Petersilge's decision to call Corrigan and Corrigan's actions during the visit didn't help my image. People began to have an initial feeling: "What does this man have to hide?" or "Why does this man have to call a criminal attorney even before his family lawyer sees him?"

On July 4th, 5th and 6th, I was examined extensively by Dr. Charles Elkins, a prominent neurosurgeon who was summoned by my brother, Steve. Dr. Elkins was a medical doctor, but Dr. Steve called him because he wanted another expert opinion. He felt that Dr. Elkins was the most qualified in the area to give it, considering my injuries.

After his first visit on the fourth of July, Dr. Elkins concluded that I had suffered a spinal cord contusion and concussion but was in no danger of death, required no surgery, and would eventually recover.

On July 6th, he tested the muscle strength of my hands and found the left one weaker than the right. He tested various reflexes, vital to determining whether there is an injury to the nervous system. He tapped the nerve centers behind the left elbow, which controls the large muscle that causes the extension of the arm. He noted that the reflex was missing.

He said he found that the right tricep reflex was present, indicating to him there was something wrong with the mechanism that controlled the reflex on the left side. He also noted that the right abdominal reflex was present and the left missing, as were both cremasteric reflexes. The latter is tested by gently stroking the inner surface of the thigh. If it is present, the scrotum will jump on the side that is stroked.

These reflexes cannot be simulated by a patient during examination. The variance in the reflexes indicated there was some malfunction in the nervous system. After examining me on July 6th, Dr. Elkins said his findings substantiated the diagnosis he had made on the day of the tragedy and that I had suffered a bruise of the spinal cord in the region of the second cervical vertebra. This injury, he said could be produced by a blow on the back of the head.

Dr. Elkins apparently conveyed his findings to Dr. Gerber, who was of the mistaken notion that these injuries had been self-inflicted and weren't as serious as my brother had indicated. He was, of course, leaning heavily on the examination by Dr. Hexter, who was nowhere near as qualified as Dr. Elkins to make a diagnosis in a neurological case.

Dr. Gerber visited me on July 5th and told me what a good neurosurgeon Dr. Elkins was. I agreed. He informed me that Dr. Elkins was really going to bat for me. Gerber spent about a half-hour talking about the prominent neurosurgeon. I don't know what the coroner was trying to get me to say about Dr. Elkins, but perhaps he wanted me to say we were good friends.

I explained to Gerber that though Dr. Elkins was a medical doctor and my field was osteopathy, we had consulted on cases and our relationship was strictly professional. I told the coroner that Dr. Elkins had asked me to come to City Hospital to discuss neuropathological cases and even suggested that my resident at Bay View come along. I went to City Hospital virtually every week. However, our relationship was not social. We had a drink on one occasion when we discussed a case, but that was the extent of it. He never met Marilyn. When he left, Dr. Gerber tried without success to imply some sort of close social relationship between Dr. Elkins and myself.

On Monday and Tuesday, July 5th and 6th, I had over ten discussions with Bay Village police and with Cuyahoga County detectives, particularly Sergeant Carl Rossbach, a big, tough man who had been on the Cleveland police force. Rossbach was a rough son of a gun, but he tried to be fair, which is more than I can say for most of the other police involved in the case.

Because of my injuries, I wore an orthopedic collar—what we call a schauntz collar. It might have made me look a little grotesque, but it protected me from neck movements which might aggravate the injury.

When I arrived at the funeral home and viewed Marilyn in the casket for the first time, I had a strange sensation that we must be sure that this is Marilyn—that I must not permit the funeral to proceed without being absolutely positive that this was Marilyn Sheppard and not some other person. Perhaps I was being dramatic, but I don't know. I think I would do the same thing again because everything was so macabre. Everything was so unreal, so unbelievable.

First I looked at her face, which had been built up by the funeral home people, then checked for a little mole on the inside of her left knee. It was there and I could recognize it. Marilyn had been bitten by a dog when she was a child and there was a little pock mark on the right side of her face. I recognized it. I was satisfied then that it was Marilyn. I held her hand for a moment, said a few words to her, and then the coffin was closed.

The decision as to an open or closed casket ceremony was mine. I demanded that it be closed. I was depressed and upset and I was a little concerned that Chip might be there, although he was in my opinion too young to attend. Because of the publicity that attended the funeral, I had a feeling he should not be there under any circumstances. Fortunately, he was left at Steve's house in the care of the maid.

Reverend Al Kreke delivered a beautiful eulogy. He described how Marilyn and I had just joined the church and how Marilyn had been baptized in our home by him because she hadn't been baptized as a child. He told of how he had just learned during the past three weeks of her pregnancy and had been the first one outside the family who was told. He didn't overdo it, but he reviewed the years of productive womanhood that had been her life and did it in a proper manner. His words were gratifying.

After the ceremony most of the people came over and shook hands with me. Somehow, this seemed to be the thing to do at the moment. During the ceremony, Marilyn's aunt and uncle, Bud and Mary Brown, with whom we were extremely friendly, sat with me, one on each side. Mary held my hand. They were very warm and wonderful. Other members of Marilyn's family were solicitous, but somehow it didn't seem genuine. This was the first time that I felt there was some feeling on their part that I could have been responsible for the murder. This shocked me. I didn't know how to handle their reaction. I didn't see Marilyn's father, Tom Reese, there, and I don't think he attended. If he did, he remained in the background.

After the funeral, I returned to the hospital. On the next day, July 8th, I was discharged and went directly to my parents' home, which was adjacent to the hospital on the east side. My brother Richard's home was on the west side of the hospital. I felt that my mother needed me and I wanted to keep track of her. I knew she was depressed. In the first place, she had lost a daughter. She had always wanted a daughter and Marilyn had pretty much been my mother's daughter.

She was also terribly depressed by the publicity, the newspaper headlines, and the fact that the police had accused me of murdering Marilyn. This was especially hard on her because she was an idealist. She was forever telling us when we were youngsters that innocent people are just not convicted of anything and that right wins out in the end. I think she felt that she had failed to prepare me adequately to deal with this tragic problem.

One of the first things I did after being discharged from the hospital was to telephone Tom Reese, Marilyn's father, and ask to see him on his boat at the Forest City Yacht Club, where just the week before Marilyn and I had helped to repair the deck of his cabin cruiser. He said he would be glad to see me. He stated he had full confidence in me and indicated that any suggestions of my having anything to do with Marilyn's murder were without foundation.

About an hour later, he called back and said he would have to delay our meeting until after the "situation" was straightened out. He said that some of the women in the family were badgering him and just wouldn't leave him alone. "Tom, are you worried about the women in the family or are you worried about what happened to Marilyn and your son-in-law and more than that, your grandson?" I asked. "Let's think about Young Sam. For Christ's sake you know, Tom, that I could not do this."

"Yes," he said, "but I can't do anything now." Reese was a tremendous man, a fine inventor. He had invented the process of transferring wood grain onto metal for automobile dashboards and other uses. But he just didn't seem able to cope with the women in the family. Rather than argue, he usually went along with what his sisters wanted. "This is the way it's got to be, Sam," he said, and then hung up. He never took an active stand against me as the weeks rolled on but in a situation like this, when a person is not for you, it appears that he is against you.

On Friday, July 9th, I voluntarily returned to our home with Dr. Gerber and other police officials to recreate what had happened to Marilyn and me on July 4th. When we reached the bedroom I was horrified at all of the blood. I was shocked to see that the murderer appeared to be outlined in blood on the east wall of the bedroom. There was blood all over the room, but there was a concentration on the east wall. And, there appeared to be a two-legged figure resembling a good-sized man or woman on the wall, with no blood on it.

I pointed this out to Carl Rossbach and he said, "'By God, you're right."

The mob scene at the house was something. Reporters were out in force, so were housewives, children, bus drivers, and maids. It was like a public park. People were tromping all over our property. It was ludicrous. And inside the house—there was little Mike Ahern, Don's son, walking around the house, fingering everything. He had come to get a turtle, which I had given to him.

I had been on my way home from Youngstown one day and saw this large turtle on the road. I knew it would get killed if I left it there, so I picked it up and brought it home. I had previously brought Chip three turtles and Marilyn put her foot down. I gave it to Mike and he hadn't received permission to take it home. So on that day—while I was going through the home with the coroner—Mike and his father came to get the turtle.

The next day, I went to the Cuyahoga County Sheriff's office in downtown Cleveland and gave a formal statement: "I have come to the Sheriff's office this morning of my own free will, I want to give the Sheriff every assistance that I possibly can in the solution of my wife's murder. I have repeated over and over again to the police what occurred in my home as I remember it. I have told the Mayor of the City of Bay Village, who first appeared on the scene. I have told the police of Bay Village. I was interviewed on the morning of July 4th by detectives from the Cleveland Police Department. I told them what occurred and they thereupon began to accuse me. I answered the questions of the Deputy Sheriff and the questions of the coroner although at the time, I was suffering from the terrific shock that I had undergone.

"On Thursday, when I had partially recovered my strength and faculties, I submitted to questioning for three hours by Carl Rossbach and Mr. (David) Yettra, county detectives, and Fred Drenkhan of the Bay Village police force. During this questioning, there was nobody present except the three officers and myself. They requested me after this interview to meet them the next morning at my home and to go over with them what happened the morning my wife was killed. I agreed to do this and for a period of approximately three hours I went over the entire matter in detail.

"There was no one who interfered in any way with the questioning by police. At the conclusion of this last examination by the police I was asked if I would make a written statement. I readily assented to this and arranged with Mr. Rossbach that I would come to his office or call him by nine o'clock this morning, and as a result of the request by Mr. Rossbach and my agreement to that request, I am here to make a written statement to you, because I am far

more interested than you are in the solution of the crime against
my wife. I am therefore making this written statement to help you
as much as I can, and after I have made my statement, I will submit
to any questions that you want."

Then, I proceeded to relate my activities on July 3rd, the dinner
with the Aherns, the jarring sound of Marilyn's screams or moans in
the night, and the subsequent events. After I had given my statement, Carl Rossbach questioned me in the presence of Mr. Petersilge. He questioned me at length about the T-shirt I was wearing
the night of the tragedy. It was missing.

Q. Did you take your T-shirt off?
A. Not that I know of.
Q. Do you know how it got off your body?
A. No.
Q. Do you know where it is?
A. No.
Q. What explanation have you?
A. I don't have any, but if I wanted to trump up an explanation I
   probably could have by now, but I don't want to alter the truth.

He asked me whether I had heard our dog, Koko, bark during
the early morning hours on July 4th. I said I didn't recall hearing
the dog bark. In fact, I don't recall seeing the dog at any time during the early morning hours after I was awakened by Marilyn's
screams.

Then he went into my relationship with Marilyn:

Q. Now, did you ever have any trouble with your wife?
A. No, no major trouble.
Q. Did you ever discuss divorce with her?
A. I already told them that I didn't discuss divorce seriously with her
   —that she had mentioned that if I ever wanted a divorce . . .
Q. There are some letters here that indicate that back when you were
   in California, your wife was writing letters showing a disturbed
   mind about—those letters were in your house. When you say you
   never discussed divorce seriously, do you mean it refers to that
   time back in California?
A. Yes.
Q. What happened at that time?
A. Well, we had our youngster and, as you know, a doctor sees and
   comes in close contact with many women, and after the delivery
   my wife became quite jealous, and this was . . .
Q. Did that continue for any length of time?
A. That improved very steadily as time went on.

Q. How long would you say—could you tell the year or number of years you had been married when that occurred?

A. I can't recall specific dates, but . . .

Q. Was it early in your married life?

A. No, I think we had been married for two years.

Q. About two years?

A. Yes, well, more than that—about four years. The youngster was born—we had the youngster after we had been married a couple of years, and it was on into the second year that he was with us.

Q. Was there any discussion after that about divorce—was there any discussion at that time about divorce?

A. Well, that's what I say, she had mentioned something in that regard and I had definitely discouraged.

Of course, I was not asked at that time, nor did I volunteer any information on Marilyn's reaction to sexual relations after Young Sam's birth, which was part of the problem. I just didn't feel it was relevant to the discussion and didn't want to see it all over the newspapers.

I answered some questions about a watch I had given a woman acquaintance in California to replace the one she had lost in early March, 1954. When I declined to divulge her name, the session ended. The statement was typed up on legal-size paper and it occupied the better part of thirteen pages. I signed it, and left the Sheriff's office convinced I had done everything possible to help in solving Marilyn's murder.

There were some, however, who didn't think so. They said their motives in pressing the issue were to obtain justice in the Marilyn Sheppard murder case. What they didn't say was that their motivation was something more than justice—it was dollars and cents— selling newspapers.

The Sheppard Murder Case was selling newspapers in Cleveland, New York, Chicago, Los Angeles . . . all over the country. From the first day of the case it was headline news across America. Several of the more sensational newspapers sent reporters to Cleveland to cover the story. Around the country, most of the newspapers played the story according to the facts that had been developed and with some of the misinformation that was being generated by law enforcement officers, especially the Cleveland Police Department.

The situation in Cleveland was appalling. The Cleveland *Press,* Cleveland *Plain Dealer,* and the Cleveland *News* launched a circulation war seemingly at my expense. They printed columns and columns of copy, some of it factual and some of it full of innuendoes and plain untruths. What was being printed in the news columns was bad enough, but what was to come in the editorial columns was unbelievable and eventually was to go down in history as one of the most colossal miscarriages of journalistic justice.

The assault was led by Louis Benson Seltzer, the most powerful man in Cleveland and perhaps in all of Ohio. He was the editor of the Cleveland *Press,* which happened to be the largest daily newspaper in the state. It seemed that Mr. Seltzer endorsed Detective Schottke's theory; that I had murdered my wife. "I was convinced that a conspiracy existed to defeat the ends of justice," he later wrote in an autobiography. "And that it would affect adversely the whole law-enforcement machinery of the county if it were permitted to succeed. It could establish a precedent that would destroy even-handed administration of justice."

Let me backtrack for just a moment. The same day I was giving my formal statement to police, Leo Stawicki of Cleveland told Bay Village authorities that about two thirty in the morning on July 4th, he drove past my home on the way back from a fishing trip. He said he saw a man in the driveway, standing to the west side of a large maple tree which was located on the east edge of the driveway. Stawicki described him as being about six-feet tall, wearing a white shirt and weighing about one hundred and ninety pounds. He said he had bushy hair, which jibed with the limited description I gave of the assailant.

Stawicki was taken to the County Jail, where I was giving my statement. I was placed in a lineup with three other men. Stawicki didn't know I was there. Police asked him whether he could pick out someone in the lineup who resembled the man he saw the morning of the murder. He couldn't and was sent home.

Another witness also came forward on that day, Richard Knitter, who lived in Sheffield Lake, near Bay Village. Knitter said he and his wife had gone to a movie, had stopped at a restaurant and were on their way home on Lake Road, when they spotted a man near the cemetery just west of my home, between the houses of Spencer Houk and Don Ahern. Knitter said the man was about one hundred and seventy-five pounds, had bushy hair, a large nose, and bulging eyes. When he reported this to Bay Village police, they showed him some pictures of known muggers. He could not identify anyone as the person he had seen during the early morning drive.

This information was never given prominent space by the newspapers, and none of the investigating agencies pursued these leads to any extent. They had decided to concentrate on me, to the exclusion of virtually all other clues.

On Tuesday, July 13th, the Cleveland *News* headlined that Dr. Gerber had asked me to take a lie detector test and that I was well enough to do it. The only discussion I had about a lie detector test was with Schottke and Gareau on the morning and afternoon after the murder.

The following day, a white T-shirt was found on a piece of re-enforced wire on the concrete pier that extends from the Schuele property, immediately west of our house. The T-shirt was under water. It was taken to Dr. Gerber's office. His aides gave it a thorough laboratory examination, and found no blood on it. They said it wasn't mine because it was a medium size, not a large. That was my T-shirt, there was no question about it in my mind. But it didn't have blood on it so they said it wasn't mine. It was a Hanes T-shirt. The authorities knew I wore both Jockey and Hanes T-shirts. I wore a large in the Jockey and a medium in the Hanes.

In the ensuing days, police searched the waters off our property for a murder weapon with a mine detector. They found none. At the suggestion of the Cleveland *News*, Dr. Alan Moritz, prominent local pathologist and crime expert, was brought into the case. I readily agreed to see him and submitted to a long interview. Police continued to dig into my personal life and reported all the details to the newspapers.

As the police continued their investigation, Mr. Seltzer and the Cleveland *Press* apparently became a little impatient and decided to take matters into their own hands. In an editorial entitled "The Finger of Suspicion," the *Press* said that the murder investigation had been mishandled for two reasons:

"One," the editorial said, was the hostility of Bay Village officials to any "outsiders" in the case. "Second was the unusual protection set around the husband of the victim, the sole witness, according to later reports, who could start the investigation on the right track. The protection was twofold. It came from his family and it came from his lawyer. It was unusual to say the least."

Then the *Press* said that the "first logical step" in seeing "that justice is done" would be a meeting of all law enforcement agencies involved. Wouldn't you know it, the next day there was a mass meeting of all law enforcement officials at the Coroner's Office.

Newsmen and photographers were admitted to the meeting, but no member of my family or my legal counsel was invited.

That was just the beginning for the *Press*. On July 20th, the *Press* printed another blistering editorial, under the headline: "Getting Away with Murder." Seltzer in his autobiography published two years later wrote, "Because I did not want anyone else on the *Press* staff to take the risk, I wrote the editorial myself. It may not have been a good editorial, but it was a hard-hitting editorial. It was intended to be."

It said in part:

What's the matter with law enforcement authorities in Cuyahoga County?

Have they lost their sense of reason?—or at least inexcusably set aside the realization of what they are hired to do, and for whom they work?

If ever a murder case was studded with fumbling, halting, stupid, un-cooperative bumbling-politeness to people whose place in this situation completely justified vigorous searching, prompt and effective police work —the Sheppard case has them all. . . .

From the very beginning of this case—from the first hour that the murder became known to authorities by a telephone call from the husband to the town mayor—from that moment on and including this, the case has been one of the worst in local crime history. . . .

In the background of this case are friendships, relationships, hired lawyers, a husband who ought to have been subjected instantly to the same third-degree to which any other person under similar circumstances is subjected, and a whole string of special and bewildering extra-privileged courtesies that should never be extended by authorities investigating a murder—the most serious, and sickening crime of all. . . .

What's the matter with us in Cuyahoga County? Who are we afraid of? Why do we have to kow-tow to a set of circumstances where a murder has been committed?

It is time that somebody smashed into this situation and tore aside this restraining curtain of shame, politeness, and hypocrisy and went at the business of solving a murder—and quit this nonsense of artificial politeness that has not been extended to any other murder case in generations.

That same day, the Cleveland *Plain Dealer,* the morning newspaper, printed a cartoon of the head of a sphinx mounted on the body of a dog with a collar around its neck. This obviously represented the orthopedic collar I wore, and it gave the impression that I was conducting myself like a sphinx by refusing to cooperate. This was not at all true.

On July 21st, the Cleveland *News* got into the editorial act, with an editorial entitled, "Time To Bring the Bay Slaying into Open."

We are forced to take note that Dr. Samuel Sheppard, husband of the victim, has rejected suggestions of both lie detector and truth serum tests, and has submitted to questioning only when his family and his lawyers have agreed he might.

But the big editorial came in the powerful Cleveland *Press*, first under the headline, "Isn't This Murder Worth an Inquest?"—then "Why No Inquest? Do It Now, Dr. Gerber."
The editorial said:

Why hasn't County Coroner Sam Gerber called an inquest into the Sheppard Murder case?
What restrains him?
Is the Sheppard murder case any different from the countless other murder mysteries where the coroner has turned to this traditional method of investigation?
An inquest empowers use of the subpoena.
It puts witnesses under oath.
It makes possible the examination of every possible witness, suspect, relative, records and papers available anywhere.
It puts the investigation itself into the record.
And what's most important of all—it sometimes solves crimes.
What good reason is there now for Dr. Gerber to delay any longer the use of the inquest?
The murder of Marilyn Sheppard is a baffling crime.
Thus far it appears to have stumped everybody.
It may never be solved.
But, this community can never have a clear conscience until every possible method is applied to its solution.
What, Coroner Gerber, is the answer to the question—
Why don't you call an inquest into this murder?

And, so he did, for the next day.

4

Upon returning home from Los Angeles in 1951 to join Dad, Steve, and Richard at Bay View Hospital, the work load piled up so quickly that the average hospital day seemed to stretch on indefinitely. Despite the fact that I was preoccupied with a wide variety of medical and surgical cases, I couldn't help but notice that a young medical technician was being attentive toward me.

The young woman's name was Susan Hayes. She was twenty-one at the time, had a nice figure in the crisp technician's gown, and a pleasant personality. Susan was rather pretty. She had brown eyes and brown hair and a little line of freckles across her nose. Miss Hayes had started as a trainee at Bay View in the late 1940's. I met her for a brief moment in mid-1949, when, returning to Ohio for a few weeks to study for the state medical and surgical examinations, I toured the Bay View X-ray department with a young radiologist. Our paths didn't cross again for two years.

During those first weeks after my return in 1951, it seemed to me that Susan Hayes was trying to attract my attention. Every time I looked up she was there. The house that Dad had rented for Marilyn and me while we looked for a permanent residence was in Rocky River. Coincidentally, it happened to be just a half block from the home of Miss Hayes. Almost every morning she came to the rented house and asked for a ride to the hospital. Just before we moved into our own home on Lake Road, she would open the garage door and sit in the car while waiting for me.

Susan also was a damn good medical technician, who was always willing to come to the hospital during emergency situations on weekends or during the evening to run blood tests and perform other laboratory functions. She usually waited at the hospital until the surgery was completed and then had a standard line, "Doctor, I have no way of getting home. Would you please take me?" Most of the doctors were indebted to her for doing an excellent blood-typing job and gladly drove her home.

One night I found myself alone in an automobile with Susan.

Marilyn was still having problems that went back to the birth of young Sam and Susan proved to be available to fill a natural need for me. Never did I tell her that I loved her or wanted to marry her. On the contrary, I told her of my love for Marilyn and Chip and that I had no intention of breaking up my wonderful marriage. As far as I was concerned, my relationship with her was a purely physical arrangement of convenience.

Susan remained at Bay View until the fall of 1952, then took a job in downtown Cleveland, which she held until the summer of 1953. She spent much of that summer in Minneapolis, while engaged to a doctor there. When the engagement fell through, she returned to Bay View in the fall of 1953, remaining there until midwinter when she packed and moved to California. Our relationship continued through much of that period, when Susan was geographically available.

Marilyn knew about this relationship but she understood and recognized why it had developed. "Look," she once told me, "I know my father has had a mistress ever since I've been able to walk, but that woman has been closer to me than my stepmother." It gave her a little insight regarding our own situation. She didn't like Susan, but Marilyn had gone as far as to permit this young lady and her mother into our home at my birthday party one night when other hospital staff members were there. Actually, Sue, her mother, and a friend crashed the party.

In March, 1954, Marilyn and I took a trip to Los Angeles. The primary purpose, of course, was for me to complete an extra special course in brain dissection. We also wanted to renew some of the old acquaintances we had enjoyed during the long time we were in Los Angeles. Marilyn and I especially wanted to see Dr. Randall Chapman, his wife, and several other doctors and their wives.

Marilyn knew I would be very, very busy. Mrs. Chapman asked her to spend the first part of our stay at their ranch, about three hundred miles north of Los Angeles. Marilyn and Mrs. Chapman left for the ranch the day after we arrived. Before she left for the ranch, knowing Susan Hayes was in town, Marilyn kissed me on the lips, and said, "Get your work done at the college, but also have yourself some fun. I'll see you up at the ranch."

I called Susan, who was staying with her friends, Mr. and Mrs. Shabala. Mrs. Shabala also was a medical technician and had worked for a time at Bay View Hospital. We were all acquainted. Susan and I had dinner with Dr. Randall Chapman, then went to a motel on a hill overlooking the city, where we spent the night. The next day I took her with me to the home of Dr. Arthur Miller and his wife, Carol, at their demand. Art had not previously met Susan.

The Millers insisted that while I was in Los Angeles I stay at their home. They also knew that my relationship with Susan was a little more than casual and they suggested, too, that she could stay in their home, if I wished. Carol Miller said she would be grateful to have Sue there to help take care of their little boy. Sue and I spent four or five nights together in the Miller home.

During this period while Sue and I were together, we went with the Shabalas to a wedding and dinner in San Diego. During the trip, Susan left her purse and wrist watch in a service station washroom. On the return trip we stopped at the station but it was closed. I left a note telling the station owner that if he found the watch and purse, I would appreciate it if it were mailed to me in Bay Village.

Meanwhile, I bought Susan another watch to replace the lost one. It cost about fifty dollars. (Later the watch that had been "lost" was mailed to me in Bay Village and I sent it to Susan's mother in Rocky River.) Aside from the wrist watch which replaced the one which had temporarily been lost, the only other presents that I gave Susan Hayes were an eight-dollar signet ring and a suede coat. I didn't lavish gifts on her—just bought the two things she asked for.

After completing my work in Los Angeles, I drove with Dr. Randall Chapman to his ranch near Monterey to join Marilyn and his wife. We spent a wonderful few days. It was during that stay that the child Marilyn was bearing at the time of her death was conceived. We had agreed that an addition was in order.

At this time, Dr. Chapman, the man who taught me much of what I had learned about neurosurgery, was having his problems. He and his wife had decided on a divorce—she spent most of the time at the ranch up north. And Chapman wanted to come to Cleveland to join my father, brothers, and me in practice. We discussed this possibility on our long drive up to the ranch.

I encouraged him because I knew the man was one of the very best surgeons and thought he could make a substantial contribution. He had me on his side, and now all he had to do was to win my father and brothers over to his cause.

Unbeknown to me for some time, he also had enlisted Marilyn. One day, while we were at the ranch, I was in the yard piling wood and stacking bricks for an outside fireplace. Dr. Chapman called

Marilyn aside and talked with her about the possibility of returning to Cleveland. He told my wife I had spent every minute of my time in Los Angeles with Susan Hayes, that I was all wrapped up with her. This was the farthest thing from the truth. He told her that he had talked me out of getting a divorce.

He said that if Marilyn helped him pave the way for a return to Cleveland with my father and brothers, that he would be sure and influence me to play it straight and be a "good boy." He made her promise that she would never tell me what he had told her. He turned it into a big thing, rather than telling her what was true—that Susan Hayes was available and that I only saw her during the evenings, after spending the day in the laboratory. Indeed, one evening while I was in Los Angeles, I helped a friend, Dr. Troy McHenry, work on his new racing car, a Porsche Spider, and didn't see Susan until I got back to the Millers.

Marilyn carried this thing back with her to Cleveland and she also became favorable to Dr. Chapman's cause. She convinced my father and brothers that it would be a good thing for him to come to Cleveland and become my partner. I had told Dr. Chapman that at the outset I would not insist, or push, for full membership in the Sheppard Clinic. I said that he and I could be partners and we would share a one-man intake until he fully proved himself to the other members of the clinic. When he proved himself, he could become a full member and share a fifth of the income, rather than half of one share. This is how much I thought of the man.

Dr. Chapman had a partnership in Los Angeles with Dr. Phillip Davis. He had assumed all along that Davis would be glad to have the whole practice for himself. Davis had a wife who also was a doctor. Between the two of them, they were in a pretty sizeable tax bracket. But Davis didn't want the practice for himself. He liked the partnership arrangement because it gave him time to teach. He balked, raised hell, and refused to free Dr. Chapman from the partnership agreement. That ended Chapman's plans to come to Cleveland.

Marilyn continued to conceal from me the conversation she had had with Chapman. She didn't have any idea of what he had in his mind. She liked him and his story sounded plausible. She confided at least part of the story to Nancy Ahern, but she didn't tell me until later.

I knew there was something bothering Marilyn and it took me weeks to extract it from her. I finally did, perhaps two or three weeks before the tragedy. Marilyn also came to the realization that there was something fishy, because I was displaying a true innocence about what was bothering her. Our life together and my joy about our second child proved Chapman's lie.

Anyway, she finally squared with me about what Dr. Chapman had told her. I convinced her that this account was not true. She knew that I had taken part in extra-marital relations, but Dr. Chapman's belief that I was considering marrying some other woman was something else. To her, at the time, it seemed it could happen. When Dr. Chapman said this was fact, she believed him. I thank God I was able to finally get Marilyn to have more confidence in me than in someone else.

I pointed out a few things to her. One, of course, was that Susan Hayes was planning to get married and it wasn't to me. There was also the fact that with my help Marilyn had solved her problem of sexual coldness and that we were having a normal relationship. Based on this, I had ceased any extra-marital affairs.

I respected Marilyn for living up to her promise, although I resented my wife making a promise to any man that would supersede our relationship. But, I did understand her reasoning because we had been so close with the Chapmans. There was no apology necessary in the way of spoken words or gestures. "Let's just be a family," I said. "Just let's be what we're supposed to be." It's amazing the effect that this had. We had been happy and going along day-to-day and enjoying parties, swimming, water skiing, and our little boy.

Thereafter, there was a new hue to almost everything we did. Daily, Marilyn tried to do something for me that would in some way overcome what had happened in the previous months. I returned these gestures like an echo. We acted spontaneously. We were surprising ourselves by how very much in love we were.

The basic point I am trying to make is that my affair with Susan —if you want to call it that—was not clandestine. It really was in the open. I did not try to hide it and I expected people to see it for what it was—a source of satisfaction for a physical need. I never tried to hide the wrist-watch incident and had it not been for Dr. Chapman, Marilyn would never have suspected that it was anything but what it was—an attempt to replace a lost item.

The police knew the first day that I had purchased a watch for some woman, a fact which I believed they learned from Nancy Ahern. I readily admitted it in my statement at the sheriff's office on July 10th, although I declined to give detectives Susan Hayes' name because there was no sense bringing it into the situation at that time.

I knew that they had done additional checking about my friendship with Susan Hayes and so the night before Dr. Gerber's inquest I told the entire story of our relationship to attorney Bill Corrigan. We were in an upstairs room of my parents' home.

Corrigan immediately asked me what I would do if I was questioned about my relationship with Sue Hayes. I said that I would tell the truth or if he advised would duck behind the Fifth Amendment. "All this means is that I was eating my cake and having it at home, too. It doesn't mean anything else. It might have given Marilyn grounds to kill me, but surely not me to kill her," I said. "Would she tell on you?" he asked. I told him I didn't know. I said that I didn't think she was the "tell type," but that "thinking" in this situation was not good enough.

He advised me to "deny any sexual relations." He said, "I believe she won't tell on you." I countered that I was not sure I agreed with him. Since Mr. Corrigan was the expert in the criminal law field, I reluctantly decided to follow his advice.

After the lawyer left, I discussed the matter with my mother. I told her what I was going to do and she was very upset about it— that I was going to lie if questioned about having sexual relations with Susan Hayes. I told her that that was what I had to do, according to Mr. Corrigan's advice. As it turned out, it was the worst piece of legal advice a man could receive.

I wasn't really afraid of a coroner's inquest. Several days before when I had refused to talk with Schottke and Gareau, Gerber threatened me. He accused me of being uncooperative. "Go ahead and have an inquest," I said. "I'm all for it, but don't say that I'm uncooperative because I've talked to the sheriff's office and I've talked to the Cleveland police, who have nothing to do with Bay Village."

Dr. Gerber had his inquest. But instead of having it at the Coroner's Office at Western Reserve University or in a court room downtown he picked the auditorium at Normandy School in Bay Village. If it was a big audience with plenty of fanfare that Dr. Gerber wanted, he got it. They might as well have held the inquest at the Cleveland Public Auditorium.

There were hundreds of card chairs set up in the auditorium and hundreds of men, women, and children crowded into the place, to say nothing of the reporters and photographers. They were everywhere. It was a great publicity show for Dr. Gerber. The crowd was hostile. The spectators hooted and booed and made nasty remarks to my parents and other members of my family. The whole thing was useless because a coroner's inquest is supposed to determine the cause of death and they already knew that.

I was out in the hall throughout much of the first day of the inquest waiting for my turn to testify, but I saw enough of what was going on to realize that they weren't going to learn anything they didn't know before. Dr. Gerber acted as judge, prosecutor, and jury and he played to the crowd.

Finally, late in the day, they got to me. I was still wearing the orthopedic collar and dark glasses because of the injuries suffered almost three weeks before. For two hours that day Dr. Gerber fired questions at me. Shortly after I took the stand, Dr. Gerber began to question me about the trip Marilyn and I took to California the preceding March. The police obviously had done some investigating on the West Coast and found out that while Marilyn was in Monterey Susan Hayes and I had both stayed at Dr. Arthur Miller's home.

"How many times did you see Miss Hayes?" Dr. Gerber asked me.

"I can't say for sure," I answered. The questioning continued:

Q. Didn't she stay at Dr. Miller's house?
A. She stayed there while I was taking a course.
Q. Isn't it a fact that you and your wife had differences over Miss Hayes staying there?
A. No.
Q. Didn't Dr. Miller state that you ought to be psychoanalyzed for bringing your girl out there?
A. Heavens no.
Q. She (Miss Hayes) just gave up her job and stayed there a week?
A. She didn't have a job.
Q. What did she do?
A. During the day, she looked after Dr. Miller's child.

The hearing recessed late that Thursday afternoon and then resumed the next morning. I was on the stand for another three hours. And again, Dr. Gerber questioned me about the California trip. Toward the end of my appearance on the stand, he asked pointedly, "In your stay at the Miller home did you at any time sleep in the same bedroom with Susan Hayes?"

"No," I replied.

"While there did you have any sexual relations with Susan Hayes?" Dr. Gerber persisted.

"No, not at any time," I answered.

The hearing was then recessed for the weekend. It resumed on Monday, July 26th. One of the witnesses on Monday was my mother. That was terrible. It tore me to pieces. My mother was a highly modest woman. She had come from a farm in Illinois and she had earned her own college education. She had been a school teacher and had taught English, Greek, and Latin. She had always been afraid of firearms and my father had sheltered her. Throughout her life she remained idealistic, and this left her unprepared for what she had to go through before that leering, jeering crowd.

Both my mother and Nancy Ahern, who also testified at the inquest on the 26th, testified that Marilyn was "upset" because of Susan Hayes, but what they didn't know and therefore couldn't say was that this disturbance had resulted from the story Dr. Randall Chapman had told Marilyn while we were in California.

The inquest finally broke up when Bill Corrigan tried several times to read a statement into the record. Dr. Gerber told my attorney he was only a spectator at the proceedings and ordered him forcibly removed from the auditorium, to the cheers and applause of the mob that had assembled. Corrigan didn't go easily. It took two policemen and a sheriff's deputy to shove him out into the corridor.

At that point, Dr. Gerber made no attempt to resume the hearing. He recessed it indefinitely. Although I wasn't there that day, I'm told that several women tried to kiss him and one actually did.

During the period of the inquest, the Bay Village Police Department had turned the investigation over to the Cleveland Police Department. As the inquest ended, Cleveland Homicide Captain David Kerr, who had been called back from a Cuban vacation by Mayor Anthony Celebrezze, to head the investigation, told the reporters that he expected an arrest to be made very soon.

As part of their investigation, they sent Thomas Parrino, an assistant Cuyahoga County prosecutor, and Schottke, my original accuser, to California, to talk with Sue Hayes. She was young and inexperienced and they threatened they would prosecute her as a prostitute or convict her of perjury or something equally unpleasant, if she didn't talk. They pressured her and pressured her and finally she called her father and he told her to tell everything. She told them much more than she had to to satisfy their needs. She told them that we had had sexual relations at Dr. Miller's home. This, of course, made me a liar under oath at the coroner's inquest. As I said before, I had wanted to tell the truth in the first place, but was advised by counsel to deny any sexual relations.

The police brought her back from California and the statement she made about our affair was made public. What could I say? I explained that I had denied the sexual relations because I wanted to be discreet and protect the young lady's reputation. Of course, those bent on sending me to the electric chair had another theory. They cried, "If he would lie to protect a woman's reputation, what would he do to save his own neck?"

If I had had my own way, that never would have happened.

5

The word was out. An arrest was soon to be made. I knew the police had never looked for any other suspect and that when an arrest was made the person arrested would be me. However, Cleveland police had a small problem. As smug as they were about their so-called case against me, they didn't want to arrest me themselves. They had the evidence, they said, but they wanted Bay Village police to perform the actual arrest. Why did they insist that Bay Village authorities arrest me on the basis of Cleveland police evidence? Cleveland police obviously were trying to protect themselves against future arrest proceedings. They were covering themselves, of course.

Bay Village police were a little apprehensive, too. The newspapers charged they were "protecting" me, but the fact remained that they weren't convinced the facts gathered by Cleveland police added up to an arrest. In their investigation, they had learned only that there was no forcible entry to my house and that I had had some extramarital relations. They had no motive and no weapon. Finally, Cleveland police insisted that Bay Village authorities in the suburb arrest me and threatened to pull out of the case if they didn't.

Bay Villiage police were getting advice from all sides, including Louis B. Seltzer and the Cleveland *Press*. On July 28, the *Press* carried an editorial under the headline, "Why Don't Police Quiz Top Suspect?" The editorial said in part:

But they haven't called in Sam Sheppard.

Now proved under oath to be a liar, still free to go about his business, shielded by his family, protected by a smart lawyer who has made monkeys of the police and authorities, carrying a gun part of the time, left free to do whatever he pleases as he pleases, Sam Sheppard still hasn't been taken to headquarters.

What's wrong in this whole mess that is making this community a national laughing stock?
Who's holding back—and why?

What's the basic difference between murder in an "ordinary" neighborhood and one in a Lake Road house in suburban Bay Village?

Who's afraid of whom?

It's just about time that somebody began producing the answers—

And producing Sam Sheppard at Police Headquarters.

The press wasn't letting up. The next day, the newspaper published a cartoon which showed that handcuffs were on officials and the police and not on the "murder suspect," who was being shielded by lawyers and friends. And then on July 30th came the most blatant blast of all.

"Why Isn't Sam Sheppard in Jail?" shouted a Cleveland *Press* headline. In later editions, the headline was changed to read, "Quit Stalling Bring Him In." The editorial said:

Maybe somebody in this town can remember a parallel for it. The *Press* can't.

And not even the oldest police veterans can, either.

Everybody's agreed that Sam Sheppard is the most unusual murder suspect ever seen around these parts.

Except for some superficial questioning during Coroner Gerber's inquest, he has been scot-free of any official grilling into the circumstances of his wife's murder.

From the morning of July 4, when he reported his wife's killing, to the moment, 26 days later, Sam Sheppard has not set foot in a police station.

He has been surrounded by an iron curtain of protection that makes Malenkov's Russian concealment amateurish.

His family, his Bay Village friends—which include its officials—his lawyers, his hospital staff, have combined to make law enforcement in this county look silly.

The longer they can stall bringing Sam Sheppard to the police station the surer it is he'll never get there.

The longer they can string this whole affair out the surer it is that the public's attention sooner or later will be diverted to something else, and then the heat will be off, the public interest gone, and the goose will hang high.

This man is a suspect in his wife's murder. Nobody yet has found a solitary trace of the presence of anybody else in his Lake Road house the night or morning his wife was brutally beaten to death in her bedroom.

And yet no murder suspect in the history of this county has been treated so tenderly, with such infinite solicitude for his emotions, with such fear of upsetting the young man.

Gentlemen of Bay Village, Cuyahoga County, and Cleveland, charged jointly with law enforcement—

THIS IS MURDER. THIS IS NO PARLOR GAME. THIS IS NO

TIME TO PERMIT ANYBODY—NO MATTER WHO HE IS—TO OUT-
WIT, STALL, FAKE, OR IMPROVISE DEVICES TO KEEP AWAY
FROM THE POLICE OR FROM THE QUESTIONING ANYBODY
IN HIS RIGHT MIND KNOWS A MURDER SUSPECT SHOULD BE
SUBJECTED TO—AT A POLICE STATION.

The officials throw up their hands in horror at the thought of bringing
Sam Sheppard to a police station for grilling. Why? Why is he any different than anybody else in any other murder case?

Why should the police officials be afraid of Bill Corrigan? Or anybody
else, for that matter, when they are at their sworn business of solving a
murder.

Certainly Corrigan will act to protect Sam Sheppard's rights. He should.

BUT THE PEOPLE OF CUYAHOGA COUNTY EXPECT YOU,
THE LAW ENFORCEMENT OFFICIALS, TO PROTECT THE PEO-
PLE'S RIGHTS.

A murder has been committed, you know who the chief suspect is.

You have the obligation to question him—question him thoroughly and
searchingly—from beginning to end, and not at his hospital, not at his
home, not in some secluded spot out in the country.

But at police headquarters—just as you do every other person suspected
in a murder case.

What the people of Cuyahoga County cannot understand, and The
Press cannot understand, is why you are showing Sam Sheppard so much
more consideration as a murder suspect than any other person who has
ever before been suspected in a murder case.

Why?

You might say, whatever Seltzer wanted, Seltzer got. And, he
wanted police to give me the third degree in hopes that I would
confess to murdering my wife.

The night of July 30th, which happened to be a Friday, I had
dinner at Steve and Betty Sheppard's home. After dinner, they suggested we take a boat ride on Lake Erie.

Members of the press had been following me all day, anticipating
that there might be an arrest. They followed me to Steve's house
and they followed us to the yacht club. I finally threw up my hands
and said, "The hell with it." And asked to be taken to my parents'
home, near the Hospital. I said they could take their boat trip and
I'd talk to the folks.

Within that past twenty-four hours, Cleveland Mayor Anthony
Celebrezze had given Bay Village police an ultimatum that either
they arrest me or Cleveland police would drop the case. Richard
Weygandt, the Bay Village solicitor, took the matter under advisement. At ten that night, he announced his decision to newsmen on

the steps of his porch. "There is probable cause to believe Sam Sheppard guilty of the murder of his wife and I believe the arrest should be made." Nobody bothered to notify my attorneys or my family.

At about ten twenty p.m., three policemen arrived at the home of my parents. Newsmen already were cluttered around the home and a mob had started to assemble. The word had already been spread far and wide by radio and television that I would be arrested and the curiosity seekers and neighbors were out in force to witness the spectacle.

They trampled on the lawn, stepped in the flower beds. There were newsmen on the porches. My poor mother was petrified when photographers used flash guns with their cameras in trying to get pictures through the windows of the house. The ugly, hostile mob shouted "Murderer," and "Go get him," as police arrived.

Dad went out on the front porch and asked the mob to leave the premises, but they just laughed at him. Police were able to remove photographers from the porch. Finally, I was handcuffed to one of the detectives in the living room, right in front of my mother and father, and was led out the front door to the cheers of the mob. The best police could do was clear a path to their vehicle. The glare of exploding flash bulbs was almost unbelievable. They put me in the car and drove me to the Bay Village City Hall.

I had expected the arrest after reading the newspaper editorials, but when the moment finally came, I couldn't believe it was happening to me. I didn't think that in America this kind of thing could happen. As we drove to the City Hall, my concern was for my parents, who had to witness their son handcuffed and led away to the taunts of the mob. It was their welfare that bothered me most.

When we walked into the City Hall, we passed several glassed-in offices. There was a light in one of the offices and through the translucent glass, I could see the shadows of several men in conference. Wearing a pair of blue pants, a white T-shirt, and a suede jacket, I was taken into a meeting chamber and left alone. The room was dark and the windows were open.

After a few moments, the meeting in the office broke up, the lights in the chamber were turned on and several men filed into the big meeting room. The President of the city council, Gersham M. M. Barber, who had publicly expressed a definite opinion against me, called the session to order. He was substituting for Mayor Houk, who was under the weather and had disqualified himself because of his involvement in the events of July 4th.

I knew that my family had called Corrigan and five times I asked Barber if we could wait until his arrival before proceeding. The request fell on deaf ears. He just went along as if I had never said anything. Finally, Barber said my attorney would see me "in due time." Then he said, "On information supplied to me, I, Gersham M. M. Barber, charge that you, on or about July 4th, did purposefully and of deliberate and pre-meditated malice kill one Marilyn Sheppard. How do you plead?"

"Not guilty," I answered. Then Barber set a preliminary hearing for August 7th. The handcuffs were placed on my hands again, I was taken to a police car and driven to Cuyahoga County Jail, a trip of about forty-five minutes, to await what Mr. Seltzer called "the third degree."

We arrived at the jail and rode the elevator to the fourth floor of the jail. They photographed and fingerprinted me and then placed me in a small isolation cell, which contained no toilet or wash bowl. I was told that an old, dirty, stained pail in the corner was to be used for a toilet. I was scrutinized by every deputy in the place. I asked myself, "Could this be Cleveland, Ohio, or is this a prolongation of the hideous dream that started on July 4th."

They put a police guard outside the cell. I guess there had been more rumors around that I had been taking dope and that's why they put me under observation. The authorities thought perhaps there would be withdrawal symptoms, if I had been taking dope. The whole thing was ridiculous. I wasn't taking dope and never had. It is a fact that an addict will do almost anything when in need of a "fix." I guess police felt that if I craved dope, I might do anything, even confess, if they would promise to give me a fix.

Meanwhile, my attorneys, Corrigan and Petersilge, had gone to the Bay Village City Hall and found no one there and the place dark. Then they came to County Jail and were refused permission to see me, even though I had been promised I could see my attorneys once I got to jail. When it became obvious that Corrigan and Petersilge wouldn't be allowed to visit me, I went to sleep, well aware there probably would be damn little of it during the next several days.

At five thirty a.m., a deputy awakened me for breakfast. A bowl of soggy corn flakes made with powdered milk and a cup of what they called coffee was shoved through a hole in the door. I ate and then went back to sleep until nine, when I was allowed to meet for a few minutes with Bill Corrigan. Then deputies took me to the 11th floor of the County jail and I was examined briefly by Dr. Spencer Braden, a prominent neurosurgeon, and a Dr. Greene, the jail physician. Police chief Frank W. Story of Cleveland was there and questioned me for a time. Next it was back to the cell for lunch, an unappetizing meal of meat loaf, potatoes, and gravy thrown into a bowl.

Then it was time for the ordeal. I was taken to the small office where authorities had recorded my original statement a few days after the tragedy. For the next twelve hours, four teams of detectives questioned me in relays. First there were Schottke and Gareau; then detectives William Lonchard and Peter Becker; then detectives Harold Lockwood and John Doyle; and, finally, Adelbert O'Hara and James McHugh.

The method of questioning and the continuous effect of the different teams was consistent with those methods used by police in countries behind the Iron Curtain. I was not beaten and drugs were not administered, but, otherwise, the experience was no different from what has been reported by men subjected to Communist methods.

It was mental torture at its worst. Physical beating would have been a pleasure to me in comparison. Hour after hour, they shouted at me, accused me, insulted me and members of my family. They tried to trick me by questioning me about facts they knew were not correct. Each time I told them I didn't kill my wife.

They called me names I wouldn't repeat. I was faced with the necessity of mustering all of my faith, courage, and fortitude to withstand this unjust attack and also of maintaining the composure to overcome the tendency to fight back forcibly. A forcible retaliation or a psychological breakdown was exactly what these people were looking for.

It was necessary for me to reach deep into past experience to come up with this fortitude combined with restraint. I recalled high-school and college football, where fortitude was necessary, but such fortitude could be expressed in contact and rough play. Dirty play on the football field was practiced by some, but controlled by the referee. There was no referee in this stuffy, smoky, room.

My thoughts drifted back to the high-school and college fraternity experiences, where as pledges we were the butt of many humiliating incidents. Especially in college, fraternity members go out of their way to test prospective members by subjecting them to beatings with paddles as well as words. A complaint would warrant more beating and to fight back would usually result in dismissal from the pledge group for lack of restraint.

The fraternity experience had taught me what I could take physically and gave me some mild indication of my psychological composure. But, in the fraternity there were fifteen other fellows going through the same thing and the goal was membership in a secret brotherhood, not a chance to sit in the electric chair. I was alone in my plight, but the fraternity background helped a great deal because we were taught as pledges to work together. I was determined to hold firm to the truth and not allow these rather stupid individuals to break my mental and physical poise.

Each pair of detectives tried to make a deal with me. They promised that if I confessed I could get off with a manslaughter indictment, which would mean a year or so of prison and then freedom. I told them that I wasn't going to confess to anything that I didn't do, regardless of the consequences. I told them this was a helluva way to operate in a democracy, in America, to try and persuade an innocent man to confess to a crime he didn't commit.

At one point, detective Lockwood said to me, "How can you put up with this ordeal?" I told him that I had faith in the truth and faith in God, that Marilyn was with me in spirit, and with that faith I could take anything they had to dish out and more. The first day's ordeal ended at midnight.

The next morning, Bill Corrigan, arrived at eight and we briefly reviewed my situation until the sheriff's deputies ordered Bill out of the jail. It was Sunday, but it was not a day of extra rest for the detectives. They started all over. "Why did you do it, Sam?" one would ask. Another, "Why did you kill your wife?" Then using a rolled newspaper they would pretend they were beating something with a weapon, the way I was supposed to have bludgeoned Marilyn and they would shout, "Down, down, down," as though they were hitting a head. Then, "Why, Why, Why—You!"

Finally, on Monday, the third day of questioning, I told them I would not answer any more of the questions; that they were trying to get me to confess and that I was not going to confess to a crime I did not commit. Then I started reading a Bible which had been given to me by Reverend Alan Davis, one of my best friends, and refused to answer any more questions.

This obviously convinced the detectives that they were barking up the wrong tree—that I wasn't going to confess to something I didn't do, regardless of their tactics or their silly offers for pleading their way.

However, on Monday evening, August 2nd, I was in for another surprise. About seven, I was handcuffed, put into a police car, and taken for a ride with Carl Rossbach and deputy David Yettra and a couple of Cleveland detectives. When I asked them where I was being taken without my consent one of them said, "You'll find out." We finally arrived at City Hospital on Scranton Road.

There were several doctors there, including Dr. Spencer Braden, (the neurosurgeon I had seen the morning after I was arrested) plus the X-ray specialist and others. They stripped me and took off my orthopedic collar. They X-rayed me, even thought I protested. X-rays taken a month after suffering the injuries would be of questionable value. The state of Ohio forced me to submit to an examination. They tested for various reflexes. In short they gave me a complete neurological examination without my consent. When they were finished sticking me with pins and twisting my limbs, I was allowed to dress and was taken back to the county jail in handcuffs.

Meanwhile, my attorneys tried unsuccessfully to obtain my immediate release from the jail on a writ of habeas corpus.

My reactions during those first few days of jail can best be expressed by this letter written to Mother:

Mother dear:

Your letters and the sermon by Reverend Tittle have helped more than I can say. Two portions that express my feelings are:

1. What Socrates revealed when, threatened with death, he said, Anytus and Meletus may indeed kill me, but hurt me they cannot. And if you can bear to hear the truth you've spoken twisted by knaves to make a trap for fools, or watch the things you gave your life to broken, and stoop and build 'em up with wornout tools, you are the possessor of poise.

These things help because I can't fight back. These men have their minds made up and did before they even talked to me. They are trying to obtain a false confession. These comments in relation to poise are so representative of Dad and reasons that I have always tried and wanted to be more like him. *We* all know how our thoughts and drives have been centered around service to mankind through Dad's inspiration. Others don't see this.

Everything I do or look at reminds me of Marilyn. At this point I would like to join her, but she would be disappointed totally if I should give up. Her total confidence and belief in my ability is another thing that helps somehow. She is right with me and with us (the family). God bless her! She was and is still the greatest! Chip is the living proof of that.

I can't help thinking of those who might have actually employed someone to do this thing to us. We know there are those who would fit this possibility. Ask Dad what he thinks of this. This of course would be something the police would have much difficulty tracing, so not considered by them. They have admittedly gone on percentage and I am therefore guilty in their eyes until *I* can prove myself innocent. This is hard to believe in the U.S.A.

I figure that you pass these communications to the others in the family so I'm not writing to the others.

Was glad to read in regard to the hospital. According to the police here —the hospital is falling apart, no patients and no spirit. Don't know how some of these fellows live with themselves. Some of them display great satisfaction in discussing their meager salary and my "great wealth" and my present position in jail.

One of my communications was taken from my pocket by David Yettra —they act as though a man has no rights.

My radio helps but has something loose in it and it doesn't work at all sometimes. Maybe Richard could bring his down and take mine and fix it. I don't need the batteries as a plug is available.

Now that they have stopped questioning me I have time to think a little and read. Am reading the Bible. I have a pocket version of *Treasure Island* I plan to read. Rich will be happy to know this. *The Cruel Sea* Rich gave me too.

Have had a continuous basal headache associated with the stiff sore neck, but it is improving.

The last question period terminated yesterday morning. All the detectives without exception have said there is absolutely no evidence of premeditation in this case. The ones yesterday denied their wish to get a false confession but for me to have faith in God if innocent. After all their statements a man almost wishes he *could* answer their questions. They attempt to mold the suspect to their impression of him. According to them, I would be better off *legally* and treated much better, if I were guilty and could explain their questions. It would be impossible for a guilty man to go through this *going over* without confession in my opinion.

Don't wish to go over and over these things and subject you to all of this but I think I'll be better off to express these feelings in writing than to keep them inside.

The baseball game is going to come on soon so I'll close. Sunday is the day we were going to the sports car races in Columbus. Marilyn and I looked forward to it.

Thank Dad for the picture of Marilyn he sent. I have it on the wall of my *comfortable room*

All my love to everyone.

Sam.

The next item on the legal agenda was a preliminary hearing at which police were supposed to show probable cause as to why I should be held over to the grand jury. The preliminary hearing originally was scheduled to be held before acting Mayor Gersham M. M. Barber of Bay Village, but my attorneys went to common pleas court and proved that Barber was prejudiced in the case and should not sit in judgment at the preliminary hearing.

The preliminary hearing was then rescheduled before Common Pleas Judge William K. Thomas on the morning of August 16th. It was the same day that county officials were taking the case before the county grand jury and apparently the prosecutor's office planned to ask Judge Thomas for an adjournment or postponement of the hearing while the case was outlined before the grand jury. In this manner, the prosecutor's office would be spared from divulging the details of its case, whatever they might be.

Sitting in Judge Thomas' court that morning I watched Bill Corrigan go before the judge, a thin, distinguished-looking man, and ask that I be released on bail. It was a move that surprised the police officials. As the late, great Will Rogers used to say, "All they knew was what they read in the newspapers."

"This man has never been connected with any crime other than those sins which many of us are guilty of," Bill Corrigan said, his voice filled with emotion. "This man is thirty years old and a neurosurgeon. Up to now, he has had an excellent reputation in the community." Tears stung in my eyes as I thought about Mother and Dad's spotless relationship and reputation.

After the hearing, Judge Thomas returned to his study while I remained in the court room and chatted with my brother, Richard. Shortly after eleven a.m., the Judge emerged from his office and stepped to the bench. I didn't know what to expect, but from the way things had been going I wasn't too confident.

"I do not pass on the question of innocence or guilt, but merely on what evidence has been presented here," Judge Thomas said slowly. "I find no evidence. Having in mind that this is an American court, operating under our Constitution and our Bill of Rights, I grant this application." Then Judge Thomas said I could be freed on a $50,000 bond.

I was elated. His action reaffirmed my faith in the American system of justice. I felt that at least there was one man who could look at this thing objectively, without fear of newspaper recriminations, and hand down a decision that was probably unpopular with the police or the press—but was quite within the law.

Deputies returned me to the fourth floor cell and within little more than an hour I was freed. As I walked out of the jail, Mike Ucello, the chief jailer, yelled to me that I had forgotten my radio. I turned and shouted, "Keep it for me, I'll be back."

Richard and I drove to my mother's home and we had a wonderful reunion. It was all too short. I knew it would be only a matter of time before they had me back behind bars and I made the most of the visiting with my patients at the hospital.

Late the next afternoon, August 17th, the Cuyahoga County Grand Jury returned a first-degree murder indictment. I was eating dinner when Carl Rossbach and two other deputies arrived at my parents' home to re-arrest me. As I said before, Rossbach was fair and square. He urged me to take time and finish my meal. When I did, I had a few private words with my mother and father, said good-bye, and stepped into the vestibule. Only then did Rossbach handcuff me. I appreciated his thoughtfulness. We returned to the County Jail. It was my last day of freedom for more years than I care to think about.

During the previous time in jail, I had started to draft a statement to the press, because I wanted to get my side of the story told and felt that some kind of a formal statement was the best way. After my second arrest, Corrigan and another lawyer who had joined the legal team, Fred Garmone, came to the cell and we worked together to polish the final draft of my statement. It was released to the press on August 18th. It said:

I am not guilty of the murder of my wife, Marilyn. How could I, who have been trained to help people and devoted my life to saving life, commit such a terrible and revolting crime?

I was severely injured in the encounter with her murderer and I am still suffering from the effects of those injuries.

Dr. Hexter, who examined me for Coroner Gerber on July 4, reported that I was injured in the right side of the forehead, both eyelids of my right eye were contused, that I could open my mouth only about 50 per cent and there were cuts inside my mouth; that there was an injury to my right chest, and that the cremasteric reflexes were absent and there was an absence of abdominal reflexes.

The absence of these reflexes indicated an injury to the brain or spinal cord. I was examined by Dr. Charles Elkins, who found evidence of definite injury to my spinal cord. These injuries were inflicted upon me by the murderer of my wife and for a time rendered me unconscious.

I have told the police and other officials who questioned me all I knew about the murder of my wife. I have done this freely and willingly because I am more interested in the capture of my wife's murderer than any person on this earth.

I loved my wife; we rejoiced that we were to have a second child, all the scandal and gossip to the contrary. We had even given our unborn child a name and had named it Stephen Allen. The last three months of our married life were perhaps among the happiest we enjoyed together.

I related all I knew to the coroner, the police at Bay Village, the detectives from the County Sheriff's office and the police of the City of Cleveland.

Some of the police from Bay Village and county detective Carl Rossbach and Deputy Sheriff David Yettra seemed to be genuinely interested in solving the crime, but the Cleveland police seemed to have made up their minds that I committed the crime and concentrated on me in solving the crime by securing a confession from me.

I was questioned on July 4 and 5 by a number of officers. On Thursday, Detectives Rossbach and Yettra questioned me for three and one-half hours. This was in my room and no other person was present except officer Drenkhan of the Bay Village police force.

On Friday, July 9, I went to my home with Rossbach, Mr. Yettra and Coroner Gerber and re-enacted for them all my actions of the evening of July 3 and the morning of July 4. They examined me with the greatest care and without any interference on the part of anyone. This activity lasted about four hours.

After that they asked me to go to the Sheriff's office and make a written statement. I agreed, and the next morning, July 10, I arrived at the Sheriff's office at 8 o'clock and remained there until almost 5 p.m. without eating lunch.

I was questioned by Mr. Rossbach, Mr. Yettra, Assistant County Prosecutors Parrino and Bauer, and detectives Schottke and Gareau, of the Cleveland police department. I made a long written statement which is a matter of record and is in the possession of the Sheriff of this county.

On July 22, 23 and 26, the coroner held a public inquest in the gymnasium in Normandy School in the city of Bay Village. All the television stations, radio stations, newspapers from Cleveland and other cities had representatives there, both reporters and photographers.

I was informed, and did not have to be informed because I knew, that inasmuch as I had cooperated with police and given them my statements and in view of the unwarranted vicious and unfavorable publicity that I had received and the editorials that had been written about me, one of which called upon the police to give me the third degree, I would be justified in claiming my constitutional privileges.

This I refused to do, and on July 22 and 23, knowing that I would be subjected to an unfriendly examination, I waived all my rights and appeared before a hostile, scoffing crowd and for five and one half hours I answered under oath every question that was asked of me.

From July 4 to July 30, I lived at my father's house. I was barred from my own home and the home of my son, and have been ever since barred from it. I have been barred not by order of any court, but by police.

The police knew where I was at all times, but on the night of July 30 I was arrested at 10 p.m. and brought before a magistrate that has now been determined to be a biased and prejudiced person. I was deprived of my counsel and was thrown into jail, and when my attorneys arrived at the jail they were refused admission.

I have since learned that the timing of my arrest and the reason that I was held incommunicado for my attorneys was because someone had the idea that I was addicted to dope and all that had to be done to solve the crime and get a confession from me was to hold me until the craving for dope would break me down.

During the succeeding week I was spirited out of jail at night, taken to the City Hospital, where I was examined by Dr. Braden in the presence of Dr. Greene, the medical officer of the Cleveland Police Department.

During the week after my arrest, I was questioned by relays of Cleveland detectives hour after hour, as long as 12 hours at a stretch, and the entire questioning had only one purpose, to secure a confession from me of a crime I did not commit. It was only after hours and hours of questioning and when the questioning became insulting and abusive that I refused to submit further.

I am not guilty.

S. H. Sheppard

Two days after the release of that statement, I was arraigned in common pleas court on the first degree murder indictment, and pleaded innocent.

The day of my arraignment, my brother Steve received word that David Kerr, the chief of the Cleveland homicide unit and a man who had a lofty reputation for solving murders, wanted to see him. I'll ask my brother to tell it the way he did in his book, *My Brother's Keeper.*

. . . I sat across from him at a small desk while he lolled in a blond oak tiltback chair and regarded me fiercely.

"You know you people are going about this in the wrong way, don't you?" he demanded.

I asked him what he meant.

"Your brother is guilty as hell and you know it," was his next sally.

"I know just the opposite," I told him, "and so do you, Captain Kerr."

"Well, I'm going to tell you something." He leaned over his desk and grimaced at me. "I'm going to tell you something and if you ever tell anyone I said this I will call you a liar. Now then—you see your brother and tell him to confess. God damn it, he can plead insanity or whatever he wants. He will do six months in a hospital and then come out cured. He can return to the practice of medicine and there will be no further difficulty."

"And if he refuses to confess to a crime he didn't commit?"

"Don't give me that crap, Doc," Kerr growled at me, "but if he is silly enough to refuse you can tell him for me that we'll burn him. That's all."

Steve came directly from Kerr's office to see me and we talked in a jail visitation room. He laid it on the line to me just the way Captain Kerr had done to him.

"Guilt is a matter of conscience—not of law," I said after hearing the story. "I would rather go to prison or even to the chair knowing that I'm innocent than to admit killing Marilyn in order to go free. Tell them I won't do it. They offered me substantially the same deal weeks ago and several times since and I have refused them. They're just trying to use you to put pressure on me and they're not going to do it."

And so, I settled back and spent the next two months waiting for the start of my trial. I still had enough faith in the American system of justice to feel that when all the facts were laid on the line before a jury, I would be vindicated.

6

The days in the County Jail were long and the nights were longer. Having been a very vigorous man, with a busy neurosurgical practice and a great deal of physical activity, jail life was confining, to say the least. Most of the time was spent playing cards, talking with other prisoners, reading a variety of books and magazines, writing letters, and keeping a handwritten diary on legal-sized pads.

My lawyers came to see me occasionally and we discussed the legal strategy planned for use during my trial, the basis of which I insisted (and Corrigan agreed) was my absolute innocence. I provided them with whatever information I could and made some suggestions. Some of them were considered—about one out of ten. Somehow I had the feeling that as time went on I was becoming less and less effective—through no fault of my own—as an advisor in my own case. Others were making decisions for me.

The first degree murder trial was set to start on October 18th, 1954, making a total of about two months between the indictment and the beginning of the court proceedings. It seemed like an eternity. There was a constant and gnawing feeling of loneliness for my son, Chip. We had been extremely close to each other, and I knew he needed me more than at any time in his life. In consideration of his welfare, seeing him was impossible. He was staying with Betty and Steve and I knew he was getting good care. That, at least, helped to ease my mental torture.

In September, Chip entered the second grade at Rocky River Elementary School, which Steve's two daughters, Janet and Carol, attended. My family gave me daily reports on his progress. In view of the drastic change in his young life, Chip was doing fine, they said, and it made me proud. I knew he would adjust as well as any seven-year-old could. He was a wonderful boy.

Chip slept through the tragedy on July 4th. The authorities questioned him shortly after the murder and came away convinced that he knew nothing about the events of the murder morning. Of course, he was not oblivious to what was happening to me. I was in jail and he knew it. Steve and Betty tried to avoid discussing the case in front of him, but when he asked a direct question, they tried to give him an answer. They informed me he knew about as much of what happened as a seven-year-old could know.

There were frequent visitors at County Jail, Betty and Steve, Richard and Dorothy, my father, and friends. But I would not permit my mother or Chip to come to the jail because mother was already too depressed over my plight and Chip was just too young. The biggest treat of all would have been a reunion with my youngster.

Eventually, I worked out an arrangement where I could call Chip once a week. It was worth every penny of the ten dollars I had to slip a deputy weekly for the privilege. For me there was no good food or liquor for sale, as other prisoners enjoyed at a price. So I had some money smuggled into the jail and gave it to friendly inmates, who made a deal for some good Italian and kosher food. One of the guards said, "This block of cells is too hot with Sheppard in it to deal with booze. Make sure he doesn't know about this chow. Got to realize that he's square."

My mood of the time can best be summed up by some of the letters and diary entries I wrote. I've changed the names of the other prisoners in the jail. On September 1st, about two weeks after the indictment, I wrote to my family:

Well another day of cards and general B.S. with the guys here. Some symphony is on the radio now and is good. The other fellows here don't care for symphony too much, but I get help from good music.

Reverend Kreke was here and we had a good talk. I'm able to give him a lot of my inner thoughts. This helps because I can't talk to the guys here and the attorneys aren't interested in my spiritual self.

I hope you, Richard or someone is calling Mary and Bud [Brown] and reading my daily notes or keeping them posted. Dorothy or mother will. I'm not writing to them because of the other writing I'm trying to do. Actually with these characters wanting to play cards all the time I'm keeping fairly busy, which is good!

Have started the *Sermon on the Mount* by Fox. It's wonderful. I keep my little Bible close to refer to it at times. It was swell of Al Davis to come down and bring the book to me. It is now that Sunday School teachings, Sunday Chapel lessons at Camp (Fred Harrington) and the sermons in the Little Church at Hanover come back and mean a lot to me. Mr. Cadi (Philosophy Professor in college) and his teachings have been close. This background is important, but as I told Rev. Kreke today, I know that we have been given strength beyond any I have ever known previously. This is strength given to me from a divine source—there is absolutely *no* question about it.

I see this strength reflected in my parents and other relatives as well which furthers this cause.

The offer by hospital employees, who are not highly paid, to help me with expenses is overwhelming. Their offers are deeply felt and appreciated! Material things become pretty minimal at a time like this. Wish I had a big steak now with a bottle of beer but things could be worse.

The pie made of the leftover fruit could have had maggots included today, like last week. There could be more bedbugs, although this would be difficult to imagine.

The next day, September 2nd, I wrote in the diary:

It was about 10 days to 2 weeks that I was here till I realized that everything I say in here is going out to the police. At that time there were only two guys here that I talked to at all. Naturally, I couldn't say anything that would be incriminating but my comments were going out as reported by certain friends (at least one convict that knows). The two fellows that I became friendly with were Bill Smith, 47, and Floyd Harrison, about 43.

Smith was in for some bad checks and was very encouraging to me, saying any thinking man would realize my innocence. Smith even wrote to his wife who works on a newspaper asking that she speak to her editor to give me a fair report, as he knew I was innocent. Harrison was and is friendly and warned me about others who might carry out reports. As soon as Smith became definitely encouraging to me he was moved out of our block for some unknown reason (Harrison had reported this and it was obvious that I had been helped, encouraged by Smith's objective evaluation). Shortly after this, I realized that Harrison is the "plant" or the stool pigeon.

When I returned after being out on bond for 30 hours a fellow named Jimmy Kay was here in the block. He is a hotel prowler and hustler but a nice sort of guy. He, Harrison and I became friendly card players and Kay spoke in the course of playing, etc. of my situation. He mentioned the fact that they don't have a thing on me and that I'm obviously innocent if I can put up with all the questioning, etc. Soon after Kay and I became friendly and he spoke of "when Sam gets out" he was moved to another block for no apparent reason.

Harrison, who is in on a pandering charge, supposedly is never moved and would be if they were merely moving guys that I enjoy playing cards with. About 5 days ago, 4 new fellows were put in here and one was a 32-year-old fellow named Palmer. He is the one who has been White Slaving (hustling) since he got out of the Navy 8 years ago. His mother wanted him to turn himself in, so he did. He was on a submarine in the war and is a nice guy. He was very outspoken. He told me of the way things are going as regards opinion in the bar rooms, eating places, etc. He said most of the men are for me, and the women are against me.

He says 50-50% but that most of the women he has talked to are divorced or have had some trouble with men.

I had little to say about my situation other than generalities but he was most encouraging, saying he'd sure like to trade places with me and that I'll be on the streets long before he will. He mentioned some of the things that must be proven for a conviction which they obviously haven't got. He's a good card player, full of jokes, and generally made life more fun here. This afternoon for no apparent reason Palmer was moved out to another cell block.

Harrison acted as though he couldn't figure out why (the son of a bitch). My biggest temptation is to beat the hell out of him, but I'm not showing a thing. I give him candy, fruit, etc., and will continue to play cards with him because there are things I've mentioned in my favor and though he may not report favorable things we probably have nothing to gain by making known my feelings (what I know).

They now are putting Negroes in here and rather stupid guys so the only person I can talk to will be Harrison. They are intent on breaking my spirit.

They can't take away my Bible and my innocence, however. They can't take away the inner strength that has been given to me. These actions merely indicate to me that they are not sure of themselves and are trying everything to twist something against me. This realization puts me on more guard and instills more "fight" in me. These police and prosecutors are trying to solve a murder and they would gladly *murder* an innocent man by false conviction to relieve political pressure on them. This is a strong way of expressing it but it is true.

One of the cellmates is a Rumanian-Russian, about 34, who is a painter. He is here on an incest charge and is the one who I said I wouldn't put anything past associated with sex. He has talked, drawn and reacted to sex since he was placed here the first week I came.

Today he called me aside and said he would like to draw some pictures of me as *he* sees me. (He's a good artist and has done some good work on the walls here.) He said he has been here, eaten with me, etc., and evaluated me for a month and he *knows* I'm innocent and wants to draw some pictures in different clothing to display the reaction and effect I have on "just" a fellow who has been thrown with me in close contact for a month.

In another letter I said:

Last night's news said that the date for trial will be set soon. It said that some of the pleas may be changed for lesser charges. How unfair can they be? The innocent man is worse off than the guilty one who can plead guilty to the lesser charge.

In other words the system is not set up for justice but for the convenience and pressure devices of the State. Under this system, a man who is guilty of murder in the first degree can possibly get away with a third degree or second degree charge whereas the poor damn innocent bastard has to defend himself on a first degree basis unless he makes a false confession. These fellows (police and prosecutors) probably feel that this method is good even though some innocent men are sent to the pen. They can say they haven't killed them, but they might as well.

The deputies around here don't know whether to talk to me or not for fear someone will report one of them. One who runs elevators likes cars and I sent out an old Hot Rod book to him a couple of weeks ago and I got word that he got hell 'cause someone thought he had been friendly to me which he had, but he had nothing to stool about. They probably think I told him some secret about Mr. Corrigan's brand of Scotch or something. The whole bunch, chief jailer and all, are so afraid to move one way or the other that they shake.

When I get out of here I'll give them something to shake about. This place is an excellent subject for graft investigation.

Food

Sanitation

Medical care

The men who are actually convicted of a crime and sent to the pen get much better treatment than do those who are held here and may be entirely innocent as I am. I should think such a place as this would be as well run as the state pen where the convicted persons are placed. I can put up with this as long as the next person but it is not fair and represents local graft which the average person has no idea exists.

For a while, my father used to come down to the jail with case X-rays to get my opinion, but jail officials cut that out, causing me to pen this observation:

Well, they won't let Dad in to go over X-rays now. The jellyfish sheriff has been told what to do again by his political associates. He couldn't stand on his own two feet and fight for right if he had to. Sometimes I wonder if they know right from wrong. The county people, I believe, would like to be fair but they are so afraid of public opinion and more of political pressure that they don't know whether to run forward or creep backwards. (Chief Jailer) Ucello hasn't been in here for a week, whereas he used to be around several times a day. Someone probably accused him of being sympathetic with me. He therefore doesn't come around. He would probably like to, but must not endanger his position.

It's a great county law enforcement agency which is afraid of political pressure and places this above justice. (That goes for city police as well.)

On September 23rd, a special venire was picked for my trial, in what might be called an elaborate ceremony in the marble rotunda of the Cuyahoga County Criminal Courts Building. I was four floors up in the building when a county official dipped into the jury drum and picked out the names of seventy-five people who were to become prospective jurors for my murder trial. The newspapers were out in force for the game of grab bag. They photographed the selection process and, what was even more amazing, the papers were given the names of the seventy-five veniremen. They published them—three weeks before the trial was scheduled to start. You can bet those people whose names and addresses were published heard plenty of opinions from friends and neighbors during the weeks until the trial began.

About the time of the venire selection, I received a visit from Cliff Lewis, who was a former quarterback for the Cleveland Browns, a good friend and my general insurance agent. I made the following notes: "He, Cliff, told me that he and his wife drove by our house on July 4th at about 1:00 a.m. He said they looked in as usual and noted the *one* small light upstairs. He said they were questioned by the police and told them this. The Cleveland detectives tried to get them to change their stories saying that more lights were on, etc. They actually tried to get them to change their report or testimony."

Jail officials wouldn't let my family visit me unless they came on regular visiting hours and then I had to talk with them through a mesh screen. However, four or five times a week, various curious people were brought through to have a free look at me. When I wasn't in evidence, the deputy jailer or jailer, as the case may have been, called for me to display myself to these privileged characters. One night they brought the jail cook down to view me and that night I noted, "I stayed behind a pillar where we play cards. Carny called me over to meet her. She asked if we got enough to eat and I said honestly "no," but tried to be polite and not offend her. It's times like these that my poise is tested the most. A great test is yet to come I know however and this writing is a method of expression (safety valve).

"One of the fellows spoke up tonight and said, 'Next time you bring someone back here, have them bring some peanuts and bananas or we won't perform.' He added that it's more fun to watch during feeding time."

And, of course, as I said before, I wrote down anything on paper that I thought might be a suggestion in aiding in my defense. On October 4th, two weeks before the start of the trial, I wrote:

The detectives said during questioning that they didn't think I had been in the lake due to the lack of sand in hair, shoes and pants. Why did they look so hard for a weapon in the lake then? If I wasn't in the lake and the weapon is not there where could I have hidden it where they wouldn't find it and why didn't I hide the jewelry there, too?

I swam in the lake almost daily and did Friday (July 2). Rarely, if ever, did I have sand in my hair. Blood in hair does not come out easily, a rush attempt to wash hair would miss. Blood spots in hair and scalp—blood beneath fingernails for a couple of days following a surgery when a glove has been broken on a finger.

Were there not wet tracks noted on the porch, etc. and on the steps to the beach? They said there was a track of blood to the basement and the tubs were still moist. (They're moist most of the time.) They think someone used the basement tubs, however.

And on October 11th, I noted, "I defy any detective or police-employed physician to simulate or self-induce my neurological status as described by competent physicians on and shortly after July 4th. This is very important, you know."

Finally, the day of the trial arrived. I knew it was serious—that my life was in the balance. I was worried, but I didn't think I would be convicted of a crime I didn't commit. I knew that reasonable doubt was supposed to be the basis for a "not guilty" verdict. I felt they didn't have sufficient evidence to arrest me, let alone convict me.

7 ⁊

I awoke early on the morning of Monday, October 18th, put on a charcoal gray suit, white shirt, and black knit tie, ate break-fast, and waited anxiously for the moment when I would be taken down to the court room. Finally, it came. Deputy Sheriff James Kilroy, a short, stocky, friendly man, handcuffed me and we took the elevator to the first floor at the Criminal Court building. We stepped off the elevator and walked down the marble corridor to the courtroom. I was all but blinded by the popping flashbulbs and the glare of floodlights used for the motion picture cameras. The scene seemed to be one of bedlam.

We made a right turn into Courtroom Number Two. It was re-assuring to see some of the friendly faces of members of my family. The courtroom really wasn't very big. At the front of the room was the judge's bench and the witness box. Looking from the back to the front, the jury box with fourteen seats—twelve for the jurors and two for alternates—stretched along the right side. Running parallel to the jury box was a long, polished wood table for the prosecution.

The left side of the courtroom bordered on East 21st Street, a dismal-looking street containing a number of parking lots used by people who worked in the court or in the Police Department Head-quarters, which stood at the corner of East 21st Street and Payne Avenue. Our defense table flanked the windows and it was in a seat along that wall that I was to hear my case argued. About three quarters of the way down the room, there was a wooden railing and behind it were several rows of benches usually open to spec-tators.

A few days before the start of the trial, Judge Edward Blythin had met with the representatives of the press and arranged for newspaper, radio, and television reporters to occupy the first rows of the spectator gallery. Reporters from Cleveland, New York, De-troit, Chicago, Pittsburgh, Lorain, and God knows where else were on hand for the trial. Judge Blythin had personally hand-written tickets for the press seats and all other spectators at the trial.

As it turned out, people—friends of mine—who wanted to come to the trial couldn't get in because there were no seats. The judge had reserved seats and upon learning this, I said to myself, "What the hell is this reserved seat business." He was practically selling tickets.

Actually, inside the bar, the judge had placed a table for special press people like Dorothy Kilgallen, Bob Considine, and some of the elite. This was totally out of keeping with the dignity of the court. Too, some of the reporters were within a few feet of the jury box. When the jurors were finally selected they could measure the reactions of the newsmen to the statements of the lawyers and the witnesses and they could hear the murmured remarks of the press and the laughter, which was sometimes bordering on raucous.

The courtroom was crawling with photographers and cameramen. They were all over the place. During the first week or so, they were even allowed to take pictures inside the courtroom before the day's activity started. Finally, Judge Blythin put an end to this general situation, but there were photographers who violated his edict of no pictures in the courtroom at any time.

On the opening day of the trial, Bill Corrigan moved for a postponement of the proceedings and asked for a change of venue—that the case be moved to another city because of the fantastic and prejudicial press coverage of the case during the summer. Judge Blythin said that the only way to determine whether a fair jury could be selected was to try to select one and he withheld a ruling on the motion for a change of venue. The trial was on.

The original venire of seventy-five prospective jurors had been reduced to sixty-four for one reason or another and one-by-one they came to the witness stand to be questioned. First Judge Blythin would interrogate them then turn the questioning over to the prosecutors and my attorneys.

"Do you have any objection to capital punishment?" each prospective juror was asked. What I wished they had been asked was, "Are you either willing to send this man to the electric chair or free him?"

A typical question-answer session with a prospective juror went something like this:

Judge Blythin: You have heard of the case? Read of it? Discussed it?
A. Yes.
Q. Do you have an opinion?
A. Yes.

Q. Is it such that it could not be changed?
A. No. I have an open mind. I'd want to know all the facts of the case.

Then Saul Danaceau, an assistant prosecutor, took over.

Q. You have read about this case?
A. Yes.
Q. You've read many stories and seen many pictures?
A. I haven't read everything, if that's what you mean.
Q. Well, nobody has read everything. But did you read a story called *Dr. Sam Tells His Own Story?*
A. No. I get the *Plain Dealer*.
Q. Did you read any statements by the Sheppards?
A. I may have. I read a lot more in the beginning than I did later.

Finally Fred Garmone, one of my four lawyers, moved in.

Q. Should you discover that the Mayor of North Olmsted is also a medical doctor, would that cause you to give an M.D. more credence than an O.D.
A. No.
Q. You said you had expressed an opinion. Where?
A. At the office where I worked until moving to North Olmsted.
Q. How many people were involved in the discussion?
A. Six.
Q. Did your opinion coincide with the majority?
A. We were divided about half and half.
Q. You came into this courtroom today with an opinion?

Garmone challenged her for cause, but Judge Blythin overruled him, and said, "That's no reason for challenge. This lady has already said she can set aside her opinion and listen to the facts." Garmone continued.

Q. Would you take that opinion to seat number twelve in the jury box?
A. I would until I heard further testimony.
Q. I assume that your opinion is quite strong?
A. Yes.

Finally, the prosecution joined Garmone in the challenge for cause and Judge Blythin dismissed the woman.

Slowly, the jury box began to fill up. It was a long and tedious process that stretched on day after day. I listened intently as they questioned each juror and let my attorneys know how I felt about each. Sometimes my opinions were respected, other times—as we shall see a little later—they fell on deaf ears.

During the selection of a jury, there also was time to draw some reactions about this cast of characters involved in the struggle for my life—the judge, the prosecutors, and my attorneys.

Judge Blythin, a man of seventy, was a former Cleveland mayor. He was a rather thin fellow who spoke with a slight Welsh brogue. He appeared to me a somewhat pompous type of person. I learned that he had a son who was a detective with the Cleveland Police Department, but I didn't let that bother me. At the outset, I was extremely hopeful that Judge Blythin would turn out to be what I thought a real judge was supposed to be. Having had this feeling of "the blind faithful," I believed that people who are guilty are put in jail or done away with and people who are innocent are not. I believed in this and this negated a lot of the effect of the Roman holiday atmosphere that prevailed in the courtroom. Although sometimes I had the feeling that I was going to be sacrificed, I tried to put this in the back of my mind, telling myself that was a barbaric custom and not the way of the modern American civilization.

But Judge Blythin was up for re-election to a six-year term, and when I found out that he was giving interviews to reporters on the courthouse steps, I began to wonder about him. Of course, we later found out that early in the game he reportedly told Dorothy Kilgallen that I was "guilty as hell." You see, like many of the prospective jurors who were questioned, he apparently had an opinion, too.

The man who was heading up the prosecution team was John Mahon, an assistant prosecutor for twenty-two years. He also was running for election as a judge and getting his name in the paper every day didn't hurt. He was a rather tall man who had tried many murder cases during his career. It was said that he had a good batting average in convictions. Although Mahon was vigorous mentally and physically at the start of the trial, he looked sick to me. His color was on the greenish-yellow side. But I really can't say anything good about him, because I felt that he knew I was innocent.

The second man on the prosecution team was Saul Danaceau, a small, rather squat, bald-headed man. He appeared to be quite intellectual, a book man who was relied on more for his knowledge of the law than for his performance in the courtroom.

Thomas Parrino, the third man on the staff from the prosecutor's office, was also the youngest. He had a large nose and thinning hair and spoke rather softly. I also had the feeling that Parinno knew I was innocent and I knew that he practically admitted that to my brother, Steve. But, he had to go along with the orders in this operation.

The Cleveland Police Department's representative on the legal team was James McArthur, chief of the detective bureau. He was rather tall with a hawklike nose and piercing gray eyes. He just looked like a tough policeman, which he was.

As for the men on my legal team, I thought of them as I would a team of doctors, as though I had legal cancer and that these were the surgeons who had to remove it. When caring for a patient, I always insisted that he or she took my orders in good faith and though he or she might wonder about the orders they must be followed. A patient may even doubt a doctor at times because the lay person didn't have a medical education and could not understand all of the orders.

By the same token, I had not studied law and could not understand it. If I was going to be true to my own feelings about medicine, my feeling was that I must put my life in the hands of my lawyers. Petersilge said I had the best legal team available and I had complete faith in him at that time. However, knowing of my innocence, I sometimes had the feeling that I could probably defend myself and be found innocent.

Petersilge was more of a civil lawyer, so the onus fell on Bill Corrigan, an old pro in criminal trials. He was a short man with a square chin and a wrinkled face, topped by a wave of white hair that showed his many years. For an older man, he was handsome. He was a colorful, flamboyant man by nature. He didn't put on an act; that's the way he was. His speech was eloquent. He was restless, moving from chair to chair on the defense side of the courtroom, or from corner to corner of the courtroom.

Nor was Corrigan acting in this case. He was deeply involved and upset in this trial. He was personally insulted, not because an innocent man was being tried for his life, but because an innocent man was being tried for his life in an atmosphere which the Ohio Supreme Court and other courts later called a "Roman holiday." Corrigan was insulted as an American and he told me he was. He said that what was taking place in that courtroom was not the true premise of justice. He reiterated time and again that perhaps as a result of my trial the courts would establish some limitation on the freedom of the press, as it jeopardized the guarantees of a fair trial.

Second on my team was Fred Garmone, a man with thinning dark hair. Although I had heard Garmone had gained a reputation for

representing several clients "on the other side of the law" I thought
he was a competent lawyer and a nice guy. Nevertheless, I can't
help thinking in retrospect that the choosing of Garmone for my
legal team was a questionable move. Not that he didn't do a good
job, but I have the feeling that his reputation hurt me. Besides this,
Corrigan had his son, William Jr., available for the research work.
Young Corrigan did the leg work and sat at the defense table.

And, of course, Petersilge was there, too, although he appeared to
me to be out of character in the courtroom. I had four lawyers there.
I think a lot of people interpreted this to mean that I had so much
money I didn't know what to do with it. That was not true.

It was some cast. The Cleveland *Press* thought so, too. The newspaper described the setting and the characters in an article on October 23rd:

> Yes, you think, they wouldn't be more true to life if this Big Trial were
> a television drama.
>
> Then it hits you again. No there's something and someone missing.
>
> What is it? Who is it? Who's still off stage? Waiting perhaps for a cue
> to come on.

In the hallway outside the courtroom you stop to talk to Detective
Chief James McArthur. He's an old-timer at Big Trials. So you ask him.
Isn't there someone, something missing?

"Sure," says the detective chief. "There always is. I'll tell you.

"It's the other side, the representative of what in this case will be officially known as the corpus delicti, in other words, the body of the crime,
in still other words—Marilyn Reese Sheppard.

"There is no grieving mother—she died when Marilyn was very young.

"There's no revenge-seeking brother nor sorrowing sister. Marilyn was
an only child.

"Her father is not here. Why he isn't, is his own personal business."

What then, you wonder, will be the other side.

It will be there, Inspector McArthur reassures. He opens a thick brief-
case he carries daily to the courtroom.

"Here," he says, "are the statements and resumes of testimony that
will be given by state's witnesses. Here are the theories and details of the
evidence found by dozens of detectives in weeks of work.

"Here is the complete story of Marilyn Reese Sheppard. How she lived,
how, we think, she died. Her story will come into this courtroom through
our witnesses. Here is how it starts: Marilyn Sheppard, nee Reese, age 30,
height 5 feet, 7 inches, weight 125 pounds, brown hair, hazel eyes. On
the morning of July 4 she was murdered in her bedroom. . . ."

Then you realize how what and who is missing from the perfect setting
will be supplied.

How in the Big Case justice will be done.
Justice to Sam Sheppard.
And to Marilyn Sheppard.

And topping that story, which appeared while a jury was still being selected, was a big black headline, which proclaimed boldly, "But Who Will Speak For Marilyn?"

It made my blood boil. My family and Marilyn's close relatives, Mary Brown and her husband, Bud, spoke for Marilyn. Dr. Sam Sheppard spoke for Marilyn like no one else could.

To get back to the trial, the lawyers and the prosecutors and the judge haggled for nine days until they finally picked twelve people for a jury. They exhausted sixty of the sixty-four available names on the venire and still had two more alternates to select after the jury was sworn in. Judge Blythin called for another special venire of twenty-four names.

On Thursday, October 28th, Blythin swore in the jury of seven men and five women. All said under oath they would weigh the evidence against me without prejudice or bias.

The jurors were: Howard Barrish, timekeeper for Republic Steel; Mrs. Elizabeth Borke, a dark-haired mother of two; Edmond Verlinger, a hardware store manager; William C. Lamb, a construction superintendent; Mrs. Louise Feuchter, a gray-haired woman of about fifty-five; James Roger Manning, a real estate salesman; Mrs. Anna Foote, an employed mother with five children; Mrs. Beatrice Orenstein, middle-aged mother of two; James C. Bird, a railroad cashier and the only college graduate on the jury; Frank Moravec, a tool-maker; Frank J. Kallorits, the father of two boys; and Louella Williams, a fifty-four-year-old divorcée and the only Negro on the jury.

I wasn't entirely happy with this group. There were three on the panel I didn't want, but my lawyers were firm. One was Barrish. He said he hadn't read much about the case until he saw he was on the venire. Then, he said, he read up on the case. I thought he had already been markedly influenced by the newspapers.

I didn't like Mrs. Borke, either. She wouldn't look me in the eye. Garmone said that he liked her because she reacted favorably to him. "She may react favorably to you, but she doesn't seem to react favorably to me," I told Garmone. I lost on that one, too.

James Bird was the other one. He had admitted during questioning that he had been in the Army with Parrino's brother. He was a man of small stature and he struck me as never having been too effective with women. Since extra-marital relations were sure to be a topic, I worried about him. When my lawyers told me that they wanted him to remain on the jury, I couldn't fathom it. But I was advised by Mr. Petersilge that Mr. Corrigan knew his business— that he felt that the man was of a higher intelligence level and should be retained.

When Blythin got around to selecting the two alternates, it was discovered that one of the jurors, Manning, who had already been sworn in had had some legal problems in the past which had not come out during his questioning. He obviously was not eligible to sit on the jury.

In a highly irregular procedure, Judge Blythin continued with the selection of the two alternates: Jack Hanson, a factory foreman; and Mrs. Lois Mancini, a housewife. By the close of the day on Monday, November 1st, we had twelve jurors and two alternates. Meanwhile, the newspapers had been muckraking Manning's life history on page one and the Cleveland *Press* predicted he would be tossed off the jury.

Tuesday, November 2nd, was Election Day, and court was in recess. Two of the principals, Judge Blythin and John Mahon, were standing for election, and both won. Mahon was to begin his term as a judge on January 5th, 1955, and he gallantly agreed to complete prosecuting the case.

With a day off from the trial, I tried to put down some of my thoughts on paper. I wrote:

Familiar music, memories of unforgettable experiences (high school, Skidmore, Hanover, Los Angeles, Big Sur and the Bay Village house we had chosen as our permanent home), stimulate the deep-seated heartache which will never die.

We had much more together (and somehow still do) than merely physical attraction, but an understanding and comradeship as well. Chip is part of this comradeship which was not based on competition, but mutual agreement usually to my decisions.

This tragedy has intensified and clarified our love, for it is this love that manifests its strength through my response to the tangible situation as it now exists. Our love is a definite part of that manifested by those who also stand by me in life (for these *same* individuals who stand by me now would stand just as firmly by Marilyn if she were in my place). These people, as Marilyn, *could never* let me down in any way, nor could we let her down, even in the face of severe criticism or danger. Therefore, in the face of severe criticism and also danger, I will not falter. I must keep that faith with those who have lived for, believe in, and who *still believe* in Sam and Marilyn Sheppard.

On the morning of November 3rd, Judge Blythin, as predicted, removed Manning from the jury because of an arrest that had occurred eleven years previously. Into his spot went Alternate Number One, Jack Hanson. It was all very neat. The prosecution breathed a collective sigh of relief. They had been in panic with the thought that the entire jury might have to be thrown out and the selection process would have to start anew. But Judge Blythin ruled that since no testimony had been heard by the jury, it was all very legal.

That afternoon, the jury business over, we went to my home in Bay Village so the jury could inspect it. I was handcuffed and rode in a car, while the jurors, prosecutors, and my attorneys went by bus. It was a long ride, through downtown Cleveland, out over the shoreway on the edge of Lake Erie, through the West Side and finally out along Lake Road, past Bay View Hospital and the homes of my father and brother, Richard.

When we reached my home, I saw that the property had been roped off by the police, but there were hundreds of spectators, members of the press, neighbors, and others ringing the yard. It was a depressing gray day and a brisk wind was blowing in off Lake Erie. The ground was covered by snow. As we walked around the yard I looked up and saw the helicopter that one of the newspapers had hired to get pictures of this spectacle, hovering overhead. The place was a mess, as it well might be when there had been no one to take care of it for four months. The house was in possession of the police and they had the only key. The lake was rough and it was impossible to see any of the beach where I had struggled with Marilyn's killer and my assailant.

Once inside, we moved from room to room. It was a silent group and the only sounds were those of Sheriff Joseph Sweeny as he pointed out various objects and rooms. It was an emotional experience for me. It had been weeks since I had been in the house, and even under the circumstances, the visit brought back fond memories of happier days. Finally, when I saw Chip's teddy bear on top of a dresser, I couldn't contain myself any more and wept.

When the grand tour was completed, we returned to the Criminal Courts Building. The trial had been going on for two and a half weeks and I was beginning to get numb mentally. It was difficult to adjust and realize this was happening to me. I wasn't aware of the amount of reaction to the case that was appearing in other cities. I realized that newspapers had sent reporters from out of town and I had seen reports on television, but I wondered what they all were doing there—what made this such a big thing.

The only reason I could come up with was the fact that I wasn't guilty and a lot of people knew it. But I was on trial for my life and I happened to be a young physician who was in a social-economic bracket, or approaching a social-economic bracket, that most people resented. This was the only way I could analyze the intense public interest my trial was creating. I wasn't too far wrong.

8 &

John Mahon, the assistant county prosecutor, stood before
the jury on the morning of November 4th, and in his opening statement he told the jury that the State would prove that I bludgeoned
Marilyn to death on the morning of July 4th as the climax to an
argument over "other women," particularly Susan Hayes. "No one
was in that house on the morning of July 4th attempting to commit
a burglary," said Mahon. "No evidence has been found that any
burglar or marauder had been there. There was disarrangement of
some drawers and papers, but the state will show that this was done
for the purpose of deception."

Fred Garmone delivered the opening remarks for the defense.
Our marriage in the months preceding the tragedy had been sailing
along on an even keel, he told the jury, and the State's theory that
I had killed Marilyn was preposterous. He charged that police officials had quickly made up their minds I was the killer and had spent
all their time building a case against me, to the exclusion of attempting to seek the real killer.

That afternoon, the State of Ohio called its first witness, Dr.
Lester Adelson, the deputy coroner. Dr. Adelson was a brilliant
man with a fine reputation as a pathologist. In his direct testimony,
he told about performing the autopsy on Marilyn. Then, over the
objections of my attorneys, he showed the jury and others in the
court, colored slides of Marilyn's wounds on a large motion picture
screen. Thomas Parrino operated the slide projector and Dr. Adelson stood there with a pointer and described the wounds.

I half-looked at the pictures. Having been subjected to seeing the
worst of the pictures during my interrogations, I was conditioned
for this horror show. But, to show these color pictures like a movie,
on a huge screen, to these strangers, was an insult to Marilyn.

That night, I wrote to my family:

Today was very tough, but somehow strength is there when needed
most. The trip to the house was also difficult, to say the very least. To
see the place we loved so much in disgraceful condition was the worst.

Knowing how Marilyn loved it so and hated exhibition seemed and does seem to mock her.

Mrs. Jane Reese, Mrs. Weigle, Senior, and Mrs. Munn (Marilyn's relatives) were in the courtroom while the pictures of Marilyn were shown. How could they??? Even Steve couldn't sit where he could see the pictures. They seemed to carry in them a slight portion of the gruesome vicarious satiation that others in the same courtroom have displayed. (News reporters, friends and relatives of the judge, and other officials.) The deputy suggested that I need not look at the screen and he chose to remain behind the screen, too.

During the opening statement, the state attorney made no mention of "proof," but rather "reasonable conclusions" and the "pointing of the finger of guilt." I always thought our free country had set up its laws based on hard clad "*proof*," not "reasonable conclusions."

Dr. Adelson was on the stand for the better part of two days. During that time Bill Corrigan showed conclusively that the autopsy had been botched beyond belief. The night before Dr. Adelson took the stand, I gave Corrigan a basic lesson on the anatomy of the head and brain. As a result of my lesson and careful scrutiny of the autopsy report, Corrigan came to the conclusion that no single blow had been severe or deep enough to penetrate the outer covering of the brain or the dura mater. He concluded that Marilyn had died of causes other than the actual blows themselves—that she had choked to death from the blood that had flowed into her lungs. He hammered away at Dr. Adelson on this point.

Mr. Corrigan tried to develop that she had been killed by a left-handed person. I'm predominantly right-handed, but, like all surgeons, I used both hands in an operation. Bill Corrigan was trying to show subtly that an athletically inclined person like myself would certainly have penetrated the outer covering with at least one of the blows, if in a fit of rage, or otherwise, as the state suggested. Believe me, if I wanted to kill someone, it wouldn't have taken the thirty-five blows, no one of which killed Marilyn.

The jury didn't get Corrigan's message at all. They might have believed his analyses if he had explained more clearly what he meant. Some things are easy to understand if they are spelled out.

After Marilyn's wounds were washed to clear the damaged area, there was no filter examination, according to Dr. Adelson's autopsy report. That's ridiculous. This is a matter of routine. Modern autopsy tables are equipped with filters and material is filtered whether you want it or not. Maybe they looked and threw it away. Perhaps something was thrown away that they didn't want, because the filtration of washings during an autopsy—especially when it's a violent death —is of essential importance.

They claimed they did not examine for sexual assault. That's equally ridiculous. Marilyn's legs were spread over the rail at the bottom of the bed. Her pajama tops were pulled up over her breasts and if there ever was a suggestion of sexual assault there it was. They knew I found her in this condition and then had later covered her. How could any competent coroner's office in any city in this nation claim they didn't examine for sexual assault when they saw a woman in this condition? Is that possible? I'm convinced they examined Marilyn and found the wrong thing, to convict me.

Specific tests could have cleared me. Both Corrigan and I were convinced that the authorities had intentionally made a botch of the autopsy, or—more likely—they did a good job and claimed to have botched the portions that were in my favor, or bore out my claims.

On the other hand, the evidence that would bear out my innocence or suggest my innocence was played down. They found a piece of nail polish in the room that didn't match any of Marilyn's nail polish. They found a piece of leather that matched nothing in the house, and a piece of a tooth. They didn't photograph these things. They just passed them around in a tiny tube—and only after Mr. Corrigan demanded that they be shown. These items were rather hard to see when presented in a little test tube.

The whole tone of Dr. Adelson's testimony struck me as though they were really trying to stack the cards against me. After Dr. Adelson left the stand on Monday, November 8th, the State called my neighbors, the Aherns. Don Ahern's testimony seemed rather wishy-washy to me, but one statement made by Nancy Ahern during cross-examination by Corrigan was very unfortunate and uncalled for. "Well, Mrs. Sheppard always seemed very much in love with her husband," she said, "but I was never quite sure about Dr. Sam."

I thought to myself, "Who gives a damn whether your wife's golf partner thinks you love your wife or not? Are we, as husbands, supposed to convince the back-fence 'gossips' of our love for our wives. These things are for home and bedroom. Those who display in public are often a fraud."

Marilyn and I had never been too expressive in public, even when we were in high school. In fact, we had agreed that it wasn't a good idea to go around hugging one another and showing a lot of affectionate expressions in the open. We thought this was not the proper thing to do. Of course, this was when we were younger, but as we grew older we carried through with this practice.

Nancy Ahern also testified that my wife had confided to her about the remarks Dr. Chapman made to Marilyn while we were at his ranch in March, 1954. I have already explained the circumstances behind Dr. Chapman's conversation—that it was a hoax, that Dr. Chapman was trying to use Marilyn and her love for me to help maneuver himself into a partnership with my father, brothers, and me at Bay View.

My attorneys protested that this was hearsay evidence and argued that it was not admissable in court. But Judge Blythin let her proceed with the story that (1) Marilyn had said to her there were clouds in her relationship with me, and (2) that Dr. Chapman had told Marilyn that I told him I was considering a divorce.

Spencer Houk—the mayor-butcher—followed Nancy Ahern to the stand. Houk testified that he had heard my brother, Richard, ask me the morning of the tragedy whether I had anything to do with Marilyn's murder. As I have previously pointed out, Richard said this never happened and so that was good enough for me.

The trial moved along. Esther Houk followed her husband, and then Fred Drenkhan, the first Bay Village policeman on the scene at my home July 4th, told of his investigation—of finding no signs of forcible entry the morning of July 4th. Police Chief John Eaton followed him and added little to Drenkhan's testimony.

On November 16th, Dr. Samuel Gerber, the coroner, took the stand and remained there in the spotlight for three days. During his testimony, he brought out the yellow pillowcase that had been on Marilyn's bed. It was covered with blood stains. Gerber said that when he examined the pillow after Marilyn's body had been removed from the bed, he found one large blood stain on the underside of it.

The coroner said the large stain had the imprint of two blades, about three inches long, and there were indentations at the end of each blade, as if they had teeth. Gerber stated flatly the imprint was that of a surgical instrument. Then, over the objections of Corrigan and Garmone, and with the consent of Judge Blythin, he flashed pictures of the pillow and the imprint on the screen. He described the imprint with the aid of a pointer. Needless to say, the mere suggestion of a surgical instrument as a murder weapon was a destroying blow for a surgeon on trial.

His logic was absolute idiocy. He never produced any surgical instrument to support his testimony, and the court never asked him to produce the surgical instrument he had in mind.

That night, I wrote to my brother, Steve:

The blood stain that Gerber refers to is obviously due to blood caught between the creases of the pillow. To substantiate this, the streak in the middle should be noted.

We knew they would try to manufacture some sort of evidence and frankly, I'm glad they have settled on such a flimsy bit of tripe.

Ask Gerber if he had located an instrument that will match the imprint? If not, why not? There are catalogs available of every surgical instrument made.

How does he know it isn't a garden tool, or some other implement?

Might be well to follow on the premise that this is an imprint and ask what, but best prove what it really is. . . .

It is not happenstance that a crease of blood (showing a previous fold in the pillow slip) is directly in the middle of the two parts of the figure displayed.

Explain this to W.J.C. [William J. Corrigan]. I have done so, but perhaps you can further explain.

Gerber's unsubstantiated testimony about the imprint of a surgical instrument on the pillow really hit my mother. Mom had been depressed for weeks, mainly because she felt she had not prepared me during my youth to deal with this kind of a vicious situation. This absolute lie really got to her. That night—in an attempt to kill herself—she took an overdose of sleeping pills. Fortunately, she failed. She was hospitalized and the Bay View records showed that she had been treated for a suspected mild stroke. Word never got out to the newspapers about the attempted suicide.

Gerber and Corrigan fought hammer and tong for the next two days with much of the questioning directed to the alleged imprint of a surgical instrument. Corrigan stressed that the imprint resulted from a crease and nothing more.

After Gerber, it was Detective Schottke's turn; he was followed by my old college pal, Dr. Lester Hoverston, who had been a house guest during the days preceding the tragedy. Hoverston and I had been friends and classmates during medical school and had worked together as interns and residents at Los Angeles County Hospital. Because of my influence, he was able to get a residency in surgery at Bay View Hospital. For the first six weeks of that time, he lived at my home. Now he was testifying for the State.

Les Hoverston testified that he and I had discussed divorce. But it was his divorce we had discussed, not mine. Never was it my divorce we were seriously talking about. As best man at his wedding, I testified for him when he divorced his wife in a Cleveland court. I was a character witness for him (over Marilyn's objections), because he was technically a resident of California at the time, and needed help.

After he got his divorce decree, he told me, "Sam, if I can ever do the same for you, let me know." One time on a trip together to perform a neurosurgical operation, he suggested that *we* divorce Marilyn and that we share a bachelor apartment and "really have a ball."

"Better find somebody else," was my retort, "because I'm having a ball now and why should any man want to change anything?" That was the extent of my discussion about divorce with him. But I suppose, in a technical sense, you could say that we discussed divorce.

Why was Hoverston such a willing witness for the State? It might be well to point out that he, too, could be a suspect in Marilyn's murder, what with having stayed at my home right up until the day of the tragedy. The fact that he had left our home on July 3rd to spend the weekend with people in Kent, where nobody knew if he had left the house during the night, could have made him look suspicious.

The State continued to spread its case before the jury. It put fingerprint experts on the stand and they testified that they found no prints in the house and there were indications that someone had tried to remove fingerprints from furniture. The thing they didn't explain was why I would want to rub the fingerprints off the furniture in my own home. I wouldn't have any motive to do this because my fingerprints surely were supposed to be all over the place. Corrigan pretty well established through cross-examination that the Cleveland police fingerprint specialists fumbled their investigation, too.

On November 24th, Henry E. Dombrowski, another member of the Cleveland Police Scientific Unit, went to the witness box and testified that during his investigation, he found what he determined to be a trail of fifty blood spots throughout the house. His testimony was interrupted by the recess for the Thanksgiving holiday.

Throughout those first days of testimony by state witnesses, the local newspapers interpreted virtually every piece of testimony that was given at the trial, most of it under blaring headlines which tended to distort what had been said. Most of them were content with interpreting the testimony that was given on the stand. The Cleveland *Press* decided to do one better. On November 24th, the day before Thanksgiving, the Cleveland *Press* ran an article under a big, black headline, "Sam Called a 'Jekyll-Hyde' by Marilyn, Cousin To Testify."

The story said:

Two days before her death, murdered Marilyn Reese Sheppard told friends that her accused husband, Dr. Samuel H. Sheppard, was a "Dr. Jekyll and Mr. Hyde."

The prosecution has a "bombshell" witness on tap who will testify to Dr. Sam's display of fiery temper—countering the defense claim that the defendant is a gentle physician with an even disposition.

One of Mrs. Sheppard's "Dr. Jekyll and Mr. Hyde" statements was made to Bay Village Mayor J. Spencer Houk as recently as last June, the *Press* learned.

Houk, according to his statement to the authorities, had expressed surprise at Marilyn's account of a display of Sam's anger.

"You don't know that guy," he quoted the murder victim as replying. "He's a regular Dr. Jekyll and Mr. Hyde . . ."

Mrs. Sheppard used the "Jekyll and Hyde" expression frequently in confidential conversations during the past several years, friends and relatives have told the murder investigators.

THE "BOMBSHELL WITNESS" IS THOMAS WEIGLE, 26, OF 15897 NELAMERE ROAD, EAST CLEVELAND, MARILYN'S FIRST COUSIN.

Weigle and his wife, Marian, and son, Gordon, visited Sam and Marilyn Sheppard's home at 28924 Lake Road, Bay Village, a Sunday in March, 1952.

The two women were in the kitchen, Weigle related, while he and Dr. Sam were watching a western movie on television. The Sheppards' only son, Sam (Chip) Jr., then five years old, was playing in his room.

Chip, Weigle said, tapped his father's arm, either playfully or accidently.

"Sam's face reddened," Weigle continued. "He whisked the boy up, tossed him across his legs, and began beating him on his back, legs and buttocks.

"As he struck the boy repeatedly, Sam said, 'Don't you ever hit me again. . . . Don't you ever do that again.'"

Thomas Weigle did not testify—as the *Press* said he would—that I was a "Jekyll and Hyde." No one knows whether the jurors saw the story or the headline and what effect it might have had on them.

Nor did anyone determine whether or not the jurors were affected by a statement made by nationally syndicated columnist Bob Considine in a radio broadcast carried by WHK in Cleveland. After a police officer gave testimony that tended to contradict details in a statement I gave to the Cleveland police, Considine likened me to a perjurer. He compared the incident to the famous Alger Hiss confrontation with Whittaker Chambers in a national spy case a few years before.

My lawers asked Judge Blythin to question the jurors to determine how many heard the broadcast. "Well, I don't know, we can't stop people, in any event, listening to it," Judge Blythin said in turning down the request. "It is a matter of free speech, and the court can't control everybody . . . We are not going to harass the jury every morning. It is getting to the point where if we do it every morning, we are suspecting the jury. I have confidence in the jury."

Later, Walter Winchell, the columnist-broadcaster, said in a broadcast carried on Cleveland television and radio stations that a woman arrested in New York for robbery (a woman I had never heard of in my life) stated that as my mistress she had borne me a child. My lawyers asked Judge Blythin to query the jurors to determine how many had heard the broadcast. Two admitted they had heard Winchell's words. "Would that have had any effect on your judgment?" Blythin asked. Both said "no." My attorneys asked for a mistrial, but Blythin turned them down.

I noted in a letter to my brother, Steve:

The way the papers grasp on every small point to twist against me and minimize the points in my favor is surely depressing and strains my composure. I can't believe the jury takes the same attitude the reporters do. They don't need to stress points to sell papers, but I only hope the jurors will not let themselves read or listen to those who do read the papers.

It's hard to believe that an American judge could threaten to bar Steve from the court for expressing his reaction and yet allow whole pages of damaging remarks to me to be printed by reporters and adverse statements by police (which were not admissible or not testified to).

I really felt helpless here with you folks running all over the place, trying to do everything and practice, too.

One of the deputies brought about 20 people to see the "monkey" tonight—half of them women. I was in the shower so they stood outside that portion of the cell range and peeked at me as best they could. That would have bothered Marilyn more than it does me.

People can certainly be crude and cruel—never thinking that they may be the next one in this spot. Everyone should spend a little time here and the situation would then possibly be improved.

Thursday, November 25th, was Thanksgiving Day, and perhaps the loneliest day of my life. No words can describe the misery I felt. I slept until noon and then joined other county jail prisoners for a "roast beef" dinner. (It was more like baked horse.) Meanwhile, the remainder of my family was together in Bay Village, and in anticipation of this family gathering, I had sent the following note:

Thursday, as you know, is Thanksgiving, and I wish to send a note expressing how happy I am that all will be together.

Though it is hard for me to personally relate myself to Thanksgiving, it is less difficult when I think of all of you. There can't help but be a question in my heart as to why this tragedy has befallen us and recalling last year at this time depresses me and leaves me feeling pretty empty. Yet I am thankful for the relative good health of all of you and the strength we all have been given during the past four months.

Without your ever present and undaunted faith with many others, and that which Marilyn expressed repeatedly in the past, this ordeal would be too much. With this faith displayed in me and my belief in Good and Truth, strength is received and the way seems to be directed.

We must be in one another's thoughts a great deal. I love *each* and all of you more than I can ever say!

It was business as usual in the courtroom on Friday, the day after Thanksgiving. Dombrowski was back on the stand to complete his testimony. Under direct questioning by Parrino, the bald-headed Dombrowski told how detectives had searched the home and had isolated a trail of possible blood spots throughout the house.

He said that by spraying most of the floor surface in my home with a fluid called Luminol, which glows when it reacts to blood and other substances, he and other detectives were able to single out possible blood spots. Dombrowski explained they worked at night and circled the spots with chalk. Later the spots were tested with Benzidine, which he said gives off a blue-green color when it comes in contact with blood.

Corrigan was at his best in cross-examining Adelson and Dombrowski. He forced the latter to admit that a variety of other substances react the same as blood does to the test. The sally went like this:

Q. What is the reaction of blood to the Benzidine test?
A. It produces a strong blue-green color.

Q. Isn't it a fact that you get the same reaction from a great many
  other things?

A. No, not a great many other things. You get it from some things.

Q. What things?

A. Certain vegetables such as carrots, radishes, and also certain chem-
  icals.

Before he was through with the cross examination, Corrigan also
elicited from Dombrowski an admission that horseradish, lemons,
limes, apples, cherries, berries, tomatoes, and lettuce and other
greens have the same results. Dombrowski admitted that out of all
the spots found, his scientific unit tested only two of them to determine if they were human blood. One proved positive—on the third
step of the basement stairs.

"Did anyone tell you there was an animal in the house?" asked
Corrigan, referring to Koko, our female dog. "I heard it the first
day I was there. Did they tell you the animal dropped blood?"

A. No, sir.

Q. Nobody told you through all the examination that the Sheppard
dog, since March . . . had dropped blood throughout the house?

A. I heard it some time in September, after I had completed the investigation.

Then Corrigan attacked Dombrowski for not giving Luminol and
Benzidine tests to the bedroom where Marilyn was murdered. "Why
didn't you examine the floor in Marilyn's bedroom?" Corrigan
boomed at Dombrowski.

"It was our opinion from the appearance of that room that it
would have added nothing to the investigation," the detective said.
"We knew the blood was there from our experience with blood."

They never checked the various blood spots in the murder room,
which is impossible to understand.

The sixth week of the trial was completed. The seventh week
began on Monday, November 29th, and the State was still talking
about blood. This time the witness was Mary Cowan, chief medical
technologist at the coroner's office. Miss Cowan said she had visited
the home several times and had isolated six blood spots. Based on
her findings, the state had found seven human blood spots in the
house and claimed that the killer had left a trail of blood. But, they
were not able to type it as being either Marilyn's or mine.

There may have been blood spots in the house, but they didn't
come from me. If I had dripped blood from a weapon throughout

the house, why wasn't there blood on my trousers, except on my knee which I had placed on Marilyn's bed when I went to feel her pulse? There was absolutely no other blood on my pants, either from spatter or from dripping, nor was there any blood on my leather belt.

Miss Cowan, a soft-spoken woman, also told the jury that she had made microscopic studies of material discovered under Marilyn's finger nails and found fibers that couldn't be matched up with anything in the house or on me. These fibers were passed around to the jurors in an envelope and they were so tiny, I doubt anyone could see them. The lady technician didn't bother to project them on the screen, as had been done with the enlarged pictures of my slain wife and the pillow.

The night after Mary Cowan's testimony, I wrote to my family:

I can't get out of my mind the evidence of a left-handed person doing this thing. The pictures and all of the set-up of the room surely fit, and I know there must be more than I am now aware of to fit this pattern . . .

It seems as if a right-handed person could not have helped but throw blood on the ceiling. You have all worked this out no doubt, but I am just giving way to my pent-up feeling on the subject. Also, most of the blows were placed on the right side of the head and the right hand and arm—presumably in self-defense—were damaged most.

It becomes more and more difficult to sit and listen to these people try to relate everything to me. They really have the witnesses coached to the teeth and put the words right in their mouths.

To get back to the right and left hand—the fact that they claim they couldn't tell whether a right or left-handed person was responsible makes me feel they think a left-handed person did it but wish to minimize this. If there was much question they'd say it was right.

If this is human blood on the basement steps—he must have gone down there to clean himself up a little and he knew he could have the light on down there without anyone seeing in, etc.

The fellows here in the cell think all is going pretty well. They think it should be thrown out but they don't think Blythin will do it. They say I'll be home to Chip for Xmas. Hope they're right. Getting kinda tired of this place.

The State moved on toward the conclusion of its case and called as its last and star witness, Miss Susan Hayes—the event for which most of the spectators had been waiting. It was Wednesday, December 1st, in the seventh week of the trial. Sue looked quite attractive for her courtroom appearance before a standing-room crowd. She wore a black wool dress with an angora knit collar. She walked slowly to the witness box and took the oath. When she finished the oath, Bill Corrigan rose and asked that she be told of her constitutional rights.

"She is not required to testify to anything that will incriminate, disgrace, or shame her," he said sharply. John Mahon fired back that "the court is under no obligation to instruct the witness."

"The court will not so instruct her," Judge Blythin said in his Welsh brogue. "I assume she knows her constitutional rights." Then Thomas Parrino, who had originally gone to Los Angeles with Detective Schottke to question Susan, led her through direct testimony.

It wasn't long before he got to the trip I had taken to Los Angeles with Marilyn in March, 1954, and the incidents at Dr. Arthur Miller's house. The questioning went like this:

Q. Where did you stay that night?
A. At the Millers'.
Q. Did Dr. Sam remain at the Millers'?
A. Yes.
Q. Did you both use the same bed?
A. Yes.
Q. State whether you had intimate relations with Dr. Sam Sheppard.
A. Yes.
Q. State whether you had any clothes there at the Miller home?
A. No, I went to the Downey residence for clothes.
Q. Who drove you there?
A. Dr. Sam.
Q. What did you do when you got to Downey?
A. I changed clothing.
Q. Where did you go then?
A. We drove back to the Miller residence.
Q. How long did you stay there?
A. Seven days.
Q. Did Dr. Sam remain at the Millers', and how long?
A. Yes—seven days.
Q. Did you occupy the same bedroom with Dr. Sam for seven days?
A. Yes.
Q. Was the first time you had intimate relations with Dr. Sam this time in California?
A. No.
Q. Referring to the time you were at Bay View Hospital in December of 1952, did you have intimate relations with Dr. Sam before?
A. Shortly before.

Q. After you quit Bay View in 1952, and the time you quit in 1954, did you have intimate relations with Dr. Sam Sheppard?

A. Yes.

Q. Where did you have these intimate relations?

A. In an automobile, and in the apartment above the Fairview Clinic.

Later in her direct testimony, Parrino asked Susan whether, in her association with me, the subject of divorce had been mentioned. "Yes, in the early part of 1953," Susan answered. The questioning continued:

Q. What did he say?

A. He said he loved his wife very much, but not as a wife, and thought he would get a divorce, but he wasn't sure his father would approve.

Q. Did he mention divorce again?

A. Later in November of 1953 when I was working in the hospital.

Q. Who was present?

A. I was.

Q. What did Dr. Sam Sheppard say?

A. He said he mentioned something about divorce to his wife.

Q. Do you recall the subject of divorce being discussed on other occasions?

A. It was never discussed, but it was mentioned.

Q. On the other times mentioned, who was there—just the two of you?

A. I'm not sure.

Q. After Dr. Sheppard left California in March, 1954, did you communicate with him—did you write letters?

A. Yes, I received about four letters and I sent about the same amount —four.

Q. Who started the correspondence?

A. Dr. Sheppard. He wrote to me first.

Q. Did he profess any love in those letters?

A. No, sir.

A few more questions and Parrino announced he was finished with her. Judge Blythin ordered a brief recess, then Fred Garmone took over the cross-examination. Garmone handled her gently, questioning her mainly about the sequence of events leading up to her "telling all" to Parrino and Schottke.

And when he finished this line of questioning, he asked, "During all the period of your activities at Bay View, the Rose Building, and the activities between yourself and Dr. Sam Sheppard, were you always aware that he was a married man?"

"Yes, sir," she answered, and she was dismissed. She was on the stand a total of sixty-five minutes. After she left the stand someone asked me whether I felt sorry for her, having to bare her soul? Sorry? How could I feel sorry for her? My reaction was that she was a silly girl. I felt that her father must be out of his mind to let her do this. She didn't have to testify at all. Other than that, I thought it was good that she testified that I told her I loved my wife.

Later two of the spectators, an attorney from southern Ohio and Fabian, the great British detective from Scotland Yard, spoke to me. Both indicated that all Susan Hayes did was to bear witness to the fact that I had pretty good taste in women and that she had had poor advice about appearing at the trial. They said that Susan had pointed up the fact that Marilyn might have had good reason to kill me, but that I had certainly no reason to kill Marilyn.

Fabian shook my hand and asked if he could come to my "victory party." I said that we would wait until the victory and then talk about it.

With the completion of Susan Hayes' testimony, the State of Ohio rested its case. I was encouraged and felt the case should at that point be thrown out of court for lack of evidence. In any event, it was our turn at bat.

9

My attorneys immediately moved for a directed verdict of acquittal. Arthur Petersilge handled most of the arguments on three motions filed on my behalf. The red-haired attorney said that my story of the events of the murder night were unrefuted at the moment. He chipped away at several points the State had made in the case against me.

Petersilge pointed out that the lack of fingerprints in the house could be discounted because the investigators admitted they did not examine a number of items in the home for fingerprints. As for my folded jacket on the couch, in which the State had put much stock, he explained that the jacket may have been removed by Marilyn or I might have thrown it off as I rushed upstairs to Marilyn's aid. Someone may have later picked it up and folded it.

Bill Corrigan interjected the point that Marilyn had died from blood in her lungs, not from the thirty-five blows, which were not powerful enough to kill. The type of head injuries she suffered, he said, were intended to disfigure Marilyn, indicating a woman may have been involved.

John Mahon rose to his feet to challenge the statements of my attorneys, and charged that the State had proved "deliberate and premeditated" malice. Judge Blythin ruled that the trial should continue—that the jury should determine my innocence or guilt. I really didn't expect anything else.

The first defense witness was my brother, Steve, and he took the stand on Thursday, December 2nd. His testimony stretched through Friday and into Monday, December 6th. Steve told of coming to my home the morning of July 4th, of finding me injured and taking me to Bay View. Steve said that in his medical judgment I had been seriously injured, which refuted the testimony a few days earlier by Dr. Richard Hexter, the general practitioner from Bay Village, who was the State's only medical witness. Dr. Hexter had tried to minimize my injury and lack of the left abdominal and left cremasteric reflex, which is bilateral. It was significant to me that the State didn't call Dr. Spencer Braden, the eminent brain surgeon who had examined me after my arrest, a month after I suffered the injuries. Obviously, he couldn't support Dr. Hexter's testimony, or they would have had him in court.

Steve testified that on the basis of the X-rays that were taken of my neck on July 4th, he concluded I had suffered a fracture of the second cervical vertebra. "It was apparent to me that Sam had both a brain and a spinal injury," he said. "I, therefore, called in a specialist, Dr. Charles Elkins, the most eminent neurosurgeon I know."

After Steve was finished, his wife, Betty, took the stand. She told the jury that Marilyn and I had enjoyed a happy married life.

On December 7th, my brother, Richard, took the stand. Richard was very proper and very professional and represented our family in the best possible, gentlemanly manner. His testimony was, in my opinion, outstanding in my favor. Not that Steve's testimony wasn't favorable, but his indignation at my arrest and being put on trial seemed to temper its impact.

Richard made one point that I have tried to stress over and over. Contrary to what Spencer Houk had said about Richard's asking me the morning of July 4th whether I had anything to do with the murder, Richard said sternly, "I am positive I never said such a thing. I could not have because it never entered my mind that my brother could have killed his wife." ("Or anyone," he told me later.)

The presentation of my case went quickly. Corrigan called eighteen witnesses to the stand on December 8th. They were staff people of Bay View Hospital who supported Steve's story of the diagnoses and treatment of my injuries.

There were other character witnesses who pictured me as an "even-tempered man with a fine reputation in the community." They testified in my behalf on December 9th. One of them was Rev. Albert C. Kreke, our minister, who made me break down when he told how he had baptized Marilyn in our home. And it came to my mind in a flash how Chip said afterwards that "Mommie had been advertised."

The two men who had gone to the police back in July with stories that both had seen a "bushy-haired" man on Lake Road the morning of July 4th, also testified that day. Leo Stawicki of Cuyahoga Heights, Ohio, said he saw a stranger near a maple tree in my driveway between two fifteen and two thirty in the morning. The man, he said, had "a long face, with bushy hair—hair that was standing up." He said that he had viewed me in a police lineup and that I couldn't have been the man because I was too bald.

Richard Knitter of Sheffield Lake, Ohio, also told the jury that he had seen a "bushy-haired" man walking in front of the cemetery about one hundred fifty feet from my house at about three fifty that morning.

Both men denied the accusation that they had come forth with their stories a week after the murder because my family had offered a $10,000 reward for information leading to the arrest and conviction of Marilyn's murderer.

Then, shortly before two p.m. on Thursday, December 9th, the court clerk droned, "Dr. Samuel Sheppard, take the stand."

There was never any question in my mind that I was going to testify in my own behalf. Corrigan had asked me only once whether I would take the stand. "Hell, yes," was my immediate answer.

"They'll put you through a wringer," he said.

"Bill, what about the wringer you put me through when you talked with me and tried to find out for yourself whether I was innocent?" I said. "Did I not convince you? Do you think these guys can put me through more of a wringer than you did?" Corrigan had really given me a grilling back in July. He questioned me up and down and around.

I had known the night before that I would probably be on the stand on the 9th. I wasn't nervous. I actually was eager to get on the stand and tell how I felt and what the story was. If anything, there was a feeling of relief. It was a feeling that now I could finally express my feelings and understanding of what happened.

When I stepped into the witness box, the bailiff administered the oath. The jurors looked at me more attentively than they had previously. All of the jurors had glanced at me from time to time during the testimony of others. Now they were scrutinizing me closely. During my testimony, I looked at the jury as a whole, but occasionally I looked at one or two individuals in the jury box. I wasn't trying to single out any one person who might be particularly sentimental or might have a child about the age of Chip or some gimmick like that. I was trying to be honest and straightforward, and that's all.

One of the first things I did under direct examination by Bill Corrigan was to clarify an incident that Tom Weigle had described and the *Press* had written about. The *Press* had said I would be called a "Jekyll and Hyde" by Weigle, but he never did say it. He did testify that two years earlier I had given Chip an "unmerciful" beating.

"Chip had become a problem in the household in that he was difficult to reprimand," I testified. "Shortly before the day Tom Weigle and his wife visited us, Marilyn asked me to talk with Chip. She was having trouble trying to discipline him because when she spanked him she couldn't hurt him. On this particular day, Chip was showing off, as youngsters do. I believe he pushed over Tom Weigle's son several times. Chip then hit me on the shoulder with his tomahawk. I gave him several good licks on the backside. I took him over my knee to give him a few reasonably good licks. Chip's pride was hurt and he ran upstairs. Later, Marilyn and I took his dinner to him." Corrigan then asked me if the disciplining had been effective. I smiled and said, "Yes."

The remainder of the first day on the stand was concerned primarily with a description of my early life, my medical training, and the early years of our marriage. It went very smoothly. I was at ease as Corrigan led me through this phase of the testimony.

The second day of my testimony, on Friday, was much more of an emotional experience. In relating the events that occurred the night of July 3rd and early the morning of July 4th, I clenched my fists and spoke softly as I answered Corrigan's questions about hearing Marilyn's cries, rushing up the stairs half asleep, finding her battered in bed, and my subsequent scuffles with the intruder. I told of calling Spencer Houk, of being taken to the hospital, and of being examined and X-rayed and questioned by Schottke and Gareau in the hospital.

About this time, one of the jurors, Mrs. Borke, a dark-haired, middle-aged woman, asked Bill Corrigan if she could ask me a question. "Go ahead," my attorney said. Mrs. Borke leaned forward and spoke to me. "Dr. Sam," she began, and then Danaceau was on his feet.

"Just a moment, here," he shouted. "You ask the court first!"

"Judge, can I ask the question?" Mrs. Borke asked.

"The law does not permit it," Judge Blythin said sternly.

We continued through the remainder of the events prior to my arrest, the session with Dr. Gerber and other officials, my written statement, right up to the night of the arrest. I told how I was arrested at my parents' home, the mob scene, and how I was denied counsel at my arraignment at Bay Village City Hall.

Then Corrigan questioned me about the grilling I had received by Cleveland police. I told about the seventy-two uninterrupted hours of questioning, the shouts and insults, the gruesome photographs of Marilyn they shoved again and again in my face, the offer of a manslaughter conviction in return for a confession. It was pretty much as I related it earlier in this book.

Apparently my testimony about the treatment I received from Cleveland homicide detectives caught Captain David Kerr right where it hurt. In a statement to newspapers after the testimony, he called me a "bare-faced liar." "If ever a person was handled with kid gloves, Dr. Sam was," Kerr said. "Lies—nothing of that sort transpired. There was no third degree, no offer of a deal—that's ridiculous. We can't make deals. That's up to the court."

It's interesting to note, that no Cleveland policeman ever got on the stand to refute what I had said. Nobody could have done it under oath.

That night, in my cell, I wrote to my brothers:

Tonight's paper has a statement by Kerr saying that my account of the Cleveland detective questioning is untrue. He also says that they never use third degree and have had no complaints in some numerous cases.

There are four young men in my cell block *now* (all younger than I am) that have been physically beaten by the *Cleveland* detectives and called filthy names.

One fellow was first beaten when he was only 15 years old, and has been treated the same way many times since. No doubt the beating this boy got at age 15 helped develop his delinquency. He is now sentenced to the State Pen. He is here to testify in another case. One boy can testify to a recent time when a friend of his was first handcuffed by Cleveland detectives, then beaten until he fell down; he was then repeatedly kicked in the face. The same boy was struck with a rubber hose by members of the Cleveland detective force.

Mr. Kerr may have bitten off a little more than he cares to chew. These boys say there are many others who can testify to such brutality. One of the fellows is 23, one 21, and two are 19 years old. How can society expect to help and rehabilitate these boys, who are *not all bad*, when such activities are allowed to go on?

I have the names and will give them to W.J.C.

Love to all,
Sam

P.S. I guess I was handled with kid gloves compared to others. (Physically, but not mentally. A physical beating would be much easier for me. Those bastards are experts in choice of torture.)

But before the State got its long-awaited chance to cross-examine me on December 13th, Corrigan had a few more questions remaining in direct examination. One series concerned the T-shirt that had been found near my property in July.

"Doctor," Corrigan started, "there was put in evidence here, brought into the case by me, a T-shirt. Was that T-shirt ever shown to you either by police or the coroner before it was brought in here?"

"No, sir," I replied.

"Did you look at it here in the courtroom?" he asked.

"I certainly did."

"Is this your T-shirt?" he asked dramatically.

"It certainly could be my T-shirt. I'm not sure," I answered.

Then before turning me over to the prosecutors for cross-examination, Corrigan posed one last question. "Doctor, have you in your lifetime ever submitted to sin?"

"I have succumbed to human frailties, yes, sir," I answered.

"Your witness," said Corrigan. The prosecutors took over.

It was a long, grueling day, but I tried my best to answer each and every question put to me by the prosecutors, no matter how hostile they were. I admitted that I had some involvement with several other women, including Susan Hayes. I also got a chance to tell my side of the story as to whether the subject of divorce had ever come up in my relationship with Susan.

"You say it was she who suggested the divorce?" Mahon asked. "What did she say?"

"She said something like, 'Some men get divorces, why can't you?' "

The questioning continued:

Q. During the latter part of 1953 did you speak to Susan Hayes about a divorce?
A. I believe she spoke to me about it.
Q. What was said?
A. I said I love my wife very much; I love my boy.
Q. What did she say?
A. About the only thing I can remember is that she referred to Dr. Hoverston's divorce and said, "Some men get divorces."
Q. Why would you be called upon to say you loved your wife?
A. She was talking about divorce.
Q. While you were in California in March, 1954, did you stay at Dr. Arthur Miller's home?
A. Yes, sir.

Q. Did you and Miss Hayes share a bedroom?
A. Yes.
Q. For how long?
A. About five days.

Under cross-examination, I also denied Dr. Hoverston's charge that I had ever discussed any plans to divorce Marilyn. It was the other way around, as I have previously stated. We were talking about his divorce. I testified: "He said to me, 'Why don't you consider getting a divorce? We could live together, enjoy living together'—something to that effect. I took it as 'misery loves company.' Do you want my reaction?"

"I'll tell you if I want your reaction," Mahon said sharply. "Tell what you said to him."

"I told Dr. Hoverston Marilyn was the finest girl I ever knew anywhere, and if he wanted me to go out playing poker, or if I wanted to go out with the boys, there was never any problem with Marilyn. I told him I felt our situation was ideal for me."

"Didn't you bring up the subject of divorce and didn't Dr. Hoverston advise you against it, making a statement to the effect that 'you might be jumping from the frying pan into the fire?'" Mahon persisted.

"No, sir," I answered. "I expect if anything like that was said I told him I had a pretty wonderful situation with Marilyn, and if he used that expression he must have been agreeing with me that Marilyn was a pretty wonderful girl."

The prosecutors kept up their cross-examination for a day and a half. The thing I can remember most vividly was the one last flurry with John Mahon. It went like this:

Q. Now, Doctor, the injuries you received—didn't you receive those from jumping off the platform down onto the beach?
A. No, sir, I think that would be impossible.
Q. Why impossible?
A. Because a spinal cord contusion is something that is the result of a rather forcible force. It would necessitate almost definitely a force from the back of the neck. That would be so unless there were injury to the top of the head.
Q. And couldn't such a blow be administered to the back of the neck if you fell on it?
A. No, sir.

"I object," shouted Corrigan. "Do you have any evidence that these injuries are self-inflicted?"

"We are asking the only man who knows," interjected Saul Dana-ceau, the assistant prosecutor.

"The witness already has answered the question," Judge Blythin said with finality. The questioning continued:

Q. Isn't it a fact, Doctor, that you beat your wife that morning?
A. No, sir.
Q. And after you had killed her, you rushed down the stairs and jumped off the platform to the beach, and fell and injured your neck?
A. That is absolutely untrue, sir, and unfair.
Q. When you testified at the inquest, was an oath administered to you?
A. Yes.
Q. The oath was to tell the truth?
A. Yes.
Q. Did you tell the truth?
A. Not in regard to Miss Hayes.
Q. You mean you deliberately lied at that hearing?

Corrigan protested that I had already answered a similar question, but Judge Blythin overruled the objection.

A. I felt—
Q. Answer the question yes or no.
A. I don't feel that I can fairly answer that question yes or no.
Q. You know whether you deliberately lied or not?
A. I felt that Miss Hayes' reputation justified that answer.

The flurry of questioning apparently took more out of Mahon than it did out of me. I noticed him slumping over the jury rail after he was finished. He was limp.

So far as I was concerned, I felt that I had done pretty well answering his questions—that the psychology courses that I had taken in college and medical school helped me cope with his type of questioning. Mahon didn't want to know the truth. He wanted to get me, and he knew I was innocent at the time. All he wanted was a conviction.

Before I stepped down from the stand, Corrigan asked a few more questions in redirect examination. At one point, he asked, "Is there anything else you want to say, Dr. Sheppard?"

Before I had a chance to open my mouth, Mahon objected. Judge Blythin, as he had done throughout most of the trial, ruled in favor of the State. "The question is too general," he said.

Corrigan put the finishing touches on the case after I left the stand on Tuesday, December 14th. First, Dr. Horace Don, who

formerly worked at Bay View and now was practicing in Iowa, told
that he had frequently gone to my home after midnight to show me
X-rays of accident patients and that he usually—if not always—
found the door open on the road side.

He also said that he was in my home the morning of July 4th
after hearing about the murder and saw a young boy in the house,
about ten or twelve years of age, touching things "all over the
house." Don said that while he was in the house he heard Dr.
Gerber say to police officers, "It is evident that the doctor did it—
let's go and get a confession."

I should mention here that years later, Dr. Don told me that some
time in 1953, Gerber said something like this to him, "So you work
at Bay View with the Sheppard boys. Some day I'm gonna get one
of them."

Another witness—and an important one—that day was Dr. Charles
Elkins, the neurologist who had examined me at the request of my
brother. Dr. Elkins had moved to Arizona after the tragedy in July,
but flew to Cleveland to testify on my behalf. He told of his examinations of me on July 4th and 6th, and stated that there were missing reflexes, which indicated a spinal cord injury.

At the end of Dr. Elkins' direct testimony, Corrigan asked him,
"Did you examine Sam Sheppard on August 6th at County Jail?"

A. Yes.
Q. What did you find in that examination?
A. I was asked by Dr. Steve to examine his brother Sam. Sam looked
   well. Asked how he felt he replied that he still had some neck pain
   and occasional headaches.

Dr. Elkins said he still found some weaknesses in the grasp of my
left hand and the reflexes which had been missing in July had returned, but were still not entirely normal. (This proved variation.)

Q. Did this examination confirm your impression of July 6th at the
   hospital?
A. Yes.
Q. What was your impression?
A. My impression was that Dr. Sam Sheppard had received a contu-
   sion of the spinal cord. He had exhibited positive signs in July.
   Now one month later, his disease had improved.

About the only negative item in Dr. Elkins' appearance on the
stand took place when he refuted a portion of Dr. Steve's testimony
regarding the finding of one blood cell in the spinal fluid. And that

would never have happened had not Steve been overzealous on a point about which he knew better—a point that I had been taught when I was a medical student. So had Steve. Dr. Van Horn Gerdine, an eminent neurologist and psychiatrist, had taught Dad, Richard, Steve, and me with too much care for Steve to come out with such a statement. I was shocked, since thereafter the defense medical testimony was tainted.

After Dr. Elkins finished, I felt there could be little doubt in any juror's mind that I had suffered a serious injury on the morning of July 4th. And I knew it wouldn't be long before the case would be in the hands of the jury.

10 ᥦᥩ

Bill Corrigan put his hand on my shoulder and said. "If Sam Sheppard had killed his wife Marilyn, it would weigh upon his soul and the soul would endeavor to throw it off, just as if he had taken poison in his stomach and his stomach would throw it off. The commission of a brutal crime is foreign to Sam Sheppard's nature."

Then he took my hands in his own and held them high in the air. He spoke almost with a whisper. "These hands. These hands that just a few hours before had worked with skill and devotion to save the life of a little child." Several people wept openly in the courtroom as Corrigan delivered his closing argument in the ninth week of my murder trial.

Each side had been allowed five hours by Judge Blythin for closing arguments. The State of Ohio was to begin, then we would have our turn, and then finally the State would get in its last licks before Judge Blythin charged the jury. First, it had been Thomas Parrino for the State. "He lied about his relations with Susan Hayes because he wanted to protect the name of that lady," Parrino had shouted. "We're not dealing with something insignificant here, ladies and gentlemen. We're dealing with murder. We're dealing with the brutal murder of Marilyn Sheppard. If the defendant would lie under oath to protect the name of a lady, how many lies would he utter to protect his own life? How many lies would he utter under oath to protect Sam Sheppard? We look to the jury for justice. The murder of Marilyn Sheppard was one of the most brutal murders in the history of crime. It was committed, we have no doubt, by the defendant. I for one do not envy your position in this case, any of you. Our task is not simple, the task of Judge Blythin is not simple —but yours is the hardest task of them all. Whatever you do, ladies and gentlemen, let justice be done. No one could ask for more."

Parrino spoke for two hours and twenty-three minutes. He attacked my story of the events of the murder morning as "fantastic." At one point, he waved Marilyn's bloody watch—which had stopped at four fifteen a.m.—and asked where I had been during the almost two hours between that time and the time I called Spencer Houk. He charged that I could not have been unconscious all that time.

To Parrino's charges, Arthur Petersilge replied, "Five months after the murder of Marilyn Sheppard, the State still does not know how she was killed, with what weapon she was killed, or why she was killed. Yet on the basis of this flimsy evidence, the State is asking that you send Sam Sheppard to the electric chair."

Then Fred Garmone stepped before the jury and told how the police had bungled the investigation, how the Cleveland police had let valid clues die, while working unceasingly to build a case against me, to the exclusion of concentrating on solving the case.

Finally, it was Bill Corrigan's turn. His voice alternating between a thunderous tone and a whisper, Corrigan held those in the courtroom spellbound as he delivered an emotional summation in my behalf. Corrigan accused the Cleveland newspapers of creating an atmosphere of hysteria. He charged that the State had evolved a theory that Marilyn was killed because she was pregnant, and he referred sarcastically to testimony that had been presented speculating that I was sterile.

"I don't care that the matter of Susan Hayes arose, or that Sheppard wandered from the path of rectitude," Corrigan said. "That didn't prove he didn't love his wife, his home, his family. I would lie under oath if I were asked to confess to some private sin intended only for the ears of a confessor. Sam Sheppard succumbed to sex, the strongest lure in the human body, as you and I know."

Then he spoke of my arrest, "Three men came to the house of his parents and manacled him and took him away. It would almost remind you of the Gestapo methods we used to read about. Then the third degree starts, and if you read about this story in a people's court in China or behind the Iron Curtain, it would raise the hair on your head. But this happened in your own city, in this very courthouse. Third degree? This young man is subject to the most grueling examination by people who know how to do it—not amateurs. They worked in teams. They never let him rest. If Sam Sheppard was guilty of the murder of his wife, do you think he could have withstood that grilling without giving them the confession they were looking for to cover up their incompetence? They threw pictures of his dead wife in his face. They insulted his mother. They insulted his father, using vile and unspeakable names. Then there would be another offering manslaughter, talking about getting it all over and going to a ball game, getting a couple of years in prison, or maybe only nine months." Then he turned and shouted, "They made a mistake and they are not big enough to admit it."

He closed his statement, reducing me to tears by saying, "We approach this holy season and I approach this case imbued with the idea that unless we American lawyers and we American jurors do our part in maintaining in this case that freedom, we have failed in our duties. I bring you Sam Sheppard. I give him to you. A more serious deposit I probably will not make again. A more serious deposit you will never receive again. I give you the body of a man thirty-one years young, an immortal pearl from which God poured forth his own love. I ask you to search your consciences thoroughly and I know your verdict will be one of not guilty. The Lord guide you and bless you."

When Corrigan finished with his summation on December 16th, Danaceau and Mahon had the last words for the State. I thought Danaceau was pleading for a manslaughter conviction when he said, "Sam may have been awake. He may have walked up to the bedroom. Perhaps there were some recriminations over these other women, some arguments, some fight. When men are terribly angry, they sometimes do things they wouldn't otherwise do." In other words, he was charging I had done it in a fit of rage.

Then there was tall, bald John Mahon with his final remarks. I sat with a crucifix I had received in the mail clenched in my fist and listened as he completed his statement.

"I say to you," Mahon said, his voice rising, "he got his injuries by jumping off a platform not in pursuit of a shadow, or phantom, or figure, but because he was pursued by his conscience because of the foul act he had just committed, and had decided on ending his life in the waters of Lake Erie. The cold water made him change his mind. Then he came to the realization of the position he was in and that is when the faked burglary was set up. In your hands, I rest the life of this defendant. I want you to give him the benefit of every doubt to which he is entitled. And all I ask on the other hand is that you be just and fair to the decent, law-abiding citizens of this community. Consider it without prejudice or bias, yes, ladies and gentlemen, and without sympathy in this case."

During its closing arguments, the State never did ask for the death penalty. Their closing arguments were incongruous. There were Parrino and Mahon asking by inference that I be convicted of first-degree murder and thus be given the chair, and Danaceau talking about the murder being committed in a blind rage. The

State didn't come right out and say "electric chair" because I think that would have weakened their case.

In looking back over Corrigan's closing argument in my behalf, I wish he had been a little less eloquent and had hammered away at some of the discrepancies in the State's case. He didn't point out the fact my pants were not spattered with blood and the absence of blood on my belt, my shoes or my person. Nor did he bring up the issue of the tooth chip, the piece of polish or paint, and the piece of leather in the murder room.

On Friday morning, December 17th, Judge Edward Blythin sat on the bench overlooking the jury and charged the seven men and five women responsible for deciding my fate. After a few opening remarks, he said in his Welsh brogue: "It has undoubtedly occurred to you that deciding what the facts are in a case of this kind is a very important function. It is, in fact, an all-important function and is exclusively your function. With it I have nothing whatever to do, and if by anything that has been said or done during the progress of this trial, or by something that is now said, or by some emphasis which you may think I place on something I now say, there is created in your minds some impression that I have formed some opinion as to what the facts are in this case, you are now instructed to disregard and dismiss such impression entirely and to proceed to arrive at your own conclusions on the basis of the instruction now being given to you. You are the sole judges of the facts in this case." Then he went on with his charge.

I felt that the entire charge was confusing. And if it was confusing to me, it had to be confusing to the jurors because all were less educated and his verbiage was very difficult to follow. The crowning blow came when he gave an analogy to show how the jurors were to define direct evidence and circumstantial evidence:

"There are two classes or types of evidence and both are involved in most cases of the kind and character of this case. They are designated as direct evidence and circumstantial evidence. Both are proper and one is as effective as the other if equally convincing under the rules of law for its application. Direct evidence is that given by a witness on the basis of the dictates of his own senses— what he himself heard; what he saw; what he did; what he said —matters which he himself knows. Circumstantial evidence is that which is furnished as to a fact which may not be the fact or situation sought to be proven but is a fact from which a fair inference can be drawn tending to prove the fact or situation sought to be shown or proven. I believe that a very simple and homely [sic] example or illustration of each of the two types of evidence mentioned may be helpful.

"Illustrating now what would be direct evidence, let us assume that I had on a certain day a very fine cherry tree in my yard. The family happens to be away on that day and when I return about five o'clock in the evening I find my cherry tree chopped down. I proceed to investigate and first make inquiry of my next door neighbor, Mr. Smith. I ask him if he saw any stranger doing anything in my yard on that day. He replied, 'Yes, I saw George Washington chop it down with an axe.' That would constitute direct evidence because Mr. Smith is relying on his own sense of sight and states what he himself saw with his own eyes. For that reason he is able to give direct evidence that George Washington chopped down that cherry tree.

"Let us now consider a case of circumstantial evidence in the same connection. Assume that on inquiry of Mr. Smith, my neighbor, he, in answer to my question, says that he did not see anyone chopping down my tree. I then ask him, 'Did you see anyone about my place today?' He replies, 'Yes, I saw George Washington walk along your driveway from the yard to the street with an axe on his shoulder.' Here is evidence of a fact which does not directly prove who chopped down my cherry tree but which permits a natural and fair assumption that George Washington can well be the person who chopped down that tree. The circumstance that George Washington was in my yard with an axe combined with the fact that my tree was chopped down would constitute very definitely a piece of circumstantial evidence to be weighed in the consideration of a charge against George Washington involved in the act of chopping down that tree."

This analogy or parallel to my situation regarding circumstantial evidence showed me that this man was totally prejudiced and was, in effect, asking for a guilty verdict.

Before he sent the jury to its deliberation room, he outlined five possible verdicts:

Guilty of murder in the first degree as charged in the indictment, which called for death in the electric chair.

Guilty of murder in the first degree as charged in the indictment, but with a recommendation of mercy, meaning a life sentence with no parole.

Not guilty of murder in the first degree—which is premeditated—

but guilty of murder in the second degree, calling for life imprisonment, but with eligibility for parole after ten years.

Not guilty of murder in the first or second degree, but guilty of
manslaughter, with a penalty of one to twenty years, with parole
available after one year.

Not guilty.

When Judge Blythin finished his charge, I wanted to stand up
and shout, "Please give me the electric chair or turn me loose. Anything in between wouldn't be right or fair to Marilyn and isn't fair
to me. I'd rather go to the electric chair than go to prison."

And so, at nine forty-seven a.m. on Friday, December 17th,
Howard Barrish, Mrs. Elizabeth Borke, Edmond Virlinger, William
C. Lamb, Mrs. Louise Feuchter, Jack Hansen, Mrs. Anna Foote,
Mrs. Beatrice Orenstein, James C. Bird, Frank Moravic, Frank J.
Kallorits, and Louella Williams walked from the courtroom. They
went up the narrow stairs to the jury room to elect a foreman and
to begin deliberating whether I was guilty or innocent, whether I
should live or die, whether I should be incarcerated or freed.

I returned to my cell on the fourth floor of the Criminal Courts
Building to await their decision. Frankly, I was elated. I felt that
the jury couldn't do anything but acquit me. Even a nut couldn't
convict me on this lack of evidence, I reasoned. I knew I was innocent. The only thing the State had was the fact that I was in the
house at the time Marilyn was murdered—nothing else. They had
no weapon. They found no blood on my hands, on my eyebrows,
on my hair, on my trousers, except for the patch on my knee. They
couldn't find any blood on the clothes I had on—and there had been
so much blood spattered in the murder.

There were the piece of leather, the piece of nail polish, and the
piece of unidentified tooth. The latter is a part of a human body.
This is like a chunk of finger left in the room. It was either Marilyn's, mine or evidence of another person's being there. I can't help
wondering why the authorities did not make a determined effort to
identify its owner.

Corrigan said he couldn't see any other answer but acquittal. I
was relatively relaxed and received encouragement from the other
fellows in the jail, and from members of my family and friends,
some of whom had to stand in line at the jail for more than an hour
to visit me. My visitors included Marilyn's wonderful aunt and
uncle, Mary and Bud Brown.

The jury deliberated through Friday and finally was sent to a

downtown hotel for the night. The group resumed their deliberations on Saturday morning and after many hours in the room, Judge
Blythin finally called them down at seven minutes after ten in the
evening and asked, "I wonder if there is some likelihood if you continue deliberation tonight you might come to a verdict?" He asked
them to raise their hands. No one did. The judge asked them if they
wanted to recess until ten Sunday morning. All raised their hands.

I was beginning to feel like a yo-yo. Each time the jury convened,
each time it went to lunch, each time it returned to deliberate, each
time it was recessed, I had to take that elevator ride down to the
courtroom. Blythin was not allowed to say anything to the jury
without my being present.

Although I didn't see it myself, the scene in the pressroom and
in the courtroom was something to behold, according to reliable
sources. Newsmen were playing cards, sleeping on benches, drink-
ing whisky while waiting for the verdict. Each time Judge Blythin
called the jury in to send them out for a meal or to recess them for
the night, there was the inevitable barrage of flash bulbs.

The handling of the jurors—when they were recessed for the night
and taken to the Hotel Carter about a mile away—was also very
irregular. While there were seven men and five women on the jury,
the group was entrusted to two male bailiffs. There was no female
bailiff to accompany them. We later learned that the jurors were
allowed to call their homes and that the calls were not monitored.
While there was a bailiff present in the room where the calls were
made, no outsider heard the conversation and no one knows what
might have been said to the jurors or whom they might actually
have called.

As I said before, Corrigan had been supremely confident when
the jury got the case, but now as the deliberations moved into Sunday—the third day—he began to hedge a little. He said that the
length of the deliberations was a "bad sign." He told me he knew
there would be two or three prejudiced persons on the jury—persons
who already had made up their minds—and that was why he had
asked for a change of venue. The white-haired Corrigan said he
had hoped that some of the more intelligent jurors would be able
to persuade these people of my innocence, but the fact that deliberations had stretched into a third day did not look good. He told me
to prepare myself and my mind for a conviction.

"What are you talking about?" I asked.

"They would have come back in twenty minutes with an acquittal, and now they have been out three days," Corrigan answered.

Despite Corrigan's initial shock, that something might be happening that I had not expected, I was still fairly confident, though weary. I still had a lot of reassurance from the fellows in jail. How could they not know my innocence? One man said, "Doc, you didn't do it or you'd have confessed and made a deal for manslaughter. But even if you had, you're going to hit the bricks!" (Acquittal.) He seemed to be speaking for many.

The jury deliberated until six p.m. Sunday without reaching a verdict. Judge Blythin again sent them to the Hotel Carter, for the third night. It was the same story again Monday. On Monday night, the jury requested more time to study the case and went to the hotel for the fourth straight night. Based on Corrigan's remarks on Sunday, the tension was beginning to become unbearable.

We played cards and chess, and chatted to pass the time on Tuesday, the fifth day of deliberations. The jury resumed its work at nine four a.m. and went to lunch at twelve twenty. By one thirty p.m. the jurors were back in the bare-walled room where James C. Bird, who had been elected foreman, led them in their deliberations. At two thirty p.m., one hundred hours had passed since they got the case on Friday, December 17th.

Unbeknown to me, the buzzer signifying that a verdict had been reached shattered the tension of the late afternoon, at four twelve. Reporters, lawyers, and other court officials ran to the courtroom.

I was half napping in my cell on the fourth floor. Mike Ucello, the chief jailer, came to the cell and said, "Okay, Sheppard, let's go." He didn't say that a verdict had been reached and since he didn't, I assumed that perhaps the judge was going to send the jury out for dinner, recess them for the night, or, perhaps, dismiss them as hung.

I got up, grabbed my towel, and rubbed my face and eyes vigorously, trying to get the sleepy look out of my eyes. As you can imagine, I hadn't been doing much sleeping in the past four nights. Deputy Sheriff James Kilroy slapped on the handcuffs and we took the elevator down to the first floor. We walked through the hall. The scene was bedlam. He took me over to the defense table, where Bill Corrigan and his son were sitting.

"They've got a verdict, Sam," Bill Corrigan said solemnly. "Steady yourself, it's not good."

"How do you know, Bill?" I asked. "How can you say that?"

"I've been through a lot of trials, Sam, and all I can tell you is what I feel. I feel this verdict is not going to be good, but I don't care what the verdict is because the record built up here will absolutely necessitate a new trial on appeal. It will demand a new trial."

Judge Blythin, dressed in a black robe, came through the door at the front of the courtroom and quickly assumed his position on the bench. The jury filed in. Blythin asked the foreman, Bird, if the jury had reached a verdict. "Yes," the foreman answered firmly. He handed the judge a sealed envelope. Blythin carefully tore it open. I held my breath.

"We, the jury," he read—and then paused momentarily—"do find the defendant," and he paused again, "not guilty of murder in the first degree." For a fleeting moment, I felt a surge of elation through my body and from the sounds of members of my family and friends, they did too. "But, guilty of murder in the second degree."

The elation turned to disbelief. I was numbed by his words. My mouth opened and I uttered an involuntary gasp. I stared at the jurors, shaking my head back and forth. Bill Corrigan leaned forward and clasped his hand on my shoulder.

Judge Blythin indicated he wanted to pass sentence immediately. "Why sentence him now, before I file a motion for a new trial?" Corrigan shouted. "Oh, go ahead. It's just indicative of the whole thing."

Blythin asked me to step forward. I did. He told me I had been convicted of second degree murder and asked me if there was anything I wanted to say before he passed sentence. I looked him squarely in the eye. "I would like to say, sir, that I am not guilty and I feel there have been facts presented before this court that definitely have proven that I couldn't have performed this crime."

"All right," Blythin answered, "but a jury has found otherwise.

"It is now the judgment of this court that you be taken to the Ohio Penitentiary, there to remain for the rest of your life."

Then I was handcuffed and led from the courtroom. "They found me guilty of murder in the second degree," I told the other prisoners when I returned to the fourth floor. I took off the charcoal gray suit I had worn throughout the trial, put on a pair of blue slacks and a blue sports shirt, and sat down to digest the shocking events of the past few crushing minutes. That evening, I put my thoughts down on a yellow, legal-sized pad. It was in the form of a letter to my family and to Mary and Bud Brown, Marilyn's aunt and uncle. Here is that letter:

You are as shocked as I, but it seems that the entire trial was almost useless. If I were guilty and confessed to it the worst I would have gotten is second degree. Everyone but those who counted I guess either had faith in me or changed their opinion as the trial went on. Many people, as you know better than I, became more and more confident as the trial went on. What happened seemed almost inconceivable, but the whole thing is inconceivable.

Corrigan seems more calm and confident than ever before, and says he will have me out of here eventually. I feel like the fight is all gone out of me, but yet I can't hang my head for something I didn't do, and I'll not let you or him down and will never stop fighting this.

My biggest concern is you folks and Chip. Please don't worry about me. I can get along anywhere, and if the appeal goes on without bail, I will request to go down to the Pen, where I can get some exercise, etc. Please don't worry about me any more than you would if I had been killed with Marilyn. Let's all be eternally grateful that Chip didn't awaken and get killed as did M. I want Steve to adopt Chip and take complete charge of him and his future, as he has already. He should be told the facts, and legal action to change his middle name to "Blake" should be initiated soon.

Mary will take care of all of Marilyn's things, and you do what you think best about the house and my things. If this sentence sticks, which we hope won't happen, but if it does, I realize that I will lose my license and in effect lose everything, but there are places in the world that need medical care and where licenses are not the important thing. There is still a lot of good that can be done in this world by me, no matter what happens. I'm still acting on my knowledge of what Marilyn would expect of me and us, so please don't feel too bad.

I can't say that I'm not crushed, hurt and bewildered, but we have been truly sandbagged and I won't lie down for it.

I love you all so very much it is beyond expression. As long as you all know that I am innocent I can face the fire of hell. They can't take my family and true friends away from me, though they have tried very hard.

Love to all,

Sam

Things were bad on December 21, 1954. But, impossible as it may seem, they would get much worse before many weeks would pass. No words can express the depth of my progressive depression during the following year. Death would have been sweet relief, but I could not do this to Chip, Richard, Steve, Dorothy, and Betty—or to Marilyn.

11

The day after the conviction, the jail authorities put me in a solitary observation cell, which they said was common practice for anyone convicted of murder. I had the feeling they were afraid I might try to commit suicide and they wanted me under the watchful eye of a deputy at all times. It was ridiculous, I thought. I was downhearted at the turn of events, but I wasn't ready to throw in the sponge yet and never would be. And I sent word of my feeling to the press in a statement issued through Bill Corrigan.

"I can stand this," I said. "I have stood so much since this tragedy happened that one more thing doesn't really mean much to me personally. But, I will keep fighting for my family's sake. I am sorry for and worried about my father and mother and my little boy."

I had plenty on my mind beside my current predicament. My mother, who had tried to take her own life during the trial, was still despondent and had taken the verdict extremely hard. My father, like other members of the family, had lost a considerable amount of weight during the long weeks of the investigation and the trial. But it soon became evident in my father's case that his loss of weight wasn't entirely due to the worry and anguish over the trial. He was extremely ill.

The day before the verdict was reached both my mother and father were taken to Bay View Hospital—mother for her emotional state and dad for treatment of what had been diagnosed as pleurisy. With Christmas just a few days away, there was no happiness in the Sheppard family.

While others were starting to get caught up in the holiday spirit, Bill Corrigan and the other members of my legal team were preparing to file a formal motion for a new trial and a stay of execution that would keep me in the County Jail until at least a portion of my appeal was heard. Meanwhile, I was putting down on paper for release to a Cleveland newspaper the reasons why I felt the jury should have freed me, rather than convict me of second degree murder. On December 23rd I wrote:

The total disregard of definite evidence that proves there was someone else in our house, who killed Marilyn, stuns and naturally depresses me.

(1) Trace of evidence in the form of fibers under Marilyn's nails can only represent the last material her hands contacted, yet these fibers could be matched to nothing in the house of mine or Marilyn's. Where did these come from?

(2) The small piece of leather found under the bed matched nothing of mine or in the house in texture or fit. The fingernail polish did not match Marilyn's brand or color. Where did these things come from?

(3) A portion of broken tooth found under the bed did not fit Marilyn's mouth. No attempt was made to check it with my mouth, but if it was part of my tooth it proves I was struck in the room. If it's not my tooth, someone else was in the room.

(4) A cigarette butt which was not entered as evidence, but found in the upstairs toilet, was finally admitted by Officer Hubach (rebuttal witness). What investigation was performed in relation to that? We'll perhaps never know as the prosecuting attorney chooses to withhold as much of the evidence not suitable to his case as possible. (Only careful cross-examination brought out the presence of the trace of fibers under the nails.) My understanding was that a prosecuting attorney was duty bound to produce all evidence.

(5) State's witnesses testified to the fact that it is impossible to remove blood from a garment by washing it. (This is an established fact.) Yet, my pants had only one area of blood above one knee where I must have put my hand or touched the bed. The blood on the walls as it was in the pictures would display the fact that the killer could not have worn those pants.

(6) Proven spinal cord injury is explained by saying I dove over the landing of the beach house, and yet my story as told by a dazed, injured person is called fantastic.

I don't know if the jurors expected my relation of the events to sound like a mystery novel or not, but a man who has been knocked senseless twice can't describe associated events with clarity.

How any fair American citizen can honestly disregard the above facts, not to mention testimony by witnesses who saw a man consistent with the one I described, in my driveway, is unbelievable.

I do not think the jurors were consciously unfair, but they should search their subconscious reactions very carefully and recognize the effect previous publicity of a prejudicial nature must have had.

If it had not been so clearly shown that I could not have performed this crime my reaction would not be so profound, since I knew I must stand guilty till proven innocent.

My innocence *was proven*, but my fellow citizens still call me guilty, take my freedom, my son, my profession, any self-respect, and actually my everything.

The day before Christmas, Corrigan, Petersilge, and Garmone filed the motion for a new trial. It contained forty points of alleged error. (A few days later they added a forty-first point.) Judge Blythin set December 30th as the date for hearing arguments on the motions.

Mail was pouring into the County Jail for me by the bagful. There were Christmas cards and letters and religious items, and almost all of it indicated support and prayers for me. As you might expect, Christmas Day provided another emotional experience, what with being cooped up in a cell, away from those I loved. Toward the end of the day, I wrote the following letter to my family:

Well, today was pretty rough, but things were not too bad as we had plenty of food with all the things that were sent in to me yesterday. The boys here are no doubt glad to have me here as fruit, candy and nuts were enjoyed by all.

The reaction displayed by so many people manifesting utter faith in me has been most inspiring and has really given me renewed faith and determination to fight on with more fervor than ever. I know you all were knocked down as flat as I was, since things looked so good 'til this.

Bill Corrigan was in yesterday and discussed with me just what had happened and what was to come. He is confident of the outcome, but feels this whole thing is far more reaching than just me and my unjust trial by the press. Bill feels that perhaps I have been the chosen one to go through this ordeal from which new legal measures will be taken to prevent such unfair and unconstitutional treatment in the future. He explained that I must maintain my mental and physical health, etc., as things progress. He explained that the police, etc., would like nothing better than to disturb my mental stability which he says has been remarkable. (Merely a stand for the truth, in my mind!) Anyway, Bill is going ahead with his end and I assured him, as I do you, that I can fight on and on, especially when you all are with me.

As Christmas came and went, it became obvious that my father's condition was deteriorating. Steve and Richard called in a doctor who specialized in internal medicine and cardiology. After a careful examination he told them he suspected that dad was suffering from cancer of the lungs, and that his days were numbered.

Word of dad's condition did little to make my 31st birthday any happier on December 29th. I spent the day playing cards with fellow inmates, listening to the radio, and reading the hundreds of letters and many birthday cards sent by well-wishers. And, of course, I was thinking about the hearing to be held the next day. I wasn't really very hopeful that Blythin would order a new trial.

Bill Corrigan put three motions for new trials before Judge Blythin in a seventy-five-minute hearing in the same courtroom where I had been convicted just nine days before. I was there. The first was based on the forty-one points of error he said took place during the trial. The second was based on the fact that Cleveland newspapers had carried headlines and news stories prejudicial to me during the trial. The third was based on "new evidence" Corrigan said he had obtained, linking someone else to the murder of my wife.

Blythin said he would rule separately on the motion based on newly-discovered evidence. He gave Corrigan and the other lawyers until January 8th to produce it, and ruled that I could remain in County Jail until the new trial issue was resolved. The hearing that day concerned primarily the other two motions. After it was over, Judge Blythin took the matter under advisement. It didn't take him long to decide the issue. On January 3rd, he turned down the motions based on the forty-one points and on the newspaper publicity and said flatly that the verdict was supported by the evidence. I wasn't surprised.

After Judge Blythin's ruling on the major motion, my attorneys dropped the motion based on new evidence and decided to proceed directly to the Court of Appeals. They made known their decision to Blythin on the morning of January 7th, and he continued the stay of execution—delaying my trip to the Ohio Penitentiary—indefinitely.

Early in the afternoon I was in my cell, at County Jail. Suddenly, one of the deputies came into the cell and removed my radio. There was no explanation. I knew something was wrong. Within moments, a deputy came in and ushered me to a small, bare-walled room. My brothers, Richard and Steve, and Steve's wife, Betty, were there.

"Who is it, Steve?" I asked.

"Mother shot herself, Sam," Steve said. "She's at peace and won't have to worry any more." I was sitting at a small, wooden table. I dropped my head in my arms and cried.

Mom had been staying at Steve's house. With Dad in the hospital and Mother aware of the graveness of his condition, my brothers felt that she should not stay alone in their home next to the hospital. I had not seen Mother since the day of my second arrest. I forbade her to visit me in jail because of her sensitive nature.

Steve said Mother had appeared in good spirits that morning when he left for the hospital. Later, Betty left the home, leaving only Mother, a maid, and Chip in the home. Around eleven a.m.,

Mother wrote a short note, locked her bedroom door, put a .38 caliber revolver to her temple and pulled the trigger. At noon, Betty hurriedly summoned Steve home from the hospital. When he entered Mother's bedroom he found her dead. A note was propped up on the dresser:

Dear Steve:
 I just can't manage without Dad—thanks for everything.
                                                    Mother.

When Steve, Richard and Betty left the jail, the authorities again placed me in an observation cell as a precaution against a suicide attempt on my part. It appeared as if they actually wished to remind me of the "easy way out."

Late in the day, I was given permission to telephone my dying father at Bay View Hospital. He told me to have courage and to continue to fight. "God bless you, son. Don't ever give up," were the final words he spoke to me. "Never." I said, choking back the tears. That night, I wrote him a note:

Dearest Dad,
 Words are inadequate, but your message to me is enough to carry me through anything!
 If you can take it, I can.
 You are a great man, and Marilyn was surely correct when she said, "A little bit of God walks with Dad Sheppard wherever he goes."
 We'll work together again!
 God bless you.
                                                       Sam

Common Pleas Judge Harry Hanna, presiding judge of the Common Pleas court, gave me permission to attend Mother's funeral on Monday, January 10th. At two thirty p.m. I left the County Jail handcuffed to two deputies. I said nothing all the way out to the Saxton Funeral Home in Lakewood. The funeral inside the home was supposed to be private, but the scene outside was anything but that. There was total disregard for personal privacy.

Lakewood police had roped off the funeral home area, but more than three thousand people, by police count, loitered and ogled in the area. Some were newsmen, but the vast majority were morbid curiosity seekers who couldn't leave us alone in this hour of extreme and overwhelming grief.

Reverend Alfred C. Kreke, the minister who had presided at Marilyn's funeral, delivered the eulogy. As part of his sermon he quoted from one of my mother's favorite passages, "The Achievement of Poise," by Rev. Ernest Fremont Tittle. This was the sermon she had sent me after my arrest. Reverend Kreke read, "If you can keep your head when all about you are losing theirs and blaming it on you, then you will achieve poise."

At the end of the sermon, Steve, Richard and I walked to the casket and prayed. There was a stranger in our midst. I was still handcuffed to Deputy Mike Ucello, who was standing behind me, intruding on our last moment with Mother. Even the most desperate men who attend a funeral from Ohio Penitentiary do not remain handcuffed at the casket.

From the funeral home, we went in cars to Sunset Memorial Park in North Olmstead. As snow fell on a frosty knoll overlooking a quiet lagoon, Mother was laid to rest, without privacy. Newsmen and the curious climbed fences and hid behind shrubs to catch a glimpse of the Sheppards in mourning. It was so incongruous. In life, Mother, like Marilyn, was so very, very modest. On the return trip to County Jail, I asked the deputies if I could stop for a moment at Bay View Hospital to visit with Dad. They refused, and we went directly to the jail.

During the weeks following the murder and through the trial, I heard nothing from most of Marilyn's relatives except Mary and Bud Brown, who came every visiting day. But when my mother took her own life, Marilyn's father, Tom Reese, and others sent their sympathy to me. The day after the funeral, I wrote to Tom Reese, Jane, and other members of the family:

You have expressed sympathy in regard to my mother's death. I appreciate this expression, which has been the only recent indication that the wonderful representatives of Mimi and Grandad Reese still exist. (Other than the visit with Lola and Rook the other day.)

My mother, as you may know, loved Marilyn as her very own flesh and blood, sacrificing for her only as a mother can or will. She knew that her son could no more physically harm Marilyn than he could little Chip or any other person.

I continued:

Mother went to her tragic death with the frightful feeling and belief that many of the blood relatives of her Marilyn had turned their backs on us both (Marilyn and I) as well as on mother and Chip.

On his death bed now is another person who loved Marilyn beyond expression. Though his mental strength to accept injustice is greater than was Mother's, it seems his physical ailment will take him from us while I am incarcerated.

Marilyn and Mother were very much alike, both feeling keenly what other people thought. This tells me how utterly crushed Marilyn would be if she knew the effect your reaction or lack of reaction has had on Mother and Dad Sheppard.

For Marilyn always knew that she could always bank on them in any situation as she could you folks. You may be sure that if she had been in my position, my entire family would have rallied to her side which would have tended to preclude a great deal of the dirty publicity which you enjoyed no more than we. They knew that neither she nor I was capable of such an act, and no newspaper or so-called detective could have destroyed the faith they had, and have, in each of us as well as the family, including Chip.

Realizing these things, I have prayed for you to evaluate and recognize the obvious bias and prejudiced methods and testimony used against me. I hoped that such study and enlightenment would stimulate you to my side, lending support to the cause of truth before it's too late. I have prayed for this as much for your sake as for mine, and surely Chip's, because my conscience is clear which strengthens me to carry on under any circumstances. I am prepared to fight endlessly for truth as Marilyn would expect of me (knowing that I'll never let her down).

It would be difficult to live in the knowledge that I had helped destroy or refused to help preserve what remains of the things Marilyn loved the very most in this world.

God bless you.

                                                                        Sam

The same day I wrote the above letter, my father was transferred to the famed Cleveland Clinic for further tests and examination. The diagnosis—cancer of the stomach. Dad knew he was dying, and asked to be allowed to spend the remaining days of his life at the hospital he built and loved, and where he could be near his sons. He returned to Bay View Hospital on January 14th.

Three days later, my attorneys appeared before the three-member Court of Appeals and asked that since I was convicted of second degree murder I be released on bail, pending outcome of my appeal. The justices took the matter under advisement, promising a decision in a few days.

About eleven on the night of January 18th, two deputies came into my cell and removed my radio. I knew why, even though they didn't tell me. Again, minutes later, my brothers, Richard and Steve, arrived and we gathered in a small room in the jail.

"You must know why we are here," Richard said, putting a firm hand on my shoulder. "Dad passed away tonight."

That night I wrote in the diary:

Dad surely had the will to live that mother lacked. If only their bodies and minds could have been put together to evolve a relatively healthy body and mind. I can't help this totally unscientific dream at a time like this.

Naturally they have put me back in the "suicide cell" again where I was placed after the verdict for a week, after mother's death for a week, and left only yesterday for my regular cell again.

This is one of two cells placed off the main hall where I was also placed the first night of my arrest July 31st. This cell, unlike those on the regular ranges, has no washbasin and no toilet. A pail is placed under a small bench at the end for toilet necessities during the night. A bright light shines into the cell and a deputy sits outside, peering in continuously.

This deputy is stationed there to see that I do a good, complete job of suicide if attempted, I gather, for there is nothing this aged, fumbling old man could possibly do if I decided to take my life, which would be ridiculous and stupid at best.

A climb to the top bars of the outer hall of the cell or even the inner ceiling of the cell and a dive on one's head would make very short work of things. Peculiar to this arrangement are windows within three inch reach of the bars from the hallway of the cell, through which a wrist could easily be jammed, the ragged glass of which could be raked and cut across the radial and ulnar arteries. Naturally these people have to treat me like their average prisoner who has no medical knowledge and is guilty of the crime for which he has been accused or convicted. For neither of the above do I qualify.

Yet common horse sense would tell a person, if I did stand guilty truly of the crime as accused, my medical knowledge would provide many ways by which suicide could be accomplished, and would be.

Actually placing me in this cell alone, save one homosexual who looks, talks, acts and reacts like a woman in the next cell, is much tougher psychologically than staying with my fellows in the cell block whom I've learned to know and enjoy.

The next morning, the Court of Appeals refused my application for release on bail. A day later—on January 20th—I again left the County Jail in handcuffs, this time for my father's funeral. Even though the arrangements had been kept secret, there was another mob scene and again little privacy.

After the funeral I returned to my cell, shaken and depressed, wondering what new and tormenting tragedy fate had in store for the Sheppard family. In little less than seven months I had lost my wife, my mother and my father, and my freedom. Nothing would bring back Marilyn and my folks, but the remnants of the Sheppard family were united in one common goal—to obtain from the courts a reversal of my conviction, and my freedom.

12 &

Throughout the months following the tragedy and during my trial, police officials kept possession of my home and members of my family were admitted only in the presence of a police officer. My attorneys tried to obtain a court order for release of the house during the trial, but were turned down. They wanted to do a detailed examination of the premises for use in the defense, but as a result of Judge Blythin's ruling this could only be done under the watchful eye of a police guard, who would just be a pipeline to the prosecutor's office.

Finally, after my conviction, the keys were turned over to my attorneys. Bill Corrigan was determined to have a scientific investigation made of the premises by an unprejudiced, independent expert. He stopped to see me in early January and asked whether I had any objection to hiring Dr. Paul Kirk, noted West Coast criminologist, to make a study of the home.

"I know you're not guilty, Sam," Corrigan said during the visit. "But if there's anything in the house you don't want uncovered, tell me or tell me not to call Dr. Kirk. Dr. Kirk is a man whose integrity is beyond reproach. He will report what he finds, regardless of how it might affect your case."

"Call Dr. Kirk," I said. "I've got nothing to hide."

Dr. Kirk was a professor at the School of Criminology of the University of California, and the author of several books and scientific papers on criminology. He was one of the nation's foremost experts in the field of blood detection and blood groupings, as well as investigative procedures. Dr. Kirk arrived in Cleveland on January 22nd, and spent four days making a minute inspection of the murder bedroom and the rest of the house. He visited me for a few minutes in County Jail. He asked me whether there were any phases of the case I felt needed closer investigation or whether there were any areas of the home that should be given special consideration.

I suggested that he thoroughly check the teen-age club room above the garage, where some of the neighborhood boys used to congregate with our permission, and also to check the garden tools and auto wrenches in the garage to determine if there were any blood spots on them. He said he had already done that and could find none.

When Dr. Kirk completed his examination, he returned to California, to analyze his findings, study the trial transcript and reach some conclusions on the murder of my wife. Naturally, I was anxious to see his report, but Dr. Kirk was a very thorough man and I knew it would be several weeks in coming.

In the meantime, I remained numb from the death of both parents. Jail life was just one long, empty day after another. Where before I had been diligent in writing a daily diary of jail happenings, I didn't make an entry from the time of my father's death until March 13, 1955, when I started writing again. My first notes said:

Have been in solitary confinement since the death of Dad, recently have been given the privilege of walking on the porch. This was a relief to me and I was unable to mask the satisfaction it brought. At the realization of this, Carney and Weitzel decided to send me back to the cell block. Having adjusted well to my solitary existence and happy to get a little air, this move struck me as tough again.

The fact, I think, actually is that most of the floor deputies but Carney, of course, had observed me closely while in solitary confinement and all obviously realized that I am no murderer. This was noted by Weitzel, etc. and though he's tried hard, the regular deputies of the higher type treated me very well when not spied on.

At any rate I again realized that though moving was a great deal of trouble due to all my accumulated spread in the larger cell, I accepted this, as everything else, as a challenge. The boys here have been the recipients of my fruit and candy for some time, though I was not allowed to come back and talk or even motion through the windows. One day I am in a solitary cell with privileges to walk on the porch, but can not talk to any other prisoner in any way. The next day, I am thrown into the cell block with twenty-three others. These people spend their time conjuring up methods to make the men unhappy here.

On March 18th, the day after I learned that a hearing before the Court of Appeals had been scheduled for May 23rd, I wrote to Steve, who was on a brief vacation:

Your letter came today. I can't put into words what it means to me to have brothers like you and Richard.

The fact that any and all pleasure events that you take part in are overshadowed by my present position is one which results only from our relationship. I want you to know that the reverse is honest, true, in that your recent trip and any other recreational activity on your part have had a beneficial effect on me. (Knowing you need same!)

As far as my lack of complaint goes, I think Dad taught us all that complaints don't help much, but it's a firm stand and the punch with guts that counts. You, Betty, Rich, Dorothy, Mary, and Bud have shown this stand and fortitude which I have also attempted to display. Mary tells me that she lives from one week to the next visiting day here, to find the strength she has continued to show. We have all inspired each other, but I want you to know that you and your frequent notes (when going has been toughest) have represented a large amount of the inspiration which has been truly necessary at times for me. [He reminded me to think of Dad.]

Called Mary and Bud tonight and Chip answered. [He was staying with them for a while.] They were having a fine time making a plane. He sounds wonderful and Mary is very much impressed by the fact that he is much easier for them to handle now than previously. His sisters [Steve's daughters] and the boys on the street are good for him. You and Betty have and are doing a wonderful job. I somehow feel that Marilyn knows and loves you more or even is helping you.

She has been very close to me for the last few weeks. It's a difficult thing to explain, but you know I think—my mental processes are not as numb as they were for so long with the repeated blows.

Mary is afraid she and Bud shouldn't go on a vacation while I'm hanging here, but have encouraged them to go when they can. The hearing is postponed until May 23rd.

"Am doing exercises daily and about pulled a muscle while chinning today. Have to work pretty hard to stay ahead of some of the nineteen-year old paratroopers they have here.

Several days later, I noted in my diary, the following impressions:

The past few days have been an experience which relates little to my case, but points well and illustrates the vicious and often stupid methods exerted here. Monday afternoon the block I have been kept in was vacated so that the entire block could be washed and cleaned. At this time I was told by [Asst. Sheriff] Weitzel that I could stay in the block while it was cleaned and I agreed, if I could help work.

He said "fine," I could work. So I started to help with the preliminaries of cleaning up the place. Tuesday a.m. I was awakened and told to get everything ready to move. (Evidently they realized that I was not going to feel degraded by living with and working with Negroes, so they were moving me.)

I was moved to A block on the same floor where I knew some of the fellows and some I did not. In about an hour, at least ten deputies, the sheriff and assistants came in here and started a shakedown (search).

All the men but six were locked in the day room, a center room be-

tween two cell ranges for eating, etc. The other six men were taken to
the hole. This is a delightful place I may have referred to before. An un-
heated cell and no bed of any type, no blankets, no toilet or bowl. They
are given one meal every three days if they are lucky and must perform
their toilet in the bucket in the cell. These men were placed there and
are there now evidently because they are suspected of something. None
of them know what they are suspected of and so they have nothing to say
and they are kept in this place.

During the "shakedown" the searchers went through each man's cell
tearing all personal belongings and other things apart. Clean clothes were
thrown on the floor. My tooth brush was on the floor and one of the men
saw one of the deputies step on it. My clothes were intentionally strewn
over the floor and everything I had just moved and placed neatly was
utterly strewn.

They had not let me bring my radio to this block because one was here.
As an afterthought, Carney took the radio. So now we have none.

Last night, the men on the range threw papers and trash all over the
floor and refused to clean it this a.m. The six remaining men on my side
of the range were moved together to another floor as penalty and that is
exactly what these men wanted. They all wanted to get away from Carney. (Naturally I was left to clean the mess.)

On April 2nd, my attorneys filed the appeal brief with the Cuyahoga County Court of Appeals. It was a massive, three-hundred-
sixty-six-page document bound in a tan cover, and in it, Corrigan,
Garmone and Petersilge cited thirty-seven errors in law.

The brief charged that Judge Blythin had erred in denying the
motion for a change of venue and contained numerous examples of
prejudicial newspaper coverage and editorials to support it.

That Judge Blythin erred in denying the motions for a directed
verdict for dismissal of the indictment because there was no substantial evidence of my guilt, but there was substantial and undis-
puted testimony that supported my story and that was inconsistent
with my guilt.

That in seven instances, Judge Blythin erred in empaneling the
jury, including his refusal to allow my attorneys to question prospective jurors on whether evidence of extra-marital affairs would
prejudice them against me.

That Judge Blythin erred in the admission of testimony, including
the presentation of the colored slides of Marilyn's battered body;
hearsay testimony by Nancy Ahern, permitting unfair cross examination of me, and permitting Spencer Houk to testify that he took

a lie detector test for the sole purpose of emphasizing in the minds of the jury that I did not take a lie detector test.

That Judge Blythin erred in the exclusion of testimony, including the restriction of the testimony on cross examination of Dr. Hexter and refusing to allow witness Don Ahern to testify that I was a deep sleeper.

That Judge Blythin erred in the conduct of the trial because of his remarks in the court in the presence of the jury, disorder during the trial, in failing to properly admonish the jury at the time they separated and in the coercion of a verdict.

That Judge Blythin erred in his charge to the jury, including his analogy on circumstantial evidence and his failure to include assault and battery in the list of possible verdicts.

And that Judge Blythin erred in overruling a motion for a new trial because the verdict was against the weight of evidence and because the jurors were separated and allowed to communicate with outsiders by telephone during their deliberations.

Next, it was up to the State of Ohio to answer the brief and for both sides to appear before the three-member court on May 23rd for oral arguments. Two weeks after my attorneys placed the appeal brief before the three-judge panel, Corrigan was again before Judge Blythin, with a motion for a new trial, charging that we had evidence that the murder of my wife was committed by a left-handed person. The basis for this motion on newly-found evidence was a brilliant report prepared by Dr. Paul Kirk, who had spent nearly two months studying the results of his examination in my home. Judge Blythin immediately set April 27th as a date for a hearing on the motion. Dr. Kirk, reached by newspapers at his Berkley, California, home said he was eager to come to Cleveland to testify at the hearing.

Four days before the hearing, I got a first-hand look at Dr. Kirk's findings and my emotions were recorded in my diary dated April 23rd.

Bill Corrigan was in this a.m. and brought a copy of most of Dr. Kirk's report. All I can say, it is terrific. It proves my innocence beyond all question. His complete thoroughness is that of only a great scientist which he is. I'm so fired up now that I can't think of sleep. I want to show this report to the whole cockeyed world, Mother, Dad, and Chip.

I want them to open these doors. How they can attempt to refute this proof is hard to see.

On the day of the hearing on my motion for a new trial, I donned
a dark-blue business suit, white shirt, and dark knit tie and was led
to a courtroom. It was my first courtroom appearance since the dark
days of the preceding December when I was convicted and denied
the original motion for a new trial by Judge Blythin. The courtroom
was crowded with newsmen, photographers and spectators. As I
was led in by Deputy Walter Apalka, I smiled and waved at my
brothers, Steve and Richard, and their wives, who were there for
the hearing.

The entire proceeding lasted twenty-five minutes. During that
time, my attorneys entered seven affidavits to support the motion,
including Dr. Kirk's statement, which I thought was a blockbuster
and proved for all to see that I was innocent of the murder of
Marilyn.

Dr. Kirk's statement started with a description of his background
and qualifications to act as an expert in the Marilyn Sheppard murder case. It told of the four-day examination of my home and the
gathering of additional exhibits for study in his laboratory in California. Then he reviewed the technical evidence presented by the
prosecution during the trial and commented:

> Careful appraisal of the technical evidence presented by the prosecu-
> tion shows it to be completely worthless as proof of the guilt (or inno-
> cence) of the defendant. Only the autopsy and pathology findings are
> really pertinent to the case. With two minor exceptions, it shows no cir-
> cumstantial value whatever. They are: (a) Water under defendant's
> watch crystal. (b) Loss of T-shirt.
>
> The first point, (a) is self-contradictory. If the watch was in the lake
> after the murder, fresh blood on it would have been removed to a degree
> which would make any effort to group it completely futile. Since it was
> considered to be sufficient for grouping, the watch couldn't have been in
> the lake after the murder, and the water must have been under the crystal
> previously.
>
> Point (b) has no ready explanation which can be shown so definitely.
> It is consistent with the story told by the defendant, as well as with the
> version presented by the prosecution. It is not impossible that the mur-
> derer removed the T-shirt to be used in cleaning blood from his own per-
> son. An unbiased observer surely would be struck by the fact that the
> defendant, if he removed his T-shirt because it was bloody, would surely
> put on another one to cover the loss of the first.

In summing up the prosecution's technical evidence, Dr. Kirk
said:

Analysis of the technical evidence offered by the prosecution shows it to be superficial, incomplete, and erroneous in interpretation. Little if any of it had a direct bearing on the guilt or innocence of Dr. Samuel H. Sheppard. At the most, it establishes that the victim was beaten to death by a weapon of unknown type; that there was some blood found in various places in the house; that the murderer attempted to give an impression of a burglary; that it was so amateurish and clumsily performed as to fool nobody; and that certain details appeared to be inconsistent with the story told repeatedly by the defendant. Even these apparent inconsistencies were so minor as to be of little value if correct, and no certainty of the correctness of interpretation was established.

Briefly, no actual proof of a technical nature was ever offered indicating guilt of the defendant, and the facts that were established and offered are even more readily interpreted in several respects in terms of another murderer than the defendant.

Next Dr. Kirk described how he traced blood spatter patterns in the murder room and how he tried to reconstruct the spatter in his laboratory by producing a dummy skull with a wood block, sponge rubber and sheet of plastic which simulated human skin and striking it with a variety of possible weapons, including a ball peen hammer, steel bar, and flashlight.

He told of finding a large blob of blood on the closet door in the bedroom and upon laboratory analysis determining that it matched neither Marilyn's blood type nor mine. And he described how he obtained a large number of human teeth from dentists and by experimentation determined that Marilyn's teeth were broken by an outward pull rather than from a downward blow.

From the known and demonstrable facts of the case, a reconstruction of the murder is possible, a limited amount of inference is unavoidable, but in the main, the facts are clear and the conclusions inescapable.

(1) The original motive of the crime was sexual. Examination of the slacks in which the victim was sleeping shows that they were lowered to their approximate final position at the time the blood spatters were made. Leaving the victim in the near nude condition in which she was first found is highly characteristic of the sex crime. The probable absence of serious outcry may well have been because her mouth was covered with the attacker's hand.

(2) The victim was not moved after being beaten. This follows from the fact that her head was at the same point as the center of the blood spot pattern. Since her legs protruded under the lower crossbar of the bed, it follows that she had drawn up her legs in a defensive action, and moved downward during the early stages of the struggle. At the time of

death or unconsciousness, her muscles relaxed and the legs straightened to a position similar to that in which she was found.

(3) At some point in the activities of the attacker, the victim obtained a firm grip on him with her teeth. His defensive action of jerking away was violent enough to break two or three of her teeth. The evidence indicates that blood welling from the resulting wound to the bitten member was thrown as a very large drop to the wardrobe door.

(4) Presumably inflamed by the resistance and pain, the attacker utilized some available weapon to strike the victim down. She instinctively turned her head (probably to her right) and shielded it with her hands which were in turn severely injured in the beating that ensued. She may also have grabbed a pillow as a shield pressing it in front of her head, and depositing much blood on it. Whether an early blow produced unconsciousness or whether her head was held down with the other hand of the attacker is uncertain, but one of these two events must have occurred.

(5) She was beaten by a weapon held in the left hand, swung low in rapid and vicious blows to her head after it was puddled with blood from earlier injury, and possibly after her actual death. Whether any beating occurred after death or not, her head was certainly beaten for some time in almost exactly the same position—the one in which it was found.

(6) The weapon was almost certainly not over a foot in length, and had on it an edge, quite blunt but protruding. The edge was almost certainly crosswise to the axis of the weapon and could have been the flared front edge of a heavy flashlight. It was not similar in any serious respect to the alleged impression of a surgical instrument on the pillow case, nor to any of a large variety of possible weapons that have been suggested by the prosecution.

(7) During the beating the attacker stood close to the bottom of the bed and balanced himself with one knee on the bed. The weapon swung to about ½ foot from the wardrobe door in this position.

(8) After commission of the crime, the attacker faked a very clumsy attempt to indicate that a burglary had been committed. This included removing watches, keys, etc. and stuffing them in a bag (the green bag) which was later thrown away during the retreat; upsetting the papers from the living room desk; disarraying the den; breaking the trophies, etc.

Then in concluding his remarks, Dr. Kirk dealt with what he called the "Defendant's Account," which bears repeating in total. He wrote:

No crime reconstruction is complete or reliable unless it is at least consistent with all the known facts. Several obvious inconsistencies are certainly present between the reconstruction and the theory that the defendant was the attacker. It remains to show that the reconstruction is consistent with the version of the events given by the defendant.

His account is vague, with few details. It is not a well thought-out story such as might be expected of an intelligent person who was faking the account. The vagueness itself is a characteristic which must be consistent with the known facts if the account is to be considered true. That a true account would necessarily or probably be vague is indicated by the following known or claimed facts:

(a) The defendant was asleep on the couch when last seen by his visitors, the Aherns. A person suddenly awakened from a sound sleep often is confused and at a loss to act or understand what is happening, especially if it is not commonplace and customary.

(b) Sworn testimony is available to indicate that he suffered a dislocation or other injury to the vertebra of the neck, sufficient to inhibit his normal reflexes. Sworn testimony is available to indicate that he suffered a blow to the face sufficiently to loose teeth, and cause swelling and discoloration around the eye. These circumstances strongly imply the probability of unconsciousness, which is certainly consistent with vagueness.

(c) On one special point, it was possible to conduct an experiment to determine whether vagueness was consistent with the fact, viz., the "light form" in the bedroom. The night light in the dressing room was turned on with a 50-watt light. All other lights in the house were extinguished. This investigator went downstairs after placing a subject in the bedroom in the position of the attacker. The subject had on a white shirt and dark trousers. After closing the eyes for a short time, this investigator ran upstairs as rapidly as possible to the bedroom door. In the very dim light a whitish region was seen corresponding to the white shirt. The head could not be distinguished, nor could portions below the lower limit of the shirt. The boundaries of the shirt itself could not be distinguished, and what was seen was as precisely what was described by the defendant as could be imagined. The experiment was repeated with the night light on 100-watts. Again the results were similar though now the boundaries of the shirt could be dimly distinguished. It was still not possible to see anything but the white shirt.

It remains to determine whether other specific points of the account of the defendant are consistent with the interpretation of this investigation. Numerous points emerge from the consideration:

1. It was entirely possible that the defendant was struck on the back of the neck by the same weapon used to kill Marilyn Sheppard. If the weapon was of the type indicated by the studies made, and was a cylindrical object with a flared end, all that must be assumed is that it was the cylindrical portion that contacted the back of his neck rather than the flare. It may be pointed out that in the experiment described in the above paragraph, the subject on one occasion merely moved around as the investigator arrived at the door, and delivered a light blow to the back of the neck without the movement being seen or anticipated by the investigator.

2. The method and clumsiness of removal of the watch and key chain from the defendant's pocket certainly appears to be the work of another person. As pointed out earlier, it would be difficult and completely unnatural for a person to rip his trouser pocket downward in removing a key chain, but this would be extremely probable if someone else stripped it from a prone body. It is also unlikely that a person removes his own watch so as to damage the band, even if he is faking a burglary.

3. The abandonment of the green bag in the woods is not the work of a person who is deliberately setting a scene as it was postulated that the defendant did. If he took time to wash off all the blood, to sponge the stairs and take other precautions attributed to him, he would not carelessly throw away the green bag where it would not necessarily be in a real burglary. Rather, its abandonment was the act of a person in an unnatural hurry as would be true of an intruder being pursued as claimed by the defendant.

4. One portion of the account given by the defendant can be accurately confirmed, viz., the return to the bedroom with wet clothing, and leaning over the bed (water spots on the sheet).

5. Another point of importance that was apparently not fully developed is the question of the amount of sand in the defendant's shoes. If he waded out into the lake to wash off blood, he would not sink into wet sand very far, and would pick up in the shoes minimal quantities of sand. Also, *he would not pick up any sand* in the pockets. If he were lying on the beach, as he stated, he would accumulate large quantities of sand in his shoes, and some in his pockets, as was the case. Further, the toes of his shoes had pressed into the insoles and linings much more sand than the heels of his shoes. While this scarcely constitutes proof that he lay face down in the water and sand, it at least is more consistent with that idea than with any alternative, for the sand would work down into the toes and inevitably more would remain there than in the heels.

6. It is not reasonable to believe that the defendant would deliberately break his own and his wife's trophies, as occurred. Under no circumstances, would this assist in establishing the events as the work of a burglar, for it is equally unreasonable for a true burglar. It is completely consistent only for someone who hated the Sheppards, or who was jealous of their athletic tendencies and abilities.

7. It is not reasonable that the defendant would mistreat his surgical and medical equipment, as was done. Even to establish the event as the work of a burglar, a doctor who likes his work (as it appears he did) would have faked the theft from the bag entirely differently, rather than merely upsetting it in the hallway, disrupting the contents of his desk, etc.

8. By no stretch of the imagination can it be conceived that the injuries to the defendant were self-inflicted. As a person who was fully aware of the danger associated with a blow to the back of the neck, and faced with almost insurmountable difficulty of delivering such a blow at all, and

certainly of doing it under control, no doctor would ever risk trying it. It is also peculiarly difficult to deliver a blow of any force to one's face. *Neither of these injuries can be reconciled with self-infliction.*

9. It is equally ridiculous to assume that these injuries were sustained in falling from the landing platform at the beach. That type of fall would inflict many abrasions, bruises and secondary injuries to the limbs, with the serious possibility of broken bones. It could not under any circumstances select the back of his neck and his face for the only injury. *No satisfactory explanation except that given by the defendant has been advanced for his injuries.*

10. The type of crime is completely out of character for a husband bent on murdering his wife. In such instances, the murder does not start out as a sex attack with the single exception of an unfulfilled and frustrated husband, which is completely contrary to the indications of this event.

11. Tests of the large spot of blood on the wardrobe door which were conducted by this Affiant establish in Affiant's opinion that it is human blood, that it is not the blood of the defendant, Dr. Samuel H. Sheppard, and that it is not the blood of Marilyn Sheppard, the murdered woman.

Two of the other affidavits were signed by a Bay View doctor who scraped the blood spot off the wardrobe door and mailed it to Dr. Kirk in California and a minister who witnessed the removal of the blood spot. The other four affidavits dealt with the padlocking of my home and the months it took before the keys were returned to my family.

After the affidavits were presented, Judge Blythin adjourned the hearing until May 4th, a week hence, to give the prosecutors time to file an answer to Dr. Kirk's affidavit.

Cleveland newspapers gave a good run down on Dr. Kirk's affidavit the day it was presented. The next day, they carried the comments of various law enforcement officials, including Inspector McArthur, Assistant Prosecutor Danaceau and Coroner Gerber. Their comments were about as I expected they would be. McArthur called the report a "good college thesis" and claimed that no new evidence had been presented. Danaceau said Dr. Kirk's conclusion was "far-fetched" and "unconvincing" and said the state's official reply in court would be very brief because there was little to answer "by way of fact." Dr. Gerber said that the affidavit was "an opus of fantasies that should have been produced by a well-paid advocate and not by a scientist."

Dr. Kirk fired back that "the State can't dispute the facts put forth in my affidavit so they charge that no new facts have been presented. And the reason they won't answer the arguments advanced in my report is because they can't answer them."

And for myself, I noted in my diary on April 28th, "The papers today tell how the prosecuting attorneys claim that there is no new evidence to answer. It is obvious they can't answer the new evidence because it is irrefutable. How can they shrug off the different blood spot? They are going to try, but how can they possibly be so stupid and unfair."

The new evidence hearing resumed on May 4th, and it was a bitter two-hour affair. To refute the claim by Dr. Kirk that the killer left his signature in blood on the wardrobe door, the State produced an affidavit by its own blood expert, Dr. Roger W. Marsters of University Hospitals. He charged that Dr. Kirk's finding was unwarranted by the facts. Bill Corrigan refuted this statement with an affidavit taken by telephone from Dr. Kirk in California that morning, in which the noted criminologist charged that Dr. Marsters was an expert on fresh blood, not dry blood. Thus, Dr. Kirk said, Dr. Marsters was not qualified to sit in judgment of his methods and conclusions.

Bill Corrigan was his fiery best in arguing before Judge Blythin. "Here is a man convicted of second degree murder," he shouted. "And he has brought in evidence that there was another person in the house. We have a statement from one of the leading criminologists in the United States. You can't ignore it. What have they done to refute it?"

"Mr. Corrigan," Judge Blythin asked, "is that new evidence or is it opinion?"

Corrigan retorted that we had been barred from my home until after the trial and that he had brought Dr. Kirk to Cleveland to conduct a "real investigation." He argued that Dr. Kirk had determined that the killer was left-handed and that he had left a blood spot on the closet door.

"The only thing we didn't show in Dr. Kirk's affidavit was a facial description of the murderer," Corrigan bellowed.

Saul Danaceau, the assistant prosecutor, droned that Dr. Kirk's affidavit contained "theories, analyses, opinions, conclusions, speculations—not new evidence." He insisted that my attorneys were free at any time to inspect the Lake Road home before and during the trial if they agreed to have a policeman present. To this, Arthur Petersilge answered that Dr. Kirk could not have conducted a proper examination of the premises with a policeman watching him.

Judge Blythin took the matter under advisement and I returned
to my cell to await the ruling. Based on his previous performance in
my case, I didn't allow myself to get overly hopeful. Whatever hope
I might have had started to ebb the next day when the Cleveland
Press followed up the hearing with a story under the headline:
"Blythin Seen Rejecting Dr. Sam's Re-trial Bid." (The *Press* always
knew Blythin's answer.)

On Tuesday, May 10th, Judge Blythin again shattered my dreams
for a new trial when he turned down the motion based on Dr. Kirk's
investigation and statement. He called our claims of new evidence
conjecture and post mortem conclusions and said that Dr. Kirk's
findings were based on his own theories.

Bill Corrigan said immediately that he would appeal Judge Blythin's ruling on the motion for a new trial to the Court of Appeals.
Meanwhile, Dr. Kirk had some harsh words for Judge Blythin's
ruling. He called it a "miscarriage of justice" and "simply a face-
saving maneuver." The small, scholarly scientist said he was not
surprised by Judge Blythin's ruling. "I don't think any of them
know the difference between facts and theory," he said in a newspaper interview. "I don't think they wanted the facts."

Two days after Judge Blythin turned down the new trial bid,
Cleveland Detective Chief James McArthur released two pictures
which he said disputed the defense claim that I could not have
killed Marilyn because the murderer was left-handed. One of the
photos showed me chatting with people at a party. I was holding a
plate of food in my right hand and eating a sandwich with my left
hand. "This shows that Sam is ambidextrous," McArthur was quoted
as saying.

The other picture showed Marilyn and myself water skiing. Marilyn was holding onto the tow bar with both hands, while I was
holding on with my left hand. "Water skiing is a tricky sport,"
McArthur said, "in which you use your strongest arm to hold on
with in case of a mishap. Sam is an athlete and would strengthen
his left arm in boxing and basketball."

I wrote in my diary that night:

Tonight's *Press* carries the story by McArthur where he discloses two
pictures and claims these prove I am adept at use of my left hand.

This is so ridiculous that I should think any intelligent person could
see through the policeman and his associates, the prosecuting attorneys.

It is obvious Dr. Kirk has *proven* that the murder was committed by a left-handed person. They can find no one to contest this so they are knocking themselves out to claim that I *could have* done it.

This is typical of the Cleveland police. To think a right-handed person would use his left hand in commission of such a brutal act is fantastic and they know it.

In regard to the pictures: If we take them and study them for a true deduction, which is not what McArthur wants, it is rather simple.

In water skiing double the man on the longer rope must be careful at all times that he is ready for a mishap to the person ahead. The shorter rope might break or a fall for any reason may be dangerous to the one on the short rope. The person on the long rope should therefore keep the hand and arm free on the side toward the short rope skier (in this case the right hand was kept free toward Marilyn on the shorter rope). [Especially since one of my skis was a slalom with a large metal fin.] Marilyn used to scoot under my longer rope (we'd cross at full speed). I changed hands accordingly.

The next step in the battle to win a new trial came on May 23rd and 24th at the Lakeside Avenue Courthouse, about two miles from County Jail. It took the form of arguments on the voluminous appeal my attorneys had filed with Appellate Judges Julius M. Kovachy, Lee E. Skeel and Joy Seth Hurd, the tribunal which made up the Cuyahoga County Court of Appeals. Though I was eligible to attend the hearing, I decided to remain in my jail cell at County Jail.

Corrigan, who was joined by Petersilge and Garmone in arguing before the three-judge panel, pointed out strongly that had I desired to kill Marilyn, I could have done it without detection. "I know a way to kill a person and leave no trace of murder," Corrigan said. "Doctors know it and I know it. Dr. Sheppard could have planned his wife's death in many ways," the white-haired lawyer asserted. "He could have easily drowned her when they were water skiing together." He said, however, that Marilyn and I were deeply in love and had no desire to harm each other. He charged that I was arrested because of "the voice of the mob," subjected to Gestapo tactics by Cleveland police, and then tried and convicted in a "carnival atmosphere" and in an "aura of prejudice."

"The State's argument is that he [Dr. Sam] is guilty unless he can give satisfactory explanation of certain things, like what happened to his T-shirt," Petersilge told the justices. "If the State can't establish them it has no legal right to place the burden of proof on Dr. Sam."

Thomas Parrino was the principal spokesman for the State. He called my story of the morning of July 4th "absurd," and hammered away at the fact that I had not told the truth at the inquest about my relationship with Susan Hayes. Both he and Danaceau said I had been tried fairly and properly and should be ordered to serve the life sentence handed down by Judge Blythin.

In my diary on May 25th I wrote, "Steve was in today and Rich yesterday. They described the hearing and how the three appellate judges seemed to react. I am almost afraid to be hopeful. It seems that every time I get hopeful it is merely a let down so I am trying to expect the worst, but I can't help a big hope and prayer for a fair break."

The following day I wrote, "I am now in rather continual prayer that the appellate judges will be fair. God, how can they overlook the obvious prejudice of Blythin. The greatest encouragement to me about the current appeal is the reaction by Art Petersilge who is always on the pessimistic side, but feels that they are trying to be fair and that a fair analysis will be consistent with a favorable result."

Corrigan went back to the Court of Appeals on May 31st with a twenty-three-page brief challenging Judge Blythin's ruling against a new trial on the basis of the newly discovered evidence uncovered by Dr. Kirk. "The person who did commit this crime is partly identified in the newly discovered evidence," Corrigan said in the brief. He asserted that Marilyn probably was murdered with a red lacquered flashlight. He said the basis for this deduction was the finding in the murder room by Dr. Kirk of red chips which previously had been identified as chips of nail polish.

Two weeks later, when arguments on this portion of the appeal were heard by the Court of Appeals, Corrigan charged that the police had failed to make a scientific investigation of the murder room and that we were compelled to hire Dr. Kirk to make a proper investigation. He said that Dr. Kirk was able to determine that the killer was left-handed. Petersilge hammered home the point that the finding of a blood spot on the wardrobe—which could not be identified as either Marilyn's or mine—proved there was a third person in the murder room.

Parrino countered that Dr. Kirk's report was based on "theory, speculation and conjectures and contradictions to what was in the trial record."

The month of June dragged slowly as I awaited a ruling on the case by the Court of Appeals. I spent most of the time getting whatever exercise I could, by reading the constant flow of letters from my family, friends, and well-wishers, by playing cards and by making notes in my diary.

On June 5th, a portrait of my father, Dr. Richard A. Sheppard, was unveiled at Bay View Hospital, and I noted: "Today was a beautiful day for the dedication. I stayed away from church again as going up there where I see the street, cars, and people on the outside causes a marked depression. As long as I stay down here and see no one I seem to get along O.K.—well I get by anyway.

"Am still 'sitting on eggs' waiting for the July ruling. This year has been hell. Hell couldn't be worse."

Entries in the diary express my mood and feelings during that period:

June 6, 1955: Letters from A. Miller today tell of his cases as usual and pictures of his recent fishing trip. He obviously has no idea of what it is like here or he wouldn't remind me of the life I love, but am denied here (namely my professional work and outdoor sports). Art means well but it's tough to hear about all the cases he's doing, fishing, swimming, etc.

Stacia K. was just here. She like everyone else is hoping, but afraid to be optimistic at all. Richard expressed the same reaction. Rich and Steve have turned over our house to the real estate guy to sell. It breaks my heart to sell the material thing that M. and I and Chip loved so much. The flowers we planted and replanted together, all the decorating that M. did to her wishes. She chose every color, the paper, kitchen linoleum, etc. Well I guess it just can't be helped with all the expenses that is inevitable. As in everything else Rich and Steve have to use the best judgment and follow through.

June 7, 1955: Steve was in today and we had a long talk. He pointed out how much worse his birthday (which was the day before) could be and that tho' he hopes next June is much happier he is thankful it is not worse. Chip is fine and that means a lot.

June 11, 1955: In the paper tonight is a picture of the house. How people do relish others misfortune.

June 14, 1955: I don't dare hope and count in any way on honesty and justice for fear that the hammer will fall again and knock me apart. I'm planning on the O.P. [Ohio Penitentiary]. This wait 'til the decision is the worst yet, mainly because it represents the continuous wonder as to whether our higher courts are what they claim to be or not.

Letter from Chip—I want to see him so bad I can almost feel him.

June 22, 1955: Father's Day card from Chip made me cry. I recall last year when M. and Chip gave me a fine new pipe.

June 24, 1955: Got to call Chip tonight and wished him well on camp trip. He seems fine and anticipated a good go at camp. He's taking my tennis racket and he and Janet [Steve's daughter] are going to learn to play tennis. He ought to become a good player as M. was.

On June 26th, I received a letter which touched me very much, it was from a youngster in Douglas, Oregon. It read:

Dear Dr. Sheppard,

You may wonder who I am, and why I am writing to you. I am a little girl eleven years old and I think of you so often, knowing how terrible it is just waiting and hoping and worst of all, going through all your suffering, for something you didn't do.

It has been nearly a year now since I first read about it and I asked my mother before to write you, and she said there was nothing I could do, and you had too much on your mind to ever read anything I'd write, but I am going to say this, I have never seen you and know I never will, but I want you to know I believe in you, and when I pray, I ask God to help you.

You look so kind and nice, and you ask Him too. I feel it will all be well with you by and by.

I am going to vacation Bible school. I go to church and Sunday school, but I like to swim and ride fast on boats, and I am going to learn to ski.

I have two brothers and a sister all around 30 years old. My sister is a nurse and administrator of a hospital and one of my sisters-in-law is also a nurse. I am planning on being a doctor, do you think that would be a good profession for a woman? My mother says it would be a hard life but I still think that's what I shall do.

I hope it makes you feel a little better to know there are others who think of you.

I wonder if you'll even get this. I don't dare hope for an answer but I'd be mighty proud.

Sincerely your little friend,

SRT

On June 29th, I noted:

We've been playing hockey the last few days, which is rough, but a good workout. Two men on a team, a goalie and a forward. The two forwards face-off in the middle of the range and try to hit the ball to opposite ends where the end cells are designated as the respective goals. The goalies protect their goals but may run up and help in a pinch, leaving their goal open. No kicking or use of hands except in blocking. It gets rough and tires us out fast, but Malone and I have outlasted all the younger guys 20-30 who haven't been here over one or two months.

So, we guess our exercises, J.R. [jump rope], etc. have kept us in fair shape.

I received a card on July 3rd from Chip, who was at camp in Union City, Pennsylvania. "Dear Daddy, I'm having a nice time. I caught a lizard. Love Chip." It prompted the observation:

A card from Chip. My most sincere passion now is to be at Chip's side, to play, work and be with him. We often did things together, but if I'm given the chance most all of my free time will be spent with Chip.

Bill Corrigan was here this a.m. He had little to say, but I think merely wanted to know that I was holding up O.K. at this time.

It was only hours away from the anniversary of Marilyn's death. My God, what a year. In the past few days, the newspapers had been rehashing and rehashing the events of the last twelve months. On the 3rd one of the deputies brought me a letter from John Blair, a Cleveland *Plain Dealer* reporter, who was waiting downstairs in County Jail. He asked for an interview or for some statement from me. For a few moments, I didn't know what to do. But, finally decided to write a note to him on the back of his letter. I felt that the paper would print something on the anniversary and my comments might be better than what they would make up. So I wrote:

July 4th reminds us of the day we American citizens were given certain rights. It is strange that this same day marks the date, following which more than one of these rights were denied a respectable American family and individual.

A recent letter from a stranger expresses this quite well. "But you must know that there are large numbers of people who believe you are innocent and who wish you complete success in your fight for freedom. I know you will soon be vindicated, Doctor. *I must believe in that in order to believe in America.*"

I miss Marilyn and grieve her loss each and every day.

July 4th came and went. At the end of the day, I sat in my cell and wrote my impressions:

Well, the day is over!

We played the rough hockey game most of the day and all the boys are sore. I was happily surprised about 3:00 p.m. to be taken down to the 1st floor where they said I was to call the Browns. Mary had called and asked to talk with me so they had me call back. We had a nice visit and they are solid as ever.

The *Plain Dealer* printed my statement, sent out yesterday, and Blair did a nice job on the article.

The *News* had a rather poor article by (Howard) Beaufait with a definite slant against me. Though the article is not favorable to me, it is obvious that even those who are against me don't have any idea what really happened last July 4th. *They just don't believe me.* This very article discloses the point that I have been considered guilty till proven innocent from the first and even now since Dr. Kirk has *proven* my *innocence* they are wondering. The boys here were upset by the article, but pointed out that in some respects it is not bad.

It is really hot and we sweat like mad while running and batting the ball. [Made of long strips of stolen sheeting wrapped tightly around moist, bundled up newspaper pages.] I haven't done much writing on the early days of our marriage anniversary because it is so depressing. God, I wish the decision would come through so I'd know what the score is.

I didn't have much longer to wait.

13 ∂∂

At nine thirty on the morning of July 12th, Mike Ucello, the chief jailer, woke me from a sound sleep and put an end to my anxiety about the Court of Appeals. He informed me frankly and without emotion that Justices Joy Seth Hurd, Lee E. Skeel, and Julius M. Kovachy had overruled my bid for a new trial on the basis of thirty-seven errors cited in our appeal. Ucello said the tribunal would rule in a week on the appeal of Judge Blythin's rejection of the new evidence motion, based on Dr. Kirk's affidavit.

The news was depressing. But, by this time, I had lost my wife, my home, my parents, and the privilege of being with my little boy. This was just another in a seemingly endless series of blows. Later in the day, when I saw the text of the opinion by the Court of Appeals on the major bid for a new trial, it was obvious to me what the second ruling would be the following week. That night, I wrote my reaction to the decision, which said that "substantial justice" had been achieved in my case.

They wrote as though they were all prosecuting attorneys. They quote statements by the prosecutors and fail to recognize the many, many points in my favor. It is now clear why they wanted to hear the case rather than have the visiting court as was requested. They wanted to be sure to sew me up as much as they could and prevent future reversal if possible. These men from their statements couldn't possibly have been fair and objective.

They mentioned my vagueness and answers of "I don't remember," or "I don't know," as being against me, whereas obviously a trumped-up story would be complete.

My mind was made up on one thing. If the Court of Appeals turned down the second motion, I was going directly to the Ohio Penitentiary to await further action on appeal. I had heard enough about the Ohio Penitentiary to learn that they at least got out in the sun once in a while. There were bedbug bites all over me. My eyes were swollen. I couldn't stand bright light. I hadn't been in a bright light for one year, and I knew if I continued on that dungeon-like fourth floor much longer, it would damage my eyes permanently. Besides, I wanted to get some regular exercise. I knew I had to get in shape for the long fight ahead.

Late in the afternoon on July 19th, the Court of Appeals delivered its second decision. It refused to overrule Judge Blythin on the new evidence matter. Like the original appeal ruling, this one also was unanimous. Judge Kovachy, who wrote the opinion, concluded that Dr. Kirk's findings were theories and speculation and could not be accepted as the basis for a new trial.

My brothers, Steve and Richard, and their wives visited me later that afternoon to say good-bye. They knew that my next stop was the Ohio Penitentiary and that I probably would be sent there the next day. Of course, they promised to continue to fight for my freedom, regardless of the expense, and would see me as frequently as possible at the penitentiary in Columbus. My brothers said they would live up to their promises to Dad on our Sheppard Clinic financial agreement.

That evening, the official papers committing me to the Ohio Penitentiary were signed, and I expected to be taken to Columbus like any other prisoner, in the van called "the gray goose," which usually left for the penitentiary about five in the morning. I spent that night in solitary confinement, which struck me as one last kick in the teeth from the County officials.

The officials had always made the point that I was being treated just like any other prisoner, so they came to the jail early that morning to bid me farewell as I was loaded aboard the gray goose. But when the gray goose left, I wasn't on it. Jail officials had decided to delay my departure and take me to Columbus in an automobile. It seemed obvious to me that this action was planned so the television newsmen could get their pictures and interviews.

By the time they were ready to take me it was early afternoon. I shook hands with the ten other inmates in the jail cell range. Then I was taken to a guard room, frisked, and shackled to another man, Michael Jacko, who had spent twenty-seven of his forty-seven years in prison and was returning to the Ohio Penitentiary to finish serving a life sentence. As I came out of the jail doors into the daylight I saw Mary and Bud Brown. They had waited for hours to see me. I shook Bud's hand and gave Mary a kiss on the cheek. They were both crying and they said to me they'd both live to see the day that I got out.

Photographers, television cameramen, and news reporters were all over the place. They were yelling questions and shouting at me, trying to get me to change my grim facial expression or attract my attention to their cameras. One had the gall to ask me to smile.

Chief Jailer Ucello got in the back seat with us and Deputy David Yettra got in the driver's seat. We drove away slowly so that several cars full of newspaper people could fall in behind. We were followed all the way to Columbus, a distance of about one hundred forty miles. Occasionally one of the cars would pull alongside to take flash pictures or TV films.

The talk on the way down was very limited. Ucello asked me if I was glad to leave the jail and my answer was that I looked forward to being more active than I had been in jail. As we neared Columbus, Ucello said he would have to tell the newsmen what we talked about. "What shall I tell them?"

I told him to say that I mentioned Dr. Paul Kirk's statement, "They are sending an innocent man to prison and I know it is true just as well as I know I am sitting here." I further requested that he say nothing further other than to give to a *Plain Dealer* reporter a note I handed him. It said, "I am innocent and those who persecute me know it."

As we pulled up to the penitentiary front entrance, the droves of photographers took up where they had left off in Cleveland. The yells and requests for statements resumed. I wanted to scream my innocence, but such an action would probably have been interpreted as hysteria. I restrained myself again.

We were ushered through a large room full of uniformed guards, with sticks in their belts, and taken to a small cage where the handcuffs were removed, which allowed the two of us to disentangle our arms for the first time in over three hours. Our personal things were brought in in bags and we then awaited a guard to take us across the central yard of the prison to the deputy or associate warden's office.

While I waited, I saw the prisoners from the various prison mills marching to and from supper. The prison band, which did quite well with poorly-tuned instruments, played while the men paraded to the mess hall. It was surprising to see men in a modern-day penitentiary marching in close-order drill. Most of the men appeared to keep step pretty well. It was also a shock to see that the white men were lined up in the front of the column, while the Negroes were lined up at the rear.

Finally, I was taken to the deputy warden's office. We walked across the prison yard and I couldn't help noticing the old buildings and the double and triple walls which surrounded us. We passed the prison garden, which had been started by Dr. John Eckstorm, a prison physician and one-time head football coach at Ohio State University. It was filled with beautiful roses, which provided a stark contrast to the dull, brick buildings. Then we turned into a newer building, where the deputy warden's office was located.

All of my clothing was checked. Underwear, shoes, and some other items of a personal nature were put in one pile. All jewelry, including my wedding band, and lucky charms and my money were taken away. I was told that they would be returned to me later to be mailed home, along with my regular clothes. Then I was taken to the clothing room, where I was stripped and a check made for narcotics. My suit was traded in for prison clothes. I was given two pairs of trousers, one heavy and one light, and two shirts—one for weekdays and one for Sunday wear. The weekday shirt had stripes and was hickory, a heavy, old-fashioned, rough-textured material, which produced rashes. The other was just a plain, blue work shirt. I also received one blanket, one sheet, a pillow case, and a ticking bag for carrying and storing my worldly goods. The numbers 98860 were stencilled on my shirts and inside the right rear pocket of my trousers. That was to be my identification number for the rest of my stay at the Ohio Penitentiary.

We showered and were sprayed with DDT powder and then put on our prison clothes. One of the most drastic things about entering the prison is the combination of putting on those ill-fitting, scratchy, crude clothes, and the heavy clang of the doors behind you as you go in. Most prisoners, I later learned, never get over the incessant clanging of doors, no matter how long they have been there. They say that a man goes stir crazy when he's had too many doors slammed behind him.

From the clothing room we walked across the yard to the Receiving Ward at the prison hospital, where I was to be in quarantine for a few weeks, standard operating procedure for new inmates. The yard is a postage-stamp sized area of grass, spotted with a few trees, between the cell blocks, the two chow halls, the deputy warden's office, and the hospital. Just in front of the west mess hall is a large water tower where they store the sulphury-tasting water used for the cell blocks. When we reached the hospital, one of the guards asked me whether I had eaten. I told him that because of the all-afternoon drive from Cleveland and our late arrival, I had

had no dinner. A "runner"—a convict who is not quite ready for honor status but who has earned a certain measure of trust—escorted me to the mess hall. He wore a red cap and a red band on his arm to identify himself as a runner.

They served fried eggs, bacon, coleslaw, jello, and some ice cream. The only egg I had been given at County Jail was a hard-boiled one at Easter, and I hadn't tasted ice cream for almost a year. Compared to the slop served at the County Jail, this tasted like it was served at the Waldorf-Astoria in New York. The food was as good as good hospital food, and this surprised me.

Upon returning to the ward, I soon learned that Wednesday (the day I arrived) had been bath day and we could not expect another bath until the following week. This was surprising because there was a double shower in the ward lavatory. It was, however, reserved for the supervisory workers in the ward.

That evening I received numerous telegrams from relatives and friends, all of which were in my behalf. They helped to ease the feeling of loneliness. I sat down and started writing some letters. The officials want the prisoners with families to write as soon as possible to encourage relatives. But they don't let you have visitors for the first month because you're supposed to be in quarantine. Here was an example of one of the many things in prison life that didn't make sense.

Here are a bunch of men brought in to be placed in quarantine or isolation so that any communicable disease can be identified and treated. And where do they have the ward? On the first floor of a hospital where cross-contamination is the easiest thing in the world. The same sheets that come into that receiving quarantine ward go into the laundry at the end of the week and then come back to some patient who may have undergone lung surgery or some other major operation.

Maybe the person who used the sheet in the receiving ward was a tuberculosis carrier. The laundering of sheets can take care of some diseases, but the tuberculosis bacillus and some other germs are not killed unless the sheets have been sterilized under pressure in an autoclave. They didn't have that kind of equipment for general laundry sterilization at the Ohio Penitentiary.

The new prisoners are taken out of the receiving ward to the out-patient department for examination, and are allowed to use the regular toilets that are used by normal inmate out-patients. As a doctor, I was appalled. One of the things we learned in medical school was trying to prevent cross-contamination. I later learned that the Ohio Penitentiary tuberculosis ward in the hospital was on the same floor as the surgery and two large surgical wards. It was the damnedest thing I ever saw.

That same evening, several convicts from various work groups, called companies, visited me and discussed the possibilities of working with their respective groups once the quarantine period was over. It was interesting to note that the men from each of these work companies were very enthusiastic about their particular group. Most of them stated that their guard or civilian director was really "a fine guy." This was of particular interest and encouragement for two reasons. It appeared that the greater percentage of the men were working at an endeavor they enjoyed and they generally got along well with those in charge.

About ten the same night a group of the new prisoners were listening to the barber's radio in the receiving ward. On a news broadcast, it was reported that Marilyn's aunt, Mrs. Henrietta Munn, planned to file suit, asking for custody of Chip, who was living with my brother, Steve, and his wife, Betty, and their two daughters, Janet and Carol, in Rocky River.

It was the first inkling I had that Henrietta Munn and her husband, Worth, had this up their sleeves. I was really shocked. No one can imagine the psychological pressure and horror I felt. It was torture to know that Young Sam was out there and I was helpless to do anything about the ordeal as to where he would live and under whose influence he would be. I knew Marilyn would have been ashamed of the Munns for this action.

This news really drained what spunk, fight, and determination I had out of me. That night I lay down on my bunk and started to think. Sleep was impossible. I asked myself, "What are you going to do? Are you going to lie down and let this happen? What would happen if you killed yourself?"

Thinking of Dad and Marilyn, I came to some pretty quick answers. If I took my own life out of despondency, people would be quick to say, "See, we told you he did it. He couldn't stand himself." That, of course, was the farthest thing from the truth.

I asked myself again what my father would have done in a similar situation, and the answer was there, because I knew exactly what my father would have done. That was to hang in there and fight though not in a vicious way. He would have encouraged my family to do the right thing. He would have encouraged me to fight and fight and fight, even if they hanged me by my thumbs or put me in the electric chair.

Personally, I didn't want to live and face a life of hell, but I decided it would be a cowardly thing and certainly not fair to Young Sam and his future, and the family, for me to take my own life. Though death would have been sweet, this would be the weak thing to do. I knew my father would never have stood for it. I dismissed the thought from my mind, but spent a long and sleepless night.

My first full day in prison began at six thirty a.m. on Thursday, July 21st. I dressed, lined up, and marched to breakfast. When our group returned to the ward we were told to be ready to go out at any time to various places in the penitentiary for orientation lectures, counseling, Bertillon, and so forth. I attended sick call and received some aspirin for the headache I had suffered regularly since my injury more than a year before. We played cards most of the day and at various times were called out of the ward for indoctrination events. Late in the day, I heard the report that Mrs. Munn had filed suit in Cuyahoga County Probate Court, for the custody of Chip. Judge Frank J. Merrick set a hearing for August 3rd and ordered that Steve and I be notified. My worry intensified.

Fortunately, about five months before her tragic death, Marilyn had written a will in which she designated Steve as "sole guardian of the person and estate" of Chip, in the event both she and I should die. If Steve was not in the picture, the will named Richard, my other brother, as Chip's guardian. This was done because both Marilyn and I were doing quite a bit of traveling by air. In the event something happened to us, we wanted to provide for Chip's future.

I suffered through several days of pure unadulterated hell, waiting for a ruling on the matter of Young Sam. When the court was apprised of the will, the Munns were told that unless Steve and his wife were judged incompetent on other grounds, or were not able to provide financially for Young Sam, they had no case. The Munns also were told privately that they didn't have a snowball's chance in hell of obtaining custody of Chip, and any further efforts would only be harmful to the child. The matter was ultimately dropped, to my utter relief.

The first few weeks were devoted entirely to orientation. We were given a tour of the penitentiary, took psychological tests, and met various department heads. We were examined and given inoculations. We were instructed as to the rules of the penitentiary and we were given several orientation lectures. In my diary I wrote that,

"These are really well done and with the good of the men in mind. The various department heads discuss their functions and answer questions. This is in the attempt to prevent the trial-and-error method, which—it seems—prevailed at one time."

Eight days after my arrival, I was shifted to a receiving cell block, and I occupied cell 4-B-1, with two other men. It was just a temporary arrangement until the orientation period was over and a job assignment was made. With the switch to the cell, I was allowed gym privileges once a week. On my first visit to the gymnasium I played basketball—a real treat—and just about ran myself out.

I continued to record my impressions in my diary, and that activity, plus reading the tremendous number of letters and cards sent to me, helped while away the endless idle hours. On July 30th, I noted in the diary:

One year ago tonight, I was arrested. What a year.

This a.m. following breakfast we went to a movie, "Deep in My Heart." Beautiful music and the type Marilyn and I used to have on the recorder most of the time—"Student Prince," "New Moon," etc. I was choked up and half bawling through most of it, but I still liked it. The music and some of the scenes reminded me of Marilyn and me and some of the wonderful times we had together. It seems like a fairy tale or beautiful dreamland that is in the distant past.

At times I think, "poor Marilyn," and at others I think, "Thank God she was never subjected to anything like this." Perhaps she is the fortunate one, but I'll keep fighting for both of us and all who have confidence in me and us (Marilyn, Chip, and me)—a family.

One of the boys here says he'll train a canary as a pet for Chip.

Most all of the men here know I am here on a bum beef (am not guilty, in other words) and they wish to help. Others get a vicarious kick out of seeing me here. Misery loves company in any form, which is natural, I guess.

On Monday, August 1st, I wrote:

Breakfast as usual, then given a pass to see the Protestant chaplain, Rev. Wall. We had a nice talk. He stated he felt a little embarrassed to see me there in prison clothes, and wished to help in any way he can.

Lunch at eleven thirty. Pass to minor surgery for shots. Chatted with boys there, then a pass to see Mr. Crist. Psychological interview. He asked if I had become bitter at the American way of life. I said not at the American way, but upset by those who do not follow it and uphold it. I told him that I am afraid for the American way of life, but that if my conviction sticks, the Christian precepts on which our country was founded will not mean much.

I took every opportunity I could to work out in the gym. I started tumbling and planned to start lifting weights and initiating a general body-building program. "A man can maintain a great deal of mental health when he is improving his physical health, producing a stronger, finer functioning body," I noted in my diary. One of the most depressing factors in stir is the physical decline.

During my first weeks in the penitentiary, I met with both the deputy warden, Mr. Maxwell, and Mr. Alvis, the warden. Maxwell told me I was going to be treated like everyone else. He asked me my age and I replied, "Thirty-one."

"Forty-one—you won't be too old when you get out of here," Maxwell said.

"Who knows I'll get a parole?" I asked.

"Keep your nose clean, son, and you'll make it," he answered, adding that I would get a parole if there aren't too many people complaining about it from the outside. We both knew that many would complain when the time came, just for the hell of it.

I might have been hypercritical of the situation, but I retorted that just a bunch of cranks would be complaining. He replied that the parole board usually was not affected by crank letters or by people who have no basis for criticizing. I couldn't believe this. Then he exhorted me to keep a clean slate, stay away from the characters and obvious trouble-makers.

"What do you mean by that?" I asked.

He said they would soon be apparent to me and he urged me to keep by myself until I could sort out the who's who in the penitentiary.

Maxwell informed me that for the first six months I would have to work in a mill or in some other cell-block type of job, and that during this period I would live in a regular cell block, which was usually the custom. After that, he said, I could work in the hospital if I desired. When I told him that I didn't want to work in the hospital, he was somewhat shocked and said he hoped that my remark didn't portend a "bad attitude" on my part.

"I just feel that it might be a little tough on me to be around surgery, which is my life's work, and yet not be able to perform surgery as I should be doing," was my reply.

Maxwell agreed that this was a valid point—that working in the hospital might be tougher than being away from a medical atmosphere entirely. I requested work on the "coal pile," but was told that "only Negroes" work the coal pile. This was my method of indicating a willingness to do any job. I was shocked to learn the coal-digger's spots were "reserved" for Negroes.

A few weeks later, I met Warden Ralph Alvis, who was honest and square, but who ran a tough ship. Alvis was a straight-shooter with all inmates who played it straight with him. He went over basically the same ground that Maxwell had covered, but in more detail and in a more friendly and logical manner. He was a man of great humility and I came to respect him very much.

When the orientation period was over, I was assigned to the vocational school as a teacher. In addition to the "coal pile," I had requested assignment to the recreation department. The classification board had other plans for me. I was to teach auto mechanics under the direction of R. R. Jones, director of the Vocational School, who had sought my services because I had an education. He wanted the best possible people for his vocational school students. Jones was a fine, friendly man, who was genuinely devoted to helping convicts rehabilitate themselves.

I probably would have been more effective as a teacher in the Capital School, which teaches high school subjects, but that was not my assignment. At any rate, it took me about a week to read the book which was used for the auto mechanics course and then answer the questions on it. Mr. Jones quickly put me to work as an assistant teacher, and later made me a full-fledged instructor.

My job was to prepare the students for practical instruction in the subject of auto mechanics. Although I had always been interested in cars and aircraft, I had never been an auto mechanic. However, I knew physics. Though not an expert on engine overhaul, it was soon apparent to me that the men got a great deal out of some simple explanation of the why and wherefore of combustion, carburation, ignition, horse-power determination, center of gravity, and other principles which had never been explained to them. By the same token, I learned a great deal about the practical aspects of auto mechanics from some of my students who *were* auto mechanics.

There were certain definite advantages to being a teacher. I was given an extra shirt to wear, one that had a fine stripe in contrast to the hickory shirt with the wide stripe. This differentiated the teachers from the students, and I was grateful for the little recognition. More important, however, was the chance to live with more intelligent men. By this time the degenerate conversation of the average convict was getting on my nerves.

Most important, I began to receive "good time" for teaching. For every four months an inmate serves as an assistant teacher, one month is subtracted from the time he must wait until he is eligible for parole. One month credit is given for every three months of service as a teacher. So a regular teacher can earn four months' good time a year, while an assistant teacher can earn three months a year.

With my assignment to the vocational school, I was shifted from the receiving cell block to a regular block. My new home was on the fifth floor and on the A side of the A and B block. Four of us were packed into a small, filthy cell. The cell was in a prison block used during the Civil War, and originally was designed for two men. The overall size of the cell was like a seven-foot cube. There were solid walls on the sides and in the back, and the front consisted of plain old jail bars.

It was originally designed so that there would be a double bunk on one side, leaving a little room for the two inmates to move around. But, because of the crowded conditions, double bunks were installed on both walls, leaving about a three-foot aisle up the middle. The bunks were suspended on hinges and chains so they could be raised during the day, for cleaning the cell. We were really crammed in there.

There was a toilet with no toilet seat and certainly no privacy. Our sink or wash basin was about as big around as a radio speaker. It was made of some kind of metal and God knows what else and it was corroded. Each night I would scrub it for about an hour, but by morning it would be grayish-black and have a metallic odor. The water came from a well and since it contained sulphur, it smelled like rotten eggs.

We called the overall odor of the cell "funky." It smelled like a combination of sweat, dirty feet, and urine and other odors, because every man has his toilet right in the cell.

There was no privacy, with four cellmates. Many times I passed up the noon or evening meal, just so I could stay in the cell by myself and meditate and be alone with Marilyn. Or, frankly, I often missed a meal in order to use the toilet without three guys watching. The worst period was Saturday/Sunday, when we were locked in the cell from noon until the next morning. With four men in the cell, there was no room to exercise. About all one could do was read or write letters.

Meanwhile, my assignment in the vocational school was going along smoothly, with one exception. There was a young student in my class, which contained everything from rapists to stick-up men and murderers. His name was Steve. He was twenty years old, but looked more like sixteen. He had been convicted of armed robbery, but there had been a mix-up in his sentencing. Steve should have been sent to the Mansfield Reformatory instead of to the Ohio Penitentiary.

Steve was quite young and immature, but responded to my teaching techniques rather well. He became more and more dependent on me for advice and help, not only with his school work, but with his personal problems as well. I advised him to appeal his case and try to get his sentence changed to Mansfield Reformatory. He took my advice and seemed to be making progress.

One day, Steve came to me and said that a rather large, muscular Negro in another part of the vocational school was trying to attack him sexually. Steve—and other students soon confirmed this—told me that this fellow had threatened him. He was what we called a "jocker," a fellow who goes around and has relations with young, innocent-looking or rather tender-looking boys.

First this man had asked Steve to take part in immoral acts. When Steve refused, this bully threatened he would rape him the first chance he got, or he would maim him with a hammer, a gas pipe, or whatever came in handy in the carpenter shop. Knowing that this kind of violence was not uncommon in the penitentiary, Steve was shaken up and very upset. He turned to me for advice.

Sit tight and do nothing, I told him. I advised him to try and keep himself busy in the more populated areas of the vocational school and stay away from the storeroom and other areas of the school where the men weren't plentiful. "Don't hang around the guard, but keep in plain sight, especially in my sight."

The next day, I approached this bully, tapped him on the shoulder, told him I wanted to talk to him, and led him to a spot that I had already picked out—around the corner from a large shelf in the storage area, which was fairly well screened. Before he knew what happened, I slammed him in the throat with my fist. He went down like a bag of cement. He wasn't unconscious, but he had a little trouble breathing for a while. Steve had no more trouble.

The days and the weeks rolled by slowly. About the only thing that went quickly were the visits by members of my family. Monthly visits were permitted for each blood relative, my attorneys, and

Rev. Al Kreke and Rev. A. Davis, my ministers. The wives of Steve and Richard were permitted to visit as long as they were accompanied by my brothers.

Under prison rules, I was allowed to write only one letter a week, and only to a person whose name was on a pre-arranged list supplied by me to prison officials. Naturally, most of my letters went to my brothers, Chip, my attorneys, and a few other selected persons, such as Mary and Bud Brown. On the other hand, I received a tremendous volume of mail from relatives, friends, and well-wishers, and was sorry I couldn't answer it all. It would have helped to while away the agonizing hours.

In his letters, Steve in a casual and offhand way, gave me a running account of how Chip was doing along with other news. He knew that Chip was the biggest thing in my life. Rather than send a large group of snapshots of my son at one time, he sent one or two in various letters, making each mean much more.

Athletics played a big part in helping to stem the boredom. Each of the cell ranges organized teams in football, basketball, and baseball, and, depending on the season, competed against each other. Due to the residual weakness and the pain in my neck, I wasn't able to play football in the fall of 1955, as much as I would have liked to. In one of my letters to my brother Richard, I wrote:

I've found basketball goes pretty well and I can protect the neck O.K., though it gets stiff.

Each range includes about sixty to sixty-five men and most teams, including ours, is made up of two ranges (one hundred to one hundred-thirty men). Naturally, all those men don't play, but many do and some of the teams are tough enough to beat many small college teams I've played against. The boys elected me captain of our group, so my recreation periods are pretty active. Last Tuesday night, we played four other teams in practice periods of fifteen minutes each. We won each time and were pretty pooped as the recreation period ended. We only get to play about once per week, so practice is what is needed. Seems like the only time we have plenty of is "cell time."

My adjustment to prison life during those first months was an uneasy one. In early November, I noted in the diary, which ultimately was smuggled out of the penitentiary, that "this place is really getting on my nerves and particularly staying in the cell." And later in the month, noted, "At times after being here for five months life seems bearable. At others it seems absolutely without reason, and surely not worth the struggle." I lived then only for young Sam and my brothers and sister-in-laws.

While my mood changed back and forth during the periods of activity and inactivity, there were those on the outside who were preparing for the next battle to free me from my wrongful imprisonment. For a time, all was not going too smoothly in that regard, either. Several people in the penitentiary, including two or three guards, suggested that I might aid my own case by bolstering my legal team for the Ohio Supreme Court appeal with a prominent Columbus attorney, Paul M. Herbert.

Mr. Herbert was a former Ohio lieutenant governor, and a man who was widely respected in Columbus and throughout the state. I met with him at the Ohio Penitentiary and told my brothers that I thought we should hire him as co-counsel for the appeal. We broached the idea to Bill Corrigan, Arthur Petersilge, and Fred Garmone, and there seemed to be no objection. The thought was that Corrigan would continue as chief counsel, but that Paul Herbert would be a co-counsel and put forth in a supplementary brief some additional arguments which were not contemplated by my regular attorneys.

However, after agreeing to this in principle in verbal conversations with my brothers and me, Corrigan wrote me a formal letter which took an entirely different tack, and hinted that I was ungrateful for the service that he had rendered to date. I answered him quickly, but carefully:

Dear Bill:
 Your formal letter received today was quite a shock to me after having discussed consulting counsel with you, Fred, Art, Steve, Richard, and again with Fred about a month ago. During Fred's last visit here I explained to him, asking that he express to you that I have complete faith in you both, but that a fresh evaluation from a local man not so close to the situation might help the cause, and surely not hinder. At that time, Fred agreed that *someone* might help, but that *you, he, Art,* Richard and Steve had discussed this and were not sure what person would be best. I understood Fred to say, and Art to say when he was here, and also Richard, that you felt that you did not need help, but would not resent consultation in any way. In fact, you told me that you were being aided by a New York attorney on the subject of Fair Trial and Free Press. It was on this basis only, and time limitation, that Paul Herbert was contacted.

There are not words to express the miserable hours I have experienced in thought (though I try to minimize this to the family, they know).

I feel worse because you, who have been like a father to me since the deaths of mother and dad, misunderstand me, or I you. You have spent far more time and energy than any gold or silver could *ever* compensate, which I know well. Your heart and soul have been in this from the start because you know I am innocent and because basic American rights have been denied a guy who might well have been your flesh and blood. This closeness and emotional tie is one reason we (Richard, Steve, Art and I) feel consultation *might* help.

No one can put himself in my position, but it might be likened to a very sick patient who requests consultation which his doctor likely does not need, but welcomes for the good of the patient, psychologically, if not medically. My hope is that you can bring yourself to consider Paul Herbert as I would another neurosurgeon whom you wished me to consult before I removed a tumor from the spine or brain of a member of your family.

The oral arguments surely could be worked as a team effort. My understanding is that the expenses have been taken care of and that you requested to wait till later for your personal fee. Whatever you wish I'll do my best, wherever I am. You must know that.

Try to see my rather helpless position and realize that the present situation is not the result of lack of confidence. As dad would say, and did many times, "God bless you."

Corrigan acceded to our wishes and Paul M. Herbert joined the legal team, first as co-counsel and then as my chief courtroom spokesman.

The first order of business before the Ohio Supreme Court was to win approval of the seven-man body to hear the case. Corrigan, Petersilge and Garmone prepared a bulky, five-hundred-four-page brief which stated that the Cuyahoga County Court of Appeals erred twenty-nine times in failing to order a new trial based on the record amassed in the ten-week proceeding in Judge Blythin's courtroom. It covered most of the ground cited in the appeal brief before the Court of Appeals, asserting that the evidence against me was so meager that I never should have been indicted. It charged that the indictment against me was the result of newspaper pressure and that my conviction was the result of prejudice fostered by news coverage and newspaper editorials.

Since Herbert was a latecomer to the legal team, this massive document was prepared without his assistance. But when it was filed in November, 1955, Herbert added a forty-page supplementary brief which charged that the case against me was based on "inferences upon inferences." To our arguments, the Ohio prosecutors answered that I had been tried fairly and without prejudice and my story was "fantastic and wholly incredible."

The Ohio Supreme Court set December 13th as the date to hear arguments on my bid to have the tribunal give the case a full review. Shortly before the hearing my lawyers asked Chief Justice Carl V. Weygandt to disqualify himself from hearing my case, since his son, Richard, as chief solicitor for the City of Bay Village, had recommended my arrest in July, 1954.

Weygandt decided to step aside in the case, saying that "whenever there is doubt concerning the propriety of sitting in a particular case, it is our policy in this court to resolve the doubt against ourselves by withdrawing." Weygandt said he would appoint an appellate court judge to fill the seventh spot on the court.

While an hour-long hearing was conducted before a standing-room-only crowd in the august chambers of the Ohio Supreme Court, I continued with my job in the penitentiary—a few blocks away. Each side was given thirty minutes in which to make a brief argument before the court. Paul Herbert made his first appearance in court for me.

Herbert told the seven justices that the evidence presented at the trial was insufficient to convict. He pointed out that in their case the Cuyahoga County prosecutors had failed to explain why, except for the smear on the knee, there was no blood on the trousers that the prosecution proved I wore at the time of the murder. He produced a T-shirt in court, wet it, and demonstrated that had my T-shirt been bloodied, the blood would have soaked through to my trousers.

"What do you know about the argument that there was no blood on the trousers?" Judge Kingsley Taft asked Saul Danaceau, one of three assistant prosecutors in the chamber for the hearing.

"We don't even know if he had his trousers on at that time," Danaceau answered.

Justice Charles B. Zimmerman asked Herbert how he knew that I had my trousers on at the time of the murder, and the lawyer replied that I had said they were on and there was no evidence presented to the contrary.

Herbert also claimed that the blood found on my wristwatch was not Marilyn's type, and that threads found under her nails did not match *anything* in the house.

The court took the matter under advisement and indicated it would rule within a month whether or not it would accept the case for full review. With the Christmas holiday approaching, I again found myself in the position of waiting, hoping, and praying. Based on my previous experience in the courtroom, I dared not be too hopeful. However, hope was hard to suppress.

The Christmas cards and letters came rolling in by the hundreds, and it was a wonderful and sustaining feeling to know there were so many people on the outside thinking about me and rooting for me. Many, of course, were from my family and friends, but the great majority were from people I had never met—people who were convinced that an innocent man was behind bars for a crime he did not commit.

There were gifts of food and other useful items sent by relatives and friends. "Food for Christmas is surely welcome," I noted in the diary. "Remarkable how satisfying a small piece of salami is, when I can recall the day when such would not be considered 'choice' at all. The relevancy of life is surely brought home in this situation."

The gym was closed from December 10th until after Christmas, which meant no exercise for more than two weeks and many, many additional hours of cell time. This lack of activity, combined with the religious sentiment expressed in hundreds of cards and letters, plunged me into a gloomy state. I wasn't bawling all over the place, but tears fell now and then and it was obvious that I was lonely among many. In prison, it's strange to be lonely and not be able to get alone and think of your loved ones and everything that's important to an individual.

My last Christmas had been spent in the County Jail and it was different. My family had been near by and visiting privileges were better in jail. There was more of a sense of nearness, even though I was behind bars. One thing that surprised me in the Ohio Penitentiary was the amount of Christmas feeling and exchanging of little presents that went on. Many of the men shared their food from home, and tried to repay little favors as they could when they had the wherewithal to do so. Men who were friendly insisted that I accept some of their "loot."

One fellow with whom I had shared food at the County Jail offered me a piece of sweet potato pie his sister had sent. I didn't want to offend him by refusing, and ate an enormous slice of the pie. When finished, I thanked him, slapped my belly, ran to the toilet and relieved the uneasy feeling in my stomach. He never knew. He was a nice guy and I'm glad the subject of sweet potato pie never came up again.

It was also surprising how humane and considerate a man could be who had lived in the underworld most of his adult life. I'm speaking of a man whose first name was also Sam, and who was a convicted bank robber. He knew that I was under pressure and he saw how I reacted to the flood of Christmas cards. This hardened criminal traded four packages of cigarettes with another convict for a little baby canary which had just been separated from its mother. Though he didn't get much money from home, he bought food for the bird and gave the canary and the trappings to me. Sam taught me how to feed this baby and how to take care of it. (Bird care had not been part of my medical school curriculum.) "Now, Sam," he told me, "that bird is going to fly on Christmas Day."

Incidentally, the canary population in the penitentiary is tremendous. Many of the convicts breed them and sell them to others, who send them out of the prison as gifts. Some of them just raise the birds and keep them. To some of the inmates, the canary may be the only real friend they've ever had. As a matter of fact, one of the basic reasons for the Halloween, 1952, riot at the penitentiary during which several buildings, including the Catholic Chapel, were burned, was that the men had been denied the opportunity to buy canary food.

I had been given and accepted some canaries as gambling winnings, and had sent them out as gifts to Chip and children in my family, but I hadn't raised them. But this one Sam gave me was different. I had been reluctant to take it at first, because I frankly wasn't in the mood for a chirping bird in the cell. Knowingly, Sam insisted, and in a few days I became quite attached to the little fellow. Feeding and caring for him surely helped my morale during the several days before Christmas. The endless cell-time became busily occupied. Bank-robber Sam was a better psychiatrist than a few I knew who got forty dollars an hour from their patients.

I named the canary Chirper because the little bird would chirp and chirp and open its beak to eat when I fed it with the tip of an ice-cream sucker stick piled with meal. And, believe it or not, this little bird did fly in the cell for the first time on that Christmas Day, 1955. When Chirper was old enough and strong enough, I put him in a little shipping cage and sent him to a young boy whose life I had saved by open-heart massage.

With the aid of Chirper I got through the Christmas holidays.

Then there was another long period with little activity during the New Year's holiday. On January 2, 1956, I made the final entry in my diary covering my initial period in prison:

Well, the New Year has come and here I am, having made adjustment in the Ohio Pen and looking to the future. The true state of my psychological outlook is difficult to describe, but it is very much the same as it has been previously with one important change. The feeling of injustice and reaction to being imprisoned for a crime I did not commit is burning with as much fire as ever, but having been here for close to six months, the future is not so uncertain (no matter what might happen).

I have always felt that I could take what "they" can dish out, but life in a place like this was a great unknown to me, which is only natural. The unknown fosters a variety of conscious and subconscious fears. Consciously I harbored a fear of the Pen. My feeling is best expressed as an uneasiness about the place, which so many had told me of and about which so many varied stories were related. Now I have made my own observations, have realized many of the pitfalls and cautiously made some friends. The outlook, if I must stay here, is not one that I cannot at least anticipate on certain standards. This outlook re this place and me is strictly selfish, but at the same time it is one which better allows me to stay alive long enough to complete my unfinished work. Therefore, this outlook becomes a means to an end. I am reminded of the poem which has meant a great deal to me, *"What is Courage?"*:

> "Courage is not just to bare one's bosom to the
>   sabre-thrust . . .
> Alone, in daring.
> Courage is to grieve, to have the hurt,
> And make the world believe
> You are not caring.
> Courage does not lie alone in dying for a cause
>   to die is only giving.
> Courage is to feel the daily daggers of
>   relentless steel
> And keep on living."

At any rate, when Rich, Dot, Steve and Bet visit me down here, I don't have to reassure them that I am O.K. psychologically. We merely talk and they know that I'm O.K.—not happy, not pleased, but stable and strong. Steve's frequent notes are a great source of strength. The knowledge that Chip is with Steve and Bet is everything to me while I'm here. I know they'll do as fine a job as we could have done for Chip.

14

"Allowed." That was the ringing word handed down by the Ohio Supreme Court on January 11, 1956. For me, it meant the first legal victory since Cuyahoga County Common Pleas Judge William K. Thomas granted me a day of freedom on bond nearly a year and a half before. The seven-member Supreme Court ruled it would review my case, but only to consider the matter of my constitutional rights as related to the atmosphere surrounding my trial. In a sense, it was only a half victory, because the high court refused to consider my other claim for a new trial, based on the new evidence established by Dr. Paul Kirk.

The news of the Ohio Supreme Court's willingness to consider even one aspect of the case was brought to me in the Ohio Penitentiary by Attorney Paul Herbert. I told him unabashedly that the words he uttered were the answer to my prayers. After Mr. Herbert conferred with me and then talked with Warden Ralph Alvis, the tough, fair-minded prison official decided to allow me to meet members of the press to answer questions concerning my reaction to the ruling. It was the first time in the history of the Ohio Penitentiary that an inmate was allowed to hold such a news conference. Convicts usually are permitted only one newsman to visit at any one time.

After Warden Alvis laid down the ground rules for the press meeting and made it clear there would be no photographers allowed, I was brought into a prison office on the Spring Street side to meet eight or so reporters who had gathered for the session.

I was dressed in my prison denims and was smoking a pipe when I came into the second-floor prison conference room. After glancing out the window at the drizzle that was falling on Spring Street I stepped in front of the group. Before I spoke, Warden Alvis said there would be no discussion of any aspect of the murder case itself and events during the long trial primarily because the case was still under appeal.

The first thing the reporters wanted to know was my feeling

when Paul Herbert brought me the news. "Well, I felt more hopeful," I said. Another reporter asked me whether I thought I would eventually gain my freedom through action in the courts or through someone coming forth with a confession. "That is something that is difficult for me to speculate on," I said. "I feel the case will be solved, that there will be a confession made."

"Has your son Chip visited you?" one óf the newsmen asked. "Chip hasn't been here, at my request," was my reply. "I don't want his picture in the paper and stories about his visiting his father in prison, much as I would like to see him."

"If you are vindicated, do you expect to return to Cleveland and lead a normal life?" another reporter asked. That was easy to answer. "I certainly can't go back to living a normal life without my wife and mother and father." I wondered what kind of a sick mind formulated that question.

Upon request, we discussed some of my prison activities—the basketball, the tumbling, and the football. Then, in answer to a question as to whether I would like to do medical work in the penitentiary, I said,

"As long as I am here my wish is to be of the most benefit to the men as I can be. If the powers that be that run the prison think I can be of better use in the hospital, I'll be glad to do that type of work. There are certain phases of medicine in which I feel I could be of great help. But that is not for me to decide." (That was my unselfish side speaking.)

When my brief meeting with the newsmen was over, I went back to school, to my cell, and to life as No. 98860. And my lawyers went to work to prepare for the Ohio Supreme Court's review of my conviction.

About a month after the press conference, Warden Alvis told the newsmen that I had a new job assignment. I was now working as a male nurse in the prison hospital. "There's a definite need for qualified personnel," Warden Alvis said. "Dr. Sheppard is certainly qualified. What should I do—put him into blacksmithing?" he remarked with his customary candor. He assured the newsmen that Dr. Sam Sheppard, "Doesn't operate—and will not operate—on anyone while he's here. But we can use his skill and knowledge in the prison hospital."

Warden Alvis said my duties included making beds, taking temperatures, checking pulses, administering anesthetics and taking X-rays. Fortunately, Warden Alvis intentionally didn't spend much time in surgery or he would not have made those statements. By the time the warden made the announcement of my new assignment, I had been working in the prison hospital for almost three weeks. And from the first day, I was doing the thing he said I wouldn't be allowed to do, performing major surgery.

The first inkling that I was destined for work in the prison hospital came when I was hastily summoned one day to the personnel office, which was headed by a big, six-foot-four fellow, Marion J. Koloski. I was surprised at the call, because I had sent no "kite," an intrapenitentiary note, asking for an appointment with any prison official.

Koloski wasn't one of my favorites. He was a man who told us during the orientation period that we should try to keep physically clean and then in the same breath said that we would get one bath a week.

"No inmate will be permitted to launder his State clothing or other State issue on a personal basis," Koloski had said. "Infraction of this rule will land you in the hole. But keep clean." It was rather difficult to do when they only laundered the clothing once or twice a year.

When I entered his office, Koloski, who spoke with a pronounced lisp, asked me how I would like to work in the prison hospital. I would like to work in a hospital back home, but not in the prison hospital, was my answer. He said that a man was needed in surgery who was acquainted with surgical techniques and sterilization procedures and especially with intratracheal anesthesia, in which a tube, usually made of plastic, is placed into the windpipe via the mouth and throat or nose and throat. This is used primarily for cardiac and lung surgery, and makes an airtight connection between the anesthetic machine and the patient's lungs.

"Don't tell me your troubles," I said. "I've got troubles of my own." Speaking selfishly, I told him I would like to stay in vocational school as a teacher so that I could continue to accumulate "good time," which I figured could get me before the parole board a full two years ahead of schedule.

"Well, we'll see," he said and then he urged me to read up on my anesthesia. I looked at him squarely and said, "Well, I don't have to read up on my anesthesia." I had to know anesthesia in and out in order to do neurosurgery. I told him that his statement wasn't too bright and he wasn't too happy about the remark. I immediately made a written request to remain in vocational school.

Two days later, I received a transfer to the prison hospital. As I was passing the personnel office on the way to the hospital, I barged into Koloski's office, without an appointment. My letter was on his desk.

"What's the big idea?" I asked. "I told you I didn't want to move. I thought that no man was moved from one job to another without giving permission unless he was being punished." I guess the prison officials felt they were giving me a promotion, and that I should appreciate the opportunity to live in a hospital dormitory, have a single bed and a bedside table, extra meals and a twenty-four-hour pass in and out of the hospital. But to my way of thinking, this didn't get me out of prison any sooner and that's what I wanted more than anything else.

Koloski asked me if I intended to "freeze-up," that is, refuse to work in the job to which I was assigned. The pressure and implications were there. If I refused the assignment, I would be branded as "uncooperative" and "incorrigible" and my record would be marked appropriately. This would have reflected on my family and on the possibility or probability of guilt or innocence and this I couldn't stand. I agreed reluctantly and went to the four-story hospital, which was a crumbling building with seventy beds right next to the brand new building which housed the deputy warden's office and the personnel office. The hospital was so ramshackle that it wouldn't be allowed to operate for one minute in the outside world if a health department official inspected it.

I went upstairs to the surgical suite on the third floor and met Dr. Roy Swenson, a mild-mannered Swede, and a very accomplished surgeon. Like all of the prison surgeons, he had a practice on the outside and came to the prison on mornings to do surgery. At this time he was just filling in as chief surgeon for Dr. Watson Walker, who was in military service.

Dr. Swenson, whom I later learned was a surgical partner of a doctor who had been my father's roommate in osteopathic medical school, told me to change into hospital clothes. He said he wanted me to assist him with a major operation on a man who had cancer of the lower bowel. I administered the anesthetic to the man, inserted a tube in his windpipe and established the man's breathing and stabilization with cyclopropane general anesthetic. Then I turned the job of monitoring the anesthetic over to another convict and scrubbed in with Dr. Swenson for the operation, as requested.

Dr. Swenson and I worked as a team in performing a rather difficult operation, which, incidentally, had been perfected years before by my father, Dr. Richard A. Sheppard. It was the first time I had been in surgery for a year and a half, but it seemed as if I had been there just the day before. For a few moments I forgot where I was. The surgery was successful and Dr. Swenson was gratified and so was the patient later. I enjoyed being with a man who could operate as well as Dr. Swenson did and working with him was almost like being with my father or my brothers.

Later that day after Dr. Richard Brooks, the medical director, Dr. Swenson, and all the other attending doctors, had gone for the day, I was summoned by the head nurse—an inmate—who said that one of the patients in the ward was dying of an acute coronary thrombosis. He knew that I was a physician and surgeon and he couldn't cope with the situation himself. We went into the ward and examined the man briefly. I then ordered the standard procedure for a heart attack of this kind including drugs and oxygen. The man started to change from blue to white and then all of a sudden he began to display a regular respiration and heartbeat. He had been in a coma. Now he opened his eyes and talked lucidly.

Just as quickly, he started to take a turn for the worse. I looked around and there was this male nurse standing by the oxygen tank. He had the hose to the patient's oxygen mask bent double the way you'd double a garden hose to shut off the flow of water for a moment. I was trying to save this man's life and the son-of-a-bitch was trying to kill the patient by cutting off his oxygen. I grabbed the man by his shirt and he dropped the hose.

"What the hell do you think you're doing," I shouted.

"This guy's a fink (prison jargon for stool pigeon) and I'm going to make sure he's not going to live," the nurse replied.

"Look you take care of him on your time, not on my time." I shouted that we were trying to bring this man around and that he had better get the hell out of the ward or I was going to throw him out bodily. He turned and left, warning me that he would be back with some "friends."

It just so happened that there were a couple of brothers in the penitentiary, whom I shall call the "Other Brothers." They were the toughest hoodlums you could ever imagine. One of them had been a boxer and the other a wrestler. They knew how to handle themselves. One of the brothers, whom I will call Ike, worked in the hospital and he witnessed the incident. He immediately sent word to the planing mill via another convict to his brother, whom I will call

Mike. Mike walked right away from the planing mill, no pass or anything, came to the hospital and gave the excuse he had something in his eye.

The two Other Brothers plus a third man backed me up that first day. They told this hose-pinching hoodlum and his friends that if they harmed me in any way they would have to deal with the three of them. ("Plus one," I added!) One of the Other Brothers told me afterward that his brother and the third man had been observing me closely since my arrival, trying to determine what kind of a guy I really was. But when I came off strongly and was ready to back up my convictions, they stopped wondering and came to my aid. They hated the patient, too, but they respected my stand.

I had become quite fearless, because I really didn't give a damn. If someone had stabbed me, I could not have cared less. I was like the guy who's flying an airplane in a war and has just lost his wife and both kids and his mother. He says "What the hell." And he's able to be fearless because he almost wishes to die.

In the days and weeks that passed, I continued to act as the chief anesthetist and assist Dr. Swenson in all of his operations. Thanks to one of the men in the surgical suite team who told me the place was a jungle, and from my own observations, I learned that some of the inmate nurses were stealing drugs from the hospital. They were taking narcotics and barbiturates for themselves or giving them to their friends. Wide use was made of sodium pentothal, ephedrine, demerol and morphine and these cons would go to almost any length to get their hands on any drug of the narcotic or stimulant types.

All of the drugs were kept in the dispensary. When we needed morphine during an operation, a guard would have to bring it to the surgery door, then watch me or one of the men give the injection. For the first few times, I was a real rube. "I'll get it for you, Doc," one of the male nurses would say. Then he would get the morphine from the guard, who was not allowed in surgery because he was not sterile. Seeing that I was busy administering anesthetic or scrubbing in with Dr. Swenson, the male nurse would ask if he could administer the morphine. I couldn't break sterile and so I told him to give it.

Unbeknown to me until later the man would pinch the patient's arm in a deft manner with his thumb and forefinger. Then he would puncture the skin and push the needle right through the pinched skin and out the other side into his own finger and then push the plunger on the syringe. Others, I soon learned, stole varying amounts of morphine by squirting the drug into the caps of bottles that had been hung up for intravenous use and then taking the caps out of surgery at the end of their shift.

As I discovered these techniques, I tried to put a stop to them. I soon realized, however, that if the anesthetic and drugs were to be protected I was going to have to get in better physical shape and learn a little about brawling. Most of my exercise had consisted of the intramural sports such as basketball. I decided that sports like basketball and baseball weren't preparing me to defend myself and decided to begin a program of protection, coupled with weight-lifting.

I knew how to use my fists, but I knew my ability didn't measure up to the capabilities of some of the men I might have to deal with in the future. I turned to the Other Brothers for help. As I said before, one had been a wrestler and the other a boxer and they knew how to fight in the ring and how to handle themselves in a street brawl. These men taught me how to fight dirty, if I had to, and their efforts will be eternally appreciated.

I learned quickly, promising myself that the next time I caught a male nurse stealing a drug he would be taught a lesson. One of the favorite drugs of the male nurses was sodium pentothal, a barbiturate which is used as an anesthetic and which induces sleep when given by injection. The men would drink it or take it in an enema and would really get a bang out of it. It didn't take long to catch one.

I was assisting Dr. Swenson in a complete laryngectomy, an operation in which the voice box is removed. The operating table was tilted sharply on the side and I had to virtually get under the table to do my job. Luckily, I just happened to look out through a peep hole in the drapes which surrounded the table and saw this male nurse, a big Italian fellow, stealing sodium pentothal by draining it out of the little sterile bottle with a syringe. He replaced it with some water, colored to look like pentothal with a drop or two of tincture of zephiran, which he carried in another syringe. Syringes were readily available in surgery.

I was too busy to do anything about it at the moment, but I asked another nurse, whom I trusted, to get me some fresh pentothal, which he did. I held it in my hand and used it as we needed it. When the operation was over and we had cleaned up, I was still fuming. Imagine—here's a guy anesthetized on the table and this male nurse replaced the pentothal that was to be given the patient to maintain his level of sleep with colored water. The one guard who was assigned to the floor was giving shots in the post-operative ward.

I called this big Italian fellow into the locker room and belted him as hard as I could. He hit the corner and just crumbled to the floor. I didn't lose my temper. It was just a punch that hit him out of nowhere. He didn't know what was coming. Up until the time I hit him, the man was unaware that I had caught him tampering with the pentothal.

He was lying on the floor gibbering, "I know I did wrong. Don't kick me." Well, I wouldn't kick a man when he was down, but that's not the convict way. He expected me to stomp on him, the way the Other Brothers would do if they had a man in this position. I didn't touch him again, but I said, "This is just a taste, just a taste. If you ever touch anything on that anesthetic table again, you're going to get more than a taste. We're not going to jeopardize the lives of any patient on the operating table and anybody who takes anything off that anesthetic table is going to have to fight me." He got the message and so did some of the others.

At the outset, I had tried to explain to the men that it was wrong to take the drugs or tamper with them. I thought I was talking to human beings and made an effort to treat these men in a human way. But I soon recognized that though a handful of the other inmates I met in the place would be human, the rest were animals and I had to conduct myself as I would in a jungle. So, that's what I did. I just used my elephant gun and told them that was just the beginning or I used my deer rifle and told them the elephant gun was coming. In other words, all this sort of man could respect or understand was overwhelming physical ability. He couldn't understand reason. He couldn't see that he might be the man on the operating table the next day. All he understood was that I could beat the tar out of him and that if he didn't do as I said that I would do just that.

Word of what I had done spread around the penitentiary and even reached the warden and deputy warden. I later learned that Warden Alvis expressed his approval, not because of what I did, but because of the reasoning behind it. Regardless of what these men did in surgery, I never told a prison official about it. It was not my business to be a stool pigeon. I would rarely even tell other doctors in surgery because they, in essence, were prison officials. It put me in a unique position. Many of the things that were going on were against my professional code of ethics as a physician, but I would never think of finking on these men. I just tried to handle them in my own way. I certainly wasn't entirely successful in thwarting the efforts of these so-called male nurses to steal drugs. In at least one instance we came within an eyelash of losing a patient because of this kind of hanky-panky in the operating room.

I will relate the first part of this story in the form of a letter written to my brother Richard, on May 27, 1956:

Dear Richard:

Last Monday night I spent the first six hours I can say I was glad to be present in this place.

One of the boys from the honor dormitory developed an acute appendicitis and we took him to surgery about nine p.m. I intubated the patient and then scrubbed in to help. All went well till the patient was being transported back to the ward. He vomited and aspirated into the trachea a large quid of gastric material (though he had been cleaned out as well as possible pre-surg. and Levine tube was still in place). The ward nurses administered oxygen to no avail and then the respirator which only moved the plug back and forth. I was called and found the patient completely cyanotic changing to the pallid phase with no respiration or pulse.

I had brought the laryngoscope tracheal and tube when called *which I used* rapidly (during which time I recall hearing one of the guards instructing someone to call the medical director to "come over and sign this man out" as he was dead. He was correct, of course, at that time). With the tube in place I initiated recurrent chest pressure with a sound thump over the prechordium [external cardiac massage] and requested the anesthetic machine to use forced oxygen and the bag for resuscitation and requested a knife so that we could enter the chest. After about ten thoracic thrusts the color began to improve and a questionable pulse was noted. The machine was connected and the bag used. The pulse soon was definite so that thoractomy [use of the knife] was deferred. Suction was used naturally via the endotracheal tube and in the maso pharynx. Improvement was rapid, but it was twenty-five to thirty minutes before the patient developed or recovered his own respiration. Recovery of consciousness was more rapid than the pharyngeal and esophagal reflexes. He was conscious and lucid about midnight but not enough reflex and no swallowing. So the tube stayed in place with close observation. At two-thirty a.m. I noted the first swallow and by three a.m. the cough reflex was fair. After careful aspiration and explanation to the patient who was fully awake, the tube was withdrawn under suction. He coughed, swallowed and breathed deeply for us and has done very well since.

A few days later, the letter returned to me and scrawled atop it was "Not permitted to go out. R. W. Alvis." But just below was written: "Was fine work. RWA."

That isn't the end of the story. What had happened to this patient was a classic example of what lengths these male nurses would go to in their effort to obtain drugs for their own use or to further their homosexual desires. I had administered the anesthetic to start the operation, then was busy assisting the surgeon and finally closed the man's incision and dressed it. I had turned the anesthetic chores over to another man. He took advantage.

This other nurse, whom I had had confidence in, had slyly taken the sodium pentothal so that he could give it to his homosexual partner and had substituted curare, a South American arrow poison which kills by relaxing respiration. When used in proper dosage it acts as a muscle relaxant for a patient. A slight amount used with an anesthetic helps the surgeon to relax the abdomen in an appendectomy. The near lethal dose of curare administered by this man as a substitute for pentothal didn't anesthetize the patient. It paralyzed him. Fortunately I was able to bring him out of it.

The next day the patient, a man named John McCormick, thanked me and said, "Thank God you were there to help me, Doc." As I said to Richard in the letter which was never sent, I told McCormick that the six hours I had spent with him was the only stretch that I could say, "I'm glad I was in the Ohio Penitentary."

Of course, this kind of conduct on the part of a male nurse, by which he jeopardized the life of a patient, could not be tolerated. I passed the word of the incident along to the chief surgeon, who—in time—arranged for the man to be transferred to another correctional institution. I later learned the same nurse was the chief go-between if you wanted a fellow inmate murdered.

As a matter of fact, I thank my lucky stars that I wasn't a victim of this man's totally unscrupulous conduct in the operating room. Just a few weeks before the curare incident occurred, I underwent surgery for removal of hemorrhoids and had to be anesthesized with sodium pentothal. My closest friend in the hospital, who was recovering from arm surgery, left his hospital bed to administer the drug. He would have knocked anyone down who tried to stop him, because he had a basic distrust for most of the other nurses. And he knew what he was talking about, having been there much longer than I. If one of the other aides had been handling the anesthetic, I might not have been around to write this book. This friend gave me many tips and much information.

My own case was not without some complications, brought about by shenanigans in the operating room. One of the nurses had stolen some sodium pentothal as part of a plot hatched by some of the others of the hospital crew. (When administered in proper doses, sodium pentothal is also used as truth serum.) These inmates administered controlled doses of the drug to me when I returned to the ward from surgery. They began questioning me about my case. They had hoped to elicit a confession from me that I actually was responsible for the death of my wife. They were going to use any private information to blackmail me.

Under the influence of this drug which was administered without my permission and under which I had to bare my subconscious, I told the truth—that I did not kill my wife. The inmate who conceived the plot and who actually gave me the drug and did the questioning was so convinced of my innocence after the experience that he later disclosed what had happened and offered any help in freeing me from incarceration. When he finally was paroled he related the story to a Dayton newspaper, which printed it as part of a series on my case.

During my week-long recovery from this surgery, my brothers, Steve and Richard, visited me and because I was in the hospital, they were given permission to see me in the post-operative ward. They were given a tour of the hospital and the surgical suite. While the conditions they saw were not like those they enjoyed at modern Bay View Hospital, I was happy that at least the prison hospital had improved somewhat since my arrival on the scene.

During my first months in the hospital I made my way slowly, adjusting to the new duties. In addition to handling the anesthesia and assisting in surgery, I attempted to do my share of dirty work —the mopping, the folding of linens, and the packaging of surgical packs. At that time, some of the inmates working in the hospital were performing a lot of minor and semi-major surgery. They were doing things for which they had no training. Had they been on the outside in a reputable hospital, they would have been charged with committing a crime. They were suturing deep lacerations of the face, legs, arms, and head; they were setting fractures, and they were treating hemorrhoids. Some of them were dabbling in removing birth marks and other markings on the body, so they would be less easily identified when they got out of the penitentiary and resumed their life of crime. One man was actually trying to see how well he could remove fingerprints and palm prints—for obvious reasons. As much as I could, I took over the minor and semi-major surgery.

I also assumed responsibility for maintaining some semblance of sterilization in the surgical suite, especially as it pertained to the instruments and the linens used in major surgery. When I arrived, the hospital had no proper method of indicating whether a pack of linens or instruments was sterilized. The men working in the hospital just relied on word of mouth from others in the surgical suite. At my suggestion, a special indicator tape was ordered. The tape looks like regular tan masking tape, but during sterilization dark brown, almost black, lines develop in it. The use of this tape helped stamp out a rash of post-operative infections which had baffled the hospital surgeons for several months. They had just been too busy to realize that faulty sterilization had caused this and it took an outsider to recognize the obvious reason.

The surgical suite was pretty well isolated, but the chief surgeon's office was only a few feet away from the tuberculosis ward. One of the nurses who took care of the tuberculosis patients was able to walk in and out of the surgeon's office and often without proper sterilization would walk back into the surgical suite to observe an operation. The guy was a nice fellow and I liked him very much but I finally told him, "Look, Jack, as a favor to me please stay out of surgery. If you like surgery so much, ask for a transfer from the T.B. ward." He remained in the tuberculosis ward, but stayed away from the surgical suite.

As time went by, I was called upon more and more to assist in major surgery, not only by Dr. Swenson, with whom I established a wonderful rapport, but also with the neurosurgeon, the plastic surgeon and other visiting surgeons who practiced in the hospital. I performed a number of neurosurgical operations by myself and also had occasion to bail out some of the visiting surgical residents from a Columbus hospital who frequently were left on their own in the prison hospital and got into situations which they were unable to handle. I was never hesitant to help, but I didn't try to impose myself. When I was asked I stepped in, and tried to make it look as if the doctor did the job.

Finally all but one of the visiting surgeons asked me to assist them in surgical procedures. Some, including the visiting neurosurgeon, summoned me to surgery regardless of where I was in the walls for any major case. One time I was off duty when one of the convicts working on the coal pile had his head split open in a fight by a shovel-wielding inmate. The visiting neurosurgeon called for me. Together we virtually reconstructed this man's head in a long and tedious operation. Eight weeks later he was back on the coal pile, throwing his share of coal.

My finest working relationship was with the neurosurgeon, for two reasons. One, of course, was the fact that this was my specialty —the thing I knew best. The second was this man's character. He respected me and my background. In front of anybody in the penitentiary—guard, official, inmate—he would put an X-ray in the view box and consult with me on the case. He was not hesitant at all about consulting with me during surgery. He'd stop once in a while and say, "Sam, what do you think about that?" Then, I'd give him my opinion. He never acted as if he was operating in a penitentiary and I was a convict. This was a big boost to me. When we were in surgery together we were two surgeons working together and we didn't give a damn who said what or where. We compared notes. I was trained on the West Coast and he at Ohio State University in the Midwest. We discussed different techniques. At one point, he even asked me to show him how to do a certain surgical procedure, which he had never performed. He did the same for me.

The prison officials learned from some of the "talkers" in the penitentiary that I was performing surgery, but they knew I was primarily doing it in the presence of their regular visiting surgeons, who were under contract. They didn't dare say too much to these outside doctors, because these men come and go from the penitentiary. These surgeons have outside contacts and if ruffled by a prison official, they are liable to make an issue out of some of the unsavory situations in the penitentiary.

Most of these visiting surgeons represented some of the best men in the medical profession in Columbus. Any one of them could have made more money on the outside in a given hour than in the penitentiary. But they willingly devoted a portion of their time, for a small fee, to the prison hospital because they were needed; because there was surgery to be done; because the hospital couldn't afford a full-time staff of surgeons. And if they were given any lip or undue abuse, they would just walk out—plain and simple. They worked too hard for too little money to be treated with anything but the respect they deserved. One skin specialist, who held a clinic for inmates every Friday, saw as many as one hundred-thirty inmates in a day. Men who work like that are hard to find, at any price.

So, when I established a man-to-man rapport with these men and they permitted me to assist in surgery, the prison officials could ill afford to make an issue out of it. Prison officials couldn't complain much anyway. Because I was administering anesthesia, I represented a sizeable saving in money, upwards of fifty to seventy-five dollars a case. Had I not been there they would have had to pay a licensed anesthesiologist that kind of money. They were really getting their money's worth out of me. For four dollars a month, they had an anesthetist, surgeon and general surgical suite handyman, who took care of the linen, cleaned up, and kept a close watch, day and night on the post-operative patients, who were left without any qualified surgeons at night.

Eventually, the chief resident surgeons—first Dr. Swenson and then Dr. Watson Walker, when he returned from the Army—put me more or less in charge of the post-operative section after they left the prison hospital for the day. Of course, in both cases, this was a gradual thing, which came after the two men realized that I wasn't trying to undermine them, that they could trust my judgment and I was only trying to help the poor fellows in the beds and on the operating table. Both eventually left orders for me to be called if any emergency developed. I had the feeling that both realized that I was just a victim of circumstances and I was still a doctor. This put me in the middle a bit, because some of the prison officials didn't go for the arrangement. Almost every night I stayed in the surgical ward until one or two a.m. just to be on hand in case of an emergency. Then I'd go down into the dormitory and have one of the other male nurses relieve me so there would be someone on hand who could spot trouble and summon me. I would sleep in my whites, so that I could get up quickly, jump into my tennis shoes and be on the floor in a moment. Many a night I went to the dormitory, found my relief asleep, decided not to waken him and returned to the surgical ward for the remainder of the night. Often, it amounted to an eighteen to twenty hour day in the hospital, what with performing duties as an anesthetist, helping with surgery, cleaning up and then taking a long evening turn in the post-operative section. I also kept up on the latest medical and surgical techniques by reading the dozen medical journals sent to me every month by my good friend, Dr. Art Miller of Los Angeles. These covered everything from anesthesia to orthopedics.

We rarely ate at regular times because of surgical schedules. As a result we generally had better meals than the rest of the men as the cooks had to prepare special meals for us. I had plenty of passes to the gym, but only had an opportunity to use them about half the time, when we were free in the late afternoon. With a tight schedule, I had very little time for reading, and spent most of my spare time writing letters and making infrequent notes in my diary, in which I noted that the existence at this hospital "can be rapidly summed up by saying the men are treated like men here."

Of course, it was also good to be called "Doctor" again. First the prison surgeons called me "Doctor," then the male nurses and the patients, and then finally some of the guards. This recognition irritated the prison officials, short of the warden. A convict is supposed to be some kind of a worm that they can step on at any time. To hear me called "Doctor" really rubbed them the wrong way. The officials held a meeting and told the guards to stop calling me "Doctor," in the ward, out of the ward, or anywhere. I frequently received packages from the outside. Invariably the "Dr." was marked out. What the dummies didn't know was that even though I wasn't licensed to practice medicine because of my conviction, they couldn't take my title away. The title of "Doctor" was bestowed upon me by a medical school and it had nothing to do with the license to practice medicine granted by the state. At any rate, this campaign to get the guards to keep from recognizing my title and the incidents with the packages just incited the rest of the inmates I came in contact with to make more use of the title. From then on it was always "Doctor" or "Doc Sam."

All in all, I was happy that I had not made a case about my transfer to the prison hospital. I wasn't particularly glad to give up the "good time" associated with teaching, but I was relieved in a way to get a little air and get a little sun and wear clean clothes every day. I had a clean pair of white trousers and white top as scrub clothes every day or twice a day, if I desired. I could take a shower any time I wanted and this was wonderful in the hot weather. We had a free pass every evening and many times after dinner. When there was time I would go to the gym to lift weights as part of my body-building program.

On the weekends, and during holiday periods when the convicts who lived in the cell blocks were kept under lock and key for long periods of time because many of the guards had weekends off, the surgical crew could come and go from the hospital at will. During the warm weather, while the other convicts were in their cells, a small group working in the hospital would play baseball or football in the yard.

And, of course, living in a dormitory, was heaven compared with the filthy seven-foot cube in which they crammed four men in the cell block, which served as a bedroom, bathroom, etc. There was a certain measure of privacy and a man could find a convenient corner and meditate, if that was his pleasure.

Certainly work in the prison hospital was not without its problems. My position was a rather precarious one from many points of view. First, I was called upon to assume medical and surgical responsibilities which—under the circumstances—were not really my province. One mistake might certainly have been disastrous.

Second, I was forced to assume the position of the protector of the drugs, a job performed for better or worse. My actions in this regard certainly put me in physical peril at times. One fellow wanted me to go in the contraband pill-selling business. Another just wanted me to save all the left-over medication for him and his associates as a "price" for being considered a "good guy." A "good guy," that is, until they could get rid of me and refill my slot with one of their peddlers. Others tried their best to persuade me to begin using narcotics, barbiturates and other drugs and stimulants, including alcohol, which—if taken—would have put me at their mercy, so to speak, especially if I began to like the "stuff," as it was called. Fortunately, as I said, I befriended three of the most solid and roughest guys in the joint and they helped to make life a little easier.

I know that although I threw all of the excess medication away, some of the rats in the penitentiary thought that I was saving it for my friends and they were not beyond spreading this kind of misinformation to the prison officials. This kind of vicious rumor-mongering once got me in trouble later.

I tried very, very hard to dissuade my prison friends, if you can call them that, from using drugs, because I knew what could happen. But they became addicted to them all the more. These men, who backed me up, knew what my ethical stand was on the subject of surgery and drugs. I know they thought more of me than to suggest that I make anything available of an illegal nature.

Third, of course, was the problem of adjusting my moral and ethical outlook to some of the shoddy and often inept performances turned in by some members of the medical staff. Men died because there were not always competent medical men on hand to treat them or because they were allowed to languish in solitary confinement without medical treatment even though prison officials knew they were mortally ill and required intensive care.

As an example, there was a man in the hospital who had a severe heart ailment and who appeared to one of the doctors (who shall remain nameless) to be on his last legs. The doctor apparently felt that he had done what he could for the man and further treatment was futile. Before he went home that night, the doctor filled out a death certificate for the man, signed it and left it under the nurses' blotter in the ward. He didn't want to come back that night and pronounce the man "dead." Even if one of the regular doctors were willing to give up on this man, one of the young male nurses wasn't. He called me and asked if I could do anything for the patient, who by this time was unconscious and was turning blue obviously from heart failure. His lungs had filled up with fluid and he was drowning in it. I administered some drugs to regulate his heart beat, which had become very irregular, and to get rid of the fluids. By the time I left the ward late that evening, the patient was smiling and talking. He lived for several months.

I did what I could to help men like this. As in the case of John McCormick, I was glad for the moment that I was at the right place at the right time so that I could live up to the medical oaths I had taken years before. I was a doctor without license, a surgeon without shingle, but I was doing what I had been trained for years to do—care for the sick and injured. I approached my responsibilities with the same dedication and conscientiousness that I had displayed when I was a surgeon making more than $30,000 a year in my own practice.

The fact that I was again doing something useful, that I was helping people, no matter how degenerate some of them were, certainly helped to pass the endless string of days, and weeks, and months, while my case was being appealed to the higher courts. Unfortunately however, this strange role as a four-dollar-a-month physician-surgeon threatened for a long time to become a semi-permanent career.

15

"From the facts in the record a reasonable inference may be drawn. The assailant was delivering repeated blows about the head of the victim. She was struggling violently to resist the attacker. She screamed. The assailant placed his hand over her mouth and a finger penetrated into the mouth, and between the teeth. The victim clamped down on the finger and it was jerked out violently, thereby precipitating the broken teeth outwards and onto the bed where they were found.

"The assailant's fingers would surely have been severely lacerated and causing much blood to emerge. There was not a scratch on the defendant's hands or fingers."

The speaker was Paul M. Herbert, tall, white-haired, distinguished-looking former Ohio Lieutenant Governor. The audience was composed of the seven black-robed justices of the Ohio Supreme Court, my lawyers, prosecutors and about one hundred spectators who crowded into the chambers in downtown Columbus. It was April 17, 1956, and the Ohio Supreme Court was hearing oral arguments on the appeal of my conviction. I was not in the courtroom but going about my regular heavy hospital duties at the penitentiary several blocks away.

"This being an extremely doubtful case," Herbert continued, "the court's charge on the general reputation for conduct of the defendant as to peace and quiet was highly prejudicial. The evidence of the state and of the entire record not being legally sufficient to support a verdict of guilt beyond a reasonable doubt, the defendant should have the judgment entered for him and should be forthwith discharged.

"If the court should not agree with this conclusion then certainly there is prejudicial error requiring reversal of the verdict and a new trial."

In the argument, Herbert also struck out at the prejudicial press coverage of the trial and said that in similar situations courts have not hesitated to order new trials. Perhaps the most significant point made in his statement concerned the blood found on my watch. Herbert pointed out that in reply to a question at the trial as to whether the blood was that of Marilyn, County Morgue Technician Mary Cowan, said, "No, sir. Her group is O." Herbert further recalled that Miss Cowan testified the test she made was inconclusive.

"If the blood was not Marilyn's or Sheppard's, whose was it? This alone exonerates Dr. Sheppard," Herbert said.

"That the public was interested in the murder mystery and that there was considerable publicity is, of course, true," the prosecutors said in their statement to the court. "But it is not true that any news agency, newspaper, or radio station slanted stories to convict the defendant, and defense counsel do not, by mere repetition, make true that which is untrue. The defendant had a fair trial before a fair and competent judge and by an impartial, unbiased and unprejudiced jury. The verdict should be affirmed."

It was again time to play an agonizing waiting game. "Many have their ideas of the outcome, but I just don't know what to think," was my written reaction at the time. "Steve and Rich are obviously very encouraged as are many others, but I have been bitterly conditioned to courts and judges."

The court deliberated the case for six weeks. At about four p.m. on Thursday, May 31st, I was working out in the gym with several other convicts when word was received that the Ohio Supreme Court had upheld the lower court decision to affirm my conviction by a five-to-two decision. Late that night, I wrote:

I couldn't help but become more hopeful. Wish they had refused to hear the case now, but guess they wanted to write a strong decision against me so that the United States Supreme Court would be less prone to hear the case. Don't want to sound or to be bitter, but when they go through all that apparent hearing, etc., to overrule laws they are supposed to enforce it is difficult to figure at best.

Haven't talked to anyone yet, but supposed we'll charge on to the United States Supreme Court, as long as the money due to the sale of Dad's hard-earned property lasts. Naturally, the whole world makes me sick at this time, except for a few persons and I guess if I knew there are more than a few.

A few days later, I received a copy of the complete Ohio Supreme Court decision. Where the Cuyahoga County Court of Appeals had rendered a unanimous, three-to-none decision to uphold my verdict, the highest court in the State had split five-to-two on the decision.

Conceding that the trial had been conducted in a "Roman holiday" atmosphere, the majority still struck down the claim that I could not have received a fair trial in Cuyahoga County due to the publicity and Judge Blythin's refusal to order a change of venue.

"The right to order a change of venue is in the discretion of the trial court," wrote Justice James Bell in the majority opinion. "And a refusal to order a change of venue until it can be determined whether a fair and impartial jury can be impaneled is not an abuse of discretion. Where seventy-five prospective jurors are called for examination and only fourteen are excused because they had formed an opinion as to the guilt or innocence of the defendant, and a jury of twelve is sworn from those seventy-five jurors before the defendant has exercised all his peremptory challenges, it is not an abuse of discretion of the trial court to refuse to order a change of venue."

Touching on the fact that jurors made telephone calls during the time they were deliberating the case, Justice Bell said that alone would not be a basis for reversal, because my attorneys had not shown I was prejudiced by this act.

Regarding the evidence presented in the trial, Justice Bell wrote, "Where circumstantial evidence is relied upon in the proof of a crime, and the jury finds that there is no reasonable hypothesis of innocence based on the facts as it finds them to be, and the facts which it finds are irreconcilable with any reasonable hypothesis other than guilt, it is its duty to convict."

However, Justices Kingsley A. Taft and William L. Hart disagreed with the majority opinion of Justices Bell, Charles B. Zimmerman, James Garfield Stewart, John M. Mathias, and Charles W. Montgomery, and said so in a strongly worded dissent, written by Justice Taft. It was the first time any judges had taken my side in the case. Justice Taft wrote:

I have grave difficulty in concluding that any reasonable man could either (1) fail to have a reasonable doubt as to whether defendant killed his wife, or (2) after the entire comparison and consideration of all the evidence feel an abiding conviction to a moral certainty that the defendant killed his wife, or (3) determine that the circumstantial evidence excludes every reasonable hypothesis except that the defendant killed his wife, or (4) conclude that the only probable or natural explanation of the proved facts and circumstances is that the defendant killed his wife.

Justice Taft attacked Judge Blythin's charge to the jury and said that I had been prejudiced by it in at least two instances. Referring to the portion of the charge that related to character evidence introduced on my behalf, he said:

A considerable amount of evidence was offered with respect to the character and reputation of the defendant. Although, as stated in the defendant's brief, defendant did philander, a philanderer may have propensities for peacefulness. If defendant did have these propensities for peacefulness, as this evidence indicates, such evidence would be evidence of a circumstance tending to indicate that the defendant did not commit the crime of violence involved in the instant case.

Any instructions by the court that would have a tendency to influence the jury to disregard such evidence or not regard it as evidence bearing on the issue of whether defendant was guilty or innocent would be particularly damaging in a case such as this where the state relies entirely on circumstantial evidence.

This would be especially true in the instant case where commission of such a violent crime would be entirely out of character and inconsistent not only with the events in his home during the preceding evening, but also with everything known about the defendant's previous life and his family background.

Commenting on the portion of the charge where Judge Blythin used the George-Washington-cherry-tree analogy, Justice Taft said:

This portion of the court's charge was most unfortunate in the instant case and quite probably had a tendency to mislead the jury. The state was contending that defendant's guilt should be inferred largely from circumstances of his presence in the house at the time of the killing. The jury was told in effect that George Washington could be found guilty of chopping down the tree because he was seen nearby with an ax in his possession; and the jury would thus be influenced by this example to conclude that, since defendant was nearby at the time of the killing and "could have" committed the crime even though the nature of the murder weapon was never identified by any evidence, then defendant, like George Washington did what was consistent with the circumstances of his presence. This is especially likely to have influenced the jury since everyone has been taught that George Washington did do what was consistent with his presence, that is, chop down the cherry tree.

Justice Taft also condemned Judge Blythin for allowing Nancy Ahern to testify that Marilyn had told her about Dr. Chapman's conversation concerning a divorce, calling it "clearly hearsay." He concluded:

It is quite apparent that in such a case as this it would be impossible to reach any other conclusion but that this defendant may have been prejudiced by the foregoing errors in the courts charge and by the admission of the foregoing hearsay evidence.

There are other assignments of error which may be well taken, but it appears to me that in a case such as this it is sufficient to recognize that it would be impossible or unrealistic to say there was no prejudice to the defendant from the foregoing errors.

Undoubtedly a retrial of this case could be conducted with less of the "atmosphere of a Roman holiday" referred to in the majority opinion. The witnesses have already testified once and so one of the principal elements of suspense, which was an important factor in generating that atmosphere, would be absent. There should therefore be less question after such a trial than there undoubtedly now is whether this defendant was accorded a fair trial.

If, as he apparently does, defendant desires another opportunity to establish his innocence, even at the risk of his life, this court should not deny him that opportunity by summarily determining that the errors at his trial were not prejudicial. On the record before this court, such a determination would represent in my opinion a mere and highly doubtful guess.

Little more than two weeks after the decision was handed down, a lengthy insert in my diary, dated June 16th, shows my frame of mind:

After reading the Ohio Supreme Court opinions I feel we have gained quite a bit by the hearing. We are in a much stronger position now than before the recent hearing. The strong dissenting opinion raises much question of United States Constitution, as well as the law of Ohio. Even the opinion against me admits errors and the fact that I was tried in an atmosphere of a "Roman holiday." This certainly could not be constitutional.

But, I'll keep fighting for what is just and right all the way. When I don't fight anymore, I will be dead! (And I surely don't anticipate that in the near future.)

The feeling I experience now is one of great pain for Steve, Rich, Betty and Dorothy. They feel this more than I do and are now hurting more than I. This is true, though it may sound strange to some people who have never felt true love for another or do not know what the word compassion means in its true sense. There are many here and probably all over the world, who "feel sorry" for me. This is not true compassion and is not something I relish or take pride in.

The relationship I feel with my brothers, their wives and Mary and Bud Brown is much different and one of which I am greatly proud. These people feel my incarceration as if part of them were, or is, locked behind these walls. They and their personalities are in truth partially cut away as long as this great wrong continues. Very few others ever share this relationship with anyone outside these walls.

The outlook from here as I sit this night looks somewhat hazy to say the least, but there are a few things I should do soon. One is to ask Steve and Betty to adopt Chip. I feel it would be best for all. This is something I've given a great deal of thought to and think Marilyn would want it that way considering the long pull ahead. Many guys have noted the various time intervals involved in a United States Supreme Court hearing, but the consensus of opinion is about eighteen months at least and this means two years anyway. Well, if I could withstand the past two years, which I'd never have believed I could, I can stand two more and more if I have to.

The outlook or chance of success with a Supreme Court hearing is something I have no idea about. If they are fair, I'll be out O.K., but this has become such a political football that I'll expect something good only when it happens.

My legal team moved swiftly to put the case before the United States Supreme Court for the fall term of 1956. The initial move, of course, was to get the nation's highest court to agree to hear the case in the first place. This is accomplished by submitting a petition for a writ of certiorari, which the nine justices study, then decide whether there are sufficient constitutional grounds for a full-scale hearing before the court.

William Corrigan personally delivered the writ to the United States Supreme Court on August 28th. In contrast to the bulky documents that were filed with the Cuyahoga County Court of Appeals and the Ohio Supreme Court, the writ was a slender, sixty-five-page booklet that set forth seven points on which I was denied due process of law. They were:

The overruling by Judge Blythin of a motion for a change of venue and continuance of the case until "the passion and prejudice" of the community could abate.

The fact that I was tried in "Roman holiday" atmosphere created by the news media.

The refusal of Judge Blythin to permit my lawyers to exercise the last peremptory challenge in the selection of the jury.

The permission by two court-appointed bailiffs for jurors to make telephone calls during the period of deliberation.

The action of authorities in seizing possession of my home immediately after the murder and retaining possession until after trial and conviction.

The admitting of the case by the Ohio Supreme Court on constitutional questions, then the failure of the tribunal to pass on those questions.

The illegal make-up of the Ohio Supreme Court. The chief justice of the court disqualified himself from participation in the case and then appointed a judge from the court of appeals to take his place. The appointment of an alternate should have been made by the justice having the longest period of service on the Supreme Court, as required by the Constitution of the State of Ohio.

The petition was well documented with samples of press coverage before and during the trial and with a description of the "Roman holiday" conditions which pervaded the courtroom and the courthouse during the trial. "Due process requires that a trial shall take place in an atmosphere of quiet and dignity, not, as occurred in this case, in the atmosphere of a 'Roman holiday,' the writ charged. "The situation of 'trial by press' is so fraught with evil that it is demanding the attention not only of the bench and the bar of the United States but all thinking Americans, including great editors of newspapers, who are apprehensive of the disintegration of constitutional rights."

"We believe that this case brings squarely before the Court the widely debated question of 'fair trial and free press.' "

Bill Corrigan was extremely hopeful that the Supreme Court would agree to hear the case in its entirety. "Something has got to be done about the way the news media affected a fair trial in your case," he said to me. Corrigan said he saw mine as a test case that might set the ground rules for all trials in the future. I couldn't help but be encouraged by the aging attorney's words, but tried to insulate myself against being overly hopeful, especially in view of the long string of setbacks suffered since July 4th, 1954.

On November 13th, while listening to the radio in the hospital dormitory, I heard the Supreme Court's answer to the writ. The high tribunal refused to hear the case. Next to the blow of being wrongfully convicted in the first place, this was the crusher. I just couldn't believe it because I had no idea that collateral attack was possible and better.

While the court as a whole turned its back on the case, there was one tiny ray of sunshine—a memorandum filed by Justice Felix Frankfurter in connection with the case.

The defendant claimed that a trial so infused and enveloped by the atmosphere of a "Roman holiday" precluded a fair trial and could not but deprive him of the due process of law guaranteed by the Fourteenth Amendment to the Constitution. The Supreme Court of Ohio rejected this claim and the defendant then invoked the discretionary power of this court to review the correctness of that decision. *This court now*, in turn, refuses the defendant the opportunity to bring the case here for review.

Such denial of his petition in no wise implies that this court approves the decision of the Supreme Court of Ohio. It means only that for one reason and another this case did not commend itself to at least four members of the court as falling within those considerations which should lead this court to exercise its discretion in reviewing a lower court's decision.

For reasons that have often been explained the court does not give the grounds for denying the petitions for certiorari in the normally more than one thousand cases each year in which petitions are denied. It has also been explained why not even the positions of the various justices in such cases are matters of public concern. The rare cases in which an individual position is noted leave unillumined the function of the certiorari system, and do not reveal the position of all the members of the court.

Heartened somewhat by Justice Frankfurter's rare memorandum, my attorneys petitioned the Supreme Court to reconsider its decision not to hear the case rather than file a writ of habeas corpus. On December 17th, the high tribunal—without comment—again rejected the appeal, a decision that suprised neither me nor Bill Corrigan. The Supreme Court of the United States had spoken with finality, or so it seemed then. It would take almost a decade for the court to virtually admit it might have erred in not hearing the case and to rectify, as only it could, one of the great wrongs of American jurisprudence.

Christmas—my third behind bars—was just a week away. My spirit ebbed, but I refused to give up hope, mainly because Bill Corrigan, a valiant old man who was equally as disappointed at the Supreme Court decision, said he would never quit working for my freedom. My defense already had cost more than $100,000 and had all but drained the sizeable inheritance from Dad Sheppard.

"I don't care if you don't have any money," Corrigan said to me after the Supreme Court spoke, "I'll fight this thing through as long as I live." Unfortunately, he didn't live long enough to see himself and his client vindicated.

16 ?

It was a few days before Christmas, 1956, and the agonizing finality of the United States Supreme Court decision was still fresh in my mind. The only thing that buoyed my sagging spirits was the work in the prison hospital. That changed instantly, too. A prison official approached me in the hospital and told me, "Sheppard you're through here." There was no explanation. Within a few hours, I was moved out of the hospital dormitory into a double cell with an old man who was awaiting transfer to another institution. It was not quite solitary confinement. The Christmas box that had come from home and my belongings were tossed into the cell like so much trash.

Word quickly filtered through the prison grapevine as to what had happened. A male nurse whom I had slugged for stealing sodium pentothal during an operation finked to prison officials that I had given sodium pentothal to one of the Other Brothers, who in turn had shared it with the editor of the penitentiary newspaper, a man I shall call Bill Moore. As a result, the fink said, Moore had lost his eyesight and was dying in the prison hospital. Ted Other was ill. Apparently this man had been reliable in the past and prison officials took him at his word, summarily dismissed me from my job, and then began investigating. It was a farce.

What really happened was this. At the entrance to the surgical suite there was a regular medical laboratory, where blood tests, urine analysis, and various other medical tests were conducted. Different kinds of alcohol were used in the laboratory, ranging from the mild to the lethal.

When they could get their hands on this alcohol, some of the inmates would mix it with various ingredients and drink the "cocktails." There was a young technician working in the laboratory and some of the convicts were trying to muscle alcohol from him, just as they had tried to get drugs from me. I had answered most of these fellows with my fists. This fellow felt he was just too small to fight and devised another method for dealing with them.

One night he left a big cylinder of alcohol, supposedly non-poisonous, outside the door. Actually it was lethal. Some of the fellows who picked up the cylinder came to me and asked what I thought. I smelled it, put a little on my finger, tasted it, and advised them not to drink it. Most of the men took my advice. But, Bill Moore said he knew better—that I didn't know what I was talking about. He proceeded to drink several swallows of this potent stuff. Ted Other, who wasn't there when I was consulted, apparently didn't get the message either, and also drank the alcohol although not in great quantity.

Shortly before they moved me out of the hospital, Ted Other came to me in the surgical suite complaining of cramps in his abdomen and trouble with his eyesight. He said his vision was fuzzy and bright light hurt his eyes. When questioned whether he had drunk any of that alcohol, he said yes. I advised him to check immediately into the hospital, which he did, prescribed a course of treatment, and obtained a pair of sunglasses to protect his eyes. I had no idea that Bill Moore was in another part of the hospital, mortally ill. In addition to saying that I had given Ted Other sodium pentothal, the finking male nurse also informed officials that I had treated my friend and had ignored Bill Moore.

Shortly after I was moved to the cell, Moore died, and became a coroner's case. A week later the results of the autopsy showed that he died of alcohol poisoning—not from an overdose of sodium pentothal, as the fink had reported. The report cleared me and also Ted Other, who worked as a masseur in the officer's rub-down room. The coroner found no oil of wintergreen—used in rubbing alcohol—in Moore's system.

Instead of admitting a mistake and restoring me to my former position, prison officials hoked up an excuse. They claimed I had been eating too many meals in the hospital. When I was busy, I frequently would eat the food on a tray that had been prepared for a patient who was just too ill to eat. All of a sudden this became a crime.

They reassigned me to the print shop and gave me a job as a sorter, where I separated sheets of colored paper. About two weeks later, Captain Corbin, in charge of prisoner classification called me over and told me in so many words that the warden was very unhappy with the way I had been treated. Corbin, an intelligent man who was strict, but fair, told me that I was not at fault in the incident and that there would be nothing derogatory put in my record as a result of it. He further indicated there was a certain appreciation among prison officials because I had refrained from notifying my family and making a fuss about it.

Corbin asked me if I knew how to type. I said I had taken a typing course in high school, but certainly wasn't proficient. He suggested that my family send down my portable typewriter and that I practice on it. "In two to four weeks I'll have you over in the personnel office," Corbin said.

About a month later, while playing in the final intra-prison basketball game of the year, I was informed that my new assignment was in the personnel office. It meant a transfer from a cell block to the prison office dormitory, a free run of the penitentiary, a shower every day, and evening and holiday passes, which meant more recreation.

The first job in the personnel office was as a timekeeper. I kept track of the number of hours worked by inmates in their various jobs. On the basis of this record, inmates were paid up to a maximum of eight dollars a month, half of which they kept in the penitentiary to purchase candy, cigarettes, etc. The other half was sent home to their families. I also prepared the daily transfer sheet, which listed new arrivals, discharges, and transfers to other penal institutions in the state. Apparently, my work was good, because after several weeks Captain Corbin made me his personal clerk.

We developed mutual respect for one another. He never gave me any bull and I never gave him any. We were on opposite sides and both knew it, but we were straight with one another. He knew that I would never fink on another inmate. Many times when he asked me a question which I couldn't in good conscience answer, I would say, "Now, Captain Corbin, you know I can't tell you that." By the same token, he knew he could trust me and when he was gone I wouldn't let anyone in his office. It was just a matter of loyalty to the man for whom I was working.

While I was settling in the job as Captain Corbin's clerk, requests started coming from the hospital for help in various situations. First, I was asked to examine potential blood donors for the Red Cross. Then, some of the doctors occasionally asked me to assist in administering anesthetic and serve as a surgical assistant. One day, in late spring, 1957, an inmate suffered a severe head injury in a brawl. The visiting neurosurgeon asked that I immediately be sent to the surgical suite to assist in delicate brain surgery. Captain Corbin agreed. When I returned, he said, "Sam, I think we'd better give up and let you go back to where you're supposed to be."

"I don't want to go back to the hospital and work for a man who won't back me up," I said, referring to the prison official responsible for the hospital, the man who apparently relayed the fink message to higher officials. Captain Corbin agreed to let me stay in the office. The requests for help became more and more frequent. He finally had no choice but to reassign me to the prison hospital. So, late in the summer of 1957, I moved from the office dormitory, which had about one hundred twenty beds, to the hospital dormitory, which had about fifteen, and remained there until I achieved honor status.

A few weeks after returning to the hospital on a full-time basis one of the prison officials approached me and asked my help in "getting" a male nurse, who apparently was giving officials a bad time. This man, whom I'll call Tom Jordan, had threatened to kill some of the fink male nurses in the hospital.

I was asked to plant a syringe filled with a drug in Jordan's pillow or mattress. Then, a guard would "find" it and Jordan would be sent to the hole. "I hate you, you son of a bitch, but I wouldn't even do that to *you*," was my answer. "You have access to the hospital. If you want to trap this man, go over and plant your own syringe." The official got pretty upset at my words, but knew he couldn't punish me for refusing in no uncertain terms something that was strictly illegal, even under the loose moral standards practiced by some of the officials. I was never again asked to participate in such a deal.

He and other officials apparently couldn't understand how a man with my education and training could come to the penitentiary and not do their bidding. They wanted to know why I associated only with the hardened element in the place. My answer was that the hoodlums and thieves appeared to be the only people around the penitentiary who could be depended upon. The more intelligent prisoners usually turned out to be rapists and child attackers and generally became finks or prison informers. A fink could get you in a jam without much trouble. If you spit on the sidewalks in the penitentiary it was all right, but if a fink reported that you fed the sparrows left-over food, they'd put you in the hole for a day and a half. I didn't want any part of the finks and chose to associate with men who were thieves and stick-up men most of whom were doing their second or third tour of duty in the prison.

Make no mistake, it is not my intention to whitewash these men.

They were not nice people and they weren't the kind of men I wanted to consider as friends. But, unlike the rapists and the like, they were not degenerate. They had an honor code among them and were good to their word. And, of course, as I have previously mentioned, some of them helped me to learn how to physically defend myself in the penitentiary environment.

It really boils down to the prison definition of a convict and an inmate. And there is a difference. In recent years, officials of Ohio's penal system have tried to get the entire prison population—guards and prisoners—to refer to those incarcerated as inmates, rather than convicts. The general feeling was that convict was a rather crude term.

As a rather natural or normal evolution of this, the prison population had chosen to use both terms—and they stand for different types of prisoners. Those who are called inmates are the cooperators, generally the finks. There are basically three types of finks: those who tell what they know directly to prison officials; those loud mouths, who always seem to be talking in front of known informers; and the dry finks—those who claim not to be stool pigeons but manage to get their message across by telling a known informer by a planned slip of the tongue.

This group is opposed to the solid passive resisters, called convicts. They won't tell officials anything, not even the time of day, or what kind of toothbrush they use. They are sharp enough to recognize the finks and to stay away from them. In short, then, the convict is the solid passive resister that is never a stool pigeon under any circumstances. He pulls his time, does his prison job, but steadfastly refuses to be a part of the prison intelligence system which officials use effectively to spy on the prisoners and keep them on edge.

The Ohio penitentiary visitors' rooms was crowded with convicts and their families. I was seated by myself at a small table, waiting for Steve and Betty to arrive for their monthly visit. A few tables away sat a masculine-looking prisoner and his attractive wife, a bus ticket tightly grasped in her hand. She was neat, well-groomed and looked to be a typical young American woman in her late twenties.

They talked quietly for a while and then suddenly the man, with whom I had played basketball, raised the level of his voice. "My wife is back in that cell," he said. "I've got more woman in my cell

than you are. Go home—leave me alone." A hush came over the
room. There was an embarrassed silence for this pert young woman.
She was aghast and didn't know how to respond to the shocking
words from her husband. Finally, tears streaming down her face,
she stood up and walked out of the room. I was ready to withdraw
from the human race.

This incident, I believe, graphically illustrates one of the major
problems prevalent in the Ohio Penitentiary and probably in all
places where men are incarcerated. That problem is homosexuality.
In medical school we were made aware of the probable causes and
the effects of homosexuality in neuropsychiatric courses. In residency, I had the opportunity to sit as an observer while neuropsy-
chiatrists counseled with homosexual patients, trying to help them
in any way they could. This medical training gave me an insight
into the problem, but hardly prepared me for the gross homosexual
conduct that goes on behind the tall gray walls in downtown
Columbus. No less than fifty percent of the inmates in the penitentiary take part in homosexual activity for one reason or another.

First, there are the inmates who became homosexuals long before
they arrived at the penitentiary. They simply like other men and
can't help it any more than a normal male can help liking women.
They represent about twenty percent of the prison population and
take the female role. For want of a better expression we will call
them "regular" homosexuals. They are the kind of people who are often driven to crime because they enjoy life at the penitentiary, where
they are "queens." The regulars—who walk, talk and act like girls—
don't have sexual relations with other regular homosexuals. Their
fervent desire is to capture a normal man who has a need. Certainly
no man knows how to express sexual gratification in a society without women, but rather than resort to masturbation to relieve pent-up
sexual drives many of the inmates turn their attentions to the long-
time homosexuals. These men, who assume the male role, are called
"jockers" in prison jargon. The jockers usually are men who are
bewildered by their sudden shift from society to prison life and are
prime targets for the regulars. Before they know what has happened
these bewildered men are hooked on another man.

The largest group of homosexuals in the peniteniary are what I
call "economic" homosexuals. These are men who have a sexual
need, but place money before it. They sell themselves like prosti-
tutes and will play either role for cigarettes, candy, money, a better
job, etc. We call them punks.

As in the case of the young man described earlier in this chapter, there are hundreds of "marriages" in the penitentiary. Jockers are "married" to the regulars. When they live in the same cell, the "wife" does the washing, presses the pants, and straightens the cell. The jockers walk around the penitentiary as if they were kings.

Instead of trying to discourage this kind of activity, the prison hierarchy encourages it. They know that persons weak enough to go the homosexual route are weak enough to be finks or stool pigeons. And prison officials are always on the lookout for finks or agents—what we called four-dollar-a-month guards. It is no secret in the penitentiary that some of the guards and officials are homosexuals and participate in activities with convicts.

Some married prisoners with lovely wives—the toughest, most masculine men you could imagine—fell over the midline and participated in relations with the regulars and the economic group. I insulted many a jocker by pointing out that homosexuality applies to the "pitcher" as well as to the "catcher." Man-to-man sex is homosexual conduct no matter which way it is accomplished, I told them, and it is not uncommon for the pitcher to become the catcher.

It is a fact that there are annually two to four killings a year inside the penitentiary, most of which are hushed up by the authorities. Most of these killings result from homosexual conduct and the jealousy resulting from it. As a surgeon in the penitentiary, I tried to save the lives of many of these victims of mayhem.

In one instance, a prison barber was having an affair with one of the long-time homosexuals. A big, rough convict started to vie with the barber for the third man's attentions and threatened the barber, saying that unless the barber stayed away from this inmate he would be killed. The barber stole a rattail file from one of the prison shops and filed it down into an incredibly sharp knife.

In the prison movie house, where some of the most blatant homosexual activity takes place, the lights are either on or off. There is no way to dim them. One night, when the lights were cut off for the start of the movie, the barber sneaked to the seat where this big jocker was sitting and before the big convict knew what happened plunged the file into him several times. When the jocker was brought to the prison hospital we found that he had fifteen stab wounds—most of them in the chest and arms—and had lost several pints of blood. We worked throughout the night to save his life.

One of the most amazing sights is to watch regulars vie for the attentions of the new arrivals, especially the more masculine ones.

Unfortunately when I arrived at the penitentiary, the stories of my widely publicized indiscretions with Susan Hayes and other women came with me, giving me an advance reputation as somewhat of a lover. This made me a prize target of the regular homosexuals.

Several of these repulsive characters approached me and suggested a relationship. I decided to put a halt to this monkey business right away. About two weeks after arriving, I slugged one of these homosexuals and fractured his jaw. By the next morning, word had spread through the penitentiary that "Sheppard does not go this route." There were no approaches made after that.

Now, we have been talking about what at least one half of the prison population does to fill the sexual need that arises in every man. What about the rest—the normal males who are plucked out of a heterosexual society and put into a society with only men? It is a fact that the normal man or woman must eat, drink, and express himself or herself sexually—in that order.

The other fifty percent just suffer. They sweat it out. They lift weights, run, coach, and participate in athletics. They gamble, mainly for pacification and sublimation. They try to keep busy and by doing so subconsciously sublimate their sexual drive. You don't concentrate on wiping the thought of sex from your mind any more than you have to concentrate to know that you are projected to women.

Of course, its much easier to sublimate this desire when you are living in a dormitory, where there are dozens of men. You can pick your friends and discuss whatever you want, philosophy, sports— you name it—or play bridge. When you are in a four-man cell, chances are you'll be in there with a bunch of ignorant degenerates, who talk about nothing but sex. That's why I was happy to go to the hospital, to work, or to teach in the school. You get away from all homosexual talk.

It's not tough for the real man to shun homosexual activity. There's no temptation at all. If a man has ever had a deep-seated love for a woman, the thought of one of these homosexuals even touching him is deplorable. If you were hungry, would you eat garbage? This may be a poor analogy, but it is the best one I know to express the feelings of the normal population.

In my case, my state of numbness due to the grief of losing Marilyn and my parents and being separated from my son was so great during the first years in the penitentiary that—except for my love for Marilyn—I rarely gave it a thought during that period. When I finally emerged from this state of numbness, I missed going to bed with women very much. But more than that I missed a real female companion, something that had been part of my life for so long.

I had the opportunity to talk with many lifers—men who had spent twenty, thirty, even forty years behind bars. Most of them felt the same way. Most of them missed feminine companionship, but would never think of substituting a homosexual for a real woman.

On occasion, some men with connections in the penitentiary were able to get a woman smuggled into the place but, as far as I know, it was a rare happening. Though I am aware of how this was accomplished, it is better left unsaid.

About the only time inmates got close enough to women to smell their perfume and feel their touch was during the monthly visit of the all-female Red Cross blood bank crew. There were six to eight nurses, all thirty to forty-five years of age, in the group. An inmate was allowed to donate blood only once every two months. My hospital work included examining the men before they donated blood and we had to check closely to make sure these men weren't making monthly contributions. Some would have gladly given blood every week, just to feel the nurse put the tourniquet on their arm and thus have an opportunity to smell the perfume.

By the end of my second year in the penitentiary, I had learned the in's and out's of life behind the big gray walls, knew who were the solid citizens (those that could be trusted) and the finks and learned what you could do and what would get you in trouble.

To my utter dismay, I discovered that one cardinal sin in the penitentiary was trying to get yourself freed without the help of an outside lawyer. Fortunately this didn't affect me. I had people on the outside fighting my case up and down the line. But the man with no resources or no family is expected to take his punishment, no matter how long it lasts, no matter whether the man feels he was wrongfully convicted or not.

There is a law library in the penitentiary, but to my way of thinking it was there for show, more than anything else. Convicts would spend hours in the library looking for legal loopholes that might free them. When they thought they had found a point of law applicable to their case they would prepare a brief on toilet paper or anything else that was handy.

It may be coincidental but if a man persisted in preparing documents to try to free himself, he might find himself in a solitary cell for an extended period of time or in the mental range, a triple-decked cell block with individual cells to house psychotic prisoners.

Friends who worked as male nurses in the mental range told me that fully fifty percent of the men in the cell block had no business being there.

The mental range is no picnic ground. In addition to the mental torture of being in this block, it is a place where physical abuse is not uncommon. Sometimes, of course, it is necessary. Some of the men in there are actually dangerous. The guards and inmates who work in the range often have to resort to physical force to restrain some of these men. But I learned that some of the nonpsychotic inmates were abused, merely because they persisted in fighting for their freedom.

In the eyes of prison officials, a man who is continually battling for his freedom is bad enough. A fellow inmate who tries to help him is worse. The so-called jail-house lawyer who has some knowledge of the law and helps another convict to prepare a brief also is a candidate for the mental range, where smoking is prohibited, no radios are permitted, and the men receive only a limited commissary.

During my hospital duties, I tried to save the lives of at least three men who committed suicide because of the hopelessness of life in the mental range. The problem of using the range as a persuasion center for convicts was also extremely frustrating for prison psychiatrists who tried to do a conscientious job, but often found the cells filled with men who had no business there in the first place. At least one top psychiatrist quit because he refused to tolerate the situation any longer.

Another thing I learned about life in the penitentiary was that some of the convicts would go to any lengths to help a man they felt had received a bad deal from the courts. The most extreme example concerned a convicted murderer who was under death sentence.

Some of the convicts felt that there were extenuating circumstances in his case and he certainly did not deserve the death penalty. They started a campaign to make this man appear to be a real psychotic. Under Ohio law a man who is judged insane cannot be executed. Faced with death in the electric chair, the man was naturally on edge. Prison doctors prescribed injections of small amounts of scopolamine hydrobromide to help calm him down. One of the prison male nurses had learned that a little pre-suggestion of unnatural conduct and a strong dose of this drug could make a man appear to be insane.

Before each injection (it was a lot stronger than the doctors had prescribed) the male nurse would suggest to the condemned man that he was a little nutty—that he was an animal and should cower in the corner and attack anyone who came into his cell or paint the walls of his cell with dung. Then he would give him a strong dose intravenously. The man would quickly go out of his head, crouch in the corner and shout, "Come and get me." He tried to urinate out the cell door on the doctors when they entered. This went on for several months. Finally he was judged psychotic and was not executed.

Fortunately, I never needed that kind of help from my fellow convicts. In my case, the only help toward freedom could come from the outside and there were those still working unceasingly to free me.

17

In the late 1940's, Erle Stanley Gardner, the world-re-nowned mystery writer, began what was called "The Court of Last Resort." *Argosy* magazine gave space every month to these inde-pendent investigations in cases where it was felt innocent persons might have been wrongfully convicted. Through solid investigation work, lie detector tests, and the magazine columns, "The Court of Last Resort" built an excellent record for obtaining pardon or parole in most of the cases it took over.

"The Court of Last Resort" first came to my attention in Decem-ber, 1954, a few days after my conviction in Judge Blythin's court. My brothers and some friends were trying to organize a group to obtain a detective service which would follow up clues that had been overlooked or not disclosed by the Cleveland police. After one of the prisoners at the County Jail described the operation of "The Court of Last Resort," I suggested to my brothers that possibly *Argosy* might be interested in my case. "This seems to me to be a very good thought," I wrote in a letter, "because besides being an excellent group of investigators they carry a name which would make people believe and there would not be present the prohibitive cost of such an investigation. Whether this group would take on the case before it has been to all courts and final sentence or not I don't know."

On January 3, 1955, a long-time friend, Seymour Rosen, took the initiative and wrote to Erle Stanley Gardner, asking that "The Court of Last Resort" consider my case. Apparently Gardner turned it down at the time because the case had not run its course through the courts.

When the United States Supreme Court struck down hopes for a new trial in December, 1956, I suggested to Steve that the *Argosy* group might now consider the case. Steve agreed and early in 1957 wrote a letter signed by Richard, Betty, Dorothy, and himself, ask-ing the group to investigate the case.

Erle Stanley Gardner and his associates studied the request, consulted with Cleveland authorities and agreed to accept the case. Their first order of business was to administer lie detector tests to Steve, Richard, Betty, and Dorothy.

During the investigation of my wife's murder there had been innuendoes and outright accusations that members of my family had been part of a conspiracy to cover up the evidence; that they had magnified my injuries suffered at the hands of Marilyn's killer; and that they had "spirited" me to Bay View Hospital without police permission. If these accusations were valid, they would certainly be verified in a lie detector examination.

On May 5, 1957, my brothers and their wives, underwent lie detector tests administered by four impartial experts in the field brought together by *Argosy* and "The Court of Last Resort" at the laboratory of John E. Reid and Associates. The interrogators included John Reid, co-author of *Lie Detection and Criminal Interrogation*, considered one of the outstanding guidebooks in the field; C. B. Hanscom, past president of the Academy for Scientific Interrogation; Dr. LeMoyne Snyder, doctor of medicine and doctor of law and internationally-renowned expert in the medico-legal field, and Alex Lee Gregory, official polygraph examiner for "The Court of Last Resort." Like Hanscom, Dr. Snyder and Gregory also were past presidents of the Academy for Scientific Interrogation. According to *Argosy*, the chances of members of my family fooling this blue ribbon panel were "one in a million."

Were any of the insinuations and charges made against members of my family true? "All four experts, after two days spent in preparation, interrogation and polygraph examinations, have agreed unanimously that none of these charges or insinuations are true," wrote Erle Stanley Gardner in *Argosy*.

"These examiners are certain in their own minds that the four members of the Sheppard family whom they examined know nothing about any murder weapon, nothing at all about any cover-up; that they did not help to remove any fingerprints, obliterate any evidence, nor have ever heard Dr. Sam Sheppard make any statement that indicates he was guilty. Moreover, the wives of the two brothers who were examined have never heard their husbands make any statement which would indicate they were not convinced of Dr. Sam's innocence," Gardner wrote.

"Of course," he continued, "all this doesn't mean that Dr. Sam Sheppard is innocent. It does mean, however, that all of the gossip, all of the speculation regarding the fact that these members of the family might have engaged in a cover-up have no foundation in fact."

In short, my family passed the test with flying colors. I knew they would, because they had absolute faith in my innocence. Had there been any reservations, they never would have risked exposure by going before a battery of experts.

Armed with the results of the polygraph tests administered to my brothers and their wives, "The Court of Last Resort" charged ahead with the investigation. High on the list of Gardner's priorities was to obtain a lie detector test for me. He was informed by my family that I was ready, willing and able—that I had always agreed to take a polygraph examination administered by competent, impartial examiners. The big problem, of course, was to obtain permission from Ohio prison officials for such a test.

Ohio Penitentiary Warden Ralph Alvis took a dim view of a lie detector test for me, despite the fact that the last time "The Court of Last Resort" administered a test in the Ohio Penitentiary the convict involved confessed to actually committing the crime after being confronted with Alex Gregory's polygraph results. In that instance, Warden Alvis had been overruled by then Governor Frank J. Lausche and the test was given.

As a result of Warden Alvis' reluctance in my case, *Argosy* mounted a campaign in its editorial columns and asked readers to write Ohio's current governor, C. William O'Neill, urging him to permit an examination within the penitentiary walls.

About this time, the case broke wide open. At DeLand, Florida, Donald Joseph Wedler, a twenty-three-year-old Florida convict serving a thirteen-year term for robbery and escape, confessed that he killed my wife, Marilyn. There had been other so-called "confessions" before but all had broken down under police investigation. A little skeptical when I first heard of Wedler's confession, I began to think this might be the answer to my dreams of freedom as facts began to develop in the case.

Wedler said that on the night of July 3rd, he took a shot of heroin in downtown Cleveland, stole a car and drove out to a residential area. He admitted that he parked the car, entered a residence and went upstairs. Wedler said he saw a man sleeping downstairs. The convict told authorities that he went into a bedroom and started rifling a dresser for money. At that point, he explained, the woman in the bed started to stir and he hit her with a pipe three or four times.

Wedler explained that as he was about to run down the stairs, he met a man in the hallway, hit him with the pipe and pushed him out of the way. On the way out of the backdoor of the house, Wedler contended he noticed a black bag which was open, dumped out the contents, but did not take anything. He said he ran along the beach in the opposite direction from where he parked the stolen car and threw the pipe in the lake.

Erle Stanley Gardner immediately wired authorities in DeLand and offered the services of "The Court of Last Resort" to administer a lie detector test to Wedler, to evaluate his confession. Sheriff Rodney B. Thursby agreed and Alex Gregory, the "Court's" polygraph expert was on his way to Florida. Meanwhile, Gardner wired Governor O'Neill in Ohio that "The Court of Last Resort" was going to administer the test to Wedler.

At DeLand, Gregory gave Wedler a long series of polygraph tests. His findings were that Wedler either murdered Marilyn or sincerely believed he committed the crime. Gardner again wired Governor O'Neill, telling him that Wedler's lie detector tests showed no evidence of deception and stating that so far there were only minor discrepancies between the true facts and the Florida man's story.

On Thursday, July 19th, Governor O'Neill notified "The Court of Last Resort" that he would permit its experts to administer a lie detector test to me, within the walls of the penitentiary. This turn of events was incredible. I was on cloud nine. O'Neill indicated that the test would be administered on Tuesday, July 23rd. Later in the week he spelled out ground rules for the test. The Governor said polygraph equipment owned by the Ohio State Highway Patrol would be used in the test and that the patrol's polygraph expert, Sergeant William George, would be present while "The Court of Last Resort's" experts administered the test. The test would be under the complete direction of Warden Alvis, O'Neill explained.

Meanwhile, a storm of protest arose from officials who originally prosecuted the case. Assistant County Prosecutor Saul Danaceau called O'Neill "ill-advised." "A lie detector test has so little value that it's a waste of time," he said. John Mahon, who was prosecutor at my trial and now was a common pleas judge, contended that I was fairly tried and convicted. A lie detector test would be of no value, Mahon charged. "I can't see why a person in the penitentiary should be permitted to undergo a lie detector test three years after he was convicted and after he refused such a test during the investigation," said former assistant prosecutor Thomas Parrino, now a municipal judge.

Coroner Dr. Samuel Gerber called the proposed test "fantastic and unusual" and urged Governor O'Neill to delay the polygraph examination until Cleveland authorities had a chance to fly to Florida and question Wedler about facts in the case. Judge Blythin urged Attorney General William Saxbe to deny "The Court of Last Resort" the right to override the constitutional courts of the state and federal government. He called the situation "nothing short of fantastic."

Meanwhile, Erle Stanley Gardner flew to Florida over the weekend and questioned Wedler. According to Gardner, "a couple of major conflicts between Wedler's story and the known facts—if we may call them known facts—developed." On Sunday night, Gardner notified Governor O'Neill that there were discrepancies in Wedler's story. The mystery writer felt that while Wedler continued to show a clear polygraph record, his confession should not be accepted as conclusive evidence of his guilt until after a further investigation and a psychiatric examination.

Gardner's latest wire to the governor was not known to me. But, my elation about Wedler's confession and the prospects of being able to take a lie detector test administered by impartial people was so great that I didn't get much sleep that weekend. As a matter of fact, fever was running high in the penitentiary. Virtually all of the men I knew gave me encouragement.

The men in there knew of my innocence. You can't hide things from people you live with and work with day after day. It was not only because I had Marilyn's picture hanging near my bunk and was fair and honest with all I dealt with. It was because I had passed every one of the tests thrown at me by the hardened convicts, most of which were unknown to me. Many a night, dormitory and cellmates would stay awake, hoping to hear me talk in my sleep about Marilyn's murder. And, as I said, I was once questioned at length by convicts while under the influence of sodium pentothal —used as truth serum.

On Monday morning, I reported for work at the prison personnel office. Captain Corbin called me over and told me the lie detector test had been cancelled. "It's too bad, Sam, I'm sorry," Corbin said. That morning, Governor O'Neill had called off the test, citing Gardner's Sunday night telegram questioning the validity of some of the points in Wedler's confession. O'Neill said that a test would be permitted for me only if we had a true confession to the murder of

Marilyn Sheppard, which had been investigated thoroughly. A pardon would be granted me only if another person was found guilty of the crime, O'Neill explained.

The news stunned me. This was a terrible blow. The lie detector test was sort of a last-shot thing and O'Neill's decision hit me with the same impact as the Supreme Court turndown. It was obvious that some tremendous pressures had been exerted on the Governor to cause him to back down. I thought about the great disappointment that Young Sam and other members of my family must have felt when they heard the news. And I thought about the real killer —if it wasn't Wedler—out there chuckling to himself.

The next day, Dr. Gerber, James McArthur, who had retired as chief of detectives in Cleveland, and Deputy Sheriff David Yettra were in DeLand to question Wedler. After four hours of questioning, Gerber labeled Wedler's story a complete hoax. "As far as we are concerned, Wedler is not telling the truth," the coroner told newsmen, "We can't pin him down on any specific details of the crime." Gerber said that as far as his team was concerned the Wedler issue was closed.

That was bad enough, but what was worse was the fact that Erle Stanley Gardner and "The Court of Last Resort" decided as a result of the rebuff by Governor O'Neill to drop the case. "We are going to fold our tent and silently steal away," the mystery writer said at a news conference. "By the time Ohio wakes up to how people feel about this case they will be damned glad to have someone to help them out of the mess they are in."

The next week, Bill Corrigan, still active in the case, went to DeLand and obtained Wedler's signature on a three-and-a-half-page confession. But, with Cuyahoga County officials convinced the twenty-three-year-old convict was not telling the truth, there was little that could be done with the document and further efforts to use the Wedler story as a basis for legal effort on my behalf were dropped.

The entire episode further chipped away at my ability to hope. Certainly I always hoped for the best, but expected the worst. The Supreme Court of the United States had refused to hear the case. "The Court of Last Resort"—my last hope—had withdrawn from the case. What else was left? I started thinking about parole—a minimum of eight years away. Seven more years behind bars was a frightening prospect. There was nothing left to do but live one day at a time—pull my time, stay out of trouble as much as possible— and try to make parole by mid-1964.

18

Endless years of incarceration are hard enough to bear even if you have been rightly convicted of committing a crime. But, there are no words that can adequately describe the feeling you endure behind the ugly gray walls when you have been wrongfully convicted and have eight more years behind bars staring you in the face.

Fortunately, shortly after "The Court of Last Resort" affair, prison officials restored me to full-time duty in the hospital. I threw myself into medical activity with greater intensity than before. Whatever spare time I had left was spent in athletics or in acting as an instructor in weight lifting and body building. By projecting myself wholeheartedly into whatever I was doing, it was quite often possible to forget why I was in the place and what the immediate future held. I was like a robot.

A few months after I returned to the hospital job, Sloan-Kettering Institute for Cancer Research began a research program at the Ohio Penitentiary in which convicts were used as guinea pigs in an effort to determine whether live and dead cancer cells would grow when inoculated into the body. Before volunteering for the dead cell part of the program, several of the men came to me and asked for my advice. I explained to them that the cells were dead and couldn't cause cancer any more than dead tuberculosis germs could cause tuberculosis. On the basis of my encouragement, many of the men participated in the program.

Inoculation with live cancer cells was another story. While medical experts had speculated that they would not grow in a healthy human being, it had never been tried. Therefore, no one really knew what to expect. On the basis of my medical training, I felt there was little danger, but couldn't be sure.

However, if the men were to be encouraged to take part in this very critical phase of testing—the first time live cancer cells had been used—action would have to speak louder than words. I immediately decided to subject myself to the first live cancer cell experiments. The man in charge, Dr. Chester M. Southam, Associate Professor of Medicine at Cornell, arranged for me to be the first convict in line for the injections. (No other convict could back out after Doc took it himself!)

There were other reasons, too, for volunteering. Dad and other friends and relatives had been cancer victims. I wanted to help in any way possible to end the suffering from this killer disease. Also I felt that a physician might be able to record some subjective findings that would be missed by the average subject. Mostly, there was nothing to lose. I didn't have any particular death wish, but I didn't give a damn whether school kept or not.

On March 21, 1958, we lined up in the prison hospital for the injections. Dr. Southam called me over and as flash bulbs popped (a prison cameraman) he injected live cancer cells into my left forearm. In all, Dr. Southam gave me three injections—one of liver cancer (one of the most lethal), one of skin cancer cells, and the third of a mixture of the two. In my right arm at spots parallel to the cancer injections on the other arm, he injected a saline water solution as a control. Nineteen men followed me in this historic experiment.

Within a few days terrific swelling developed in the left arm and armpit. It was traceable to a foreign protein reaction as my body was producing antibodies against the cancer cells.

Dr. Southam and his associates studied us closely for approximately two months. To help in the study, I recorded daily notes, which included my temperature and blood count, skin color and other physical reactions. While my system was overcoming these live cancer cells, my overall body and muscle tone was phenomenal. I could lift heavier weights than ever before and throw a football and baseball farther distances than I ever dreamed possible. During this period, there was a remarkable decrease in muscle aches and pains when I did opposing types of exercise, such as playing baseball and lifting heavy weights on the same day.

The swelling in my left forearm disappeared after a wrestling match but a painful, swollen lymph node in my left armpit remained. Near the end of the study period, Dr. Southam performed a biopsy on the left wrist area, and removed some muscle tissue samples. He found that the body had overcome the cancer cells. We decided not to biopsy the armpit area. We both felt that the swelling was due to the trapping of the cancer cells by the lymph glands, which is part of their function. That's what it turned out to be. Thank God!

There were similar reactions in the other men, but not one of the twenty of us developed cancer from the live injections. It was a meaningful milestone in cancer research and we all felt a sense of pride in having helped prove conclusively that the healthy human body can ward off live cancer cells when introduced by injection. Cancer experts had long believed that man had a natural immunity to cancer. This experiment helped to substantiate the theory.

My participation was duly noted on my prison record, but it won no favor for me in terms of special treatment. In fact, it didn't even help me get honor status in what is considered regulation time for a person sentenced for second degree murder. Normally, prisoners with good records are moved to honor camps around the state or to the prison honor dormitory within three to four years after entering the Ohio Penitentiary. When I arrived at the penitentiary, prison officials told me I would be treated the same as anyone else. Though B. C. Sacks, who succeeded Ralph Alvis as warden, conceded that I had an exceptional record, it took five years for me to win honor status.

The shift to the honor camp outside the penitentiary walls came early in July, 1960. It coincided with another legal setback in the never-ending effort to free me from false imprisonment. In 1958, Bill Corrigan had launched a battle to have me freed on a writ of habeas corpus, charging that Cuyahoga County authorities had suppressed evidence favorable to me during the 1954 trial. This maneuver dragged through the Ohio Supreme Court for about two years, but in the end produced exactly what all of the other appeals had spawned—nothing.

The honor dormitory was an oblong, three-story building outside of the main walls of the penitentiary. Offices, a kitchen and dining room were on the first floor and several four-man rooms were on the second and third floors. There were no doors to the rooms, except to the dispensary. Draperies separated the rooms from the hallway. Prisoners could have fabric sent in from the outside for the windows and the doorway. Inmates were allowed to have throw rugs and radios of any kind. No individual television sets were permitted in the four-man rooms, but there was a large set in the dining room.

My job in the honor dormitory was first aid man and as such I was given a room of my own which also served as the dispensary. I was responsible for treating minor ailments, deciding whether a man was sick enough to be sent inside the walls to the prison hospital, and dispensing medicine. A short time after moving to the new surroundings, I helped a convict who was well-versed in dental work to make the switch from the penitentiary to the honor dormitory. I let it be known that I didn't care to handle dental problems in the dormitory and indicated that this man would be a welcome addition. He was permitted to move from the penitentiary proper to the dormitory and shared the big combination dispensary-bedroom with me. He was amazing. He had never gone beyond the fifth grade in school, yet was proficient in extracting teeth and making dentures.

If you can call any form of incarceration pleasant, life in the honor dormitory was better than anything I had been subjected to in the county jail or in five years at the penitentiary. The pressure was off. There were only a handful of guards and there was little regimentation. I was permitted to eat when I wanted to and could go out into the yard anytime to work out with weights or shoot baskets.

In addition to handling the dispensary, there were always many other jobs to do. Frequently, we left the camp grounds in a truck to haul potatoes or onions that had been donated by some farmer with a bumper crop or to pick up and deliver used desks that had been given to the state by companies which no longer needed them.

From time to time when we were on these delivery trips outside the camp, we would stop at stores along the way to purchase various items we needed. It was not strictly legal, but we got away with it anyway. Honor men who lived in Columbus often stopped off at home to see their wives. Others had an opportunity to visit houses of prostitution. They were allowed to carry money and wear a watch, something not generally permitted behind the walls because these could be used to bribe a guard.

Frankly, paid women were available to me when I attained honor status, but while other men with me on deliveries or pickups stopped at houses of prostitution, I went to a bar and had a shot of whiskey and a beer. It's not that I didn't want to go with them. I did. But I felt that the moment of pleasure wasn't worth jeopardizing my possible freedom or the reputation of my son or my brothers and their wives. They had already been through enough because of my indiscretions. To do something like that while an honor man would be pure idiocy and would have displayed a base disregard for the respect of my family. This seemed to supersede all with me.

It was also interesting to see the marked change in most of the men who had been economic homosexuals in the penitentiary when they were given honor status and moved to the dormitory. More than half of the economic homosexuals suddenly became "men" again. They were the men who took the most chances when it came to having relations with real women. Perhaps they had a guilt feeling about their conduct in the penitentiary and now wanted to prove they were really heterosexual.

At the honor dormitory, it was possible to get any kind of food desired. The commissary chief and the man who did the marketing, both inmates, were always willing to make extra purchases for the men, as long as they shared in the goodies. Mostly though, I used this method for getting fresh or frozen strawberries and ingredients for pizza, which was prepared by the cook. For five dollars we usually had enough pizza to feed the entire dormitory.

My travels were not restricted solely to the Columbus area. Though I had never played anything but an infield position in baseball while a youngster, I was able to make the honor camp baseball team as an outfielder. The team traveled throughout the state, meeting other honor camp teams.

In short, one had the feeling of limited freedom and it was refreshing. But it didn't last long. In January, 1961, they transferred me to the Marion Correctional Institution without asking me whether I wanted to go or not. Marion was a medium security institution which had everything but a wall. In place of a wall, there was a double barbed-wire fence. It meant moving from a situation where there was virtually no restriction—only supervision—to a place where you had most of the rules of a penitentiary. I tried to pull all the strings I could with friends within the Ohio Penitentiary to have my transfer cancelled, but the best that could be done was a delay until after the Christmas holidays.

When I arrived at Marion the circumstances behind my transfer were explained. Dr. R. E. Hershberger, chief medical officer, had asked for me to aid in surgery at the institution, which had some one thousand four hundred inmates. The Marion Correctional Institution had complete hospital and surgical facilities. Apparently, Dr. Hershberger was under pressure from Ohio penal authorities to make more use of his surgical facilities.

Dr. Hershberger was quite frank with me. He said he needed me there to help with surgery. What he really meant was he needed me there to do the surgery. Dr. Hershberger further said that in return for my cooperation, he would help set up a school at Marion for training male nurses and would help me get good time for teaching at the school. It seemed to be an ideal situation, even though Marion would be more restrictive than the honor setup.

At first, they placed me in a dormitory with fifty other men, but within several months I was given a cell. At Marion this is an advantage as there is only one man in a cell. It's like having a private room. As things turned out, I became a one-man surgical department. There were no specialists called in from the outside as was done in Columbus and I performed all types of surgery under the watchful eye of Dr. Hershberger. This arrangement continued for two years.

In the meantime, Dr. Hershberger followed through on his promise to help establish a nursing school. The course was set up according to the standards set by the State of Ohio and other fine practical nursing schools. We taught everything connected with practical nursing—how to give an enema, how to assist with surgical cases, how to assist with intravenous injections, and of course how to maintain sterile conditions. A classroom mànual using the United States Navy manual for medical corpsman, was prepared for distribution to the students.

Several outside experts came to Marion to lecture the trainees, including a laboratory technician, a psychologist, a dentist and oral surgeon, a specialist on disease control, a professional social worker and a minister, who discussed family care following death. The first class agreed unanimously to donate their eyes to the local eye bank in the event of death. It was a demonstration of how deeply these men had become involved in a community feeling of wanting to help somebody.

The nursing school was not without its problems. The chief headache was in handling the men who wanted to goldbrick their way through the school and expected me to pass them, regardless of their performance. There were two men in particular who tried to muscle their way through the school and they met with solid opposition from me.

One morning while I was preparing for surgery these two guys came at me with knives in their hands. Fortunately, a good friend came along at the right time. He saw what was happening, pulled a knife which was strapped to his leg and slammed it down on the stainless steel instrument counter.

"I haven't had a good knife fight for several months now," he shouted at these two hoodlums. "I'm ready to fight and so is Sam, even though he doesn't have a knife. I think it's an even fight. Let's get on with it." Knowing that he was probably the most expert knife-wielder in the place, the two backed off.

Unlike the situation at the Ohio Penitentiary, there was virtually no problem in surgery with male nurses trying to steal drugs. There had been so little surgery performed before my arrival that those who worked in the hospital had had little access to the drugs and, therefore, no chance to get hooked on them.

At Marion, there was plenty of time to participate in basketball and baseball and to make trips around the state with our institution teams. Also, eventually I was able to set up my own small business in the institution. In the honor dormitory at Columbus there had been an opportunity to do some leather work, making purses and clutch bags. This helped maintain the dexterity of my hands and it was enjoyable work.

At Marion, one of the inmates had a virtual monopoly on making religious jewelry, which was sold along with other prisoner-made handicraft in the display cabinet at the entrance to the institution. I learned that this man wanted to sell his little monopoly and decided to buy it.

The price for the business and stock, which included some silver chain and religious medals, was sixty dollars. I scraped up the money by taking what was left in my prison work account and by swapping my radio (one of the best in the place) for an old television set and some cash. Since I was under a semi-honor status, this was all done with the blessing of prison officialdom. I was in business and quickly set about to turn a profit.

With a few dollars left over after purchasing the business, I sent to a mail-order religious supply house for two rosary kits. One of the sets had sterling silver beads and the other crystal beads. I became intrigued and wondered whether it was proper to use more than one color bead in a rosary. I put the question to Father Cosmos, the Catholic priest at Marion, who told me that as long as the bead pattern was correct, more than one color could be used. I began producing rosaries with two colors of beads. They became very popular with the inmates and with prison visitors.

Business became so good that I was able to buy beads, sterling silver wire and chain in bulk and crucifixes separately. One man ordered twenty rosaries as Christmas gifts. Most of the crucifixes sold for $9.66, a reasonable price, which provided for a modest profit. [I also made other types of religious jewelry—Ten Commandment necklaces for those of the Jewish faith and religious medals and crucifixes for Protestant buyers.]

Most of the jewelry work was done at night and on weekends. My main tool was a surgical hemostat that I filed down. My new business was a great dexterity-builder for a neurosurgeon and soon made me financially independent once again. It produced enough income to keep me in tobacco, candy and other incidentals and enabled me to send an occasional twenty dollar bill to Young Sam and to buy gifts for my family and friends. After I had built up a little reserve much of the jewelry was sold at cost. Many of the men in the prison wanted religious items to send home to children and to relatives, but couldn't afford the price. When a man said he wanted to send a religious medal home, he got it for the cost of the materials.

The one-man-to-a-cell setup at Marion permitted me the privacy to perform the delicate jewelry work and also allowed me to be more selective of my friends than in the penitentiary. I could come and go as I pleased, have inmate visitors in the cell any time until ten p.m. Actually the cell was more like a room. There were no bars at the front of the cell and there was a regular door.

The busy surgical schedule, teaching in the nursing school, the jewelry business, and participation in athletics kept me on a treadmill. Keeping busy was the only way I knew to maintain my mental health as the weeks and months moved slowly toward the day when I could apply for parole.

During the six-month stay at the honor dormitory and the first year at Marion, there was no legal activity by my attorneys. Bill Corrigan had indicated in mid-1960 that he would appeal the Ohio Supreme Court's turndown of the habeas corpus bid to the United States District Court, but he never did.

Corrigan, my dear friend and defender, suffered a mild stroke early in 1961. From that point, the white-haired lawyer's health ebbed slowly until he died in the summer. I mourned him like a member of the family. He went to his grave with an unyielding faith in my innocence and sickened with frustration that the courts of this land should allow such a miscarriage of justice to survive.

For the next several months, my legal ship was rudderless, but for all intents and purposes, it didn't matter. There appeared little anyone could do to upset the conviction that had kept me in Ohio penal institutions for more than seven years. However, in November, 1961, a young lawyer named F. Lee Bailey of Boston flew into Cleveland for a meeting with my brother, Steve. The session had been arranged by a mutual friend who suggested that Steve listen to the young man's ideas about future moves to free me.

Bailey, an ex-Marine Saber-jet pilot who had attended Harvard and Boston University Law School, was on his way back to Boston from California and planned to spend only a few hours in Cleveland before continuing to his home. Steve and Bailey talked for few moments in the main lobby of the Cleveland Airport. Bailey was not yet thirty, but Steve was impressed with his knowledge of the case and some of his ideas. My brother persuaded him to change his travel plans and have dinner and spend the night at Steve's house in Rocky River.

As Steve related in his book *My Brother's Keeper*, the two talked long into the night. Bailey said that if he was retained he would press for a lie detector test for me. The expected favorable results, he reasoned, would pressure the governor and the Ohio Pardon and Parole Commission to grant clemency.

If prison officials refused to grant administration of a polygraph examination, Bailey said he would petition the Ohio Supreme Court to force them to permit a test. That failing, the case then could be taken to the federal courts again. Steve indicated that he was all for Bailey's plan, but that the final decision would be mine. Bailey and Steve decided to drive to Marion the next morning to discuss it with me.

Steve showed Bailey to the guest room and then returned to the living room, where he found his wife, Betty, less than enthusiastic about reopening the case, which had lain dormant with virtually no publicity for a year and a half. Her reasoning, according to Steve's account of the conversation, in *My Brother's Keeper*, was that things had quieted down—that their daughters were doing well in school and that my son, Chip, was settled at a private school. Steve quoted her as asking, "Do we have to stir everything up again?"

To his everlasting credit, Steve told Betty that as long as I was behind bars he would never give up the fight to free me. The next morning, Steve and Lee drove to Marion for an unscheduled visit. After some hesitation, prison officials allowed them to confer with me and we spent several hours discussing my case and in general conversation.

Lee Bailey's aggressive, but articulate, presentation made an immediate impact on me. He did not look much beyond his twenty-nine years, but he handled himself like a man many years older. Frankly, I was a little skeptical that he could succeed in his plan—a natural reflex action from being disappointed so many times. There was no hesitation on my part, however, in agreeing to any form of lie detector test he could arrange. The big question was: Could he get state penal officials to grant the test or force them to do it through the courts?

Throughout 1962, Bailey was no more successful than Bill Corrigan, Paul Herbert and the others had been. He gave generously of his time without remuneration and at his own expense piled up thousands of miles traveling between Boston and Ohio and made hundreds of telephone calls. He made numerous speeches and radio and television appearances in Ohio, telling all who would listen that I was innocent and should be released.

His arguments won many friends for the Sam Sheppard cause in Ohio, but failed to impress the warden of Marion Correctional Institution, Maury Koblentz, director of state correctional institutions, and Governor Michael V. DiSalle. One by one they turned down his pleas that I be allowed to take a lie detector test. The Ohio Supreme Court didn't think much of the idea, either, and turned down his bid on December 27th, 1962, just as the high tribunal had refused to overturn the conviction and later had ruled against Bill Corrigan's habeas corpus action.

The setbacks in trying to get a polygraph examination for me only fired Bailey's indomitable spirit and made him more determined to win complete exoneration for me. But after spending eight and a half years behind bars (including the year in the County Jail), exoneration was secondary to me. All I wanted to do then was get the hell out of the Marion Correctional Institution—for at least two good reasons.

19 ❧

While life may have been difficult for me during the interminably long years of imprisonment I never lost sight of the fact that this was an even more difficult period for a youngster who was not equipped—by virtue of his age—to cope with the situation as well as I. He was my young son, Chip, who within the space of a month lost both parents and spent the most important years of his life growing up with foster parents, Steve and Betty Sheppard.

Chip adjusted beautifully to his new home life, although it marked a radical departure from the life he had had with Marilyn and me. With us, as an only child, he was spoiled a bit by Marilyn and by the neighborhood high school kids and our baby sitter. He played basketball with me and other boys in our driveway basketball court. He was a constant companion in the boat while we water skied. Sports was a big part of our life. This all changed at Steve's house. Steve was more academically inclined and rarely, if ever, engaged in athletic activity with Young Sam.

There was more discipline in Steve's house than there had been when Sam was with Marilyn and me. In his new home, Chip had to help with the family chores—empty the waste basket, help set the table, and the like—and all of these things were new to him. At Steve's house, Chip has recalled, you couldn't have dessert unless you ate every drop of food during the regular part of the meal. He conceded that since he was growing up, some of these items probably would have been part of his regimen had we remained a family unit.

"I kind of took pride that I was fairly good at Uncle Steve's house," Chip told me. "In all the years I lived there, I was only spanked once and that was for something that really wasn't my fault."

At our home to avoid confusion, Young Sam was called Chip. The name stuck and most of his playmates called him by that name. However, after he was at Steve's home for about two years, my brother and Chip agreed he couldn't go on using the nickname throughout life. That his name was Sam Sheppard and he should use it.

The next day the nine-year-old stood up in his school-room and firmly announced to his classmates that from now on his name was Sam Sheppard, not Chip Sheppard. You can imagine how proud I was when I heard about it.

Surprising as it may seem, Young Sam says he underwent very little taunting from his schoolmates about the fact that his father was in the penitentiary. He says he never got into a fight about it. I was thankful that there was no known constant harassment by other children. Sam, of course, knew I was in the penitentiary and visited me there but admits he didn't grasp the significance of what had happened until he was in the sixth grade. "By then, it all just seemed so unreal," he said.

His first visit to the Ohio Penitentiary came after I had been there about a year. It had actually been more than two years since I had seen him and touched him, and for both of us it was an emotional experience. From that point on, Steve and Betty brought him two to four times a year. I cherished every visit, although for a time he was still too young for us to communicate in meaningful terms.

At first, most of the correspondence with Young Sam from the Ohio Penitentiary came in the form of letters to Steve and Betty, with excerpts for Chip. But, in early spring, 1957, I wrote my first direct letter from the penitentiary to him:

Dear Sam (Chip),

Your most recent, fine letter came the other day and I was very happy to receive it, as I always am to hear from you or one of the other kids. In this way, I know that you are thinking of me and that is a big help.

How are you doing while Steve and Betty are away? I hope fine as usual and I guess all is well or you would have told me different in the letter.

Perhaps you are surprised to have me writing directly to you for the first time. Well, since you and the girls have been writing to me, it has become obvious that you can read and write, though I know you could when I came here, but you couldn't be on my mailing list at first because many fellas of seven aren't able to read and write as well as you did. Anyway it is straightened out now and I'll write to you about every three weeks now so I can answer your letters for a change and I'll try to answer the letters that the girls send through mine to you. O.K.?

Your last letter told of your going out to see how good you are in baseball after the long layoff over the winter. Ha. Ha. I did the same thing last week and I wasn't too hot myself, but we went out again today and

I find that I'm doing a little better. We'll both improve as we get a little practice.

I was glad to hear about your nature scrapbook and I also got word of your objection to the increase of the game birds which are to be shot. That is fine and I had three or four chances to shoot deer, but they are such beautiful and graceful animals that I couldn't shoot. A friend of mine always goes hunting with a camera-gun, rather than with one with bullets, and when he sees a bird or deer or whatever he is hunting he shoots a picture, and then he has a nice collection of pictures of the animals that he could have shot, but didn't. I feel as the friend of mine does and I think that perhaps you do too, though we have never talked about it before. We'll give it some thought when we want to go hunting together.

Please give my love to Janet and Carol and tell them that I miss them very much as I do you. Wish we could get into baseball shape together this spring, but guess we'll have to wait for another.

Love,
Dad

A few days later, I received an answer:

Dear Dad,

As you know we had a contest about our scrapbooks at school. There was a tie for first place. I was one of the people.

In school we are writing to great cities to get information about them. I'm writing to two places. We also made poems to be put in the hall. Tomorrow at church there will be a ground breaking for our new church.

I'm very glad you can write to me.

Aunt Betty and Uncle called they are fine. They are having fun.

Janet is in the school choir they need a coral speaking group to put in a prowgram. I'm in it. All my love.

Love,
Sam

From that point on we corresponded regularly, building the only kind of relationship we could under the circumstances. Though we were one hundred forty miles apart and there were only a few visits a year we kept in close touch by mail. It helped both of us to ease the aching loneliness.

On May 18, 1957, Chip's tenth birthday, I wrote:

Dear Sam,

Well, here it is Saturday and the 18th of May (your birthday). Ten years ago today we were pretty happy with our new little boy. I had to stay with Mommie for pretty near eight hours before you decided to come along O.K. and then I helped with the big event. Grandma and Dick (my father) were on their way to Los Angeles to help take care of you and I was all excited after you came. I drove home in Los Angeles after I was sure you and Mommie were O.K. and on the way I went through a red light and bounced a fender on the car on a large curb. I got a ticket for the red light and had to fix the fender later.

Grandma and Dick came shortly and took over. Grandma taught us all about taking care of babies and Dick just smiled and beamed over you (HIS FIRST GRANDSON). Well ten years look pretty short looking back at time, but it looks pretty long when you look ahead at it. I have a card for you and have had it for a long time, but I didn't send it last week so it will be a little late. Please forgive me, but know that I didn't forget and never will.

A month later, Sam came to the Ohio Penitentiary for his second visit, before leaving to spend the summer at camp. In my next letter I wrote:

You seemed to enjoy our visit almost as much as I did and that is quite a lot. I know that you didn't enjoy the part when Steve and I had to talk business and about some of the situation, but you understood that we hadn't seen each other for a long time and had to get some things straight. . . . Though we couldn't cover everything by a long sight, I was glad we had the chance to talk as we did when you were here. I want you to know that I am very proud of you and think you are doing a fine job in every way. I will keep up the same and we will never let one another down. Sometimes it takes the tough situation to bring out the best in a person. Well, the pay lists are rolling in now and I have to get back to work, but I wanted to send you a short letter to tell you how I enjoyed our visit and what a great guy I think you are. All my love, Dad

As the years rolled on, I gave Young Sam whatever fatherly advice I could. As Steve would not encourage him along athletic lines, I tried to interest him in physical fitness and sports in general. At my suggestion, he started lifting weights when he was ten. Since I was active in body building programs at the penitentiary, I tried to pass along helpful information. But, it certainly was a poor substitute for being there in person. I longed to work with him, play ball with him, run with him, and give him the kind of encouragement Dad Sheppard had given me when I was a youngster and became deeply interested in sports.

Although Young Sam ultimately became a good distance runner in track, he is and always will be bothered by the thought that he might have become much better in that sport and others had I been there to work with him and encourage him during the formative years.

As Young Sam grew, the tone of my letters changed. He was not without problems and I tried to bolster him. Steve had always wanted a son and although he was not the kind of father I would have been, as far as athletics went, he did become quite close to Chip.

In the spring of 1960, there was talk in the family about sending Chip to a private school. I was against it, because I felt his mental well-being would best be served by his being around members of the family where he could have some measure of love and affection. Although he had little choice Young Sam was unsure as to whether he wanted to remain in public school or go to a private school.

On April 4, 1960, I wrote to him:

Dear Sam,

How is everything going with you and the girls? There is very little new on this end so nothing to write about; other than I think of you every day and pull with you as you face the various problems that do crop up. I somehow feel that you are, in a way, here with me too at times when I feel low or there is some tough work ahead. Things seem a little easier when one or more people are pulling with and for you. Though the rough spots are still rough and no one can take the direct jolts that are cut out for you or me but just you and I. So I try to take my bumps and jolts the way I'd like to see you take yours. This lightens the load in some way. You must feel it too.

Much love,
Dad

In the fall of 1960, Chip entered Culver Military Academy. I still wasn't sold on the idea from where I sat but there was little I could do. One thing that bothered me was that due to his rigid schedule and the distance from Columbus to Culver, we would be able to see each other only two or three times a year. Our visits had become more frequent and meaningful. The thought of long periods of separation bothered both of us.

Being the son of Dr. Sam Sheppard, convicted wife-killer, posed a few problems for Young Sam at Culver. Most of his classmates and teachers just ignored my imprisonment and treated Chip as if he were just any other student. One instructor who knew Chip was from Ohio, but apparently did not know he was my son, thought he was being funny in class one day and kept referring to Sam as "Dr. Sheppard."

"I didn't say anything about it that day," Sam told me. "But I decided if he did it again the next day, I would get up and walk out of class—just like that. Then I would come back after class and see the teacher. Evidently, somebody told him who I was. The man actually apologized to me and never made another joke about it again."

About the only other incident that occurred at Culver came in a Spanish class when a pimply-faced kid who had read something about my case in a newspaper asked Sam in a voice loud enough for the whole class to hear whether he was related to the jailbird, Sam Sheppard, who had killed his wife. The teacher was out of the room and Sam asked this kid in a nice way to be quiet. The boy persisted and said something about Chip being the son of a jailbird, wife-killer. Sam, who was just a shade under six-foot and pretty well built, got up, walked slowly over to the classmate and said softly, "Shut up . . . or I'll smash you." The kid shut up.

Chip readily adapted himself to the new surroundings. By his own admission, he quickly became "gung ho" for the military portion of his training and did so well at it that he ultimately achieved the top military rank in his class. Meanwhile, Steve kept urging him to hit the books—to forget about athletics. However, in the fall of 1961, his freshman year, Chip made the cross country track team and developed a burning desire to compete. He barely missed getting a letter as a freshman, but did earn his "C" in cross country during his sophomore year.

Steve's feelings on the subject were outlined in a letter to Sam's counselor.

I was pleased to receive your letter of April 5, 1962. I am certain that we have achieved our goal and that I can depend upon your good judgment and experience in the educational field to make certain that Sam is exerting maximum efforts in the direction of scholastic achievement.

I wish to reiterate, however, that this next fall when Sam returns to Culver, if he is accepted, that competitive athletic endeavor will hinge entirely on the grades which he receives at the end of his term this spring. I would like to make it abundantly clear to him that as far as I am concerned competitive sports are extra-curricular activity, certainly no more important and probably of even less importance than ballroom dancing, for example. Unless he achieves and maintains, therefore, a grade point average equivalent to a B and no mark on his report card lower than a C, I shall be forced to the conclusion that excessive attention and energy is being directed toward activity in competitive athletics.

I feel certain that I may depend on you and other men at Culver to continue to impress on Cadet Sam Sheppard the importance of achieving scholastic goals first.

Very truly yours,
Stephen Sheppard, D.O.

I didn't exactly take the opposite tack. I felt grades were important, but so were athletics. There was little I could do about it on a direct basis, but I kept encouraging Young Sam to continue training, giving him tips for diet and body building. In the spring of 1962, Chip won his first competitive interscholastic race in the mile, and when the news reached me, I was bursting with pride. "Congratulations and wonderful going on winning your first track event," I wrote. "It's hard to make good time when the pace is slow. So don't worry about times too much right at this stage. Just go out and win the races. I know you have won races and events before, but this was the first win with 'outside competition.' That first one is a bit of a thrill. Stay right in there and your times will improve; it will seem almost overnight."

I'd have given a million dollars for the chance to see him run. That was not possible. So, I had to rely on his descriptions of the races. Our mutual interest in track helped to forge an even stronger bond between us. "We are very close now like it used to be," I said in a letter a week after his first track victory. "I find myself wanting to write to you daily."

A few weeks later, he was fifteen years old, and it didn't seem possible that nearly eight years had passed since that horrible morning in July, 1954. Thanks to the parents of a Culver friend, Chip's fifteenth birthday was complete with cake and the trimmings and when he told me how much he enjoyed it, I wrote to him:

Thanks so very much for your quite wonderful letter of May 20th. To know that you truly had a nice birthday means a great deal to me. I should like to thank your friend's parents; not for you, but for me and Marilyn. (She would have had you calling her Marilyn long ago if she was with us, so let's do as she would have asked or wished.) You two, in fact, we three, were such buddies and M. was so young at heart; she would just have been like an older sister to you by now. (We seem like brothers ourselves, No?)

Each time Young Sam came to visit me at Marion, I marveled at how rapidly he was developing both physically and mentally. His wavy blond hair and glasses gave him a scholarly look, but due to his conscientious training program he was a fine physical specimen. When Chip first visited me back in 1956, his attention span naturally was limited. After a few minutes of conversation, he would be off wandering around the Ohio Penitentiary visiting room. As the years dragged on, we had more and more to talk about during his visits. Now, he was able to come alone, and we had a lot to talk about without Betty and Steve. "Wish it was last weekend so that you would be here on Monday," I wrote in May, 1962. "I know your visits have become more than just important to me, to say the least and think that it is this burning desire to spend more time with you that made me jump at the chance to 'make it easier' for you to visit each month with me. After seeing and talking with you, however, it is quite obvious that you want to see me about as much as I do you; which is quite a lot. This way, as I said before, you can jump a bus any month Uncle Steve or Rich can't make it."

In the fall of 1962, Chip entered his sophomore year, ran cross country track and worked as diligently as possible to get grades that were acceptable to Steve. Apparently he didn't, because on April 11, 1963, Chip wrote, "I've decided that I shouldn't go out for spring track. I told Uncle Steve I'd get a B average and I guess I'd better do that."

Sitting out that season didn't appreciably affect his class standing, about the middle of a group of two hundred thirty. He was industrious and worked hard. It was obvious that he was working almost to his limitations. He ran cross country track in the fall of 1963, and from that point on the issue of competitive athletics was settled. With the concurrence of school officials, he was allowed to compete in spring track in his junior and senior years and made a letter both seasons.

In his senior year, he captained the cross country team and was president of his class. "Everyone likes Sam," his counselor said in a newspaper interview. "He's easily one of the two or three most popular boys in the school. And he is also very effective. He gets things done."

The counselor's sentiments were echoed in a letter I received from the father of one of Sam's roommates. "I know you will be interested in knowing that your son is doing a thoroughly outstanding job at Culver," the father wrote. "As the Regimental Sgt. Major he has the highest rank of any cadet in his class. He is obviously most popular. I found him quiet and reserved, but certainly most enjoyable to be with. I know that my son thinks the world of him and they are very simpatico roommates. You have every reason in the world to be extremely proud of your son and his accomplishments."

So, despite the barriers that were thrust in his path as a seven-year-old back in 1954, Young Sam has emerged for the most part as a well-adjusted young man. Certainly the ordeal of growing up without a father and mother had its effect, as did the publicity which attended the case and followed Young Sam wherever he went.

He is a loyal, sensitive young man who has some serious doubts about the kind of society that could unjustifiably imprison his father. At times he is a little cynical, which can be traced to the entire episode and, frankly, to living with Steve, who has that trait. He is quite reserved in showing his affection for people, even those very close to him. Sam became a man and learned how to accept responsibility long before others of his age and he feels he is a better man now for it. Some boys would be broken. He seems to have been tempered rather than broken.

I think he has come through adversity with flying colors. But, I would give anything to be able to turn the clock back and to have had more than a pal relationship with him all those years. Words cannot accurately describe what we both missed. We both feel this.

20

The beautiful, twenty-four-year-old woman sat in a waiting room of a dentist's office in Dusseldorf, Germany, in late December, 1954. Ariane Tebbenjohanns, the wife of a steel company heir, intelligent, blonde, slender—mother of an infant daughter—picked up a magazine and began thumbing through it casually. Suddenly, her eyes caught the headline on a story about the Sheppard murder case in Ohio, some four thousand miles away. She began reading the story, which posed a series of questions about the case: "Is this man the killer?" "Does he have a Jekyll-and-Hyde personality?" "Was the community prejudiced because of his wealth? Because he committed adultery?"

As she read the article, Ariane apparently just couldn't rationalize the method of the killing or the act itself with my education and dedication to medicine. It seemed to her that the fact I liked tailor-made suits, drove foreign cars, and was reasonably successful at the age of thirty had aroused people's jealousy. Even from the sketchy facts in the story, she came to the conclusion that my case was being tried in the newspapers—that authorities were trying to hang a murder rap on me for committing adultery. She wondered to herself, "How could this happen in America?"

After the dental appointment, Ariane went to the home of her mother, told her about the article and spent the afternoon discussing it with her. Her mother's advice was to forget it as there was nothing she could do. In Ariane's case, that was easier said than done.

Several days later, she learned of my conviction. She wanted to write me a letter and express her sympathy and outrage—as many from around the world had done. But she was unsure of her English usage and didn't know how to go about writing to an American in jail. She continually postponed writing the letter.

In March, 1955, Ariane and her husband, Olaf, went to the Riviera, where they met an American couple from New Haven. The Sheppard case was still very much in Ariane's mind and she questioned them about the case. The American eye specialist and his

wife told her they were acquainted with the case and felt that I
had been railroaded as a cover-up for someone else. "What are you
going to do about it?" Ariane asked. They assured her there was
nothing they could do.

Ariane and Olaf spent much of the next three weeks with their
new-found friends. Time and time again, Ariane brought up the
subject of the Sheppard case. Finally, the Americans asked her to
stop talking about it. However, this sensitive young woman could
not get out of her mind the thought of my languishing in prison for
a crime she felt I did not commit. Over the next few years she made
several starts at writing to me but each time she tore up the letter.
During her annual trips to the Riviera, she implored every American
she met to write to the Governor of Ohio protesting my conviction
and imprisonment. "How can you relax in the sun here," she would
ask vacationing tourists, "while an innocent man is sitting in a dingy
cell, with no one to fight for him."

"Stop talking about Sam Sheppard," her husband would say.
"Can't you talk about anything else?" "It's crazy Ariane; it's hopeless," her mother told her numerous times.

In 1957, Ariane divorced Olaf Tebbenjohanns. The divorce had
nothing to do with her interest in the Sheppard murder case. In
fact it took another two years for her to write the first letter. It was
early 1959, and I had been vegetating in the Ohio Penitentiary for
nearly four years.

She didn't know where I was, but remembered the name "Sheppard Clinic, Cleveland, Ohio," from the original article and sent the
letter to that address. It reached my brother, Steve. In that letter,
Ariane said she was sympathetic to my cause and asked whether it
would be possible to write to me. Over the years Steve had received
hundreds of letters from women espousing faith in my innocence
and asking whether they could correspond with me. Occasionally,
he would bring some of the letters to the penitentiary during visits,
primarily to buoy up my spirits with the fact there were still people
in the country and, in fact, the world, who believed in my innocence.
But I never cared much—as far as I was concerned, I was through
with women.

Steve brought the letter to me during his next visit. I read it and
sensed that the tone was different from most of the letters that had
been sent by well-wishers. I told Steve to write Ariane, tell her of
my desire to hear from her again and, ask for a picture of her. "My
brother is interested in what you are doing, and he wants to know

more about your life," Steve wrote. "Since prison regulations forbid him to write anyone other than his immediate family, Dr. Sam suggested that your communications come to me and I will take your letters into the prison on my next visit."

We began a three-way correspondence. Ariane would write to me, care of Steve. Steve would bring the letters to the penitentiary, I would read them and tell him what to write in return. Most of her letters were light, telling of incidents that happened to her during her travels through Europe, about her family, and her daughter, Iris. Through Steve, Ariane learned about prison life.

When I received her picture, I was amazed that someone as beautiful would take the time to become interested in a convicted murderer in a prison thousands of miles away. To me, she was Sophia Loren, Doris Day, Marilyn Monroe and Liz Taylor all wrapped up in one. No, that is an understatement—she was unique and life once again began to take on some meaning.

The three-way correspondence continued for almost two years. I found myself waiting desperately for Steve's next visit, so that I could read Ariane's latest letter. In 1961, when I was transferred to the Marion Correctional Institution, Ariane was permitted to write me directly, but for about a year my replies still had to go through Steve. Then, in 1962, the Marion officials permitted me to put her on my approved mailing list. At last, we could correspond directly.

The correspondence had a remarkable effect on me. It pulled me from the depths of the depression, where the never-ending series of setbacks had pushed me. When she received a picture of me and wrote back that I was getting too fat, I began to work out with more determination than ever before. It was not uncommon for me to do five hundred pushups as part of my body-building campaign.

I read her letters, meticulously written in white ink on a parchment-like red stationary, five and six times a day, carrying each new one with me until the next one arrived. She sent me a little lock of her hair and I carried it with me in a transparent packet.

When we began corresponding directly with one another we both realized there might be something more to our friendship than a woman's concern for a man who was falsely imprisoned. The first time I acknowledged to myself that there was a deep affection for this beautiful woman came when I sent her a picture and inscribed it, "All my love." Before that, neither of us had ever mentioned "love." In her letters, Ariane had been very careful in trying not to arouse me. She felt it was not fair to build up the hopes of a man who did not know when he would be getting out of prison. But she could tell by the tone of my letters that I was very much encouraged by our relationship.

During 1962 Ariane had a lingering feeling that she might be falling in love with a man she had never met. In the summer of 1962, while on the Riviera again, she acknowledged in her diary it was fact. "It's preposterous," she wrote. "The idea sounds abnormal, but I've become so obsessed with the thought of Sam that everything else seems insignificant. Even my beautiful Riviera and the crazy life I lead here is no longer attractive."

In December, she decided to do something about it. She would come to the United States and try to visit me. She would find out whether our relationship was friendship or love—and live with it. She wrote to Marion officials and asked permission to see me, but they refused. Determined to see me, she decided to come anyway. She would stand in front of the institution door until they let her in.

On Christmas Eve, 1962, she wrote, "I know how terribly lonely you must be tonight. And how you long to sit around a warm fireplace with Young Sam and admire the Christmas tree decorations, while listening to the Christmas music. I know how you long to once more be a father to your boy and to be able to select his gifts yourself. How I wish that these years in prison have not turned you against the human race."

The next night, she wrote in her diary, "For over a year, I am inwardly in love with Sam Sheppard. A man I've never seen. A man I know little about, except that the world thinks he is a killer. In January, I am going to America to see him. What will this meeting be like? Will it be the great moment in my life for my fluctuating, penetrating heart which has always been so full of fantasy and dreams?"

I didn't know exactly when she was coming, but I wanted to see her. Through the help of some friends at Marion, the edict against her visiting me was lifted, though she didn't know it at the time she left Europe. The letter advising her of visiting privileges arrived after she departed.

The whole thing seemed unbelieveable to me. I asked myself, "What does a beautiful, wealthy woman with the world in the palm of her hand—with more suitors than she could handle—want from a guy like me?" I was afraid to let myself believe that she was really coming. It was just a defensive reaction, resulting from the myriads of previous disappointments. I was even afraid to believe that

Ariane existed in the first place. Since I had no idea exactly what date she would arrive, there was very little apprehension.

Ariane arrived in New York on January 13th and spent several days in the city. She was actually afraid to call my brother, Steve, and kept putting it off for a week. Finally, on the 20th, she called and said she would arrive in Cleveland in two days. Steve picked her up at the airport and on the way to her hotel, asked her pointedly, "What would you say if my brother would fall in love with you? Have you ever considered that possibility."

"Yes," she answered. "That's why I am here. Because I too think I am in love with him and want to make sure. I think it is unfair to build up any dreams in his mind under these circumstances."

"Then I must tell you frankly," Steve said, "that I am under the impression that my brother is already in love with you."

During that first meeting, I learned, Steve told Ariane that he had discussed our relationship on numerous occasions. And he had. "Ariane has not made any promises to you," he told me shortly before she arrived in this country. "All she said was that she'd visit you. Maybe this is just one of her madcap extravaganzas—visiting a man in prison. It could be a foolish notion of a rich girl with too much time on her hands and nothing sensible to fill it with. Maybe she just wants an excuse to visit America and you're it."

Steve told Ariane about making this statement to me. "But, I had the distinct impression that my brother was not listening to a word I was saying," he related. "That's why I asked you the question. I'm sure you know that I'm very close to my brother, and if I can help it, I don't want him hurt any more than he has been. If this is only one of your gags to amuse yourself," Steve continued, "nobody objects to that. All I ask is that you make this clear to my brother —that you are only visiting, that you like him, but that's that."

"Yes, these are my sentiments, too. Otherwise I wouldn't be here now," Ariane answered.

The next night, Ariane boarded a train for Marion. Since I was on semi-honor status, we were allowed to have lunch together, and she carried with her on the train a large bag filled with cold meats, cheeses, bread, butter and fresh fruit. It was nineteen degrees below zero that night and to make matters worse the train's heating system broke down. By the time Ariane reached Marion after midnight she was half frozen.

She was up early, so that she could be at the institution by nine in the morning. She grabbed a cab, stopped at a doughnut shop, purchased a dozen doughnuts, and proceeded to the prison. When she stepped up to the counter, a guard asked, "You're coming to see Dr. Sam, aren't you?"

"Yes," she answered.

"Well, have a seat there," the guard replied. A young Negro man, about twenty-two or twenty-three, was pacing the waiting room floor. He was dressed in civilian clothes, as he had just been released from custody. His parents apparently had promised to pick him up, but were very late. A prison official came out and told him that if they didn't arrive that day, he could spend another night at the prison. The young man said he would rather spend the night out in the cold.

When the official left, Ariane told the rather disappointed youth that she would be finished with her visit by mid-afternoon and that if his parents hadn't arrived by then, she would give him enough money to take a taxi to town and spend the night in a hotel.

"Oh that won't be necessary," he said, "because my parents promised." A few moments later they arrived. The young man walked out the door and embraced his parents in the wind and snow. Ariane stood at the window and watched, so touched by the emotional scene that she failed to hear the loudspeaker booming, "Sheppard visitor."

Finally, a guard came up to her and said, "Didn't you want to see Dr. Sam Sheppard?" She said yes, the guard checked her purse and the bag of food, and led her to the visiting room.

I had no idea Ariane would be visiting me on that day. Having worked late the night before, a guard had to wake me from sound sleep, to tell me there was a visitor to see me. It was so cold in the place, that I had on a sweater and a bathrobe. Three blankets and the rug from the floor covered me in the bed.

"There's a woman out there to see you in a mink coat that will knock your eyes out," the guard said.

"Oh, bull," I answered, thinking the visitor was one of my lawyers or a minister. He finally convinced me that it was Ariane. I dressed quickly and hurried to the visiting room and sat down on the edge of a big table, with my back to the doorway. I tried to pretend that I was relaxed, but wasn't to say the least.

When she walked into the room, I stood up and walked toward her, with a big smile on my face and said, "Hi, how about giving me a big kiss." She gave me a kiss on the cheek and I knew she was real.

She had platinum blond hair and exquisite features. She was wearing a smartly tailored suit and, just as the guard had said, she was draped in mink. She was even more beautiful than in the pictures she had sent me. "Which table would you prefer?" I asked. We finally selected one by the window, sat down and started to talk. We both relaxed and it was as if we had known each other for years. We both knew it had been love before first sight.

I told her about intimate things of the past. I didn't know whether she wanted to know something about the case, and some of my feelings about it, but told her whether she wanted to know or not. I was surprised how much she knew about the case—names, events, dates.

After a while, one of the guards brought in the bagful of food Ariane had carried from Cleveland. Suddenly, she remembered she had forgotten to slice the bread. "We need a knife," I said to one of the guards. "Could you get us one? Or could you cut this bread for us?" The guard brought a sixteen-inch bread knife and left it with us. "Hey, you're trusting me an awful lot," was my comment. "You must have confidence in me, haven't you?"

"Come on, Doc," the guard answered. "You're not fooling me. Stop talking nonsense." We all got a big laugh out of it.

As we became more engrossed in the conversation, we found we were talking about our mutual futures. I was telling Ariane of a tentative plan in which I would go to India to establish a clinic, if and when my sentence was commuted or parole was granted. Suddenly, the conversation stopped for a moment and then I spoke again, "Ariane, I'm in no position to propose to you. Although, I would love to ask this question more than anything in the world."

"I wish you would go ahead and ask, Sam," she replied. "Because the answer is going to be yes."

"I even have something I can give you as a symbol of our engagement," I said, then got up from the table and placed a sterling silver chain and dove of peace—with "Sam-Ariane" on the back—around her neck. I was so nervous I could barely fasten the clasp. My hands were trembling. I bent down closer to her neck and smelled her perfume. "What kind of perfume are you wearing?" She told me and I replied that it reminded me of a fragrance I had smelled years before.

It took every bit of restraint I could muster to keep from grabbing her in my arms and kissing her. But, there were guards peering at us through a large window above and they were a restraining influence. Ariane gave me a large gold coin in return.

Shortly before the end of the visit, the Catholic priest, to whom I had shown Ariane's Christmas letter, came into the room to meet Ariane. He had been so impressed by the letter that he insisted on seeing her. We had a nice chat and he said that since Ariane had come so far to visit me, he would see what he could do about arranging for her to visit me briefly the next day. But the superintendent refused the request.

In all, we spent four and a half hours together. As the moment for her departure neared, we both stood up. Ariane kissed me on the cheek. Guard or no guards, I grabbed her in my arms and kissed her on the lips—so eagerly I almost broke her back.

It was three fifteen p.m., when she turned and left. We were engaged, but neither of us knew when we would see each other again. In the short span of little more than four hours, we both knew that we were deeply in love—that fate had ordained a future for us together.

For me, life as I had known it ended early on July 4, 1954, when Marilyn was murdered by the savage who invaded our home. It took nearly eight and a half years of adversity and imprisonment for me to begin feeling like a human being again. It was like a Cinderella story in reverse—as if Ariane had tapped me with a magic wand and said, "You're alive again."

21

Lee Bailey had encountered little success in his efforts to win a lie detector test for me as the first step toward exoneration, but significant progress was made on another front and there was at least a slight chance that my prison term would be shortened. After more than a year of written and verbal communication with Governor Michael V. DiSalle and the Ohio Pardon and Parole Commission, my brother, Steve, and Lee succeeded in petitioning for a hearing of commutation of my minimum ten-year sentence. The petition called for commutation of my second degree murder sentence to manslaughter, thus opening the way for immediate parole.

The hearing was scheduled for January 29th—five days after Ariane's visit at Marion—at the Ohio Pardon and Parole Commission headquarters in Columbus. While he strongly believed I should forego early release and work toward total exoneration, Lee Bailey agreed to plead my case before the commission. I, too, wanted my name and record cleared, but after eight and a half years in prison, my first inclination was toward winning freedom so I could marry Ariane immediately and Young Sam could join us as a family.

Having conditioned myself to hope for the best, but expect the worst, I refused to allow myself the pleasure of being overly hopeful that the board would act favorably. And I tried to impart the same feeling to Ariane during her visit. A turndown, I told her, probably would mean waiting another two long years before I was eligible for parole.

Ariane returned to Cleveland after our first meeting, told Steve and Betty of our secret engagement, accepted congratulations, and asked if she could attend the commutation hearing. Steve reasoned that the public would find out about our romance sooner or later and there was no good reason for hiding it. He told Ariane that if it was all right with Lee Bailey for her to attend the hearing, she could go. He telephoned Bailey in Boston and told him of our engagement. Bailey agreed to her attending the session.

Bailey felt that if Ariane was going to be in Columbus, it would be best for the press to be notified in advance. He let the word out on January 28th, the day before the hearing, and bedlam resulted. Ariane was besieged with calls from newspaper reporters and television newsmen. She answered questions as politely and completely as she could. She realized that poor press relations during my trial had hurt my case and she made up her mind to be sincere and try to win over the news people as friends. Some of the newsmen and women immediately labeled her as a fraud—an actress who had been engaged by the Sheppard family to build sympathy for me during the clemency proceedings. It didn't take long before most recognized that she was the real thing—a woman with a cause.

No one was more surprised than I that the word was out about our engagement. When Ariane left Marion, it was agreed that for the time being the engagement would remain a closely guarded secret, shared by us, a few relatives and my attorneys. Even Young Sam didn't know about it. He was told of our romance by the chaplain at Culver, who had heard the news on the radio. This was a hell of a shock for Chip.

On the next day, January 29th, Ariane walked into the Ohio Pardon and Parole Commission headquarters in Columbus with Lee Bailey and was greeted by a barrage of newsreel cameramen, photographers and reporters. Shades of the "Roman holiday." Again, she managed to be polite in face of some barbed questioning by cynical, unbelieving newsmen.

Once the hearing was underway, Bailey reluctantly plead for commutation of my sentence. "I would rather he stayed in (prison) so I can litigate and prove him innocent," he told the commission. "If he is freed, the question of guilt becomes moot." Then he added, "I'm his attorney, not his soul . . . he is asking for commutation of his sentence."

Lee apologized to the commission for the "sensationalism" that had been created by Ariane's entrance into the Sheppard story, but said that she had been in communication with me for a number of years and had met with me at the Marion Correctional Institution for the first time the previous Thursday. He added that we planned to marry when I was freed. Bailey told the commissioners that on the basis of my fine record since being sent to prison in July, 1955, I was deserving of early release. He asked the group to recommend to Ohio's new Governor, James Rhodes, that my sentence be commuted to manslaughter, paving the way for quick release.

Cuyahoga County, which had extracted more than a pound of

flesh from me over the years, was represented by Gertrude Bauer Mahon, an assistant county prosecutor and widow of John Mahon, who had prosecuted my case in the first place and in the middle of the trial won a seat on the common pleas bench. Mrs. Mahon pleaded with the commission to reject the bid for early release, describing me as an unrepentant killer. Ariane, who sat passively through the hearing, broke into tears when Mrs. Mahon vigorously protested commutation of the sentence. After three and a half hours of arguments, the commission took the matter under advisement, indicating it would have a decision within a few days.

The night after the hearing, Ariane was interviewed on one of the Columbus television stations and her deportment proved to be a great morale builder for the men at the Marion Institution. The newscaster asked her whether she would accompany me to India, if my release was granted and I established a clinic in Mahreha in one of the most rugged areas of India. Ariane answered firmly that she would go with me wherever I went.

Most of the men at Marion must have been watching the interview, because when she made that statement, a spontaneous cheer went up in the place. The men slapped and banged the walls and hollered. Even the hardened gunmen and safe-crackers were touched by her statement. They knew this was a solid woman—a woman worth living and fighting for. I started to cry.

Of course, the news of the engagement also touched off some good-natured kidding, especially since it had come after our first visit. "You're a pretty fast worker, Doc," one prisoner said.

That night I also saw a film clip of Ariane being interviewed. It prompted me to write the following to my family:

As I viewed Ariane facing that mob of unfriendly cameras, I was struck hard by the fact that her display of love and loyalty was exactly what Marilyn would have shown, if given the chance. From time to time, the "sob sisters" have asked, "But who will speak for Marilyn?" smugly knowing in their minds that no one can actually speak for a dead person. However, for those few who really and truly would like to have a statement from Marilyn (such as you Chip), Ariane said it all, in her way, on Tuesday in Columbus. This is just part of why I have come to adore Ariane so fervently and completely.

Within hours after the hearing was over, a newspaper broke the story that Ariane was the half-sister of Frau Joseph Goebbels, the wife of Adolph Hitler's former minister of propaganda and one of the most evil men in the Nazi regime. Before all the facts were accounted for, Ariane was being accused of having been a Nazi herself.

Ariane and her sister, Magda, had the same father, Oskar Ritschel, but not the same mother. The sister was about twenty years older than Ariane, who was only about a year old when Magda's marriage to Dr. Goebbels took place, against the wishes of her father.

Ariane's father was a wealthy industrialist who had no use for the Nazi party and Dr. Goebbels. At that time, it was virtual self-destruction for a German to be an industrialist and not a member of the Nazi party. Herr Ritschel apparently managed to get away with it only because the German propaganda minister was his son-in-law.

Ariane recalled that as a youngster she could remember her father and Dr. Goebbels having violent arguments over the policies of the Nazi party. On more than one occasion, she recalls, Dr. Goebbels shouted, "If you weren't my father-in-law, I'd throw you in a concentration camp." Son-in-law or not, the Ritschel family lived in constant fear that harm would come to the mild-mannered, industrialist-inventor.

Herr Ritschel died in 1941 when Ariane was twelve. Members of the Nazi party boycotted the last rites, an indication of the contempt in which they held him. Ariane was only fifteen when the war ended. She was kept hidden in an attic for several months in a home in East Germany so that she would not be raped by the invading Russian soldiers.

No, Ariane was not a Nazi. Due to her age when the war started and ended, she couldn't have been one if she wanted to. But, misinformation published in the newspapers gave people the impression that she was. It took her a long time to convince the skeptics that though her older half-sister (who later committed suicide with Goebbels) had married a top-flight Third Reich official, Ariane detested the Nazis with a passion.

My concern for Ariane and the treatment she was getting in the press virtually obviated any anxiety that had built up over the impending decision by the Pardon and Parole Commission. I didn't have long to wait for the verdict. On January 31st, two days after the hearing, the commission voted four-to-none against recommending that Governor James Rhodes commute my sentence to manslaughter, thus clearing my way to an early release. In turning down the plea, the commission said it had found five black marks on my record, including three reprimands for oversleeping. In short, then, the commission turned me down because I overslept three times in nine years.

The commission ruling was only in the form of a recommendation to the new governor. He could have acted as he pleased. But Rhodes chose to follow the advice of the commission and closed the clemency matter.

On the day of the commission ruling, Maury Koblentz, Ohio's Commissioner of Corrections, visited me at Marion. His first act was to cut off visiting and mailing privileges between Ariane and me. The confrontation with Koblentz took place in the office of the Marion Superintendent.

"You'd better send that blonde back to Europe," Koblentz said to me.

I was in no mood to take any guff from him or anyone else. "Listen Koblentz," I retorted, "if you call her 'that blonde' again, your wife is a - - - - -." He told me he would put me in the hole for that remark. "Go ahead," I told him, "but don't ever make any reflections on my fiancée." The Superintendent was sitting there and didn't know what to do.

"You might as well send my son along with her (Ariane) because this is my life and reason for living," I continued. "After all these years, she is the reason I have some get up and go. Now I feel like a man again. Don't ever tell me to send that woman back because I'm going to call you some names you won't like. You can't hurt me as long as this girl is behind me."

Koblentz also apparently was upset because Ariane said as long as I was in prison she would continue to air my case in the national press and even suggested that the Russian press would be interested in a system of American justice that keeps an innocent man in prison for nine years. Ariane said that as long as Dr. Sam remains in prison —Radio Free Europe lies.

He said that if he were me he would encourage—in fact tell— Ariane not to create publicity. I suggested to him rather forcefully that if he didn't want additional publicity, he should restore Ariane to mailing and visiting privileges, especially since by attaining honor status I had earned the right to have her write and visit me. "You'll get very little publicity that way," I said. "But, if you want a lot of publicity, just keep on this track. This is no ordinary gal."

"Is that a threat," he retorted. "No," I replied, "that's a promise.

I know of what this woman is capable of doing. I know that she is not going to knuckle under to you or anyone else."

Koblentz returned to Columbus and indicated to newsmen that he felt the whole engagement story might be a hoax. He said that after a two-hour interview with me, he still questioned the validity of the engagement story and thought it might have been concocted to create sympathy for me. He said that in separate interviews, I had told conflicting stories about the engagement. "I asked him if he had proposed and after a long discussion with him, he said, 'In a way I did, and in a way, I didn't,'" Koblentz told newsmen. "I asked him if he had talked marriage at all and he said 'yes,' contrary to what he told prison officials. He said he told her he wasn't in a position to marry anyone but told Mrs. Tebbenjohanns if he were she'd be the one. I asked Sheppard if he didn't definitely propose to her, did she propose to him and he said, 'In effect she did, yes.'"

Koblentz got his answer on the engagement the next day, after Steve and Betty visited me in Marion. Steve brought a selection of engagement rings from a jewelry friend in Cleveland for my inspection. I picked out a two-stone ring in a simple yellow-gold setting and told Steve to give it to her for me that night. He did and we were officially engaged.

Steve said he was surprised to see me so cheerful in the wake of the commission turndown. He said that prison officials and guards were a lot less friendly when he arrived than they had been in the past, before all of the publicity about Ariane. "We're in the doghouse," I told Steve and Betty, "We've focused attention of the public on the prison system of this state. Tell Ariane I adore her."

We discussed Koblentz's visit of the previous day. Koblentz was furious, I told Steve, and added that there definitely was the prospect of some action by the corrections chief, but it didn't worry me. "Who can lower the boom on me any more than has been done already?" I asked. "How can I be any more in prison, or any more free than I am, as long as I know Ariane loves me."

The next day, Steve received a letter from Koblentz, directing him not to visit me again until he cleared the visit with Koblentz's office. The letter had arrived too late to stop Steve from making the February 1st trip to Marion. Koblentz said he wanted to discuss an important matter regarding my rehabilitation before Steve visited with me again. My brother agreed to meet Koblentz in Columbus on February 8th.

Meanwhile, the newspapers were having a field day with Ariane's visit to Marion. It was described as a "lover's lane" meeting, a tryst and you name it. From the tone of the articles you would have thought we turned the Marion visitor's room into a bedroom. The only affection shown during the entire four-and-a-half-hour meeting was a kiss on the cheek, a kiss on the lips and some hand-holding— all under the watchful eyes of prison guards who peered at us throughout the entire period.

Koblentz's action was not long in coming. About four in the morning of February 5th, an officer woke me in my cell at Marion. "Sam, I'm sorry, but I hate to do this," the prison officer said. "We've got to take you to Columbus and we've got to get you there before six o'clock." They put leg, arm, and neck chains on me and led me to a car for the trip to the Ohio Penitentiary. It was as though I was John Dillinger.

All of my belongings were left behind, including more than one hundred fifty dollars worth of jewelry material, my typewriter, and other personal items. The office said the material would be sent along later in the day. When the belongings finally reached me, a number of things were missing. Officials had conveniently left the cell door open and other prisoners helped themselves.

We arrived at the Ohio Penitentiary at six o'clock in the morning and I was put into solitary confinement. Apparently Koblentz didn't want press coverage on my arrival and felt that by getting me there before the regular prison reporters arrived, he could avoid it. He obviously wasn't proud of the way my transfer was being handled, but evidently felt that he had to get me back in a maximum security situation so that he could dissuade Ariane from pursuing our romance any further.

Koblentz later announced my transfer to the press, but didn't say I was brought back in chains. He said he had ordered me back to the Ohio Penitentiary for violation of prison rules in my romance with Ariane. This, despite the fact that Marion officials had given written approval for Ariane's and my correspondence and for her visit to me. Koblentz said the transfer also was effected because of the "continuing efforts by persons related to or associated with Sheppard to defy or circumvent, directly or indirectly, an order which revoked visiting and mailing privileges of Mrs. Ariane Tebbenjohanns."

What may have been the clincher as far as Koblentz was concerned was a letter written by Ariane to me at Marion on February

2nd. The letter was returned to her as undeliverable. Ariane was desperate to communicate with me. She was a fighter and wouldn't give up. She rewrote the letter and sent it to the Columbus *Dispatch*, asking the newspaper to publish it so that "Sam has a chance to hear from me. I can think of no other way."

The letter was published in the Columbus *Dispatch*:

My dearest Sam,

As I have no permission to write to you or see you I am trying this unusual way to tell you how constantly my thoughts are with you. I am so excited since Steve last night put your engagement ring on my finger. How thoughtful of you—I really was content with the small silver chain of January 24th. I am so sorry there was so much noise over our engagement. I did keep it so secretly for nearly five days. I am so worried that this is harmful for you. The three of us went out for a quiet celebration dinner and as people saw the ceremony on TV they all congratulated me.

I do hope so very much to see Mr. Koblentz soon. You know, I can understand him because he has an important responsibility. But I am sure if I get a chance to talk with him that I can convince him of my reality and sincerity and I shall apologize for the big noise about me.

And you be a good boy, darling, as always—I am always at your side.

All my love,
Your Ariane

I didn't know anything about the letter until after I was taken back to the penitentiary. A convict who worked in the deputy warden's office showed me a copy of the letter. I was proud as could be that Ariane had used such imagination to communicate with me. Incidentally, she never did get a chance to talk with Koblentz. She requested appointments, but he ignored her.

Koblentz wouldn't discuss the matter with my fiancée, but he did have a heated conversation with Steve on the morning of February 8th, three days after my hasty transfer. According to Steve, Koblentz accused him of creating much of the publicity which from time to time had embarrassed the prison administration in connection with me. He charged that Ariane had created a "great and needless" disturbance.

"Before you go, Dr. Sheppard," Steve quoted Koblentz as saying, "I want it clearly understood between us that I want no more publicity on this or any other matter. I think we should come to an agreement on that." Steve said he then asked Koblentz whether Ariane could visit me once more before she returned to Germany. Koblentz said there would be no chance for her to visit. When Steve asked him when Ariane and I would be able to correspond, Koblentz responded with a cold and final, "Never."

Steve was then permitted to visit me at the Ohio Penitentiary. He relayed to me Koblentz's edict. My reaction was that they should keep up the publicity barrage and let the world know how I was being treated. "Steve," I said. "I could have settled for six months back in 1954 if I had been willing to lie and say that I killed Marilyn. Do you think I am going to give up now? They've already done everything to me they possibly can—I'm telling you to keep going, no matter what."

Then I told him to tell Ariane to "hold fast," not to leave the country, no matter what pressures were brought to bear. I would correspond with her one way or another. When Steve left the penitentiary, the press was out in force. He was asked to make a statement, and he did. "We will press on in every way and at every opportunity in our attempt to gain the freedom of my brother, Dr. Sam Sheppard," he said. "He has urged us to continue the fight on his behalf and we intend to do so."

Most of the editorial voices in the area were silent concerning my treatment, preferring instead to buy the Koblentz line that the entire Ariane episode was a well-conceived plan to win sympathy for me at the time of the commission hearing. But there was at least one dissent raised in the press and it came in the form of an editorial broadcast by WKRC in Cincinnati, a Taft Broadcasting Company station.

Entitled, "Injustice," the editorial said:

There is no doubt that justice, American style, is the finest administration of the law to be found anywhere. But in a few cases, an apparent injustice stands out in such a way as to almost negate the good legal procedures. And we question whether even an isolated injustice should be permitted in a land that prides itself on its quality of justice.

We speak of the Sam Sheppard case. We'll omit any comment on the original muddling in the investigation of this sensational murder. Let's update the Sheppard story.

Last week, Sheppard attorneys asked the Ohio Pardon and Parole Commission to reduce the charges against him to manslaughter—a perfectly legal, plausible and probable action under American justice. The commission voted no, the governor concurred. Again, a perfectly legal, plausible and probable action under American justice. Enter the apparent villains! The alert press heard rumors that there was a woman in the lonely life of Sam Sheppard. The press uncovered her name—thirty-three-year-old Ariane Tebbenjohanns, a German divorcée, pretty and blonde, and related to one of Hitler's notorious rats, Dr. Paul Joseph Goebbels.

Now, it's highly doubtful that Sheppard, his attorneys or his family, welcomed this revelation at such a sensitive time in Sheppard's long battle for freedom. If there was a culprit, it was the press—always alert to the activities of famous men, be they murderers or generals.

But the State Commissioner of Corrections, Maury Koblentz, seems to feel that Sheppard and his family have planned it this way. Mr. Koblentz has ordered Sheppard out of the limited freedom of the Marion Correctional Institution to the tighter security of the State Pen. He has banned Mrs. Tebbenjohanns as a visitor, and ruled that Sheppard cannot receive mail from her, or read newspapers for fear some obliging editor will publish a letter from Ariane to Sam.

Furthermore, Mr. Koblentz has informed the Sheppard family that the state will not tolerate any more sensational developments in the case. Mr. Koblentz attributes his actions to, quote, "The continuous efforts by persons either related or associated with Sheppard to defy or circumvent, directly or indirectly, an order, which revoked the visiting and mailing privileges of Mrs. Tebbenjohanns." It is felt, says Mr. Koblentz, it is felt that Sheppard had knowledge of such efforts.

Is this American justice? No hearing, no witnesses, no trial, no jury, no judge—it is just felt.

As Commissioner of Corrections, Mr. Koblentz ought to realize there are at least two facets of the human mind and soul that are beyond correction: the desire for freedom and the involuntary ability to fall in love.

This was one hell of an editorial. It showed that there were some people on the outside that could look at the situation with some insight. It gave me a lot of courage and guts, to put it bluntly.

Once it became plain to Koblentz that Ariane was not going to whimper, pack up, and leave, I was informed that no punitive action would be taken against me—that I had done nothing wrong, but was returned to the penitentiary only because of the publicity Ariane had generated. I could have any job desired, including the hospital, prison officials said. Since winning parole was uppermost in my mind, I requested and was given an assignment as a teacher in the regular prison school, enabling me to accumulate good time toward eventual release. My assignment was in the high school section and the courses included mathematics, biology, chemistry, and botany.

Prison officials made out a new mailing list for me and it included my family and son. I was asked to list a friend on the list and the suggestion was made that Mary and Bud Brown be put back in that category. I used this—more or less as a test and put down Ariane—

my fiancée—as a friend, knowing damn well they had absolutely no legitimate reason to rule her off the list. But they did anyway. Thereafter, I refused to list a friend.

They asked me who should be notified in case of death and to whom my body should be sent. I named Ariane. They didn't know what to do. "We can't do this," they told me. "Don't notify anyone," was my answer. I just refused to give them the satisfaction of naming my brothers or my son.

The hypocrisy of prison officials was unbelievable. Early in February, Young Sam wrote a letter to Ariane, in answer to her first letter to him. Mistakenly, he mailed a letter to her to me and sent a letter meant for me to her. Prison officials would not let me forward the letter to her. So, he wrote her again:

Dear Ariane,
I'm sure that since my dad loves you I will also once we get to know each other. It was somewhat of a shock when I heard, but it sounds great. I think you will find that I am not really much of a letter writer, but I will try to do better. I'm sorry that I am a little short on time right now and I have yet to write dad so I will write you a longer letter soon.
All my love,
Sam (little)

It took me about two weeks from the time of my early morning move back to Columbus to communicate directly with Ariane. The first letter was smuggled out of the penitentiary by a fellow convict's lawyer in a packet of legal documents.

The letter, dated February 19, 1963, said in part:

My beloved Ariane,
Though I wrote to you yesterday, the letter was returned as I expected. The letter is still in my possession and I hope to give it to Lee Bailey or some Atty. as soon as one of them gets on the ball and gets down here to see me. There is some other pretty important business which should be discussed with them relaitve to "hypno-analysis" which is the reason for the messages (Requesting to see Lee). Naturally, I do wish to send word to you and receive same, but I hope Lee doesn't think that I would ask him to come from Boston just to send a love letter or messages to you. If he does think this, however, HE IS RIGHT—I WOULD ASK HIM TO COME FROM AFRICA JUST TO SAY "I LOVE YOU ARIANE." So since he knows me pretty well and Steve knows me better, likely they think my requests are relative to lesser important (in their opinion) business. I hope you are sending me some sort of mail every day so that it may be proven that your mail has actually been returned. This is illegal, you know, since I signed an

O.K. TO CENSOR MY MAIL ONLY. Nothing on the waiver blanks says anything about returning mail unopened or opened, for that matter. One of my friends here had some similar difficulty a few years ago and he took the thing to court. . . .

What do you think about our getting married while I'm still locked up? We'd sure get to visit and write. It would be both wonderful and frustrating at the same time and I'm sure you know what I mean. I don't think we could really miss each other any more than we do now though and this may be the best way to establish visiting and mailing on a normal level. If we should consider this is the practical thing to do (to hell with the practical thing—WILL YOU MARRY ME HERE?) the Catholic Church is the only one which seems to be courageous enough to try here. This means converting. It was about one p.m. when one of the hacks (guards) brought me a pass to see the Warden (M. j. Koloski). We had quite a talk—'til quarter of four. Midway in the discussion he said, "You really do love that gal don't you. I've never seen you so affected emotionally." . . . Koloski is a pretty good guy, but he works for Koblentz and he is looking for an "out" without giving much in return. Though he says that, "If your fiancée can control your brother and your Atty. Bailey for another week or so, I think I can talk Mr. Koblentz into some agreement. This situation is obviously not fair to your Ariane and you." He added that I must refrain from sending messages to you via Steve's letters for now or he'd have to return them to me for rewrite. I was in the process of testing to see just how far I could go with these messages to you and now I know.

Now, DO YOU HAVE YOUR VISA APPROVED YET TO STAY DURING THE NEXT TIME PERIOD? If so and you can stay . . . stay right with me and possibly spend some time working on the India situation if the parole authorities think it is workable. And also you must have a chance to see Chip and spend some time with him, for he needs you too. When you can get down to Gatlinburg, Tennessee and see Mary and Bud Brown this should be done, too, and if you could take Chip with you, you would be giving them a gift beyond their dreams.

Assuming you are staying for a reasonable period, I will tell Mr. Koloski that you will contain things until he can talk with Koblentz. . . . Darling, be sure you get your visa okayed or whatever, as soon as possible because they will try to have me call you off during this period, then try to mess up your visa so that we would have little or no time to raise hell until you must go. You must have given this some thought and I know you have the MOXIE to handle things, but we have got to stay ahead of these ————. You're too much of a lady for me to print the name.

On the publicity side of things I think it would harm nothing if you continue or resume to let TV, radio, and reporters for the papers inter-

view you. IF THEY GET AN O.K. FROM KOBLENTZ. Be your charming self
with the news people; if they are not given an interview or whatever they
want within reason, let Koblentz take the blame. (It's his rap and let
him take his own rap, as the saying goes around here!) In fact, I think
you should encourage interviews, just as soon as permission is granted
from K. Kill Koblentz with Kindness and the news people will KILL HIM
WITH WORDS. If he does O.K. one or more interviews, say exactly what
you think. [He O.K.'d the interview.] Don't hold back in any way. If
anyone wants to know why you must have permission from Koblentz in
order to give an interview, tell them straight that if you don't, "He will
further punish Sam, his family and me." My love, all of it, your Sam.
YOU ARE THE MOST WONDERFUL THING THAT HAS EVER HAPPENED TO ME!
THE WORDS I LOVE YOU ARE SO INADEQUATE, BUT THEY WILL HAVE TO DO
UNTIL I TAKE YOU IN MY ARMS WHEN WE ARE FINALLY ALONE. THIS LOVE
FOR YOU, ARIANE, WHICH IS BEYOND WHAT I THOUGHT WAS POSSIBLE, IS
INTENSIFIED BY SEPARATION! NEVER LEAVE ME.

                                                                    Sam.

There was no easing of the mail or visiting ban by Koblentz.
Steve wrote to Governor Rhodes and asked for help and I followed
with my own letter, but the governor preferred to leave the matter
in the hands of Koblentz. With no allowed channel of communications, I again had to resort to smuggling a letter to Ariane. This was
carried out of the penitentiary in a cigarette lighter. I typed the
letter on two sides of onionskin paper, folded it neatly and tucked
it into the bottom of one section of a cigarette lighter. Then I
replaced the cotton and put the two sections together. When one
of my visitors wanted to light a cigarette, I handed him the lighter.
He lit the cigarette and casually put the lighter in his pocket, as if
it were his own. The next day the letter was in Ariane's hands. It
said in part:

My very dearest, darling,
    Like you, I am compelled to write to you every day so that I may say
again and again, ARIANE, I LOVE YOU. Your question sent via the Atty.
was so wonderful because it expresses the little fear that creeps into my
mind too. "Darling, will you love me tomorrow?" YES, YES, YES, MY BE-
LOVED. I shall love you forever—even beyond death our love will live on
and be remembered with the great loves of all time. You know this is
true dearest, but I, like you want to know—will you love me tomorrow?
Ask Betty to tell me, dear Betty.
    You know that I would rather write to you in longhand, but use the
machine so that more message can be placed in a small space. Also typing is safe until such time as I might sign this letter, anyone could have

typed it up, you know better, but you are intelligent, lovely, beautiful, loyal, wonderful, exotic & LOVED. (OH HOW YOU ARE LOVED.)

Anyway, Baby, I just received some information which might be what we are looking for at present. Hold onto your hat because I hope it's the answer. In two states that I know of, Nevada and Missouri, people have and do get married "by proxy." Wouldn't you and the rest of the family like to make a trip to Missouri? It would be nice. This proxy business is a bit frustrating in a way, but just so we can get your citizenship and our visits, I'm sure you will reserve the marriage consummation for a date later when I may take my rightful place in your arms.

The next smuggled letter went out just a few days later. A veteran convict, was due to make a court appearance in connection with his case. Though, I impressed upon him the danger of smuggling out a letter, he insisted that he be allowed to try. "They'll search you upside down—with and without your clothes," I told him. But he insisted and we conjured up a scheme, which worked.

I wrote the letter and stuffed it into a small, plastic pill bottle, slightly smaller than a package of Lifesavers. Then, I took a package of Lifesavers apart, put a couple of Lifesavers at each end of the plastic tube and rewrapped it with foil and the colored wrapper. It looked perfect. It should have. I worked about four hours on the package with a little set of surgical forceps.

The next morning he left for his court appearance. The first thing officials did before they allowed him out of prison was to shake him down damn good. He emptied all his pockets, tossing his comb, wallet and the package of Lifesavers on the counter. They looked in his pants cuffs, the inside seams of his shirt, his trousers, underpants, belt. They made him strip and checked his ears, nose, and other parts. All the time, the message they were searching for was right on top of the counter in the pack of Lifesavers. Satisfied that he had no message they let him go to court with his attorneys.

When he arrived at the courtroom, he broke open the Lifesavers, opened the bottle, took out the letter, smoothed it out and put it into an envelope he had carried with his legal papers. The address was written inside the envelope. He copied it on the front of the envelope, then scribbled inside, "My daughter's expecting and if it's a girl, her middle name will be Ariane."

The letter reached Ariane. It was written on onionskin paper, with one side of the message typed in black and the other in red, so that both sides were legible:

Mi Querida,

Words just cannot express my consuming love for you. I live for you now and the indication that you feel the same way about me is even more intoxicating than ever. Steve and Betty may think I over-express these thoughts in my letters, but those letters are to you, Darling (my dearest). The statements to the other members of the family are thrown in merely to say honestly; this is a letter to the whole family. Betty, Steve, Dorothy and Rich are likely surprised at some of my statements because I never have been a wordy sort of guy. I never wore my heart on my sleeve, as Betty has likely told you. . . .

You're wonderful, do you know this? How can you be so beautiful, lovely, and smart as well as loyal, is hard to figure. Most girls are beautiful and dumb, or smart and ugly, or some mixture like that. You are proving to a lot of people, including most of the cons, that there are fine, wonderful women left out there in the world. The guys who have lost their women because of their troubles, or have been let down by their wives, leading to their trouble, have recovered faith in womanhood. (They hope that some day, somehow, they might find a gal like you. The great emotion called "Hope" has returned to them.) To the guys who have wives and girls that are sticking to them, you have and are showing the world and themselves just how fine their gals are. (These fellas live day-to-day with the agitators telling them their wives will send "Dear John letters" and divorce them any day.) You my beloved, have actually cut down a great deal of this type of talk and agitation. Now you know a little more about how the guys here feel about you, but to hell with them; I LOVE YOU. . . .

Now darling, the facts are that the more ORGANIZED HELL, like the Taft editorial, that is raised out there, the less pressure on me here. . . . Anybody else should be encouraged to attack this one person on the prejudice theme. You should not make any statement. K. is going to try to hurt me with the parole board. This is a known fact and we can never make him like us or Steve. If he is openly and repeatedly accused of the prejudice theme and it is stated that he is presumptuous enough to threaten my parole, which he has through ————, he will be rendered less and less effective. Three and a half years ago the head nurse at the hospital paid one of the local "trigger" men to knife me when he could find me alone in the shower or locker room. Learning this, I sought out the trigger man, (whom I hardly knew), asked him to come into the ring a minute to show me something; whereupon I beat the bejesus out of him. I made it known that he was supposed to knife me; for this reason he couldn't afford to "fill the contract" that he had made. The same principle holds here.

If we should be married by proxy, it will be obvious that this was forced by this prejudice ruling. It will not hurt me with the Parole Board.

So, Baby, I think that you should quietly turn the news people loose (with no statement from you since Mr. K. won't let you), quietly get married in Nevada; then quietly present yourself to the Office of Correction for O.K. for visit. If no O.K., get a court order as my wife, which I consider you now anyway. Believe me, My BELOVED, the above is the way. I'm not encouraging pressure merely to prove my love for you. I wouldn't endanger my parole.

I was certainly happy to get this letter out to Ariane, but no happier than the convict who took it. Beating the shakedown artists was the high point of his many years in prison. He didn't stop talking about it for days. That's the convict mind, I guess. He had a heart disease but no lack of heart.

The original idea for a proxy marriage—discussed in the smuggled letters—was conceived by a chaplain at the Ohio Penitentiary, who informed me that it was legal in the state and offered to help in any way he could. Somehow word of his suggestion reached prison officials and he was told that if I ever called at the chapel again, he would be relieved of his post.

With the prison chapel out of the question for a proxy or regular marriage, we cast around for another method. As the letters show, we came up with the fact that proxy marriages were allowed in at least two other states. Word of our plan was relayed to Koblentz by my brother, Steve, as a form of a threat. Steve apparently felt that when faced with prospect of a proxy marriage, Koblentz might relent on the question of visits and mail privileges. Steve also leaked word of the possible proxy marriage to the press. Koblentz moved quickly to head off the wedding, by pronouncing in no uncertain terms that a proxy marriage would be put on my record and held against me when it was time for parole.

That was enough for Ariane. While I was willing to risk the commissioner's wrath, she decided against it, feeling that the action in the face of his warning would seriously jeopardize my parole. When she was interviewed on a television news show and asked why she decided against going through with the marriage, Ariane told the reporter point blank about the threat to my parole. Then she said she dare not talk about it further, for fear of reprisal to me.

Most of Ariane's correspondence with me during this period immediately following my return to the penitentiary came in the form of messages brought by my relatives and attorneys and in the form of greeting cards, which were unsigned. Some bore fictitious signatures and were mailed from different parts of the country by her friends.

Several convicts who were released during that period carried messages for me. On several occasions, relatives of other convicts called Ariane and asked whether they could relay a message through their sons or brothers from Ariane to me.

Shortly after the Lifesaver letter, we decided that smuggling letters was risky business. Eventually, I would be caught and it would give prison officials an excuse to hang something on me. Guards befriended me and asked whether they could carry a letter or message out of the penitentiary. I trusted a few of them and on occasion they helped. To most, however, the answer was "No."

We worked out a clandestine method of correspondence, using a code in my letters to my family and my lawyers. A friend's attorney passed along the code and the instructions that all my letters should be forwarded to Ariane. At first, we used every third word in a sentence as the code word. While I had implicit trust in my friend and his attorney, I felt it was dangerous for too many people to know the code. When Young Sam came to visit me a few weeks later, we changed the code to a four-two combination. In other words, when you circled the fourth word of the first sentence, the second word of the second sentence, and then repeated this process throughout the letter, the message came through. Sometimes the code started with the first paragraph and other times with the second.

As an example, of the four-two code, here is a letter I sent to Lee Bailey, which in turn was given to Ariane. The code words are capitalized. Bailey did not know of this code; he sent my letters on to Ariane as he had been asked to do.

Dear Lee,

Finally got the material that was promised last week. Typed it up. Progress with care, but let's keep progressing. I have the most curious feeling of solitude and multitude.

Typing this law, **my** outlook should be pretty much like you pointed out when you were last here. My **destiny** may not mean something, but it would seem more likely, out of this place. In these cases **rests** a great deal of encouragement and though you must have most of them— I'd like to be sure and Jacques will wish to file them when you are through or have noted same. Seems **with** this type of federal law adherence just since 24-1-63 which applies to more than one of our claims; surely eventual relief with result. Do **you** still feel as strongly as you did?

Bet Alex and **you're** working pretty hard on all the technical angles so that no mis-step can be claimed. It's not only **the-pride** in your work; we understand that it is not possible to slip and try again. Reminiscent **of-my** specialty of neurosurgery; we just don't say, "Oops—slips—we'll try again." It seems that **life** or any portion thereof should be just as precious in a court of law as it is in the operating room. You **and** Alex do feel that way it seems; but you are rare attorneys.

Hope you can **delight** Betty and Steve by arriving in Cleveland in time for the trip and race. You **of** all people they claim will make a good crew member on the new craft. Sam agrees. It is really **my** opinion that more speed and faster curves would be more fun, but right now the sail-boat would be heaven. The **existence** of such things and all that goes with them is difficult to envision at times. Let us hope, **I** will not have to conjure up in my mind the memory of such things too much longer. I **love** to know the family is having a good time, but let's face it; I'd like to be with them physically for a change.

Please stop, if **you** will, to see me when you are in Ohio this next month. There's **so** much to talk over.

Fraternally,
Sam

This letter to my family also included a coded message to Ariane —in the third word method:

Dear Folks,

It's Friday morning and from what Steve said in one of his letters, he and Sam might be here this afternoon. I'll have to shave for a change and try to be ready so there will be no waiting. I got my hair cut real short and all the guys around here have to give an opinion. They vary from one extreme to the other and I still think the best idea is to shave and wear whatever color goes with my gal's shoes for the evening. Now what color would I wear with those "robin-egg" shoes? Silver, I guess.

Tell Sam **I** am really glad for him, and with him over the record he is establishing. He will **have** prepared himself much better than we, his uncles and Dad. We have **seen** how very much this will mean when it comes to medical school. He'll have **only** a part of the struggle which I experienced in college to catch up with the other pre-medical students. I think **you** kids know how I feel because you seem to react the same way. Many think **I** could not have done such a fine job with Chip as you and Betty have. This **I have** thought about and can't help but agree with. I have **dreamed** of the day that he and I can go skiing, fishing, working, and just being together. This will **only** be a brother or a "rappie" type of relationship, many of ·my friends tell me here, not the father-son relationship which has been viciously taken from us. Well, as **you** know it could be I think because we are sort of like rap-partners (partners in deviltry) or brothers. He and **I** are not bothered by the strains of the father-son relationship. And though **desire** to be with him and all of you burns in me constantly, we're both thankful for the fine relationship that you (Betty and Steve) have ushered along. I think **only** a guy in my situation could appreciate this and then I know that this is not true because the rest of you must understand perfectly; like the trip down to Gatlinburg; in order to come through every time just as I would have it. So to **you** again and again our eternal thanks.

Afternoon and **nothing** has happened yet so I guess the visit will come another day when your schedule permits. Young Sam **has** likely already got more than he can do with work, the new boat on the way, and everything that goes with it. Who is **the** lucky person that will get to train the new crew member? Sam will **power** the team of instructors since he'll want to spend a lot of time with Willi anyway. Say, perhaps **to** talk of instruction is silly since Willi may be a good sailor (like me— ha-ha-ha). On my **part** the water skis are much more stimulating, but I recall sailing with you and Steve when no one else would go out. It seems **you** were learning to sail and the weather was not good. You said **from** what I remember that we'd give each other lessons and everything would be O.K. 'cause you had read the book. That's good, **me** and you running around on the rocks of the breakwall with a high wind blowing (we had a ball). How did **they** ever score that race that we won? Surely you **can** recapture our first victory in the *Raven*. "We can't **take** credit for this win," you said, "we cut off some of the middle legs." That was **my** first thought that we really hadn't won. It seems **life** is like that often times since the converse is often a fact. Often track, **but** other sports too, the winner doesn't know he has won until someone informs him. It is **not** the big things so much as the many little things that I remember.

Some of **the** events might seem stupid or silly like the tree house we built every summer. However the **unfathomable** implications become more and more interesting. I would **love** to lean over the unstable tree house again and help you spit. Spit good **and** at the same time I'd grab your belt with one hand and a sturdy branch with the other so you wouldn't fall to the ground like the first time. My great **devotion** to you and Betty is difficult for me to express. We hope **that** you get the full impact of what is meant. You know **I** tried to explain during our last visit so that you must understand. You must **feel** very much the same on this subject; though Betty is right and we must not get too far out of kilter here or anywhere. Thanks Betty **for** keeping us straight most of the time. Let's hope **you** will have some help with this task in the near future.

Here lately **during** the last hours I have visited the twilight zone more constantly than ever. At the **time** of our visits, currents seemed to flow between us—feelings without words; emotions without language. This poignant **eternal** emotion is more deeply motivated than I realize myself so how can it be expressed with satisfaction?? Some of **our** best bards have tried through the ages and they had the same problems. I would **love** to be an eloquent guy now and I used to think such people were bags of wind. Guess I **will** have to be satisfied or get into some books quickly. As we **live,** "always learn something," as Dad use to tell us. He was **on** the ball—to say the least; I wish Jacques could have known him other than through us. Reminds me; **I** want to thank Mary, Irwin, and Jacques for the cards that arrived today. You know I **love** to get them on Friday so we can look at them all weekend. Say it, **you** are right, "Just like a school boy." It seems **so** remarkable—fantastic magic.

All my love,
Sam

Willi and Jacques were code names I used for Ariane. The cards from Mary, Irwin and Jacques were all from Ariane, but were signed with fictitious names. That was my way of letting her know that the cards were received. She sent a flood of cards for every occasion. Occasionally, she would write a letter for Chip to send over his signature and this contained the code we were using at the time.

I sent coded letters to everyone—my lawyers, my family, my son, my minister, and Art Miller, and would tell them all—"Send this letter to my fiancée." I couldn't even use the name "Ariane" in my correspondence. (Koblentz rule.) Only my family knew there was a code in the letters. Others thought that I wanted the correspondence to go on to her so that she would know what was going on, which was partially true.

It was extremely difficult working with the code, to make sense in the letters. Sometimes I just rambled along, groping for thoughts that would permit me to get a key word in the right place, so that the message to Ariane would have some continuity. At times, my family and friends must have thought I'd gone off my rocker. It was a tedious task at best, but it was far less risky than trying to smuggle letters from the penitentiary. We used their own mailing system to beat the problem. This urgent need to correspond and our mild success brought us even closer.

While Ohio correction authorities were extremely unfair to Ariane, federal immigration authorities were just the opposite. Hundreds of callers besieged the United States Immigration and Naturalization Service, accusing Ariane of being a Nazi and demanding that she be thrown out of the country. "You don't know the pressure we are under," one official told Ariane.

Ariane's original visitor's permit was for four weeks, but immigration officials quietly extended it for several months. The fact that my fiancée didn't pack up and flee in the face of the massive criticism heaped against her and the cries of "fake" and her sincerity in discussing my case, began to convince people she was for real.

"Ariane's Persistence Is Convincing the Skeptics" said a headline in the Columbus *Dispatch* in April, 1963. "Ariane Tebbenjohanns, imported fiancée of Dr. Sam Sheppard, Ohio's best known convicted wife slayer, is wearing down skepticism with persistence," the story said. "It had seemed all too pat when the blonde and beautiful Ariane, wearing an air of continental ennui, romped into Ohio in late January, on the eve of Dr. Sam's commutation hearing. . . . Unofficial betting was that Ariane would, after the publicity flurry died down, fly off to the east as inconspicuously as she had arrived, but the betters were wrong. Ariane is still in the Cleveland area, living at a motel, and in close contact with Dr. Sam's brother, Dr. Stephen Sheppard."

The fact that she took a genuine interest in my son, Young Sam, also helped to prove that she wasn't some freak hired for a publicity stunt. During spring vacation, she and Chip met in Columbus for the first time and they hit it off instantly. She took him to Tennessee for three days to see Mary and Bud Brown and had a fine time. Ariane told Young Sam that she did not want to wipe out the memory of his mother, Marilyn. She said she didn't want to be a second mother but wanted to be his friend. "We have only one thing in common," she said. "And that is love for your dad."

During the spring vacation, Ariane drove Young Sam to the penitentiary for a visit. Ariane waited in the car. Young Sam was like a cupid. He spent much of the visiting period repeating Ariane's messages to me and then relayed my words to her. After the visit she stood outside the walls in a parking lot where I could see her from one of the prison windows. It was my first real glimpse of her since January 24th. It was short, but like a shot of adrenalin to my morale.

Ariane decided to return to Germany, wind up her affairs, and immigrate permanently to the United States. She departed on May 10th. Immigration officials had promised her there would be no problem in her re-entering the country. Apparently United States agents had checked thoroughly into her background, found that she had never been a Nazi and that there was nothing that would keep her from being a desirable American citizen.

Shortly after Ariane arrived home, she received a letter from

Young Sam for Mother's Day and inside was a Culver Academy pin. This token of affection touched Ariane deeply. Before she left, Ariane made out a stack of cards, with phoney signatures, and gave them to a friend who mailed one or two a week to me. It was her way of keeping in touch while she was away. And it avoided alarming prison officials, who might have become suspicious if the steady flow of cards had stopped when Ariane left the country. I continued to write her in the coded letters which were forwarded to her.

Shortly after she arrived in Germany, Ariane received a small package. She tore off the outer wrapping, the colorful gift wrapping and bow and opened the box. Inside was a black bra and black panties. I had given a departing convict money for the present and his wife had selected them and mailed them to Ariane. It was my way of saying to her that I wasn't a vegetable anymore.

On May 26th, her birthday, she received twenty-six long-stemmed red roses. The card was addressed to "Mrs. Sam Sheppard." The order for the roses was wired to Germany by the attorney of a fellow convict. On visiting day, I gave the convict thirty dollars in cash and asked him to pass it along to his lawyer, with instructions on what and where to send. When Ariane got the roses, she telephoned her mother. "Forget about all birthday presents," she cried. "I got my present. I don't want anymore."

Ariane spent almost two months in Germany making arrangements for her departure and return to the United States. Until things settled down in the States Ariane decided her daughter, Iris, should continue to live with Ariane's mother. What with packing all of her belongings, handling business details, and saying good-bye to family and friends, it was a hectic period for her.

About a month before her return, Young Sam visited me at the penitentiary. As we sat across from each other at a table, I tried to slip him a card for Ariane. A guard spotted the attempt. As he approached me to take the card, I tore it up and put the pieces in my mouth. I ate that card but Young Sam had already pocketed three others. I told him to permit no search of his clothing on the way out which the warden "asked" to do. Young Sam warned him about illegal search and thereupon walked out.

It is not definitely against the rules for a convict to pass written messages to visitors. However prison officials moved quickly to reprimand me. They sent me to the "hole" in the maximum security cell block for three days. The hole is a tiny space between two doors in the solitary confinement area. It actually is a little passageway, about the width of the doors and about eighteen inches deep. All you can do is stand or lean. You can't sit down. Stints in the hole range from one to four days. It's pure medieval torture. I know for a fact that at least one man died after spending four days in there. When I got out after three days, I couldn't stand up. Prison officials also restricted my visiting privileges, decreeing that for the next several months visitors would be separated from me by a heavy wire mesh screen—not a table.

This infraction was duly publicized in the newspapers by prison officials. A friend called Ariane in Germany and told her that I was in the hole for trying to smuggle a letter to her. She swung into action. From four thousand miles away, she wrote thirteen letters —to Koblentz, to Warden Ernest Maxwell, to newspaper reporters and to anyone she thought could help get me out. Koblentz never answered her, but Maxwell wrote and said that prison officials were concerned because I was different from the way I had been during the earlier days of my imprisonment.

Actually, by the time the letters arrived in the United States, I was already out of the hole. I later told Ariane that my stay in the hole gave me a chance to really prove how much I loved her and it wasn't really so bad after all. It really was one way to be alone and think things out.

Ariane returned to the United States late in July and rented an apartment in Rocky River. She had a sizeable income from the estate of her late father and so there was no immediate need for her to take a job. Instead, she spent unsparingly of herself and her funds lecturing—without fee—to organizations through the state. She freely discussed her background, how our romance started, and why she felt that an innocent man was languishing in prison. Then she answered any and all questions from the audience. "I am doing it for him," she would say when asked why she had undertaken such a tiring speaking schedule. "I like people to realize why I believe he is innocent."

With her logic and persistence and the keen legal mind and aggressive attitude of Lee Bailey, it wasn't long before the tide of public and legal opinion began to flow in my favor. People sensed that Ariane and Lee must know they had the truth on their side to wage such a tough battle. Even those who had never met them realized that two people like these made life worth living. And to me, the reassurance that such genuine humans existed, quite apart from my personal stake in their fight, gave me courage.

22

Clarence Earl Gideon was arrested in Panama City, Florida, in 1961 and charged with breaking into a poolroom. Penniless, Gideon asked the court to appoint counsel to defend him on the charge. The judge refused, saying that Florida law provided indigent defendants with counsel only if they faced the possibility of a death sentence. Gideon tried to defend himself and failed. He was convicted and sentenced to a Florida penitentiary.

Convinced that he had been wrongfully convicted, Gideon spent hours in the prison library, studying law books. Finally, late in 1961, he wrote a petition to Chief Justice Earl Warren of the United States Supreme Court, asking that the high tribunal hear his case, which was based on the refusal of the Supreme Court of the State of Florida to grant him a writ of habeas corpus.

The Supreme Court decided Gideon's case had merit and appointed the prominent Washington lawyer Abe Fortas, now Justice of the Supreme Court, to represent him. Fortas did a brilliant job and in March, 1963, the Supreme Court ruled in a landmark decision that Gideon had been denied a fair trial, adding that every state must provide counsel to an indigent prisoner charged with a felony. Gideon later won acquittal at his retrial.

The Gideon decision was the most important of a group of key rulings, in which the Supreme Court broadened federal review of criminal cases. In effect, the decisions virtually instructed United States District Courts to re-examine previous state convictions, making sure the constitutional rights of defendants had not been violated.

At the time of the sweeping Supreme Court edict, Lee Bailey already was preparing a writ of habeas corpus to be presented to a United States District Court, charging my constitutional rights had been abridged. To him, the high tribunal's decision was heaven sent. "As soon as I read about it in the newspapers, I was sure school was out," Bailey said. "And when I later read the legal opinions in their entirety, I was certain of it. Much of the precedent we were hoping to set with Sam's case had already been decided."

Lee Bailey rushed completion on the petition for a writ of habeas corpus. In April, it was filed with United States District Judge Mel G. Underwood in Columbus. The document claimed there were twenty-two separate violations of my constitutional rights. These included:

Arraignment on July 30, 1954, without an attorney, despite the fact counsel was retained and refusal by authorities to delay arraignment until counsel could arrive and advise me.

Hostile publicity disseminated by news media, which was encouraged and generated by law enforcement officials; denial of a change of venue causing me to stand trial in an atmosphere of a "Roman holiday," and no granting of repeated motions for postponement of the trial until "the prejudicial effect of massive and sustained hostile publicity" had subsided and an impartial and unbiased jury could be obtained.

Publishing of jurors names thirty days before the trial started and then failure to sequester jurors once it got under way.

Judge Blythin failed to adequately caution jurors during trial to disregard opinions, advice, rumors, alleged information and pressures to which they were exposed.

Action of the Cleveland *Press* in "deliberately and with malice" printing articles and editorials during the twenty-six days after the murder implicating me and criticizing law enforcement officers for failing to make an arrest. The influence of the Cleveland *Press* and its editor, Louis B. Seltzer, "coerced law enforcement officials into fraudulently and maliciously" causing an inquest to be held and arresting me.

Judge Blythin was running for re-election and assistant prosecutor Mahon was seeking election to the bench during the trial and were "overly attentive to the wishes of news media which might commend or criticize" them.

Seizure of my home after the murder which prevented discovery of evidence by my investigators.

While deliberating, the jurors were allowed to make telephone calls from the hotel, where they were locked up during the trial.

The refusal by Judge Blythin to grant me a new trial; suppression of evidence by authorities; admission of testimony by two policemen to the effect I had refused to take a lie detector test; deprival of last preemptory challenge in impaneling a jury, and illegal makeup of the Ohio Supreme Court after Chief Justice Carl V. Weygandt disqualified himself.

Justice moved slowly in Judge Underwood's Court. He was an older man and there were rumors that he might be retiring. Month after month, he took no action on the petition. He didn't even schedule a hearing. However, Ohio officials apparently felt that when the petition finally came up for hearing, it might well meet with success and freedom for me could eventually open the way toward a law suit for my years of incarceration.

In October, a prison chaplain, whom I had always felt was a guard in cleric's clothing, approached me and told me he had a friend who could intercede for me with Koblentz and the parole board. The chaplain, who tried to divorce himself from any involvement in this obvious offer of a deal, said he thought an early parole could be obtained if these conditions were met: (1) drop my fiancée, Ariane; (2) drop my Boston attorney, F. Lee Bailey, and (3) discontinue the efforts of my brother, Steve, and all others to win freedom through the federal courts. I told him "thanks" indicating I would think about it, to mislead him. My true intention was to go all the way with Ariane.

On October 16th, I wrote a letter to Lee Bailey, which like all my letters, was sent on to Ariane. In the four-two code, it told of the offer:

Dear Lee,

The number of cases in our file must be getting large. Let's hope that **one** day soon we'll know what to expect. Something **official** or specific is what I mean, as you know. Hope this hearing **offers** the chance to review all of the evidence so it will be in the Federal record for appeal. The **deal,** as I understand things, is that the more complete this hearing is, the greater basis for appeal. I feel strongly **for** this reason that we must request an Evidentiary Hearing with separate finding of fact for each allegation and conclusions of law.

The **parole** board sees me in December of 1964, as of now and sooner if teaching continues. The most important **issue** to one judge might be the least to another. It **is** a written opinion therefore, on each strong point that should encourage conformance now or later on appeal; an appeal must be filed within thirty days of the certificate of probable cause issuance from what I'm told and that the certificate must be applied for right away on denial, right? Pretty sure that **you** agree, but doubt that we'll have the chance to talk face-to-face until the hearing, so don't mind if I spout on about some things that you know all about. Quite **naturally** they (Attorney General) would like to preclude the very strong appeal which we can present if currently denied.

Some time ago, I stated to you that I had the distinct feeling that, "you are going to walk me right out of this place," well this premonition is stronger than ever (perhaps because Federal law is on our side). I'll **worship** the law if this is the case and be tempted to study for the Bar or Medico-Legal aspect. Thanks for being **you**. You're **so** wonderful, is about all I can say.

Two weeks later, I wrote to Lee again, and as usual there was a message for Ariane:

Dear Lee,

You said that **you're** going to attack the weight of evidence and that is a good idea. In **my** reading these cases looked worth checking. We have good **reason** to do this, but I don't expect such wonderful fortune. It's **for** the Court to find the facts supporting conviction. We know their **existence** is not questionable; they are absent as Judge Taft pointed out.

United States v Di Re, 332 U.S. 581, 593-595

Johnson v United States, 333 U.S. 10, 13-15

Giordenello v United States, 357 U.S. 480, 486

You **never** know when one of these cases we dig up will help. We know you **would** seldom go home if you did all your own research. I **honestly** think you must not sleep anyway with all your activity. You've a great **deal** of stamina both physical and mental. Now **relative-to** the arrest and hearing without my counsel. Alex did tell **us** (you know) that Mayor Houk's testimony established this clearly. The **more** definite this is (in the record) the better; though there is no question about the fact. I feel that **every** strong point like this must be clearly proven, even if new testimony is needed. The **minute** we let up on any of these; well —we must not relax.

A short time later, one of the prison officials, who shall remain nameless, called me into his office and rather bluntly told me that I'd better lay off my legal activity or I would be buried for the rest of my life. "It's better to be a live coward than a dead hero," he said.

"That's what you think," I answered. "Because you're a coward and I'd rather be a dead hero. You be a coward and stay alive and if you can shave every day, that's up to you."

He threatened to put me in the hole for talking back. "Go ahead," I said. "What are you going to do—put me inside a prison inside a prison. I couldn't care less. I'm living for the principle. I'm living for the people outside, not for my own good or a soft spot."

"The only reason I don't put you in the hole, Sheppard, is because I think you want to go," he retorted.

"You said you wanted to talk to me man-to-man," I replied. "And then you get all upset when I tell you you're a coward. If you think it's better to be a live coward, you've proven it, but I'll be a dead hero if I have to be." He sent me back to my cell.

As the year 1963, drew to a close, the future was still uncertain. In December Judge Underwood had turned the petition for a writ of habeas corpus over to Judge Carl Weinman in Dayton, but he had not yet had time to schedule a hearing. I was about to spend my tenth Christmas behind bars, but I had the hope it might well be my last. I received one of my best presents early in the month, when Ariane came to Columbus with a visitor and stood on the street where I could see her from a prison window. I told her how I felt in a coded letter sent to Steve and Betty.

While I continued to write coded messages to Ariane in my letters to my family, and lawyers, we were also able to work out an arrangement which enabled us to correspond through another convict. The new system was given to Ariane late in the year by a released convict, who visited her in Cleveland. He also gave her an hour-by-hour run-down on my typical day in the penitentiary, so that she would know what I was doing practically every moment.

He told Ariane that the wife of a convict I'll call Wayne Smith had become legally separated from him while he was in prison and had stopped writing. He told Ariane to start writing to "Wayne Smith"—using our code—telling him that she was sorry she had left him, that she wanted to make up and everything would be fine from then on. The letters then would be turned over to me and I would write an answer, using our regular code.

It was extremely difficult for Ariane at first. She was well-versed in the English language, especially in frequently used slang. But she didn't know Wayne Smith's age, what he looked like, how many children he had, his physical makeup, and she didn't know how many times he had been married. She had to practice writing like Wayne Smith's wife hundreds of times so her handwriting looked typically American. Ariane's own writing has a European flair.

She lived in constant fear that she would make a mistake that would give away the plot and that Wayne would be punished. She didn't know he was pulling a long term, was nowhere near parole, and didn't care. He is out now, too; we're happy we didn't queer this.

Ariane wrote most of the letters on a typewriter, but occasionally when she was out of town, she would have to write by hand. She was left-handed and trained herself to write with her right hand. It took her six to eight hours to compose each letter. Wayne's wife last lived in Chicago, so we used an ex-convict and friend in that city as the relay point for the letters. Wayne and I kept our meetings to a minimum, so that prison officials couldn't put two and two together. Wayne was in a dormitory and I was in a cell, so it wasn't too difficult. We usually exchanged letters in the yard or dining hall.

My partner in this venture had a few problems at the outset. He was sharing a dormitory room with several men, who knew that his wife had left him. All of a sudden she came back and they were curious to see what she was writing. "I don't know what she is writing about," one of the inmates told Wayne. "It doesn't make much sense."

"She sure talks a lot about decorating that house," Wayne would say to me. Ariane kept referring to new draperies and a new love seat. Of course, the last was a way to get "love" in the code. Ariane later found out that Wayne had a son. When she took a trip to New York, she kept writing, as if Wayne's wife had taken the trip. "I bought our son a guitar," she wrote. And I knew that she had purchased a guitar for Young Sam.

Typical of these letters was one Ariane wrote to me, via Wayne, in December, 1963:

My darling Wayne,

I must say, I don't know where this last week has gone to—we did everything in such a hurry, honestly I didn't even find time to go to the hairdresser, so I look disgusting. I **need** not explain all this to you 'cause you knew the schedule. But I suppose, **you** only have a very vague imagination of how quickly time or let's better say a day (for time to me doesn't seem to pass at all) can pass when active "on the outside." Now, **every** day we have made a definite plan just to make sure to get everything done. I love every **minute** with Bobby, I only wish I had more of him—but while you read this I have taken him back again. And **of** course, I am always real sad driving back home alone—why do children have to grow up, I never liked that. If you'd seen **the** boy driving off in the car alone to a date—it made my heart feel real warm and good. Each **night** he took it (needless to say I gave him extra money)—and you know that for the first time in his life he could give a girl a real treat. Last night he **and** a guy went to a party with the car—with no particular girl—so that all the girls could see him and the car, ha-ha. So during the **day** I have been busy getting it into shape for his nightly escapades (car wash, oil change, heating repaired, etc.) so it was all fit again for him. But **I** think it's about time he starts practicing to drive the little car, because it doesn't have so many different moods like the other (princess), it's more reliable, but I guess, he prefers the other one. But I could **sleep** better at night if I knew he would be out in the stick-shift car.

We have been **with** you in everything we did this past week, you must have felt our intense thoughts—not one single hour passed without mentioning you—and it looks as though Bobby is absolutely in love with our new home (am I relieved). He's **your** guy all right, the way he loves our room.

I bought him **handkerchiefs** and all that junk he needs, also a beautiful night-blue blazer for Xmas which he had to try on now. But **I'll** have another little surprise for him; an I.D. bracelet—I know you gave him yours—but he does not wear it because he's too afraid to lose it. I plan to **hold** it till the last moment, to make sure he doesn't know anything about it. Perhaps **you** realize how difficult it is for me to get something he really likes—oh by the way I also got him some beautiful ties and a pair of antique cufflinks with crests engraved which he picked out himself. I could talk **forever** about our boy, I started calling him a guy, like I call all his friends at school, they all took me to the messhall for dinner, so you can imagine how the whole hall including teachers were staring. So, **once** we got started we also bought some records, how could we avoid that! So here am **I**, without my two guys, more lonesome than I was last week, yet trying to smile.

You'll **get** a little Xmas package from me, so I want you to understand, Wayne, that I can't send you very fancy stuff because I have to mail it and lots of things could spoil and arrive in pieces. But I hope **you** will like what I send, you sure do realize how difficult this all is for me, don't you Wayne—but I do wish you a good Xmas, too, and remember, Xmas has only twenty-four hours and they will pass just like any other day—so let's not make it too important (never dreamed I could be so realistic, ha-ha, hope you still smoke Pall Malls, will send some, too.

I still love you so. . . .

Of course, in this letter, Ariane was able to get across to me that she had picked up Young Sam at Culver, had driven him home for Thanksgiving and he had used her Ford Thunderbird. She also had a Volkswagen, with a stick-shift. With this cover Ariane could safely write some love "straight" to her supposed husband.

Poor Ariane was under terrific strain. Everywhere she went she had to prove herself—that she wasn't a phoney or a Nazi. Not being able to write or visit me legally nagged at her soul. To compound matters, she learned that her ten-year-old daughter, Iris, or Müecke as she was called, was ill with yellow jaundice in Dusseldorf. This made the thought of spending the Christmas-New Year holidays without her loved ones harder to bear.

Ariane was wound up like a spring. A few days before the holiday, she was in the apartment and suddenly had the feeling she couldn't breathe. She called friends, who summoned a police ambulance. The officers administered oxygen on the way to Bay View Hospital. At the hospital, a doctor diagnosed her trouble as a bad case of nervous exhaustion, released her after a few hours, and warned her that she needed a few days of hospital rest soon or she was risking a nervous breakdown. The day after Christmas she returned to the hospital for several days of treatment and rest.

Alex Martin, one of our lawyers, heard she was hospitalized and called her. He suggested that he go to Columbus, tell me, and reassure me she was on the way to recovery so I would not worry. Naturally, I was concerned but I was glad I learned about it from him, rather than from the newspaper story which broke a few days later. A Columbus newspaper man who interviewed Ariane by telephone quoted her as saying, "I guess my nerves just forsaked me . . . All year I've been trying to fight all my worries and troubles and tried to smile. The whole Christmas time is not an easy time. I wanted to go home but Sam doesn't like for me to fly and I didn't know what to do." Ariane told the reporter that her illness had forced her to cancel a march around the Ohio Penitentiary on Christmas Eve, to show her love for me.

My extreme worry and concern over Ariane gave me dizzy spells almost ten times a day. They persisted until Ariane was obviously doing well again.

23 &

Federal Judge Carl A. Weinman wasted little time in getting to the long-delayed petition for a writ of habeas corpus, once the matter was thrust into his able hands by Judge Underwood. His first act was to call a pre-trial conference for January 17th, at which the ground rules for the legal battle were established. Lee Bailey flew in from Boston and was joined by Alexander Martin of Columbus and Russell Sherman of Elyria for the possible stipulations with State attorneys in Judge Weinman's Columbus office. Assistant Attorneys General John Cianflona and David Kessler represented the State of Ohio.

All sides also agreed during the session that I would remain in the Ohio Penitentiary and not appear in court in any of the pre-trial conferences; that all preliminary proceedings would be by pre-trial orders agreed upon by counsel and/or by order of the court; that a history of the case and a stipulation of all issues to be considered by the court be filed on or before January 24th, a week later.

After the first pre-trial session, Lee Bailey told newsmen that my chances of winning release—through the courts—was greater than at any time during the nine-year history of the case. Cianflona of the attorney general's office conceded that I could be a free man, if Judge Weinman ruled favorably on any one of the constitutional claims cited by my attorneys.

There obviously was much cooperation and understanding between the State's attorneys and those representing me at the session. They went about the job of setting the ground rules for the case without the fanfare, emotion, and shouting, which had marked my other legal battles. Judge Weinman told them what he wanted to accomplish—narrowing down the list of twenty-two issues into a smaller group of stipulations, which both sides agreed should be the basis for the ultimate decision. With the judge's hand firmly on the tiller, the lawyers set about through a series of pre-trial conferences to give him what he wanted.

Lee Bailey's report on the pre-trial hearing was encouraging, but there were no guarantees as to how Judge Weinman would rule. I hoped that Judge Weinman eventually would rule in my favor, but if some other vehicle for getting out of that hell-hole without compromising Ariane came along, I was ready to take it. The door appeared slightly ajar on February 24th, when Dr. Samuel R. Gerber, who had—as Cuyahoga County coroner—done as much as anyone to put me behind bars all these years came out with a remarkable statement. Gerber said that he recommended to Attorney General William Saxbe that I be granted a parole when my case came up in the fall. He further said he would not oppose a parole for me should it come before that.

Gerber had called Attorney General William Saxbe a few days before his statement was released to discuss my case and the recent United States Supreme Court rulings. Published reports said that when Dr. Gerber suggested to Saxbe that he propose to Governor James A. Rhodes that he parole me, Saxbe replied, "That's a hot thing for the governor to handle." Saxbe then suggested that Gerber take up the matter himself with the governor. Instead of calling the governor directly at that point, Gerber decided to put his position in writing. He sent a letter to Saxbe, saying he would not oppose parole for me. When he learned of the letter, Governor Rhodes told Saxbe to turn it over to the Ohio Pardon and Parole Commission.

"Recommendation of parole of Sam Sheppard at this time should in no way be interpreted to suggest that I have any doubts as to his guilt in causing the death of his wife," Dr. Gerber said. "However, in my long experience in the investigation of homicides I have come to recognize the futility of life imprisonment for persons such as Sam Sheppard. Up until the time of the homicidal act, he was a respected and an apparently responsible citizen. The homicidal act was the result of the spur-of-the-moment incident. I believe sincerely," he continued, "that this is the time to indicate to Sam Sheppard that society and the State of Ohio recognize the element of human frailty in the act that resulted in his imprisonment."

It was an amazing statement from a man who nine and a half years previously had tried his damnedest to put me in the electric chair on a first degree murder charge. When informed of Gerber's statement, Lee Bailey, in Boston, responded with characteristic candor. "Hogwash," he said. "Mr. Gerber has so violently opposed any consideration of Sam Sheppard that I doubt his sincerity. . . . I suspect that Mr. Gerber is under the illusion that a parole would terminate the habeas corpus action. The only way it could be killed,"

Bailey explained, "is if Sheppard is paroled and discharged from parole restrictions."

"He would no longer be in the custody of the State of Ohio. I question whether the federal courts would consider the habeas corpus under those conditions. No matter what action the state takes," Bailey said. "We will bring to account the people who caused Sam's conviction and who profited by it, of which Samuel Gerber is one, and the Cleveland *Press* is the other."

The next day, several other adversaries fell into line. Frank Story, who was Cleveland police chief when his department participated in the murder investigation, said, "I feel justice has been served. As one of the prime investigators and having access to information not always available as evidence, and through my frequent conversations with Dr. Sheppard, I was, and am, convinced he was guilty of manslaughter." Story continued, "I have felt for a number of years that Dr. Sheppard should be placed on parole. I don't believe he will ever commit another crime and, if this is true, certainly it is not rehabilitation but revenge that keeps him in prison."

Warden E. L. Maxwell of the Ohio Penitentiary said he saw "nothing wrong" with Sam Gerber's proposal, adding that if the court wanted me to do more time it would have given it to me. Even the Cleveland *Press* gave qualified support to Gerber's suggestion and wound up a lengthy editorial by saying, "Sam Gerber's standing as an internationally famous and sincere student of crime and criminals is unchallenged. Penal and parole officials of Ohio should match his objectivity.

"They should examine Sam Sheppard's record as a prisoner and treat him exactly as they treat other parole candidates guilty of the same charge. If they find an imminent parole is called for, they should parole him."

Encouraged by these statements, I wrote a four-line note to the Ohio Pardon and Parole Commission on February 28th, asking that my bid for executive clemency and immediate release be reconsidered. After nearly ten years behind bars, I wanted out. Late that day, a telegram arrived from Lee Bailey in New York. It read:

SAM, AS I INDICATED LONG AGO, AS SUCCESS BECOMES APPARENT AND IM-
MINENT, AUTHORITIES WILL EXERCISE GREAT PRESSURE TO AVOID DISASTER.
YOU ARE VERY CLOSE TO TOTAL EXONERATION. DO NOT UNDER ANY CIRCUM-
STANCES ACCEPT A COMPLETE DISCHARGE FROM CUSTODY. SIMPLE PAROLE
IS O.K. THESE INVITATIONS ARE SPONSORED ONLY BECAUSE OPPOSITION HAS
LEARNED THAT YOU WILL BE FREED WITHOUT QUESTION. INSIST THAT ANY

OFFERS OF CLEMENCY BE PUT IN WRITING STATING REASONS THEREFORE.
IF DIRECT PRESS CONFERENCE IS ALLOWED, I WILL COME AND BE PRESENT.
MAKE NO DEALS WITHOUT ADVICE STEVE OR MYSELF. END OF ROAD RIGHT
AROUND BEND. DON'T FOLD NOW. CHIN UP.

LEE

Bailey's point was that if given a parole, we would continue with
the litigation, because if I were on parole on a conviction of second
degree murder I would still be under technical incarceration for life.
Parole is merely honor incarceration. And I would be under full
control of the officialdom of the State of Ohio. With executive clemency, my sentence would have been reduced to manslaughter and
would be commuted to time served. Prison officials indicated to me
that if I agreed to drop the court action, I could get commutation
to time served, which would release me from custody and the possibility of a lifetime of reporting to a parole officer.

I wanted to marry Ariane and be with my son, Young Sam. I
wanted out of prison, with no parole. I couldn't have had my medical and surgical license reinstated as a commuted felon, but I didn't
feel I needed that to make a living. I felt I had other talents and
could learn a new profession, even if it meant digging ditches. With
no-strings-attached release, I could leave the country and possibly
obtain a medical-surgical license in a foreign land, where doctors
are at a premium. Thus, I indicated to prison officials that I would
accept a commutation of "time served," and end the legal fight.

However, my relatives and some other people told the Akron
Beacon-Journal that I was not buying any deals—that I was willing
to spend additional time in prison to wait for the ruling on a writ of
habeas corpus. It was easy for them to say because they never spent
a day in prison in their lives. Just one day in that penitentiary can be
enough to get yourself killed or permanently maimed. Strange things
happen in there and the only people who can control what occurs
are the convicts, not the guards, the warden or Koblentz.

Statements such as those by my relatives put the pardon and
parole commission and governor in a difficult spot and seemed to
more or less preclude their taking favorable action in my clemency
bid. I tried to get word to the governor that at this point I would
accept freedom and forget about exoneration. Attorney Alex Martin
made this point clear to one of the governor's aides and I wrote a
letter to Governor Rhodes to reinforce that position.

Lee Bailey came to the penitentiary to see me on Saturday, March
7th, and I told him plain and simple, that my fervent desire was for

freedom. He acceded to my wishes, and later told newsmen, "We are in complete agreement as to what to do and the (Sheppard) family agrees. Sam will go forward with the clemency hearing request with a hope for a favorable result. He wants to be out now. The habeas corpus action would take a year. He wants to walk out now." Bailey said he was confident I would win quick freedom.

On March 13th, the following letter from the Ohio Pardon and Parole Commission was handed to me:

Dr. Sam H. Sheppard
No. 98-860 OP
Columbus, Ohio
Dear Sir:
Replying to your request of February 28, 1964, the Commission has determined that a rehearing of your case at this time is not in order.

Yours very truly,

OHIO PARDON AND PAROLE COMMISSION

J. Arthur Shuman, Chairman

Though I was bitterly disappointed again, the curt note seemed to settle the future course—continue the habeas corpus action and plan for a parole application in the fall, when I would officially be eligible. Ariane's disappointment was mirrored in a coded letter she wrote to me via Wayne Smith the next night.

My darling Wayne,
Last Friday night **my** mother called to ask about you and give me all the news. Her **heart** has been causing her some trouble lately, but otherwise she is fine. She said she **almost** packed her things to come down here, but then the maid got sick. She **broke** her thumb and can't do a thing for a while. I told grandma **if** she really plans to come she'll have to announce it sooner anyway. I **only** said this to make sure I am here when she comes; she knows I love to have her any time. This last week, **I** stayed home most of the time. I **could** stay home forever in this nasty weather. This snow does **hold** up everything, I couldn't even clean the porches for a week now—disgusting. If **you** were here I'd make you go out and do it—ha-ha. How about it **now** are you still anxious to come home?

Tomorrow, **I'm** going to have dinner at mom's (I lost five pounds in the last two days, so I can afford that, see!). I am often **with** them Sunday afternoons and we talk so much about you. Actually, **you** are our only subject. She insists that **in** there is the only place where you are safe, she says I am a "terrible brat" and that you couldn't possibly realize what you're asking for. And **there** would be no help for you once you'd be out, in fact you'd want to go back there, rattle at the gate and scream, "Let me in again"—ha-ha—we have some fun that way, but it's all full of anticipation and love for you. I always reply, let's wait till my guy comes home. You'll be so happy to be home that you won't even notice what a "brat" I am, ha-ha. I know, you're courageous too, so you won't be chicken and run away, and I promise to be real good and sweet, O.K.? She's too funny sometimes. Whenever I am sad, she finds some way to cheer me up. So to me she has been a great comfort many times.

I promise to write more soon. No more nonsense for today, O.K.?

I love you so . . . and that's no nonsense either!

The following day, a telegram arrived for me from Lee Bailey in Boston:

DEAR SAM

AS A RESULT OF JUDGE WEINMAN'S ORDER I HAVE CONFERRED THIS DATE WITH STEVE, ARIANE, RUSS, PAUL AND ALEX. WE HAVE NEW LOCAL COUNSEL BENJAMIN L. CLARK OF COLUMBUS AND ARE PROCEEDING TOWARD HEARING WITHIN LESS THAN 30 DAYS. MR. CLARK WILL VISIT YOU MONDAY. I WILL BE IN COLUMBUS WEDNESDAY OR THURSDAY. GIVE NO STATEMENTS FOR PUBLICATION UNTIL THAT DATE AS THESE MAY JEOPARDIZE FEDERAL ACTION. ALL LOOKS GOOD.

On Tuesday night, March 17th, Lee was the guest of writer Jack Harrison Pollack at the Overseas Press Club Book Night in New York City. The subject for discussion was the book, *The Minister and the Choir Singer*, on the famous Hall-Mills murder case. On the panel were the book's author, the lawyer, William M. Kunstler, NBC newsman, Gabe Pressman, Irene Corbally Kuhn, who covered the Hall-Mills case and Dorothy Kilgallen, who covered my trial.

During the discussion, Miss Kilgallen offhandedly remarked that while she was covering the Sheppard case in Cleveland, she was summoned to the private chambers of Judge Edward Blythin, who was donning his robe before going to the bench. It was just before the start of my trial.

"Miss Kilgallen," Dorothy quoted the judge as saying. "It's nice to see you. But why should a company like Hearst send a journalist of your stature to a small town like ours to cover what appears to be an open and shut case. Sheppard's guilty as hell. There's no doubt about it."

A writer in the audience immediately spoke out, criticizing Miss Kilgallen for not having mentioned this obvious bias on the part of Judge Blythin ten years ago. "If you had reported Judge Blythin's prejudicial statement at the time instead of keeping silent, it might have changed the venue and the entire complexion of the case."

"Things said to a journalist in confidence should be kept in confidence," Miss Kilgallen replied quietly.

Harrison Pollack rose to his feet and informed the audience that with him was F. Lee Bailey, "the brilliant young attorney on the Sheppard case." Bailey was asked to say a few words and, according to Pollack, the rest of the evening was spent talking about my case rather than the Hall-Mills murder case.

After the session broke up, Lee told Pollack that he might be able to use Dorothy Kilgallen's remark. The next day, Bailey—back in Boston—telephoned Attorney General William Saxbe's office in Columbus and requested that Dorothy Kilgallen's statement be made part of the permanent record in the writ of habeas corpus petition.

Later the following statement given by Miss Kilgallen was inserted into the record by stipulation. (Both sides agreed to the fact and truth of Dorothy Kilgallen's statement without a formal deposition swearing.)

He was very affable. He shook hands with me and said, "I am very glad to see you, Miss Kilgallen. I watch you on television very frequently and enjoy the program." And he said, "But what brings you to Cleveland?"

And I said, "Well, your honor, this trial."

And he said, "But why come all the way from New York to Cleveland to cover this trial?"

And I said, "Well, it has all the ingredients of what in newspaper business we call a good murder. It has a very attractive victim, who was pregnant, and the accused is a very important member of the community, respectable, very attractive."

And I said, "Then added to that, you have the fact that it is a mystery as to who did it."

And Judge Blythin said, "Mystery? It's an open and shut case."

And I said, "Well what do you mean, Judge Blythin?" I was a little taken aback because usually, I have talked to many judges in their chambers, but usually they don't give me an opinion on a case before it's over.

And so he said, "Well, he is guilty as hell. There's no question about it."

And after that we talked about the accommodations. He, I believe, again expressed astonishment that people like Bob Considine and people from foreign newspapers were on hand. Theo Wilson was there with an-

other man from *The News*, whose name I don't recall, Hank something
or other.

And the judge seemed genuinely surprised that there was so much interest in this particular case, which to him seemed to be a mere formality.

Another statement included along with Dorothy Kilgallen's was
that of Edward T. Murray, a clerk in Cuyahoga County Common
Pleas Court. Murray said that in July, 1954, he and a lawyer, who
was now deceased, were discussing my case. Three or four other
persons were present, but Murray could not remember their names.
Murray stated that Judge Blythin walked into the room and discussed the case with them. Murray said that as the judge was leaving, "He made the remark that Sam Sheppard was as guilty as he
(the judge) was innocent."

Judge Weinman and the lawyers had made steady progress in
resolving the issues in the case and the Dayton jurist scheduled a
final pre-trial conference for May 6th, at which time it was to be
decided whether oral arguments would be needed in the case. There
was some speculation that Judge Weinman might free me some time
that week. It was heightened by a screaming headline in *Parade,*
the nationally distributed Sunday supplement, which asked, "Will
Dr. Sam Sheppard Go Free This Week?"

On Monday I received a coded letter from Ariane. "Won't be in
Columbus Tuesday and you'll get suit. I have not too high hopes.
It seems too good to finally be true. I long to have you more. I love
you so."

Ariane had purchased a new suit for me to wear, if and when I
was released from the penitentiary. But Judge Weinman quickly
quashed any rumors that my release was imminent. He declared
that it would take more than two months for him to reach a decision
in the case, once he had all the final arguments in hand. The fact
that oral arguments might not be needed due to mutual stipulation
on all points, seemed a good indication.

Late that week, all the final papers were filed. Lee Bailey and the
other attorneys had crystallized the original twenty-three stipulations. Twenty-two were in the original petition, and the twenty-third
was added after the Kilgallen statement, into nine points. The
State's brief denied, as was expected, the allegations that I did not
receive a fair trial and that my constitutional rights were violated.
The series of pre-trial conferences had been so successful and the
material submitted to Judge Weinman was so complete, that he

decided there was no need for oral arguments. He decided to take the case under advisement immediately and to base his decision on four points which represented consolidation of the nine issues in my final brief:

Was the newspaper publicity before the trial and/or during the trial such that it violated my constitutional rights?

Did the trial judge, by failing to disqualify himself after making certain statements regarding my guilt, violate my constitutional rights?

Did the trial judge, in permitting police officers to testify that I had refused to take a lie detector test and in permitting Spencer Houk to testify that he had taken a lie detector test, violate my constitutional rights?

Did the action of the bailiffs in permitting the jurors, during deliberations and without authority from the court, to hold telephone conversations with persons outside the jury room, violate my constitutional rights?

I began the inevitable waiting game as Judge Weinman pondered the thirteenth legal appeal made in my case. I guess the word that best describes my mood is expectant. I expected the worst and hoped for the best. Newspapers speculated that the writ of habeas corpus action was a huge gamble on my part because if freed, I most assuredly would be ordered to stand trial again after having spent almost ten years in prison and when only four months away from parole consideration. Another jury, they reasoned, might send me to the electric chair. A new trial was what I wanted the most now, because it would give me a chance to completely vindicate myself and open the way for my return to my neurosurgical practice.

While Lee Bailey was extremely optimistic, I proceeded with the task of making a parole plan which could be submitted to the Ohio Pardon and Parole Commission in October. Although there was no guarantee of a parole then, I wanted to be ready. Even at that time, the commission could rule that I was not ready for release and order me to stay indefinitely. After all, my sentence was for life, with a minimum term of ten years before parole.

A prospective parolee must show that arrangements have been made with someone of good moral character and enough financial means who has agreed to take the parolee into his home or find him a job and a place to live. The Browns, my family, Ariane, Rev. Al Davis, Dr. Art Miller, and Dr. Harvey Silver discussed three possible alternatives. One plan was for me to live temporarily at Dr.

Richard Sheppard's home and to obtain a job as a sales representative, preferably with a drug or surgical supply company. There was no immediate thought of me working in any capacity at Bay View Hospital. This would have placed heat on everyone concerned, since it was well known that I performed much surgery while in prison.

A second proposal was that I live in California with a long-time friend Dr. Harry Silver. Both Dr. Silver and Dr. Arthur Miller, another wonderful friend, had tentative jobs for me as a surgical instrument salesman and as a general mechanic with a boat-building firm at Balboa Harbor.

The third tentative plan was for me to move to Gatlinburg, Tennessee, near Mary and Bud Brown. Bud, an architect, was seeing if he could line up a job with the Tennessee state highway construction group. None of these things had been committed to writing, because no plan was firm and the formal papers were not due to be filed until about six weeks before the date for consideration. Some pretty damn fine people were going to bat for me.

Meanwhile, I continued to pile up good time, by teaching in the prison school. Helping some of the men with little schooling gave me a great sense of accomplishment. It was often close to the same feeling I had when I was able to save someone's life on the operating table. One of my most satisfying moments in prison came through an old Negro man, who had been unable to read and write until he was in my class. I worked with him, encouraged him, and gave him extra homework to do in his cell. "The more work the bester," the old man drawled. "Then I don' have to think about them bars." Slowly but surely, he learned to read and write. After thirty-five years in prison he could read his letters from home and write back. One day he came up to me. He had a broad smile on his face, a letter clutched in his hand. "You know, Doc," he said softly, "I could open this letter, and read this here letter myself, my own self. God bless you, Doc." And he cried a little.

I continued a vigorous program of physical activity. Trips to the gym were not as frequent as they had been in the days when I was working in the office or the hospital or when I was in the honor dormitory or at Marion. I was just a regular convict, living in a four-man cell. There were no special gym privileges. Two of us did the next best thing and exercised for hours on end in the cell. During the daily exercise routine, it was not uncommon for me to do five hundred pushups and five hundred situps, four hundred squats, four hundred reverse pushups. Plus a half hour of intense isometric exercises.

The workouts, teaching schedule, parole planning, and composing coded letters, kept me very busy during the weeks Judge Weinman poured over the mass of legal documents which had been submitted to him. The days and weeks dragged along and finally it was July 15th—approximately the date Judge Weinman had set back in May for reaching a decision.

24 ❧

Young Sam, just back from attending Outward Bound summer camp in the mountains of Colorado, looked tanned and fit as he sat across from me in the Ohio Penitentiary visiting room. It was July 15th and he had come to Columbus with Ariane, who was waiting for him in the car. It was good to see him again and I listened attentively as he described his experiences at Outward Bound. He told me how each boy had spent five days alone in the rugged country, without food or water, and how he survived by catching fish and birds for his food. He received an award for his performance as top man in accomplishment during his session. He also described how he won the camp ten-mile marathon run, a pretty hefty feat for a boy of sixteen, especially over a hilly and mountainous course.

Of course, I asked him about Ariane—how she smelled, how she looked, what messages she had for me. He memorized two or three messages from me to her. We discussed my case and Young Sam wanted to know when a decision was expected. "It should come within a week," was my answer. When the visit was over, we stood up and shook hands. "Don't worry Dad, I'll take care of her," he said as he turned and left the visiting room.

I went up to the cell range, hoping to catch a glance of Ariane. But one of the prison officials, who had almost caught me doing this the last time, warned me they had stationed guards near the windows. Seeing them, I went directly to my cell on the fourth range, where all of the school teachers stayed. As I reached the cell, a fellow in the next cubicle, named Gregg, shouted to me: "Nice going, Doc."

"Yeah," I answered, "I'm sure glad my boy got that award."

"Your boy?" Gregg asked. "What do you mean your boy? You're going home."

"Now wait just a God damn minute," I answered, "this is something we don't kid about."

Gregg was an emotional guy and by now tears were streaming down his face. "You made it, you made it," he said, his voice choking. Then other guys down the range started shouting to me that they had heard on the radio that Judge Weinman had ordered me freed.

I was dumbstruck. About all I could say was "God damn." I walked into my cell and the three other cellmates said they, too, had heard the news on my radio. One of the fellows, Harry, who stood barely five feet tall on his tip toes, said, "Doc, I'm telling you I couldn't be happier if I were going out tomorrow." That's saying something!

I sat down on the bed, put on the earphones and listened to newscast after newscast to get the details. Ariane and Sam were driving toward Cleveland when a radio announcer interrupted the music with a bulletin, about Judge Weinman's ruling. They were so stunned they could barely go on. In fact Ariane had to pull to the side momentarily and catch her breath.

That afternoon at his Dayton office, Judge Weinman issued an eighty-six-page decision, setting me free on $10,000 bond. He ordered that the State of Ohio or Cuyahoga County had sixty days to retry me or my release "shall be final and unconditional and the bond cancelled." He made it clear in the opinion that he did not make a judgment on my guilt or innocence, because that was not the question before him.

"The Court," he said, "has considered the question of whether or not petitioner received a fair trial and in regard to that question has found five separate violations of petitioner's constitutional rights, i.e., failure to grant a change of venue or a continuance in view of the newspaper publicity before the trial; inability of maintaining impartial jurors because of the publicity during the trial; failure of the trial judge to disqualify himself although there was uncertainty as to his impartiality; improper introduction of lie detector testimony, and unauthorized communications to the jury during their deliberations. Each of the aforementioned errors is by itself sufficient to require a determination that petitioner was not afforded a fair trial as required by the due process clause of the Fourteenth Amendment. And when these errors are cumulated, the trial can only be viewed as a mockery of justice."

Judge Weinman said that while he was well aware that many State Court judges had affirmed my conviction on appeal, he had no hesitancy in reaching his conclusions after reviewing the evidence submitted.

"The order which follows," he said, "is somewhat atypical in that it permits petitioner's immediate release, but this case is unusual, for petitioner has been incarcerated for almost ten years as a result of a trial which fell far below the minimum requirements for due process."

As I heard the words over and over, I just couldn't believe it. Supper call came and went. I couldn't eat so I just passed it up. Later, I munched on crackers and ate some beans which I bought at the range commissary. The story didn't end with Judge Weinman's decision and I didn't want to leave the radio, fearful that I might miss some later development.

Almost from the moment of Judge Weinman's bold decision, Ohio and Cuyahoga County officials made it clear they were going to fight his ruling and attempt to prevent my release, which would come the next morning as soon as my family or Ariane posted the $10,000 bond. Attorney General William Saxbe, who was in San Francisco for the Republican National Convention, told newsmen that he planned to appeal the decision. Cuyahoga County Prosecutor John T. Corrigan charged that Judge Weinman's ruling "makes a hash of justice" and said he would do everything to keep me in jail.

Corrigan said he would go to court early the next morning in an effort to obtain an order staying my release. That failing, he said, I could be arrested on the original indictment as I walked out of the prison gates. That's the kind of news I heard as the night wore on. I didn't begin to sleep all night. I didn't know what the morning would bring, but the daytime range guard came on duty, banged his night stick on the bars of one of the cells and shouted, "Sheppard pack your shit. You're going home, you son of a bitch." Then he handed me a pink slip, which meant release. I was already packed. My cellmates had shined my shoes and helped me pack.

Virtually everyone in the range wanted my pink blanket, which Ariane had soaked with Arpége perfume. It smelled real good. First, I was going to take it out, but changed my mind. Harry, who had cleaned my radio and shoes took it and petted it like it was a nice cat. First I went to the deputy warden's office and left my belongings and then walked over to the school to pack the stuff I had there.

I lingered at the school long enough to meet Wayne Smith, and chatted with him a few moments. We agreed that Ariane would write him a letter saying that she was divorcing him and that would put the situation back to where it was before we started. I then

turned over to him all of the candy, cigarettes, and canned foods I
had accumulated, thanked him, and left.

Then it was on to the dining hall. Clutching the pink slip in my
hand (which gives access to any place in the penitentiary) I walked
alone into the mess hall which was crowded with convicts having
their breakfast. Hundreds of men began yelling and clapping as I
waved the pink slip back and forth to show it to one and all. Half
of the guards seemed to be clapping, too, while the other half
banged their sticks on the wall to restore order.

"Give that girl one for me," shouted one convict. "Drink a quart
for me," yelled another. I sat down and had a cup of coffee with a
few O.K. guys. It was loaded with sugar because I knew I was over-
stimulated and had to unwind. At this point food didn't interest me
and it was my hope the coffee would sustain me as the day wore on.

From there I went to the clothing or dress-out room, where a
safe-cracker tailor handed me a baggy-looking suit made in the
prison garment shop. Prison officials wouldn't allow me to wear the
new suit Ariane had bought for me, though they did allow me to
put on a new shirt and tie she had sent in. The prison suit looked
awful and I'd have changed outside the door, if it hadn't been for
the fear they would re-arrest me for indecent exposure.

While I was in the clothing room, a guard and a convict wheeled
in all of my belongings in a cart, including some of the illegal letters
and cards received from Ariane, some of my letters which had been
rejected by the prison censor, legal documents, and other personal
material. Most of this kind of stuff is usually taken from the average
convict before he is allowed to leave.

I was feeling big and bad by then, especially as I had heard on
the radio that Lee Bailey had arranged for federal marshals to be
on hand outside the prison gates to arrest Cuyahoga County sheriff's
deputies if they tried to arrest me. "What the hell do you think
you're doing?" I shouted at the guard.

"Doc, I've got to shake you down for the last time," the guard
answered. I told him he was taking part in an illegal search and
seizure of my property. "What do you mean?" he asked.

"If you touch one more thing in my personal bag," I yelled, "I'm
going to call my attorney and have him call a United States marshal
and you'll be in a federal penitentiary."

"Oh, Doc," he sighed in a sort of an unbelieving tone.

"Oh, Doc, my ass," was my reply. "Now you just try me." He
finally dropped the stuff and walked out of the room, leaving me to

go out with my personal belongings uninspected. It's doubtful this ever happened before in the Ohio Penitentiary.

As I went across the yard from the clothing room to the deputy warden's office, almost every convict going along the way shouted a greeting to me, urging me to keep up the fight. More than three hours passed in the deputy's office, while we waited for the final order for my release. All the while, I kept hearing reports on the radio of the legal moves being attempted by state and county authorities to prevent my release.

Just before noon, the order came for me to be released. Out the front gate we went. As I walked across the prison yard to the series of gates leading to the honor dormitory, a spontaneous cheer went up from every office, cell block and factory in the penitentiary. Even the projectionist from the auditorium was out in the yard yelling and clapping. This kind of conduct, of course, is not permitted. It was so spontaneous and smacked of such good will, prison officials could do nothing about it. It touched me deeply, because I felt it represented the fact that most of the men were very much in my corner and knew of my innocence because I lived with them. Convicts are not fooled; they know.

The last stop was the honor dormitory, where several of the men stood in line to shake my hand before an official ushered me into a small office. Warden Maxwell, Maury Koblentz, and a representative from the Ohio attorney general's office were there. We straightened out my prison account, which included money which had built up over the years of working. It is given to a convict when he is released so that he has a little money to start with. My balance came to two hundred eighty-seven dollars.

When we approached the last gate, Warden Maxwell extended his hand and I shook it. Koblentz, who had given Ariane and me such a hard time extended his hand and I walked right past him.

Outside the gate there was an overwhelming surge of people. Not only newsmen, but well-wishers. One woman shoved forward and pressed a crucifix in my hand. There were so many microphone wires on the ground I had trouble making any headway through them.

Maxwell and a guard were with me and we pushed our way through the crowd to a state automobile. The guard assisted me into the car and the three of us drove to the Federal Building in Columbus, where bond was being handled by my brother, Richard. When we arrived, I stepped out of the car and shook hands with

Richard. At that moment we were both thinking of our parents. I
tried to mouth something—"I wish Dad was here"—or something
like that, but the words would barely come out. "Sam, I know,"
Richard said. His wife, Dorothy, embraced me and kissed me and
together we walked down the crowded halls to the bonding room.
Lee Bailey was there.

The hallways were crowded with secretaries, other employees,
and people who wanted a look at the spectacle. Richard posted
bond and then Warden Maxwell handed me a check to close my
prison account and asked me to sign a receipt for it. Turning to
Lee, I asked if I should sign. "Sure," he said, "Mr. Maxwell wouldn't
cheat us." With my signature on the dotted line, Maxwell and the
guard made their exit. What a beautiful sight.

For the first time since August, 1954, I was a free man. I felt elated
though I could not express it outwardly. There was an urgency to
see Ariane, who had stayed in Cleveland at the suggestion of my
family. I wanted to get the hell out of there, eat a steak, and get
with my family and my girl, especially my girl, go swimming and
do all of the things which I had been missing for so many years.
Actually, I wasn't so much in a daze as I thought I would be. I
wanted to do things before this breath of freedom suddenly came
to an end and I knew there was a good chance of that. I had to
accept the possibility of a return to the penitentiary.

Before doing these things, there was one more piece of business.
Lee had agreed to hold a news conference and federal officials
turned over a large hearing room in the federal court house for the
purpose. It was jammed to the doorways with reporters from newspapers, radio stations, television stations, and magazines. I sat on a
platform at the head of a room, with Lee at my side, and started
answering questions. I guess I was a little hesitant at first, but once
we got going the words flowed smoothly.

The questions covered the gamut. When a reporter asked me how
I felt about the federal court that freed me, my reply was, "Thank
God for the federal courts." Another wanted to know my plans regarding Ariane. "I'd marry her today if she were here and we had a
license." One odd question was asked about the suntan on my face
and hands. "We are told Dreyfus was in such shape when he left
Devil's Island" I said. And so it went for several minutes, until Lee
called a halt. One important point I did make was the fact that,
"There are other innocent persons in prison."

We drove from the federal building to a motel in northwest

Columbus. My first move was to get Ariane on the phone. She told me she heard the news of my release while at her hairdresser, started crying, and ran out with her hair half-combed. We agreed to get married as soon as possible and she said she'd drive to Columbus immediately.

Meanwhile, state and county authorities were trying their damnedest to put me back behind bars. At the request of Prosecutor John T. Corrigan, the state attorney general's office obtained a temporary stay of release order from Judge Lester Cecil of the United States Sixth Circuit Court of Appeals, pending a hearing in Cincinnati where the court sits. I had just finished some orange juice and a steak and was changing into my bathing suit for a long-awaited swim when a reporter telephoned to tell Bailey of the order to return Sheppard to the Ohio Penitentiary. "Don't tell me I have to go back," I cried to Richard in near panic. Lee told me to forget about the swim and sit tight. He began telephoning to find out what had happened. I started a note to my beloved Ariane.

About the same time, a friend called Ariane and told her that authorities were going to re-arrest me. She packed hurriedly and sped toward Columbus. "All the way down, I kept hearing he was about to be arrested," she recalled. "I was so scared I wouldn't be able to make it on time." She made it with state police help.

The next three hours were frantic. I sat there helplessly, expecting a United States marshal to knock on the door and tell me he was returning me to the penitentiary. Lee Bailey made several telephone calls to state and federal officials, trying desperately to find a way for me to remain free.

In the midst of all the commotion, Ariane, who must have set some kind of a speed record between Cleveland and Columbus, pulled up at the motel entrance, left the motor running, and jumped out of the car. She bolted through a group of reporters and photographers awaiting her arrival and ran to the Bailey's second floor suite. The door opened and she virtually came flying into my arms. It was only the second time we had ever been together.

Nearly eighteen months had separated the two visits. It was pure ecstasy to have her in my arms again.

The scene at the motel was bedlam, with news people all over the place. In an effort to have the newsmen and photographers give us some privacy, Lee Bailey arranged a press conference for Ariane and myself. Fortunately, I was able to shed the baggy prison suit and wear the suit Ariane had bought for me. She looked stunning in a white, sleeveless sheath and dangling earings.

In front of the large group of newsmen, Ariane presented me with a pre-wedding present—a tiny watch imbedded between two hinged gold coins. "All I can give you just now is me," I replied. And at that point I didn't know how long it would last, because there was speculation an arrest would be made the next morning.

At the outset of the conference, Bailey told the newsmen, "We are not making any plans to leave here. We are waiting to honor the order if and when it comes. We could leave the state and nobody could stop us, but Sam doesn't want it that way." We told the group that we would be married as soon as permitted, answered several questions, and then went to dinner. We talked far past midnight, saying to one another things that had been in our hearts for the past eighteen months but could not be expressed because of Maury Koblentz. When we finally retired for the night, I roomed with Lee and Ariane stayed with his wife, Froma.

The pressure of an immediate return to the Ohio Penitentiary faded on Friday. The alert Lee Bailey had obtained a copy of Judge Cecil's order and noticed a mistake in the terminology. This caused another delay in the state's plan to have me reincarcerated while it appealed Judge Weinman's order. After several hours of uncertainty, we were notified that the United States Appeals Court would take up the matter of my remaining free on bond the following Wednesday, July 23rd, in Cincinnati. The hearing site later was switched to Akron.

With at least four more days of freedom assured, Ariane and I took off for Chicago to be married. With us were Lee Bailey, his wife, and Paul Holmes, a Chicago *Tribune* reporter and attorney, who had written a best-selling account of the murder case in which he raised serious doubts about my guilt. It was afternoon when we departed and we were followed by a caravan of cars bearing newsmen. Ariane was behind the wheel and took a zig-zag route across Ohio and Indiana trying to shake the news hounds. One by one the cars dropped out and when we arrived in Chicago shortly before midnight only one was left behind us.

Before checking into a hotel, we stopped and had the blood tests required for marriage. Early in the morning, we went to the license bureau, where I paid for the license with some of the money earned in prison. I had wanted Young Sam, who was about to leave with Steve and his family on a Great Lakes sailboat race to come to Chicago to be best man at the wedding. Steve objected, saying he didn't want the boy involved in the publicity which would surround the wedding. I suggested that we leave the decision up to Sam, who said he wanted to come. But Steve persisted and finally Lee Bailey suggested that we go along with him. Steve was right.

The wedding took place in the bridal suite of the Conrad Hilton. Lee Bailey was my best man and his wife, Froma, was matron of honor. The ceremony was performed in the living room of the suite by Nicholas Kure, a magistrate of the Circuit Court of Cook County. While I knew no legal proceedings were scheduled until Wednesday, I half expected someone to come dashing into the room during the ceremony and arrest me. In a few moments we were Dr. and Mrs. Sam Sheppard.

After the ceremony, the room was overrun by news people. We patiently granted interviews, posed for pictures and then finally had some privacy. Ariane telephoned her mother to tell her we were married.

That evening we were stopped by a television reporter as we walked out of the hotel to do some window shopping and have dinner. He asked us a few questions, then suggested we have dinner with him and a friend. He took us to a French restaurant and we had an enjoyable wedding supper. The next morning, a columnist for one of the Chicago papers, telephoned and invited us to have dinner with him and his wife at the Pump Room. We accepted. At the Pump Room I wanted to dance. Ariane thought I'd forgotten how during the ten years in prison and made excuses. "I'm too tired," she said. After I persisted, she finally agreed and was surprised how well I did.

"You thought I couldn't dance, didn't you?" I asked her.

"You must not have had such a rough time in prison after all," Ariane quipped. "I bet you guys danced together."

The dancing was indicative of the way everything went after I got out of prison. It was as if life had begun again after a long sleep. It was as if I had never been away from normal civilian life.

On Monday morning we flew to New York City. When we reached Newark Airport, we were greeted by a tremendous throng of news people and well-wishers began cheering to indicate they were with us. Fortunately, there was adequate police protection and after we answered a few questions for the reporters the police escorted us up the ramp.

One of the local reporters, an acquaintance of Ariane's called to her that he had his car and would drive us into the city. Ariane and I climbed in front, Lee Bailey and his wife, Froma, got in back, and we were off to the Pierre Hotel. There was another press conference and more interviews before we finally were left alone in early evening. We had dinner in the room and stayed up and talked all night.

We spent Tuesday in New York, then flew back to Cleveland early Wednesday morning for the all-important hearing in Akron, about thirty-five miles away. Frankly, my mood was a little uneasy as the plane approached Cleveland, the city that had been so unfair to me. I just couldn't forget the mob that appeared in front of my father's home the first time I was arrested. When this uneasiness turned to hostility, Ariane tried to calm me, by saying that there were many people in Cleveland who had reconsidered and changed their minds about me over the years.

There was a sizable crowd on hand as we stepped from the plane but it was a friendly group. There were cheers, but no cat calls. Helen Waterhouse of the Akron *Beacon Journal,* a wonderful woman reporter who had befriended Ariane when she came to this country, was the first to greet us as we walked down the ramp. Ariane and I both embraced her. We had some time before departing for Akron, so we drove to the apartment Ariane had rented in Rocky River. Again we were followed by a parade of reporter's cars.

When we arrived at our apartment, one of the newsmen suggested that I carry Ariane over the threshold. Though a disc in my back had been bothering me, I picked her up, but couldn't get the door open. When I finally opened it, I took off my shoes and walked in my stocking feet. After all those years of walking on hard floors, I wanted to know how carpeting felt under my feet.

Ariane gave me a quick tour of the apartment. It was beautifully decorated with pink carpeting, French provincial furniture, and white draperies. It was like heaven. Then Helen Waterhouse, Lee Bailey, Paul Holmes, Ariane, Ben Clark, the attorney from Columbus, and I sat down in the living room to chat. It was nine o'clock in the morning, but it was already hot and humid. "Who'd like a drink," I said, then went to the refrigerator, took out some ice, opened the liquor cabinet and started pouring as if I'd lived in the place all my life.

We stayed for about an hour, then drove to Akron, for the fateful hearing before the three judges of the United States Court of Appeals. I left the apartment reluctantly, not knowing whether I'd be back that day—or when. We checked into the Akron Tower Hotel, had lunch, and then went to the courthouse, which was crowded with reporters and curiosity seekers. The crowd—in the hundreds—was so great that we had to lock arms with a uniformed United States marshal to get into the hearing room.

The hearing on whether I was to remain free on bond was scheduled to start at two p.m., but got under way twenty minutes late in a courtroom that was unbearably hot and stuffy. So hot, in fact that by the time the argument started I had sweated right through my necktie.

Bailey based most of his arguments on Judge Weinman's eighty-six-page opinion, which had freed me in the first place. "This man," he said, "did ten years for what a federal judge says is a mockery of justice. We want to retry him very badly," Bailey continued. "We want to prove his innocence. He is not a professional criminal. You don't think a $10,000 surety bond brought him here do you? He came because he wanted to." Bailey also said that Dorothy Kilgallen's statement on Judge Blythin's prejudgment of my guilt was "new evidence," which was not known by previous attorneys representing me.

Cuyahoga County's side of the story was argued by Prosecutor Corrigan and Gertrude Mahon. Corrigan argued that the two statements included in the brief filed with Judge Weinman—by Miss Kilgallen and Court Clerk George Murray—which indicated Judge Blythin was prejudiced, represented hearsay evidence which impeached "the honor and integrity" of the late jurist. The prosecutor added that "Twenty judges—more than a jury"—had upheld the original verdict of the trial court over the years. Gertrude Mahon charged that Judge Weinman's ruling "is not based on the trial records. The entire records show that Sam Sheppard's constitutional rights were protected."

Before the three justices went into deliberation, Judge Cecil, who had granted the stay order after my release, asked, "Mr. Bailey, does he [meaning me] plan to settle down and not make a public spectacle of himself?"

"A spectacle was made of this case long before now," Lee Bailey answered sharply. After fifty-seven minutes of arguments, Justices Cecil, Weick, and Clifford O'Sullivan retired to deliberate the issue. They were out for two hours and twenty minutes and it seemed like a lifetime to me.

After the three judges filed back into the courtroom, Presiding Justice Weick started to speak. I held my breath. The sweat was pouring out of my body. They were the words I wanted to hear. The court denied the Cuyahoga County motion that I be sent back to the Ohio Penitentiary.

Judge Weick said that the court was not now ruling on the propriety or the impropriety of Judge Weinman's ruling and was "not passing on the merits of the case nor the district court ruling." That, he said, would be done in the fall when the United States Court of Appeals ended its summer recess and began holding regular sessions. In the meantime, he explained, Judge Weinman's voiding of the second degree murder conviction was being stayed, pending a later hearing.

Until the issue was decided, he said I would be under federal court custody and must within three days post a new $10,000 bond in Columbus. The hearing was over and freedom was assured for at least several months. I got up and ran to Ariane, threw my arms around her and muttered, "We made it." Tears were streaming down her face.

There was a large group of well-wishers outside of the courthouse as we left. Some of them shook my hand. An old Negro woman pressed up close to us and as she held out her hand, shouted, "God bless you, Doctor, and God bless your wife." Tears were running down her cheeks. I reached across and grasped her hand and said, "God bless you." Ariane and I were so touched we both began to cry.

We drove back to the Akron Tower, where Lee Bailey put me through my seventh press conference in seven days. "We haven't had time to think of what we're going to do next," I said. "We have to think of final vindication." Then pointing to a small flight bag at my feet, I said, "I had it packed—just in case I had to go back to the penitentiary. I can't destroy this girl with all this uncertainty."

One of the reporters asked Ariane why she had cried when Judge Weick handed down the ruling. "Did you misunderstand the judge?"

"No," she answered. "I was over-strained and I was so relieved, I was crying from relief and happiness."

We dined with friends in Akron, spent the night at the hotel, then returned to Rocky River. On Friday we drove to Columbus, where bond was quietly posted. Then we returned home to begin living as normal a life as possible, under the circumstances.

The future was still uncertain, but I wanted to make the best of whatever time there was, to become a father to my son and a husband to my new wife. Lee Bailey promised I would never spend another day in jail, but he knew, and I knew, that it would take a long and frustrating legal battle to fulfill that promise. It promised to keep the Sheppard murder case in the courts well into a second decade.

25 ❧

A leaden sky hung over Washington, D.C., and a slight drizzle was falling as we drove slowly along the streets of the nation's capital. Ariane, Young Sam, Lee Bailey, his wife, Froma, and I were on our way to the United States Supreme Court for a date which had eluded me for nearly a dozen years.

The cab driver stopped across from the court. We walked slowly toward the imposing white marble building. Ariane, Young Sam, and I had driven to Washington from Cleveland and spent the night at a small motel outside the city to avoid the press. But there was no avoiding the press this morning. As we approached the long series of steps leading to the court, we were besieged by photographers, reporters, and television cameramen. Walking hand in hand, Ariane, Young Sam, and I smiled at each other and continued slowly up the wide marble approach toward the sixteen massive columns which guard the entrance to the building. My eyes for several seconds focused on the words etched in marble above the first two rows of columns: EQUAL JUSTICE UNDER LAW—the bywords of the Supreme Court of the United States.

After passing between the columns, we entered a doorway, climbed another small flight of stairs, passed through a second set of heavy metal doors and were inside the main hall of the building, a long, wide corridor, lined with marble columns and leading directly to the court chamber.

At the front of the chamber, under four massive columns, was the bench; behind this polished mahogany dais were nine empty chairs, each of a different size and shape, but each upholstered in black leather. Flanking the bench were the desks for the Clerk and the Marshal. Immediately in front of the bench were two rows of shiny mahogany tables for lawyers arguing cases before the court. Left of these tables were rows of black-upholstered chairs for lawyer-spectators and immediately beyond were rows of benches for members of the press. On the right side were seats reserved for the families of the supreme court justices. Separating this entire area from the rest of the chamber was an ornate brass rail, behind which were several rows of upholstered benches for the general public.

After exchanging greetings with the other members of my legal team, Ariane, Young Sam and I sat down in the first row of the public gallery and waited nervously for the proceedings to begin. My day before the United States Supreme Court had been scheduled for Thursday, February 24th, but had been postponed for four days.

The delay was fortunate because I was back in Rocky River on the 24th, bedridden with the flu, and would have missed the Supreme Court hearing, the culmination of a legal struggle which had started on a wintery day back in 1954, when a jury pronounced me guilty of murdering my wife.

Sitting there waiting for the hearing to begin, I couldn't help but think back to this seemingly endless struggle—especially the agonizingly slow and emotionally painful battle since my release from the Ohio Penitentiary on July 16, 1964. We had enjoyed a two-and-a-half-month respite from the courts after the United States Court of Appeals in Akron ruled that I could continue free on bond. It was a period during which I learned how to live like a human being again and became reacquainted with my family and friends.

On October 8, 1964, we were back in court—this time at the Sixth United States Circuit Court of Appeals in Cincinnati, where three judges heard arguments on the validity of Judge Weinman's ruling freeing me in the first place. Judge Clifford O'Sullivan, who had been at the Akron hearing, presided and was joined by Justices Harry Phillips of Nashville, Tennessee, and Justice George Edwards of Detroit, Michigan, in hearing the case. For nearly two hours, the justices heard arguments on the state's petition that Judge Weinman's ruling be revoked. Then the justices took the matter under advisement and we returned to Rocky River to wait, wait, wait.

No one knew how long it would take for the Court of Appeals to reach a decision. Speculation ran from ten days to one hundred twenty days. We were on pins and needles. After my first real taste of freedom in ten years, the thought of going back to the Ohio Penitentiary was frightening to say the least, but it was also a very real possibility. We did not know whether each day or each moment would be our last together for months—or possibly years. Ariane and I began living in split seconds, cherishing every minute of freedom. Every ring of the telephone sent a nerve-jangling shiver to the pit of my stomach.

Sleep was difficult, especially during the week when the Court of Appeals was in session and could hand down a decision at any time. Periods when I drifted off into deep sleep were often marred by the nightmare of finding myself back behind bars in the penitentiary. I would awaken in a cold sweat, not knowing where I was—in my bedroom or in my cell. By the end of each week Ariane and I were both drained emotionally. Our nerves were ragged. About the only relaxed hours we had were during the weekend when the court was not in session. But by Sunday night, the tension began to build again—as our thoughts turned to what might come the following week.

Ariane became pregnant and we were both worried about her mental torment. My back, injured in a scuffle in prison, still ached. Finally, I decided on surgery for two ruptured lumbar discs. Dr. Theodore Classen and my old friend Dr. Arthur Miller operated successfully on November 7th. Art Miller, who came from Los Angeles, would not accept my offer of paying his plane fare back home. He was to leave shortly for Vietnam where he had volunteered as a surgeon. I recovered without complications.

No decision came in November and in the days preceding Christmas. When the day of December 24th passed without a ruling, I knew I would be able to spend my first Christmas at home in ten years. Ariane, Young Sam and I exchanged presents on Christmas Eve and retired for the night. Early Christmas morning, Ariane—three months pregnant—had a miscarriage, largely the result—in my opinion—of the psychological fear of my rearrest. It was just too much for her. We were both heartsick.

January came and went. Inquiries to the Court of Appeals brought word that the justices had a heavy case load and would get to my case in the normal sequence of events. February, March, April—the freedom was wonderful, but the waiting was awful. On the morning of May 5th, the telephone rang. It was Lee Bailey. He had bad news. The Court of Appeals had voted two-to-one to overturn Judge Weinman's decision and ordered me back to the Ohio Penitentiary. We had twenty days to reply to the court order, Bailey said, meaning twenty more days of freedom, unless he could obtain a continuance.

Bailey told us to leave the apartment immediately, get in the car, and go into seclusion. He was fearful authorities might misinterpret the ruling and try to arrest me immediately. I hung up the phone, turned to Ariane and said, "Well, all my worries have come true."

We were both shocked and the thought of possibly going back to prison was more than I could stand.

The majority opinion, signed by Justices O'Sullivan and Phillips, said that while the publicity in my case "was not of a nature calculated to inspire confidence in the objectivity and good taste of the public news media" my constitutional rights had not been violated. Judge George Edwards dissented, contending errors by Judge Blythin in communications to the jury should give me a new trial.

Lee Bailey had made it clear he would take the case all the way to the United States Supreme Court. By the same token, Cuyhoga County authorities were adamant that while the appeal went on, I should be back in prison and indicated they would fight any attempt for continuation of bail. Bailey immediately petitioned the Court of Appeals for a rehearing and I was allowed to remain free, pending a decision. It came on July 14th, and as expected, the Court of Appeals denied a rehearing, giving Bailey five days to file a notice of appeal to the United States Supreme Court.

It was touch and go for us until Bailey obtained permission from the Court of Appeals—over Cuyahoga County objections—for me to remain free on bond until the Supreme Court acted on the case. Ariane, Young Sam and I breathed a collective sigh of relief. It meant another several months of freedom and assured life.

On August 24, 1965, Lee Bailey filed a petition with the United States Supreme Court, asking for a review of a case that twice before it had refused to hear. This time, the American and Ohio Civil Liberties Unions filed arguments on my behalf as a "friend of the court." The big question, of course, was: Would the high court decide to hear the case? If it refused, there was little doubt I would be back in the Ohio Penitentiary by year's end to serve out the remainder of my sentence—life.

We were relatively at ease until early October, when the Supreme Court ended its summer recess and began deciding on its docket for the new term. Once the new session started, it was the same old story for us. We knew that the Supreme Court handed down decisions on any of the first four days of the week. Those days were pure hell. It was like waiting for the Court of Appeals ruling, only worse. We knew that after the Court of Appeals there was the Supreme Court. Lee had always said he felt he could keep me from going back to prison until after the highest court had ruled on the case, though I wasn't so sure myself. Now there was nothing left after the Supreme Court.

As we sat day after day in the apartment and waited for the court to decide whether to hear my case, Ariane and I both had the feeling it was like being in a jail—a beautiful jail. The Supreme Court quickly weeded out several cases early in the session, but mine was not one of them. The longer the question went without answer, the more ominous it seemed to me and the more intense the pressure on both Ariane and me. Others felt that the fact the Supreme Court had taken its time to decide whether it would hold a full-scale hearing on the case looked good for me.

We didn't eat regularly or sleep regularly during the week. On weekends when we went out for a quiet dinner or two, there were always people asking us questions, offering their best wishes, reminding us of what we had hoped to forget for a few fleeing moments. At home, the telephone rang constantly. The callers usually were reporters, asking whether we expected a ruling soon. The calls, at all hours of the day and night were so hard on our nerves we finally had the telephone company give us an unlisted phone number.

Late one morning in November, a few days after we had the unlisted number installed, my brother, Richard, appeared at the back door of our apartment and rang the doorbell. We hadn't had the opportunity to give either Richard or Steve the number. Fearing that our telephone was being tapped, we didn't want to convey it over the phone. Ariane and I went to the back door. Richard was standing there, a serious look on his face. My heart was in my mouth, as I quickly opened the door.

"It's all right, Sam," he said. "It's all right. You're going to make it to the Supreme Court.

I breathed a deep sign of relief, grasped Richard's hand and the only word I could speak was "Thanks."

"I know, Sam, I know," Richard answered. After the initial blush of excitement, I telephoned Lee Bailey at his Cape Cod home. His wife, Froma, answered. "Aren't you happy?" she cried. I assured her I was ecstatic and extremely grateful to her husband and the United States Supreme Court.

When Lee got on the phone, I expressed similar sentiments to him. "We're in the last lap, Sam," he said. "Stay with it and keep your head above water." We discussed the possibility of my taking a job so that I could provide some money for the expenses connected with the Supreme Court hearing. During the months since my release, we had lived on funds received as an advance for writing this

book and from Ariane's income. He said that writing the book probably was a full-time job and I should stick with that. He told me not
to worry about the expense. He would advance the money. Lee said
he didn't know when the case would be heard, but that it would be
in two to three months and that there was a lot of work to be done
in preparing a magnified brief.

When we ended the conversation, Ariane and I just sat and shook
our heads. Young Sam was on a world cruise and we wished he
could be with us at the moment to share our happiness. Our prayers
had been answered. I felt stimulated to say the least. I was very
encouraged, very hopeful for all of us. But it wasn't only a selfish
feeling. I had the impression that we were going to obtain something really big—something for the good of American justice.

We had a good night's sleep for the first time in weeks. The pressure was off for a while and would remain off until the Supreme
Court hearing. We could relax and gird ourselves for the emotional,
stomach wrenching period that would follow the Supreme Court
hearing on the case.

Lee Bailey, Ben Clark, and Russell Sherman—my legal team—
worked long and hard preparing the final brief in the following
weeks and filed it with the high court. The state answered. The
Supreme Court set a date. There was the brief postponement I
mentioned before. Now, one year, seven months and twelve days
after my release, we were seated in the marble-walled United States
Supreme Court to determine once and for all whether the trial
which resulted in my conviction and my spending nine years in
prison was fair.

The clock above the bench showed a moment before ten a.m. The
marshal and the clerk, dressed in cutaways, took their positions at
their respective desks. Promptly at ten a.m. the marshal pounded
his gavel on the desk. Everyone stood.

Then he droned, "The Honorable, the Chief Justice and the Associate Justices of the Supreme Court of the United States." Simultaneously, the nine justices walked through the wine-colored draperies
behind the bench and stood behind their chairs while the marshal
sounded the traditional chant that opens a Supreme Court session:
"Oyez! Oyez! Oyez!"

Then Chief Justice Earl Warren and the eight associate justices
who flank him—Tom C. Clark, Hugo L. Black, William O. Douglas,
John M. Harlan, Byron R. White, William J. Brennan, Jr., Potter
Stewart and Abe Fortas—took their seats. They handled routine

business for several moments then began hearing the arguments that would help them decide my fate.

Lee Bailey stepped before the bench and began his argument with a detailed account of the murder scene and my story of what happened that fateful morning. "As he entered the room," Bailey said in a resonant voice, "to attack or grapple this form, he was struck from behind and rendered unconscious."

At this point, Chief Justice Earl Warren asked the first of many questions that would be posed by the justices during the session. "Was there any question about whether this form was a human being or not?" Justice Warren asked.

"Sheppard said he could not be sure," Bailey answered. "It had a white top. I think it was a human being, the question being whether it was a male or female."

From then on, the speakers were constantly interrupted by the justices probing for answers to questions.

Bailey contended that prejudicial editorials, cartoons and headlines published by the Cleveland *Press* in effect instigated my prosecution by Cleveland police, controlled their action and predetermined the verdict. But Bailey insisted that his case did not rest on the finding of law violations by the newspaper.

"Do you mean you are not pressing the point with respect to asserted excessive or prejudicial newspaper publicity?" asked Associate Justice Abe Fortras.

"No, your honor," Bailey replied. "What I mean is this. That although trial by newspaper represents a serious problem, we have sufficient remedies within law which were not exhausted in this case without coming to the question of what must be done to silence the press."

Attorney Bernard A. Berkman, chairman of the Greater Cleveland Civil Liberties Union, with whom Bailey shared his argument time, also asserted that the impact of the news coverage "should have been controlled. Our argument is not to shackle the press," Berkman said. He added that the court should, "Describe with particularity the kind of publicity that could be inherently prejudicial."

When Bailey was asked what new material he brought that was not before the Court back in 1956, when it refused to hear the case, he cited the deposition taken from the late Dorothy Kilgallen, that Judge Blythin had told her before my trial started that I was "guilty as hell" and that the case "was open and shut."

Seven of the nine justices joined in several sharp detailed questions about the document and the issue of a trial judge's prejudgment of guilt. Justice Hugo L. Black asked Attorney General William Saxbe of Ohio if he believed my conviction should stand even if the trial judge was prejudiced.

Saxbe said flatly that Judge Blythin was not prejudiced. "Even if he had been," the attorney general said, "the conviction should stand unless prejudice was passed on to the jury."

Chief Justice Warren asked Bailey why my attorneys had not challenged Judge Blythin on the issue of bias. Lee assured the jurist that they would have had they known Judge Blythin's "frame of mind."

In his formal statement, Saxbe said, "I submit, this was a trial by the book. It was a good trial. To allow Sheppard to attack his conviction now with an emotional issue that obscured the overwhelming proof of guilt, subverts the jury system." John Corrigan, the Cuyahoga County prosecutor, echoed Saxbe's statement, telling the justices, "We have on trial the jury system of the United States."

The entire hearing lasted two hours and twenty minutes. I was relieved when it was over. My feeling was that Saxbe and Corrigan had been unconvincing in their arguments concerning prejudice by Judge Blythin—that if the case was decided on the basis of what was said on that day, we would win it. Of course, my feelings weren't important, nor were those of my attorneys, who shared my views. What mattered was the reaction of the nine justices to the day's arguments and the written words in the briefs that had been submitted earlier.

At a press conference after the hearing, a reporter wanted to know my emotions now that the hearing was over. "I can't afford to have too much emotion," was my answer. We dined that evening with Lee Bailey, then left for Cleveland later that night. We drove part of the way, spent the night in a motel and were back in our Rocky River apartment the next day, well aware that the next month or so would be the toughest yet from an emotional point of view.

The first few weeks were bearable. We knew that the Supreme Court would take more than a month to reach a decision. Ariane, Young Sam and I tried our best to forget about it and to enjoy life from day to day. As the weeks clicked by and it became apparent a decision could come any time, the tension became unbearable, especially Monday, the day when the Supreme Court usually handed down decisions. We rarely slept a full night during the week because the Court frequently had sessions Monday through Thursday and there were those nightmares again when I did sleep—nightmares of returning to prison.

We had foolishly given our unlisted phone number to some news people. Late Sunday afternoon, the calls would start. "Do you expect a decision tomorrow?" "If a decision comes tomorrow, will you be available?" We assured them all that we were not going anywhere—that they knew as much about when a verdict would come as we did. On Monday mornings, reporters, armed with transistor radios, would congregate in a nearby restaurant, waiting for a radio report of the verdict. They hoped to be first at the apartment to get a reaction from me.

April and May passed and there was still no decision. The longer the wait, the more tense and restless I became. My emotional state was best explained in a note written to a friend in mid-May. "You must know that I am really shaking in my boots," I wrote. "Was truly scared for the first time in my life following the Cincinnati hearing with O'Sullivan presiding. Now I'm more optimistic, more hopeful, and more scared."

June arrived and we knew the end of the waiting road was virtually at hand. The Supreme Court had tentatively scheduled its summer recess to begin on June 13th, if it could clear its docket by then. Otherwise, it would start no later than June 20th. The Court left no question but that it would have a decision before it recessed. There were three possible Mondays left for the announcement. The first of the Mondays was June 6th.

We passed Sunday, June 5th, quietly, both aware that it could be the last day we would have together for some time. Our hearts were heavy. There was the persistent feeling of helplessness. We had no control over our destiny. The anxiety, which had been mounting all day, was heightened—if that was possible—toward evening when the telephone calls from newsmen started. They wanted to know whether we would be at home the following day.

Darkness came, but sleep did not. Ariane, Young Sam and I felt we would have our long-awaited answer on the morrow.

26

The brisk rap on the front door of our apartment and the ring of the telephone came almost simultaneously. It was eleven forty-five a.m. on Monday, June 6th. Half a dozen newsmen in cars had lined up in front of the apartment. Her heart pounding a mile a minute, Ariane picked up the telephone. Young Sam raced for the front door. I was lying in bed, resting. A surge of fear charged through my body.

The caller on the telephone was a newsman. His facts were sketchy, but he breathlessly told Ariane that the Supreme Court had ruled in my favor. Simultaneously my son received the same word from the newsmen assembled in front of the home. He slammed the door, dashed to the head of the steps and shouted upstairs, "Acquittal or retrial, Dad."

Our prayers had been answered. The United States Supreme Court, which nearly ten years before had refused to hear the case, had voted eight-to-one (with only Justice Hugo Black dissenting) to set aside the 1954 murder conviction because the trial Judge, Edward Blythin, "Did not fulfill his duty to protect Sheppard from inherently prejudicial publicity which saturated the county." The high court remanded the case back to Judge Weinman, with instructions to issue the writ of habeas corpus and order that I be released from custody unless the State of Ohio retried me within a reasonable time.

The initial reaction by Young Sam, Ariane and myself was one of quiet elation for the moment. There were no whoops and hollers. Each of us paused for a moment to thank God in our own way for giving us this long-sought victory and a chance for my complete vindication.

The feeling of elation on my part quickly turned to one of relief. It was a rather strange feeling. It was not one of over-excitement or nervousness. I was quite relieved in a personal way to know that the Supreme Court had given me a chance to vindicate myself and to straighten out the matter of my innocence once and for all. On the other hand, there was some anxiety over the prospect of having to put my family through the ordeal of another trial. Twelve years of hell had conditioned me to what would take place in another legal test, but I had mixed emotions about what it would do to my loved ones.

Shortly after we heard the good news, a call came from Lee Bailey's office in Boston. One of his associates told us to "get lost" for the rest of the day—leave the apartment and get out of the county. The aide indicated that while there was no justification for local arrest, no one knew what hasty action local authorities might take and what interpretation they might give to the Supreme Court verdict. After all, while a new trial was ordered, the indictment handed down in 1954 still was valid.

As we walked to the car we were confronted by dozens of newsmen, photographers, and television cameramen assembled on the front lawn, and we talked with them as a family.

"Sure, I'm relatively happy," was my initial reaction. "I'm encouraged. I want to be free. I want what is proper for complete vindication. However, I don't wish to put my family through the tremendous ordeal." Making it clear that a new trial was up to the prosecutor, I said later, "I alone do want it as a way of absolutely vindicating myself, but I hesitate to subject my family to it."

When asked whether I expected to be rearrested, my comment was, "They don't have enough evidence to arrest me, let alone take me to trial."

Then we left Rocky River, visited a friend in Lorain and had a prolonged lunch at the Castle-on-the-Lake in Lorain. It was late afternoon before we were able to get the full story of the United States Supreme Court ruling and see first-hand the far-reaching decision which in the future would protect other Americans from the kind of prejudicial publicity that surely had helped send me to prison for a good portion of my lifetime.

The twenty-nine-page opinion was written by Justice Tom C. Clark. After discussing the known facts in the case, he proceeded to outline press activities which he said marred the "judicial serenity and calm" that any defendant deserves. He cited numerous examples such as:

A newspaper editorial criticizing a random poll taken by my attorneys of people on the streets as to their opinion of my guilt or innocence. The editorial had called the survey "mass jury tampering."

A radio debate in which newspaper reporters accused my lawyers of putting roadblocks in the path of the prosecutors and said that I had conceded guilt by hiring a prominent criminal attorney.

The "But who will speak for Marilyn?" story which appeared on page one of The Cleveland *Press*, while the jury was being selected.

The fact that hundreds of news media representatives went to my home while the jury inspected it and the fact that one newspaper hired a helicopter to get pictures of the scene.

Bob Considine's radio broadcast heard on WHK which likened me to Alger Hiss and the refusal of Judge Blythin to ask how many jurors heard it.

The eight-column headline and story, "Sam Called A Jekyll-Hyde by Marilyn, Cousin to Testify!" No such testimony was ever produced at the trial, the opinion pointed out.

Walter Winchell's baseless broadcast that a New York woman—described as my "mistress"—had stated that she had borne me a child. Two jurors admitted they heard the particular broadcast, but said—when questioned by Judge Blythin—that it would not affect their judgment in the case.

A newspaper story under the headline, " 'Bare-Faced Liar,' Kerr says of Sam," resulting from a statement issued by Homicide Captain David Kerr after I testified that Cleveland detectives had mistreated me during my "third degree" ordeal. Kerr, the opinion pointed out, never appeared as a witness at the trial.

Justice Clark's opinion also cited the fact that during deliberations, jurors had been allowed to make telephone calls from their hotel rooms and that bailiffs could hear only the jurors' end of the conversations.

"There can be no question about the nature of the publicity which surrounded Sheppard's trial," Justice Clark wrote. He continued:

Or is there doubt that this deluge of publicity reached at least some of the jury. On the only occasion that the jury was queried, two jurors admitted in open court to hearing the highly inflammatory charge that a prison inmate claimed Sheppard as the father of her illegitimate child.

The court's fundamental error is compounded by holding that it lacked power to control publicity about the trial. From the very inception of the proceedings the judge announced that neither he nor anyone else could restrict prejudicial news accounts and he reiterated this view on numerous occasions.

Since he viewed the news media as his target, the judge never considered other means that are often utilized to reduce the appearance of prejudicial material and to protect the jury from outside influences. We conclude that these procedures would have been sufficient to guarantee Sheppard a fair trial and so do not consider what sanctions might be available against a recalcitrant press nor the charges of bias now made against the trial judge.

The carnival atmosphere at the trial could easily have been avoided since the courtroom and courthouse premises are subject to the control of the court. As we stressed in Estes, the presence of the press at judicial proceedings must be limited when it is apparent that the accused might otherwise be prejudiced or disadvantaged. Bearing in mind the massive pre-trial publicity, the judge should have adopted stricter rules governing the use of the courtroom by newsmen, as Sheppard's counsel requested.

The number of reporters in the courtroom itself could have been limited at the first sign that their presence would disrupt the trial. They certainly should not have been placed inside the bar. Furthermore, the judge should have more closely regulated the conduct of newsmen in the courtroom. For instance, the judge belatedly asked them not to handle and photograph trial exhibits lying on the counsel table during recesses.

Secondly, the court should have insulated the witnesses. All of the newspapers and radio stations apparently interviewed prospective witnesses at will and in many cases, disclosed their testimony. A typical example was the publication of numerous statements by Susan Hayes, before her appearance in court, regarding her love affair with Sheppard. Although the witnesses were barred from the courtroom during the trial the full verbatim testimony was available to them in the press. This completely nullified the judge's imposition of the rule.

Thirdly, the court should have made some effort to control the release of leads, information, and gossip to the press by police officers, witnesses, and the counsel for both sides. Much of the information thus disclosed was inaccurate, leading to groundless rumors and confusion. That the judge was aware of his responsibility in this respect may be seen from his warning to Steve Sheppard, the accused's brother, who had apparently made public statements in an attempt to discredit testimony for the prosecution.

Defense counsel immediately brought to the Court's attention the tremendous amount of publicity in the Cleveland *Press* that "misrepresented entirely the testimony" in the case. Under such circumstances, the judge should have at least warned the newspapers to check the accuracy of their accounts. And it is obvious that the judge should have further sought to alleviate this problem by imposing control over the statements made to news media by counsel, witnesses, and especially the coroner and police officials.

In summation, Justice Clark wrote:

From the cases coming here we note that unfair and prejudicial news comment on pending trials has become increasingly prevalent. Due process requires that the accused receive a trial free from outside influence. Given the pervasiveness of modern communications and the difficulty of effacing prejudicial publicity from the minds of the jurors, trial courts must take strong measures to ensure that the balance is never weighed against the accused. And appellate tribunals have the duty to make an independent evaluation of the circumstances.

Of course, there is nothing that prescribes the press from reporting events that transpire in the courtroom. But where there is a reasonable likelihood that prejudicial news prior to the trial will prevent a fair trial, the judge should continue the case until the threat abates, or transfer it to another county not so permeated with publicity.

In addition, sequestration of the jury was something the judge should have raised sua sponte with counsel. Ohio has now adopted the requirement that juries in capital cases be sequestrated during the proceedings without motion from defense counsel, apparently as a result of the Sheppard experience. If publicity during the proceedings threatens fairness of the trial a new trial should be ordered.

But we must remember that reversals are but palliatives; the cure lies in those remedial measures that will prevent prejudice at its inception. The courts must take such steps by rule and regulation that will protect their processes from prejudicial outside interferences. Neither prosecutors, counsel for the defense, the accused, witnesses, court staff, nor enforcement officers coming under the jurisdiction of the court should be permitted to frustrate its function. Collaboration between counsel and the press as to information affecting the fairness of a criminal trial is not only subject to regulation, but is highly censurable and worthy of disciplinary measures.

Since the state trial judge did not fulfill his duty to protect Sheppard from the inherently prejudicial publicity which saturated the community and to control disruptive influences in the courtroom, we must reverse the denial of the habeas corpus petition.

Newspapers around the country hailed the Supreme Court decision in their editorials, "The Sheppard case has long been one of the scandals of American jurisprudence," said the influential *New York Times*. "A complaisant judge, irresponsible police officials and a sensationalist press combined to turn the trial of Dr. Samuel H. Sheppard, accused of murdering his wife in 1954, into a latter day Roman circus. The Supreme Court has rectified that injustice by ordering the trial verdict set aside."

The Washington *Post* called my trial, ". . . altogether incompatible with civilized standards of justice. It is a monstrous misfortune that the incongruity of this trial was not authoritatively recognized years ago. . . . The proceeding has remained a reproach to American justice."

"To put it mildly," said the Louisville *Courier-Journal,* "the U. S. press did not distinguish itself by fairness or moderation during the months preceding and during the trial."

The Akron *Beacon-Journal* said, "The U. S. Supreme Court has ruled that Dr. Sam Sheppard did not get a fair trial and we can't say we are surprised. When U. S. District Judge Carl Weinman held to the same effect, two years ago, his opinion was so convincing that we predicted that in the end it would prevail."

As might be expected, the Cleveland papers were less than enthusiastic. "Zealously guarding a defendant's right to a fair trial," said the Cleveland *Plain Dealer,* "the U. S. Supreme Court has narrowed the field open to the free press. These justices accepted some unfortunately weak evidence and agreed with the defense's version . . . that it was a hippodrome of news coverage . . . but the public has an important stake here, too. No rule should allow judges to control or gag the only voice of criticism the public can count on to lay open perversions of justice."

And the Cleveland *Press* editorialized:

As for the role publicity played in the Sheppard case, The *Press* cannot, of course, speak for all the newspapers and radio and television stations whose actions came under the critical scrutiny of the court.

But it certainly is pertinent to recall the fantastic public interest this case generated, not only here but throughout the world.

The *Press's* news coverage reflected this interest.

And its editorials were critical of police work which seemed for a time, to be confused and inert.

If there were excesses, as the court contends, they should be viewed against the circumstances of a case which, as the *Press* once said editorially, became "too much a part of our lives."

It was to discuss the Cleveland *Press* and other developments in the case that Lee Bailey flew to Cleveland that Monday night after the Supreme Court had spoken. He was picked up at the airport by Steve and taken to his home for an important strategy meeting. It was after dark by the time Ariane and I arrived.

Back in August, 1964, about a month after my release, Bailey had written a letter to Louis B. Selzer, then editor of the Cleveland

Press. A copy of the letter was obtained later by a suburban newspaper, *The Sun Press,* and published:

This is to advise that claim is hereby made against you by my client, Dr. Samuel H. Sheppard, for damages suffered by him as a result of your misconduct and that of the *Press.* The damages were occasioned by gross defamation, and by the deprivation of his civil rights to a fair trial which arose directly from your interference with legal processes in the case of State v. Sheppard, Cuyahoga County Common Pleas, 1954. A further claim for malicious prosecution will ripen when this case is finally resolved in Dr. Sheppard's favor through the failure of the County to try him again, and will be presented at that time.

The letter further said in part:

By your callow and ruthless acts, you robbed Dr. Sheppard and his entire family of each ounce of human dignity you could slice away. You took a man who was immersed in the greatest personal grief, and smothered him in your own brand of muck. You caused, brutally, the death of both of his parents. You stole from him his right to a fair trial in a fair court, and did each thing in your power to cause his conviction, despite his obvious innocence, for the most heinous of crimes, with his life nearly as the prize. You sought, and nearly took, all that this man had. The fair measure of malice of this kind is reciprocal. I now seek as compensation all that you have—and I refer to yourself, the *Press,* and Scripps-Howard. Our *ad damnum,* if suit need be filed, will reflect the net asset value of these three defendants.

You may have your attorneys contact me if you desire. However, to avoid wasting attorneys' valuable time, let me be clear in stating that no offers will be entertained which do not tender both substantial sums— very substantial—and some arrangements for the total vindication of Dr. Sheppard. If this cannot be done through negotiation, we will trust an unpressured jury to see that justice is done.

The nearly two years of litigation which followed that letter had precluded any action on it. But now Lee Bailey was ready to act. He had come to Cleveland, he said to me in Steve's den, to file suit for damages the next morning against the Cleveland *Press.* It was obvious that others in the room, Steve and the lawyer, Russell Sherman, agreed with Lee's plan to sue the newspaper and Louis Selzer, who had retired earlier in the year.

We explored the matter in some depth and then discussed the prospects of a new trial. The decision as to whether or not a retrial would be held was in the lap of John T. Corrigan, the county prosecutor, who was squarely on the spot. Bailey had made it clear as soon as the Supreme Court decision was released that we demanded a new trial so that full vindication could be accomplished. Bailey said at that meeting he was confident we could easily win acquittal.

I raised the question of expenses for a forthcoming trial. Ariane had done so much in the past and my feeling was that it wasn't fair for her to further drain her inheritance to pay my legal expenses. And, Lee had done so much in the past that I couldn't expect him to continue pouring out his own funds for me. Some money could be raised, I said, by selling a portion of the expected royalties from this book. Lee was adamant in advising me against that plan. He told me not to worry about it—that, if need be, he would take care of the expenses, and that we would settle the account when I was completely vindicated and working again as a surgeon. My credit was still good with Lee Bailey.

The meeting lasted into the night. When Ariane and I finally got home, we couldn't sleep. We stayed up the rest of the night talking about the ramifications of the Supreme Court decision and how our loved ones might be affected by a new trial. Later in the morning, we took Lee Bailey to the airport, then settled back to wait again. This time on Prosecutor Corrigan's decision on whether or not there would be a new trial.

Corrigan said he would have a decision before the week was out. He indicated to the press that it was a difficult one to make. Numerous court decisions had been handed down in the years since my conviction, limiting evidence admissible in criminal cases.

There was the problem of availability of witnesses and how much they could remember after twelve years. And, of course, he knew that my case would be much stronger now, especially with the introduction of Dr. Paul Kirk's report, prepared after the Cleveland police had relinquished my home. Even with these problems confronting him, we felt there was little Corrigan could do but put me on trial. To do otherwise, would indicate that he was backing off from Lee Bailey's challenge, indicating that the state was unsure of its case.

Corrigan poured over his law books, conferred with previous witnesses, police and other officials on Tuesday, Wednesday, Thursday and early Friday morning. At mid-morning on Friday, he said his decision would be announced at a press conference in his office at noon. Television and radio stations hurriedly installed cameras and microphones in his office. At noon, the prosecutor began his press conference.

Ariane, Young Sam and I sat in our bedroom, eyes focused intently on a television screen. "I am mindful that this is a government of laws and not of men," Corrigan said clearly, in clipped tones. "In keeping with that principle, I have made a determination that society has been the victim of a most heinous crime and society demands redress.

"However, society also affords to an individual a fair, impartial and objective trial before a jury of his peers and so we will present this case to them for their consideration."

The prosecutor indicated I would be tried on a charge of second degree murder, rather than first degree murder (which carried a possible death sentence) of which the jury acquitted me twelve years before. To retry me on the charge of first degree murder, he reasoned would place me in double jeopardy.

Unlike first degree murder, second degree is a bondable offense, and Corrigan said he would have no objection to my remaining free on a $10,000 bond, prior to and during the new trial, which he said would begin early in the fall.

We flicked off the television set. Ariane and I walked downstairs, opened the front door and sat down on a wrought iron bench in front of the apartment to face again the questions of the ever-present newsmen. A reporter asked me whether I was ready to stand trial again. "I'm ready to go right now," was my reply. "I would be glad if it was tonight, or even this afternoon."

In answer to a question as to whether or not I would take the witness stand in the trial, I answered, "You're damn right. I wonder whether it [the case] won't be thrown out of court for lack of evidence before the defense case is presented." I answered questions for twenty minutes, alternately talking and swigging on a bottle of Coke. Then we turned and went into the house for lunch.

A newspaper account of the press conference said that there were few smiles at the session. In many ways it was not a happy moment. Sure, I was anxious for the chance to vindicate myself. But Ariane and I were mindful of the effect a long trial would have on our loved ones—Young Sam, her daughter, Iris, her mother, my brothers, their wives and children. The children were too young to recognize the effect of the first trial. Now they were almost grown up. Young Sam was planning to go to college in the fall. Richard's daughters were to be married.

Most would not be anywhere near the courtroom during the trial, but as relatives of Dr. Sam Sheppard, they could scarcely expect to escape the glare of publicity which would attend the second trial. In my mind, this was a terrible thing for me to impose on the people I loved the most in the world. Could I be worth all this misery? I knew I could take it, but for the sake of my loved ones, my wish was that the trial could be held in private, so they wouldn't have to undergo a psychological beating.

There were many questions to ponder during the summer months as we waited for the start of the new trial. Would there be a change of venue? How could it be kept from becoming another Roman holiday? Who would testify for the state? Would a jury acquit me —as I was confident—and finally put an end to a nightmare that began on July 4, 1954?

27 &

Lee Bailey wasted little time in beginning preparations for the second trial of the State of Ohio vs. Sam Sheppard. Early in July, the dynamic young attorney, whose case load had grown to include a half dozen of the country's most highly publicized murder cases, flew to Cleveland in his recently acquired twin-engined airplane. He brought with him Andrew J. Tuney, Jr., a handsome detective-lieutenant in the Massachusetts State Police.

Tuney, a slender Bostonian, was considered one of the sharpest homicide investigators in Massachusetts, if not New England. He had headed the now famous "Boston Strangler" bureau, set up by the Massachusetts attorney general when Boston had been terrorized by the strangulation murders of thirteen women. The "Strangler," now languishing in a Massachusetts mental institution, had retained Bailey as his lawyer. Bailey was attempting to induce Tuney to resign his official position and work with him on homicide trials across the country, in which he was rapidly becoming involved. The first trial on Bailey's busy schedule was mine, and Tuney was being given a look at the other side of the coin—the defense.

During a meeting with Bailey, Tuney and other members of my family, we discussed the evidence that had been presented at the first trial and the length of time it would require to go through it again. Bailey said he envisioned a rather swift trial that would take nowhere near as long as the ten-week proceeding that resulted in my original conviction.

"More than half of what was brought out in the 1954 trial was patently inadmissible as evidence," the attorney said as we began our conference. "And half of that which *was* admissible was irrelevant nonsense. We are going to distill the evidence into one tight lump that will show beyond question that somebody murdered Marilyn—and that's all it will show. That's all it ever did show."

"It's all right with me," I replied, "but if that is so, I should get the directed verdict Chief Justice Taft said I was entitled to twelve years ago. Why should the State bring this case to trial again if they are going to get thrown out of court on their ear?"

"Sam," Bailey said with a wry smile," it's not that simple. "Just because you are entitled to legal exoneration doesn't mean you are going to get it, as you know too well by now. There are several things we may be facing. "First, Corrigan has given no promise or opinion to his constituents that you will be convicted, so perhaps he is just going through the motions to show that he tried. Second, finding a judge who has the sheer guts to throw this case out of court and into the face of the Cleveland press is going to be difficult, unless we can force the case outside of Cleveland. And third, the prosecution may invoke its 'desperation kit.'"

"What the hell is a 'desperation kit'?" I asked.

"It's an old chestnut sometimes used by prosecutors who can't make out a case any other way," Bailey explained. "The prisons are combed until some psychopathic scum wearing a human skin is found who will come into court and swear that you had admitted to him that you killed your wife."

There was a sinking feeling in my stomach. It never occurred to me that any prosecutor would go this far, and I demanded to know how they could do it in my case.

"You know damned well I never said anything of the kind to any- one," I said. "You know that some of the convicts tried to get a confession from me years ago while I was under sodium pentothal during an operation and came away convinced that I was innocent."

"Of course, I know it," Lee snapped impatiently, "and every in- mate in both penitentiaries knows that you are innocent. Nonethe- less, it is a possibility and one I want you to keep in mind. Testi- mony of that sort would rob you of a directed verdict before even the most honest judge, and you have to face that fact."

While I was pondering the unhappy possibility that such evidence might be used against me, Bailey jolted me again. "There are two more things," he said firmly. "First, I may ask you to stay off the witness stand; second, I intend to use this trial to attempt to show who killed Marilyn, and why, even though it may mean throwing some stones you might not want thrown. I want you to understand that."

I was a little confused and asked Bailey to explain his remarks. "Why shouldn't I testify?"

Bailey, never one to mince words, spoke slowly, but firmly. "Sam, you're going to have to face a fact. In Cleveland you're a phenome- non, not a case or a person. You are also the source of a great community guilt. I have never met one adult in five years in Cleveland who didn't have an opinion as to your guilt or innocence, no matter how ignorant he or she might be of the facts in the case. I will meet them for the first time when we go to select a jury—people who *say* they have no opinion. But the feeling is there. It runs deep and it's dangerous.

"If the state doesn't put in a case," he continued, "you would do them a great favor by testifying. Then the jury could find that you were lying, and this would give the state's case greater weight on appeal. No defendant should ever testify unless there is some proof against him. You have told what you know until you are blue in the face. If the jury doesn't buy it as the police give it to them, they won't buy it just because you testify to it. It is something we don't have to decide now, but give it some thought."

I reluctantly agreed to consider the possibility, but was adamant that no stones be thrown at my dead wife, even though facts had been developed over the years that reflected unkindly on Marilyn. It was a position I had taken twelve years before when it had been suggested to me that evidence of this kind might be available which would be helpful to me.

Finally, Bailey shrugged impatiently. "We'll leave it out if you want, Sam. You're the one who has got to go back to prison if you get convicted because you won't let the truth come out. But bear this in mind: If *I* lose your case, I'll stick with it as long as is necessary to set things right. If *you* lose it by overriding my judgment, you're on your own. You wouldn't remove a tumor from my brain if I insisted on telling you how to operate. You're a good doctor, but no lawyer. It's up to you."

I knew Bailey meant what he was saying. I gave him a long look. It was nearly five years since I had first met him. For the first time I noticed the change. His eyes were still bright, but there was gray filling in at the temples, and the facial lines had gotten deeper, due in part, no doubt, to Sam Sheppard. I knew that so far he had always been right in my case, and his expression was dead serious now. Lee Bailey wanted to end this case almost as badly as I.

I glanced over at Andy Tuney, whose experience in such matters had become very apparent in our short acquaintance. I looked at my son, Young Sam, who was sitting with us as we talked. He had loved his mother as much as I had. I could see that he agreed with Lee. No one spoke for a few minutes. Finally I broke the silence.

"I guess you're right," I sighed, feeling very tired—twelve years tired. "You're the doctor. Cut wherever you have to, if you have to. I guess Marilyn knows I tried it the other way."

The meeting broke up and Bailey and Tuney returned to Boston to continue preparations for the trial. Bailey and Tuney flew across the country interviewing witnesses who had testified for me in 1954. They found Dr. Charles Elkins, the neurologist who had determined the extent of my injuries, in Tucson, Arizona. They talked in California with Dr. Paul Kirk, whose intensive investigation had proved that someone other than myself had been in Marilyn's room on the night of the murder. Meanwhile, Bailey's staff in Boston began boiling down the seven thousand pages of testimony into the essential facts, indexing and cross-indexing every important name and point.

Ariane and I began to review my testimony and all the evidence that had appeared. It was not a pleasant task. It was more like plunging back into a nightmare. There were times when I couldn't force myself to think about the case at all. However, little by little the pieces began to fall back into place, some of them more clearly than before.

Suddenly, it was September and on the eighth of the month I was arraigned before Common Pleas Judge Roy McMahon, in the same courtroom where the original trial had been held. It was obvious that Cleveland's appetite had diminished very little in twelve years, for there was a throng of newsmen awaiting me when I arrived. But there was a difference—a very great difference—in the way they acted.

Judge McMahon had issued an order which, in unmistakably clear terms, limited the activities of the press corps. He ordered them not to interview the parties or counsel. He barred cameras and recording devices from the courtroom. The proceeding itself was a picture of decorum, and took only a few minutes.

"How do you plead, guilty or not guilty?" Judge McMahon asked as I stood before the same bench where another judge, Edward Blythin, had sentenced me to life imprisonment nearly a dozen years before. "Not guilty," I shouted loudly. Judge McMahon reset bond at $10,000, and although he did not set a definite date for the start of my second trial he promised it would be soon.

As Ariane, Young Sam, Lee Bailey and I left the courtroom,

newsmen asked why I shouted "not guilty" before Judge McMahon. "I've always said it that loud, but nobody would listen," was my reply.

Three weeks later, it was announced that the trial had been assigned to Judge Francis J. Talty, one of the most junior jurists sitting in the Common Pleas Court. Local newspapers ran stories recapping his background as well as his curt statement: "The Sheppard case will be tried like any other lawsuit."

Lee Bailey began his own quiet probe into Judge Talty's background. He had told me many times a great deal would depend on the man who presided at my trial.

"Just give me a good, solid, courageous judge, Sam," he had said, "a man cast in the mold of Carl Weinman, and I'll give you an acquittal so spanking clean that the world will hang its head in shame for the time that has been stolen from you."

Our first move before Judge Talty was to argue for a change of venue, on the grounds that because of the fantastic publicity the case had attracted in the Cleveland area it was impossible to get a fair trial in Cuyahoga County. Lee Bailey and Russell Sherman appeared before Judge Talty on Wednesday, October 12th, and argued that the trial be held in a locale other than Cleveland. To substantiate their arguments, the two attorneys filed as exhibits huge scrapbooks of clippings from 1954, and several issues of the Cleveland *Press* from January, 1966, which carried a series of articles containing vigorous statements from members of the first jury, who insisted that I was guilty. The trial was scheduled to start on Tuesday, October 18th, and Judge Talty took the matter under advisement, saying he would have a decision on the motion in two days.

Later that day, Steve, Lee and I conferred. "Let me tell you what I know about your judge," Bailey said as we sipped some coffee. "I have information from several sources, but more important I have met him and looked him in the eye. You never know enough about any man until you look him in the eye. Brother Talty has a good eye.

"As a matter of fact," Bailey went on, "just about everything I have learned so far is good. He is reputed to be a strong man, one who takes no nonsense. He knows the law, or enough of it to grasp quickly that which he doesn't know. And he intends to give you a fair trial. That's about all you could possibly hope for in this city, and maybe a little bit more."

"I take it," said Steve dryly, "that your Ouija board discloses that there will be no change of venue, no matter what happens."

"That is the word of the Ouija," said Bailey, his eyes twinkling. "I can't say that Judge Talty knows how he's going to rule—he may well still have an open mind, or think that he does. But I know how he's going to rule, and you can count on it."

"Why is that," I asked.

"Because this man has the blood of an advocate," Bailey replied, "and if I don't know much else, I know how that blood runs. Judge Francis Talty is going to do just what I would do if I were in his shoes. The gauntlet has been thrown down. We have said that even *he* can't get you a fair trial in Cleveland. His answer is 'I sure as hell can, and I will.' His reaction is no different than mine was five years ago when all the wise old lawyers told me your case was hopeless. Sometimes I think stuck with it just because they said it couldn't be done. Your judge is just as stubborn, I think. You watch."

On Friday of that week, Judge Talty said he would defer making a final ruling on the matter of a change of venue until the process of jury selection was attempted. The trial, he said, would proceed in Cuyahoga County, although he deferred the starting date until October 24th.

Ouija was right.

28

The dingy gray building that housed Cuyhoga County's criminal court was all too familiar. The barred floors above the courtrooms had been my "home" for the better part of a year when this case began and the memory of what had gone before added to my apprehension as I walked up the steps of the courthouse with Russell Sherman on the morning of October 24th. Once inside the building, we climbed the steps to the second floor and turned down a corridor toward the courtroom of Judge Francis Talty.

I was reminded of another day twelve years and six days before when I approached a courtroom across the hall for the start of my first trial, manacled to a deputy sheriff. I will never forget the sense of degradation I felt then as hordes of news photographers descended on me to record my entrance to the courtroom. This time, the only photographers present were outside the court building.

Judge Talty had stiffened Judge McMahon's original order considerably, ordering all photographers and movie cameramen to stay outside the court building. The jurist also ordered all newsmen not to seek information from counsel, parties or witnesses, and banned just about every quest for information beyond attention to what happened in open court. He also assigned a number of seats to newsmen—this time outside the bar enclosure—and ruled that all others would be admitted by special pass. When he got a look at the order assigning news seats, Bailey merely shook his head.

Of the fourteen seats assigned, only two went to news media outside Cleveland, and these were given to the Associated Press and United Press-International wire services. All the rest were given to newspapers, television stations and radio stations in the local area. Gone were the *Chicago Tribune*, the *New York Times* and just about every other large metropolitan daily that staffed the trial in 1954. Gone were the Considines and the Kilgallens.

"It would appear," Bailey said to me before the start of the trial, "that the people of Cleveland may learn of your acquittal, if and when it comes, but it is doubtful they will ever know how it happened. I have little hope that Cleveland news media, now on the defensive will file objective reports of the proceedings. The U.S. Supreme Court never intended that your case should give trial courts this kind of power and we never asked that it should. I'm going to object to the order." An objection was made before Judge Talty and was immediately overruled.

It occurred to me then, and I continue to wonder about it, that all the mighty proponents of a free press took Judge Talty's order lying down, and with only a few mild whimpers of protest. Although I feel that I was badly abused by irresponsibility and callousness on the part of the news media in this case, I have no doubt that freedom of speech and publication is important to our democratic way of life.

Lee Bailey said, and I believe, that the restrictive order was patently illegal, however well intended. I knew that letters of protest had been written to Judge Talty and even to the Supreme Court of the United States. Yet not one newspaper or radio or TV station appeared with lawyers to fight for the right to hear and report the trial. It seemed very much as though those who were so brave when it came to blackening an individual in print, when he cannot fight back, were somewhat lacking in plain old guts when it came to brass tacks—that is, a lawsuit to enforce their rights.

As I turned into the courtroom that morning, without the eye-searing glare of flash bulbs and strobe lights, it became quite obvious that at least the press would be harnessed in the second trial; that the court proceedings would be conducted with dignity and there would be none of the Roman holiday activity that attended the first trial in 1954. Judge Talty also had laid down strict rules governing the times when reporters could enter and leave the courtroom and I was all for it.

I took my seat at the defense counsel table on the far side of the courtroom, near the windows, which looked out to the west and gave a view of the tall buildings that dot Cleveland's skyline. The view was much better than that of the parking lot that I had looked at for ten weeks in 1954.

I had expected there would be a great deal of psychological trauma associated with the second trial, but I was ill prepared for the mental torment I was undergoing. First, there was an overpowering feeling of loneliness. Young Sam was away at Boston University and Ariane was in Germany, where she had gone a few weeks before the start of the trial to help her mother care for her ailing stepfather. It was as if my two arms had been amputated. I was like a ball team without a cheering section. I just didn't have too much spirit, although I was confident of a favorable outcome of the trial.

Second, I was more aware of what was happening to me than in 1954, when I was totally numb during the proceedings. I had spent ten years behind bars and wanted no part of further incarceration. I had a new wife, had become reunited with my son and family, had a daughter to help and had tasted of the finer things in life after years of doing without them.

The feeling of trauma on that first day was certainly worse than anything I experienced during the first trial, even though there was no chance of my going to the electric chair, as there had been when I was tried on a first degree murder charge. In short, it was just like living hell.

As the prosecution and my lawyers set about to select a jury, I realized that at this point I was the only holdover in the cast of characters assembled in the courtroom on that day. In place of the thin-faced Welshman, Blythin, Judge Talty sat on the bench. A one-time basketball star at John Carroll University, the forty-six-year-old Talty was a handsome, gray-haired former trial lawyer.

Gone were sallow-looking John Mahon, Saul Danaceau and Tom Parrino, prosecutors in the first trial. Replacing them were Prosecutor John T. Corrigan, a rather tall, well-built man with fresh red cheeks, wavy, semi-blond hair, and one glass eye resulting from a World War II injury; and his assistant, Leo Spellacy, who looked much like Corrigan but was a little shorter.

Missing were white-haired William J. Corrigan, his son, Fred Garmone and Arthur Petersilge, my original defense team. They were replaced by youthful F. Lee Bailey and Russell Sherman. Though he was only thirty-three, Bailey, short and somewhat stocky, was an imposing figure in the courtroom. He was impeccably attired in an Eastern-cut suit with the ever-present vest. A gold pocket watch was tucked in a vest pocket. When he spoke, his tone was resonant and the words often eloquent and sure.

In contrast, Russ Sherman was tall and athletic looking. A former football tackle, Sherman had a boyish-looking face topped by a crew cut.

Each prospective juror was questioned at first by John Corrigan, the prosecutor, or Spellacy. Most of those questioned admitted to some familiarity with the case, although a startling number asserted that they had never had expressed any opinion as to my guilt or innocence. When questioned closely on this point by Bailey, several were able to "remember" that perhaps they had made a remark at one time or another. Ultimately, more than half of the prospective jurors were eliminated because of these opinions.

Bailey had objected vehemently to the presence of the jurors already selected during the questioning of those who were trying to qualify. His logic in this objection was simple, and, to my mind, irrefutable. He took the position that simply listening to the questioning procedure, and thereby learning that most of Cleveland had already decided my case without a retrial, was likely to prejudice those who had come with open minds. Although I found much to admire in Judge Talty in the ultimate course of the trial, I found very little excuse for his adamance in refusing to accede to this reasoning.

The judge also refused to allow Bailey to ask each juror who admitted to an opinion just what that opinion was. This seemed odd, too. Bailey felt that if a citizen admitted that he was convinced of my guilt, this would tend to show for the record that any change of venue requested should have been granted. Counsel also felt that if a citizen indicated that he felt, from what he had heard of the case, that I was innocent he should remain on the panel so long as he would agree that if evidence presented in open court was persuasive, his opinion would not prevent him from voting to convict. After all, the law said I was presumed innocent, and it appeared to me no ground of disqualification that a prospective juror should agree with the law. But because of Judge Talty's ruling, we had to challenge every juror who evinced an opinion about the case, with no way of knowing what that opinion happened to be.

There was one exception. A Polish gentleman named Supkovich was being interrogated as a possible alternate juror, and he stated quite frankly that he had entertained an opinion as to my guilt for some time. The prosecution got him to say that he could lay his opinion aside and decide the case on the evidence. He was then passed for cause.

Bailey had been using a question that skirted the ruling of Judge Talty and nonetheless gave us some indication—by the way in which it was answered—as to which way the prospective juror's opinion was leaning. He would ask: "Does the opinion you have had cause you to have difficulty in according Dr. Sheppard the presumption of innocence to which he is entitled?" At the same time, he would stand behind my chair, his hand on my shoulder, forcing the juror to look at both of us. It helped to weed out some of those who had professed the ability to overcome twelve years of prejudice.

When Bailey asked this question of Mr. Supkovich, the reply was: "I have no doubt of it!" I wanted to run up and shake Supkovich's hand. Corrigan challenged for cause, on the grounds that Supkovich was prejudiced in my favor. To my astonishment, I heard Bailey say, "The defense joins in the challenge." I later asked why.

"Just tactics, Sam," he said, "tactics pure and simple. I knew Corrigan would get rid of him with a peremptory challenge if necessary. As long as we had to lose him, it might as well appear that we want unbiased jurors, not those loaded in our favor. We demonstrated our fairness by agreeing to excuse him. I hated to lose him as much as you did, but if he had to go, at least we salvaged something in the process."

One man said he had indeed harbored an opinion before and during the first trial and that he had read and believed in the Cleveland press. However, he asserted that after the first trial smoke had cleared and he was able to view the entire matter in retrospect, his opinion had changed. This was as much as he was allowed to say.

Bailey liked him and passed him for cause. Russ Sherman had some doubts and I was uncertain myself. We debated closely as to whether he would be struck by a defense peremptory challenge. Some day I must look him up and find out how he really felt. Perhaps he would have been a good juror—a very good juror. Choosing jurors is such a chancey affair.

An elderly lady named Mrs. Grodjinski, who proudly announced that she was a great-grandmother, broke up the courtroom when Corrrigan asked her whether she knew personally any of the principals, including Judge Talty. She beamed and turned toward the bench. "I never met the judge," she declared, "but I sure voted for him." The judge blushed, then smiled. He had run a very strict court since the empaneling began, but he was hardly in any position to land on Mrs. Grodjinski. He muttered a soft "Thank you," and order was restored.

When Bailey examined her he stood close to the chair in which she sat, asking a few simple questions. He had already decided to accept her. Then, when no question was before her, she leaned over and whispered in a voice most could hear, "I don't know

whether or not I'm really qualified to be on the jury, since I only
went to the eighth grade in school." Bailey flashed a broad smile
and whispered back reassuringly, "Well, Madam, despite your
eighth-grade education you are a very alert lady and certainly a
qualified juror." Judge Talty, obviously without very much enthus-
iasm for his task, gently warned Mrs. Grodjinski that she was not
to volunteer information. The prosecution may have been tempted
to challenge her at this point, but Messrs. Corrigan and Spellacy
were smart enough to know that they would be looked upon as
bullies if they did and would be accused of being afraid to try a
case before a solid, kindly lady. Mrs. Grodjinski stayed.

The sixth juror to be seated was a young, intelligent attractive
blonde named Carol Reese. Her name, of course, prompted the
immediate thought that she might be some relative of Marilyn's,
through marriage. She was not. She was temporarily seated in the
jury box and listened intently and carefully as the other prospective
jurors were questioned. Long before a panel of twelve had been
seated, Bailey told me to enjoy the view of the attractive woman,
since Mrs. Reese was not long to remain. He was right.

The prosecution challenged Mrs. Reese just as fast as they could
when it came time to lodge what are called the peremptory challenges—challenges with no reason shown. At the next recess Bailey
said to Lee Spellacy, with a twinkle in his eye, "I can see that your
boys don't care to fight this out on a man-to-man basis." Spellacy
grinned and answered: "Hell, Lee, we're just trying to help you
keep your attention on the evidence. No sense in burdening you
with attractive young ladies to stare at." A short while later another
pretty young woman qualified, and was quickly challenged by
Corrigan.

One of the jurors indicated in questioning that he was a third-
year student at Cleveland-Marshall Law School. Corrigan queried
him closely, trying to get him to say that he would have difficulty
clearing his mind of law that he knew from his education and
considering only such law as the trial judge should give in his
charge. The student insisted that this would be no problem. Corrigan passed him for cause.

For the first and only time in the entire *voir dire* selection,
Bailey said: "It will not be necessary to question this gentleman;
pass for cause." At the first opportunity, the State challenged
peremptorily. The tactic was obvious. Bailey had indicated that
we would very much like a man on the jury who knew what was

going on, and who would not be easily fooled by legal tricks and maneuvers. The prosecution did not want such a man, and had to get rid of him. I cannot help but think that those jurors who saw this transaction must have begun to understand that we were prepared to present evidence rather than just a smoke screen.

Day after day during the first four days of the trial, it continued to be living hell for me. I was constantly reminded of the first trial and all that went with it, including the horror of being accused of killing someone I loved and the realization of the way Marilyn died. I needed Ariane badly, and I told her so when she called early in the week. She said she would be back before week's end, and she was, arriving after the fourth day of jury selection. I met her at Cleveland Hopkins Airport and so did more than a dozen newsmen. The three weeks she had been gone seemed like an eternity, and it was wonderful to have her back again.

She was in court the next day, and I was a different man. Part of my cheering section was there and it made a difference. We smiled at each other frequently and winked occasionally. We spoke to each other without uttering words. While she had been away, I didn't eat or sleep regularly. I guess I was feeling sorry for myself because I was so lonely. Ariane got me back on the right track, and it didn't take long for me to pull my emotions together. I began to hold my head high and have guts. Ariane was a reminder of all the people who had faith in me. She reminded me of Chip, Iris and Marilyn.

It took little more than a week to seat a jury of twelve and two alternates, seven men and seven women. Bailey was in good spirits because we had what he considered to be a good and intelligent jury. He was especially pleased with one of the last selected, a thirty-three-year-old quality control engineer named Ralph Vichill. Bailey felt that one juror with a scientific background would be able to understand some of the complex scientific evidence we had to present and to interpret it for the others if necessary.

The other jurors were William Nicholson, in the advertising business; Carl D. Lindbloom, an agent for the Internal Revenue Service; Russell D. Jefferson and Charles W. Stephens, both letter carriers; Miss Betty Peters, a bookkeeper for a candy and tobacco firm; Arthur Wyckoff, a supervisor with the Federal Reserve Bank; Mrs. Yolanda Cowan, manager of a hosiery department in a shopping center; Michael A. Spinelli, a repair-shop superintendent; Mrs. Norma Koch, Mrs. Francis Grodjinski and Mrs. Sarah K.

March. The alternates were Mrs. Cecile Horneski and Mrs. Marian Pipoly.

With the jury selected, Judge Talty made a final ruling denying a change of venue and ordered the jury sequestered at the Statler Hilton Hotel, for the duration of the trial, the first time in the memory of veteran court observers that this had been done in a second degree murder case in Ohio. Bailey, who had been staying at that hotel, moved to the Hollenden House Hotel. The trial was on.

The first order of business was a trip to the Lake Road house. It had been almost twelve years to the day since I had been in the house, and the thought of making the trip again under the same circumstances as my last visit caused some apprehension. The house held some wonderful memories and one horrible one, too. Once we arrived, there was little time for emotion. Like the jurors and the prosecutors, Bailey was seeing the inside of the home for the first time and kept me busy pointing out significant places— the bedroom where Chip slept during the night of the tragedy, the murder room, where a coat of paint had long since covered the horrendous, blood-spattered walls, the den, and then the stairway to the back.

After the visit, there were opening arguments, in which Bailey eloquently told the jury, "You will be satisfied that Sam Sheppard did not kill his wife and you will have a pretty good idea who did." Then it was on with the testimony. Most of the witnesses who paraded to the stand had appeared at the first trial. However, there were vast differences in the way they were handled, and in some instances, what they had to say.

First to appear for the state was Dr. Lester Adelson, the head pathologist in the coroner's office. He had performed the autopsy on Marilyn. In 1954 Dr. Adelson had been cross-examined by William J. Corrigan for three days. Bailey questioned him for about ten minutes. The fact of homicide was established.

J. Spencer Houk, the former mayor-butcher, now turned automobile salesman, appeared next, followed by his ex-wife Esther. They had divorced in 1962, and Houk had remarried. The line of questioning they faced on cross-examination from Bailey was quite different from anything they had seen before.

Why, Bailey demanded to know of Houk, did he not immediately call the police when he received my early-morning call saying simply, "Spen, get over here quick. I think they've killed Marilyn!" Houk did not immediately call the police. Bailey also posed some other pointed questions: Why did he not take a weapon with him when he came to my aid? Why had he brought his wife, when he did not know who "they" might be, whether "they" were armed and dangrous, or how many "they" were? How had Esther known that Marilyn lay in her bedroom, since I did not mention the fact when they first arrived and before Esther dashed up to the bedroom? Why did they not call the police immediately upon seeing my condition, instead of examining Marilyn first?

The answers given by both Houks were generally vague, with very little explanation offered other than "We never thought about it at the time." When their testimony was completed, Bailey had begun to lay the foundation for what was to become a strong and recurrent defense theme: The investigation had left many important questions unanswered and, worse, many questions unasked.

The "star" witnesses for the State of Ohio during the first trial had been homicide detective Robert Schottke and Coroner Samuel Gerber. Both these men appeared and both contributed very little to the question on trial: Who killed Marilyn Sheppard? Why the two were considered "stars" in 1954 has never been clear to me, but it became apparent now that such status, if it ever existed, had utterly evaporated.

Schottke was a sergeant now, but no longer attached to the homicide bureau. He had made a name for himself early in the investigation for having been courageous enough, within twelve hours of the murder, to accuse me while I lay in a hospital bed of having committed it.

Bailey objected vehemently to evidence of this accusation, on the ground that it was meaningless since it had been denied. But Judge Talty permitted Schottke to relate the event all over again. Up until this point, Bailey's cross-examination had been careful and deliberate, but conducted in a low key. The stocky attorney gave Schottke both barrels.

He had said that he knew what I had told others concerning what had happened and also that he knew I was in the hospital, presumably injured. He had talked to me on the morning of July 4th, and had looked around the house and premises. He had been present when one of the young boys found the blood-smeared watch, ring and key, and had never thought to have them finger-printed immediately upon their discovery.

"Did you realize that Marilyn's killer had probably left prints on those items of jewelry, Mr. Schottke?" Bailey shot out.

Schottke admitted that this was probably true.

"And did you think it important to ascertain just what prints were there before accusing *anyone* of this murder?"

Schottke did not answer at first, then nodded grudgingly.

"Was there some reason that you made no effort to check these prints before you threw an accusation at a man who had just lost his wife and was lying in bed in a hospital?" Bailey demanded to know.

Schottke could furnish no reason. Bailey pressed on now, with fire in his eye.

"Officer Schottke—you knew Sam was in bed with possibly serious injuries. You knew that his neck had been X-rayed. Did you make inquiry as to just how badly he had been hurt?"

Schottke said that he had made no inquiry at all.

"You knew, did you not, that if these injuries were serious beyond the point where they might have been self-inflicted, then Sam could not be guilty?

Schottke conceded that this was so.

"Then it appears, does it not," said Bailey, smoldering with indignation, "that you accused the doctor without troubling yourself to determine whether or not he *could* be the guilty one?"

At first there was no answer. Then Schottke nodded. He left the stand, no hero now, as a man who would recklessly throw out an accusation of murder as just part of the game.

When Coroner Gerber took the stand, he looked uneasy. Much water had passed under the dam since 1954, and Sam Gerber was accountable for a good deal of it. He had shown slides and lectured all over the country about my case, always trying to show why he thought I was guilty. He had written a book with the same objective, but had been unable to publish it. He had always claimed that I had been responsible for Marilyn's murder, but when it looked as if I was going to be released by Judge Weinman in 1964, he wrote a letter to Attorney General Saxbe stating that in his opinion the killing was only manslaughter. And he tried to send me to the electric chair in 1954.

Gerber's testimony was routine. It was much briefer than at the first trial, but there was one startling difference: This time when he was shown Marilyn's blood-soaked pillow, with the so-called "impression" still visible, he simply stated that the impression was of some *object*. Gone was the ridiculous but nonetheless damaging statement that a "surgical instrument" could be seen.

When Bailey rose to cross-examine Dr. Gerber, I noticed a slight smile playing around the corners of his mouth and eyes. He had waited a long time for the opportunity and he was loaded for bear. He reasoned that Corrigan and Spellacy wanted no part of Gerber's "surgical instrument" nonsense, and had told him to omit it. He also felt that with a little goading, Gerber would disregard these instructions. Sure enough, when pressed as to what he really saw in the pillow imprint, the corner burst out: "It looked like a surgical instrument to me."

"Well, now, Dr. Gerber," said Bailey, beaming from ear to ear, "just what kind of surgical instrument do you see here?"

"I'm not sure," replied the aging doctor-lawyer hesitantly.

"Would it be an instrument you yourself have handled?"

"I don't know if I've handled one or not," said Gerber.

"Of course, you have been a surgeon, have you, Doctor?" asked Bailey.

Gerber admitted that he had not.

"Would you by chance have with you at the moment the instrument you say you see?"

The coroner had no instrument with him.

"Do you have such an instrument back at your office?"

Gerber shook his head.

"Have you ever seen such an instrument in any hospital, or medical supply catalogue, or anywhere else, Dr. Gerber?" Bailey asked, bearing down.

"No, not that I can remember," Gerber answered, in his monotonous tone.

"Tell the jury, Doctor, where you have searched for the instrument during the last twelve years."

"Oh, said Gerber, in the most startling admission of the trial, "I have looked all over the United States."

"My goodness," said Bailey, feigning surprise, "then, please, by all means, tell us what you found."

Gerber shook his head sadly. "I didn't find one." Corrigan and Spellacy looked as if they were ready to muzzle their star witness with the blood-smeared pillow. Judge Talty looked amused. He was a trial lawyer for eighteen years and was obviously enjoying Bailey's brilliant and destructive cross-examination.

"Now, Doctor," said Bailey, tightening his voice and staring right through the little coroner, "you know that Sam Sheppard was and is a surgeon, don't you?"

Gerber nodded.

"And you didn't describe this phantom impression as a surgical instrument just to hurt Sam Sheppard's case, did you Doctor? You wouldn't do that, would you?"

"Oh no," said Gerber piously. "Oh no." Just why Sam Gerber did speak of this "instrument," a statement which at the first trial he volunteered on direct examination, he never saw fit to explain. Perhaps this was because neither Corrigan or Spellacy saw fit to ask him.

Bailey then turned to attack Gerber on his personal bias in handling that part of the investigation which he took in charge.

"Did you, Coroner Gerber, tell a young intern about a month before Marilyn Sheppard was murdered that you intended someday to 'get' the Sheppards?"

"Any man who says that is a liar!" Gerber shouted.

"On the day of the murder, didn't Dr. Charles Elkins, a prominent neurologist, tell you that Sam was badly hurt?" Bailey inquired.

"No, he didn't," Gerber retorted.

"Didn't you permit several children to go through the house on the morning of the murder?"

Gerber denied vociferously that this was so.

"Didn't you tell a newspaper reporter within a week of the crime that you were satisfied that the killer was a woman?" Bailey demanded.

Gerber again denied having made such a statement.

We produced a witness to contradict him on each point. Two doctors, a stockbroker, and a newslady testified for the defense, and each swore that Gerber had made the statements as claimed. Thus, the jury was left to consider the credibility of Gerber, on the one hand, against that of the four who said that he had not uttered the truth, on the other. No matter what their final conclusion may have been, it was my opinion that when Gerber left the courtroom this time, his status as a "star" witness was gone.

As the trial moved along and I followed accounts of what I had seen in the courtroom, in the *Press* and the *Plain Dealer* daily, it was obvious to me that those papers were covering some other trial with a defendant of the same name. Prosecution witnesses who testified against me were repeatedly decimated on cross-examination for the way the investigation had been conducted, for sheer incompetence and obvious bias, and for trying so hard to sweat a confession from me that obvious clues pointing to other suspects were trampled underfoot.

Those who had strutted off the stand victorious in 1954 now had little to be proud of, and no proof of anything shown. None of this ever reached print in Cleveland. For all that one could glean from the articles, this was a replay of the same warped record that had spun in 1954.

Once again, it appeared to me that the community was being prepared for the notion that I might get away with something, but that the guilt was there.

Detective Grabowski, the fingerprint expert, appeared and testified that he had found no fingerprints in the house at all. This saved us some trouble, for we had intended to produce him if the state did not. Of great importance was the fact that Grabowski found evidence that many of the surfaces that in the normal household would normally be expected to have fingerprints had been wiped, indicating that someone wanted fingerprints destroyed. Of all possible suspects in the case who would not have to be concerned about having his or her fingerprints found in the home, I was the only one. Bailey made it a telling point in the case—one for which the prosecution never had an answer.

When another detective, Henry Dombrowski, took the stand to offer some photographs and explain what he had done by way of scientific investigation, he spent much time on cross-examination trying to explain why most of the scientific investigation was never done. The murder room had been carefully photographed. None of the blood on the walls was ever typed or tested. The blood-spatter pattern was never reconstructed, and the position of the killer was not ascertained.

To make matters worse, Dmobrowski had not even begun his work until the case was nineteen days old. He attempted to explain this delay, but the long and the short of the matter was that so many bickering agencies had had their fingers in the pie that the sum total of the investigation amounted to very little.

The prosecution was counting heavily on Mary Cowan, Dr. Gerber's assistant and the head of the morgue laboratory. She had found blood stains in various parts of the house; some of them were human. She had examined my watch and Marilyn's, and photographed both of them before the blood stains were wiped away. There had been whispers in the corridors to the effect that the prosecution had some sort of bombshell to dump in our laps, and

Mary Cowan told us—or tried to tell us—what it was.

"What did you observe about the blood on the defendant's watch?" she was asked by Corrigan.

"I saw a spatter," she said, "as if the watch were hit with flying blood." She then flashed a colored transparency on the screen, and pointed out what to her seemed to be little droplets of blood at various points on the rim around the crystal and on the band.

Bailey turned and whispered to Russ Sherman. "This is a switch. Last trial they said the moisture under the crystal got there when Sam was in the lake. Now they point to the blood and show that the watch must have come off his wrist before he was in the lake. Let's watch this one closely—I don't like the shift in the wind."

It was obvious what the prosecution was trying to do with their new theory. If the jury could be convinced that the blood on my watch was in fact "spattered," they might well conclude that it could only have gotten there while I was beating Marilyn, and her blood was flying about the room.

To my mind, the photograph fell far short of showing what the prosecution was trying to read into it. An Mary Cowan admitted on cross-examination, most of the blood on the watch was smeared, and the droplets that appeared might have gotten there in ways other than the "spatter" she claimed. After all, I knew that whoever had removed my watch had torn it from my wrist and had probably done so shortly after knocking me out as I ran up the stairs. Since Marilyn must have been alive when I heard her scream, many of the blows she suffered must have been struck after I had been felled. Assuming that this caused blood to fly around the room—and it is certain that every blow did—the fact that some landed on my watch, wherever it was, didn't prove much.

Nonetheless, it was clear that the prosecution would lean heavily on Miss Cowan's testimony, and her "spatter" theory. I did not know at the time that the prosecution had fallen into a little trap.

Bailey took Miss Cowan through much of the same material that he had used in cross-examining Dombrowski. He emphasized repeatedly that apparently the investigators had all allocated specific tasks to "the other department," as a result of which the important work was never done at all. He drove in especially hard on the blood pattern in the room, and the failure of all concerned to take any serious note of it. Miss Cowan said that she had very little experience with blood-spatter patterns and crime reconstruction, and that she didn't think that they were of great significance in any case. She balked visibly when she was reminded of her claimed ability to diagnose the spatter on my watch and finally admitted that divining the probable source of flying blood was a difficult matter.

She also balked when it came to deciding whether the murderer was right- or left-handed. At first she said that there was no way to tell. Bailey led her carefully through many of the photographs taken by Dr. Kirk. He got her to admit that they in fact fairly represented the murder room as it had appeared when she first saw it. She admitted further that the absence of all blood from the northeast corner of the room could only be interpreted as meaning that whoever beat Marilyn to death was standing at the foot of the bed when doing so. Then, pointing to the large blood spots on the closet door, he got her to agree that these came no doubt from the back swing of whatever weapon was used. Finally, he said to her, "Does it not appear, Miss Cowan, that this weapon was swung in a left-handed arc?"

Mary Cowan's eyes blazed. She was standing only a few feet from me, glaring at Bailey. "It would seem so," she said. The prosecution thus unwillingly adopted a left-handed killer.

When we left the courthouse that afternoon, Russ Sherman looked worried. He queried Lee about the probable weight of the so-called "spatter" on my watch. Bailey looked like a Cheshire cat.

"I rather think, gentlemen," he said, "that the prosecution's bombshell will blow up in their faces. If they had examined that photograph meticulously, they wouldn't have used it. Something very small but there, nonethless, is strong proof that Sam is innocent. We will point to it at an appropriate time."

The State of Ohio rested its case with less evidence than it had in the first trial, and we asked Judge Talty to dismiss the case as insufficient. There was no direct evidence, Bailey said. The circumstantial evidence was not sufficient to point to any killer, and certainly not to me.

Bailey argued the motion for dismissal, quoting the opinion of Ohio Supreme Court Justice Kingsley Taft, who said in 1956 that the State of Ohio had shown with its own evidence that I was innocent. "The prosecution has less evidence now than it had then," said Bailey. "No possible motive is shown, no evidence is submitted which points to the defendant and only the defendant, and he ought not to be required to answer what amounts to a failure of proof. I think that this court has an obligation to discharge him, and I ask Your Honor to so rule, unless and until my opponents are able to recite to Your Honor those facts and circumstances which support a prima facie case of murder again Sam Sheppard."

John Corrigan did not respond to the challenge. He suggested that my stories to officials were inconsistent, and mentioned that my watch was an important piece of evidence, although he did not say why. His entire argument took three minutes and two seconds. My heart fell. It was apparent that he was confident that the judge would rule in his favor, or he would never have been so brief. What would the people of Cleveland think if John Corrigan had permitted the Sheppard case to be thrown out over such token opposition? If he had thought that he could lose the motion, he would have opposed it vigorously and at length. I asked Bailey what he thought of Judge Talty's summary denial of the motion.

He shrugged. "Sam, I don't know. I thought he might grant it. He didn't. He's been more than a good judge so far. I assume he acted the way he believes, and that he has a right to do."

I slept fitfully that night, unable to avoid an uneasiness that the courts of Ohio were still no place for me.

On the following day we opened our evidence. We began with a witness who will not be named in this book. As I have earlier indicated, Bailey insisted that we bring out *all* of the facts, no matter to whom they might point with the finger of suspicion. I objected then, but succumbed to a professional judgment. However, what my lawyer felt must be produced in evidence is one thing. What I decided to use in this book is another. If one or several readers remain unconvinced of my innocence because I have omitted this material, that is a small price to pay. The jury was asked to determine only my guilt, not that of anyone else, no matter how strongly the evidence might point up the true killer. Hopefully, some day another jury will be given an opportunity to say, that the killer of Marilyn Sheppard is known, and is guilty. This is a matter for the future.

Our heaviest reliance was placed upon Dr. Paul Leland Kirk, a fine scientist. As it turned out he was one of the most devastating witnesses Cleveland has ever seen. It took Bailey more than half an hour just to get his background and qualifications into the record. I saw several jurors perk up when he mentioned that he served the United States as one of the developers of the Manhattan

Project," which produced the atomic bomb during World War II.

He began by explaining in considerable detail the techniques used by criminologists in the scientific reconstruction of crimes. He dwelt at length on nature of human blood, explaining how it is grouped, typed, subgrouped; how it flows and dries; how it flies through the air when propelled; and how the direction and velocity can be deduced from study of the spatter.

He then detailed at length his examination of the physical evidence in the case, and particularly his minute examination of the murder room. He had photographed virtually every square inch of that room, and had made meticulous notes of his observations. He had made drawings scaled to a fraction of an inch. Looking for an answer to the many questions that the murder of Marilyn Sheppard had posed, he had made tests and experiments with blood that had never been made before. As I listened to his calm, complex, but always lucid testimony, I wished bitterly that the authorities who butchered the investigation of my wife's death had had the services of such a man as Paul Kirk. He was a man with many answers —answers which, once given, seemed to cry with their own simplicity. It is ironic that Dr. Kirk is more often with the prosecution than with the defense, but that is the fact. Unfortunately, when he entered my case the prosecution already had its conviction, and could not stomach his findings no matter how correct they might be.

Once a man is convicted in a highly publicized trial, it is much more important to protect the victory than to let the truth out and admit a mistake. I am convinced that if Dr. Kirk had entered my case at the outset, as he would have if Cleveland had asked him, I would never have been arrested. As it was, he had to strain to get into evidence information that most police investigators would have drooled to have obtained.

I cannot explain with appropriate adjectives just how this evidence flowed from the witness stand to the jury, but it was something to watch. The spectators' section was packed, as usual, but on this day the seats inside the bar were filled with Ohio lawyers who had come to watch this phase of the case. I had often heard Bailey and Andy Tuney discuss the Kirk evidence, and the need to present it smoothly enough so that constant objection would not interrupt and spoil its impact. By this point in the trial, I knew that both Corrigan and Spellacy were astute lawyers who knew their business, and who fully appreciated the destructive effect Dr. Kirk's evidence could have on their case against me. They would be on their feet if a question had the littlest word out of place. Many times I saw them, sometimes in unison, start forward in their seats, ready to rise—then hesitate. Because I had been over this evidence in conference with Lee, Tuney and Dr. Kirk, I had some understanding of what narrow paths in the rules of evidence had to be walked in order to give Dr. Kirk the impact he deserved.

I don't know how well the jury may have understood the tension and the drama that existed between the lawyers as the evidence unfolded, but I saw it, felt it, and often held my breath. Because of the care that had been taken with Dr. Kirk in preparation, and the obvious rapport he enjoyed with the lawyer examining him, his testimony poured in and flooded the position of the State.

He was on the stand the better part of a day. By the time direct examination had been concluded, he had established pretty clearly that: (1) whoever killed Marilyn had stood at the foot of the bed from beginning to end; (2) had used a left-handed swing, the arc of which could be completely resurrected from the blood trail left on the walls and furniture; and (3) had deposited a spot of his or her blood on the closet door, a spot that could not have come from Marilyn or the weapon which beat her to death. Beyond this, Dr. Kirk repeatedly refuted with fact those things that the prosecution had sought to suggest as possible theory. When Bailey turned Dr. Kirk over to the prosecution for cross-examination, he did so with a flourish.

We had talked about possible cross-questions on several occasions, and before Dr. Kirk began his evidence I had wondered out loud how the State might attack him. Bailey grinned at me and said, "Sam, this is the worst kind of expert witness to face. He's at the top of his field, his methods and procedures in arriving at his opinions have been fastidious, and he's an honest and experienced witness. Corrigan has shown himself to be a helluva lawyer. If he really is good, he won't fool long with Dr. Kirk. He'll ask a couple of questions and sit down. Remember, the best cross-examiners are those who know when not to cross-examine.

Corrigan asked Dr. Kirk less than a dozen questions. He sought several times to suggest weakness in Kirk's opinions, and each time was rewarded with a polite, patient and logical answer that strengthened rather than weakened the opinion challenged. Corrigan knew better, as Bailey thought he would, than to continue. He stopped asking questions and sat down.

From this point the testimony moved swiftly. In contrast to the first trial, where the record was cluttered and the jury bored with needless detail and nonsense between the lawyers constantly bickering with one another, the pace was swift. Counsel on both sides pressed on quickly, and to the point.There were few objections, but when they were raised Judge Talty ruled unhesitatingly and decisively. I began to appreciate, as this trial wore on, that this was the way lawsuits ought to be tried.

Dr. Richard Koch, my dentist, testified that he had seen my teeth a short while before the murder and two weeks after. He said that he found two of my teeth to be broken off well into the enamel, and he produced X-ray films to demonstrate—before and after— the damage I had suffered. He also said that my mouth was badly cut. He testified that in his opinion the damage to my teeth could not have been self-inflicted. He was not cross-examined.

Bailey read from the old trial record the testimony of two doctors who were unavailable. One, Dr. Clifford Foster, had examined me on the morning of July 4, 1954, and detailed injuries to the mouth, face and neck. The other, Dr. Gerry Flick (who passed on several years ago), was our radiologist at Bay View and had discovered in his X-ray films a chip fracture in a cervical vertebra in my neck. As he read in Dr. Flick's testimony, I saw Bailey begin to break up. I had forgotten a very humorous few minutes in the 1954 trial.

For reasons I will never understand, Bill Corrigan had begun his direct examination of Dr. Flick by demanding to know what was printed on a certain envelope that Dr. Flick was examining when he took the stand. Dr. Flick avoided answering. Bill Corrigan examined the envelope, and found that the only writing on it was Dr. Flick's name and address. He demanded to know why Dr. Flick needed to refer to an envelope so inscribed in order to respond to a question asking his name. Dr. Flick was evasive.

"Don't you know your own name without looking at the envelope?" Corrigan asked.

"Of course I do," snapped Dr. Flick.

"Then why are you looking at the envelope?" Corrigan insisted.

"Because," Dr. Flick replied, "I like to be careful."

As Lee Bailey read this testimony to the jury, he fought hard to keep a straight face. The colloquy was funny enough as cross-examination, but when it appeared that we were ridiculing our own defense witness, it was impossible to hold down a good belly laugh. A ripple of laughter went through the courtroom, and even Judge Talty could not restrain a puzzled but broad grin.

Although all our witnesses gave good strong accounts of what they knew, I think that none was more helpful than Max Don, a man I had known as a young doctor. Max had been a close assistant, and had filled in for me as police surgeon in Westlake and Bay Village. Frequently at night he would bring X-ray films to my home so that I could examine them, recommend treatment, and come to do emergency surgery if necessary. Max had made it his practice to walk in the Lake Road door, which was unlocked, and stand at the bottom of the stairs calling my name until either Marilyn or I heard him. He knew that anyone who wanted could walk into my house at any time of day or night, and he told the jury so without hesitation. He also had some testimony to give about Dr. Gerber.

It so happened that in June, 1954, two restaurant owners named Coreno had been shot in a holdup in Westlake, and I had removed a bullet from the spine of another. Max had assisted with the surgery. A few days later, one of the Westlake police officers was asked to take a suspect to the Cleveland police station for questioning. Westlake was short-handed, and Max was asked to ride along.

When he got to the Cleveland Homicide Office, Gerber was there. Max had never met him before. Gerber introduced himself, and asked the name of the hospital with which Max was affiliated. Max said that he was on the staff at Bay View.

"Oh, said Gerber, "you're one of the Sheppard clan?"

"Well," replied Max, "if being on the staff of Bay View makes me one of the Sheppard clan, then I guess you're right."

Gerber turned to walk away, and, as he did so, said over his shoulder, "I'm going to get those Sheppards one day."

Then, on the day of the murder, Max had gone to my home after I was brought to the hospital, and had been asked to join in the search for the weapon. He agreed, and with several police officers combed the interior of the house for nearly two hours. Gerber was there the entire time. At one point Max saw a ten-year-old boy approach Gerber and ask if he could go into the house and look around. Gerber smiled his assent, and the youngster scampered inside. It was fun for the boy, but a poor way to protect the evidence.

Later the same morning, Max heard Gerber say to one of his homicide detectives: "It's evident the doctor did this. Go down and get his confession." By virtue of Dr. Don's testimony, Samuel Gerber was shown to be a man of quick judgment, a man who was prepared to designate culprits and assign the taking of confessions even before his inquiry had gotten off the ground. It is small wonder to me that the Supreme Court of the United States has cast a jandiced eye on confessions, if they are this quickly sought by officials.

It was not what Max Don said that was so important, but the way that he said it. Max, a handsome man in his middle thirties, is one of those people whose sincerity and integrity become immediately obvious. What the jury did not know is that Max, now practicing in Oklahoma, was to be the first resident in neurosurgery that Bay View had ever had, and that he was to take over part of my work when he had qualified. If he felt any bitterness because of what he had lost by my arrest and imprisonment, he did not permit it to show on the stand. His polite, attentive, and pleasant manner discouraged cross-examination.

Our last, and certainly one of our most important, pieces of evidence came from Dr. Charles Elkins, the neurologist and neurosurgeon who had been my mentor in the early days of my practice. Although he was a medical doctor, and his colleagues did not favor his giving time to a doctor of osteopathy, he was always ready to advise me in difficult cases. When I was brought to Bay View on the morning of July 4, 1954, there was no other neurologist to examine me for brain or spinal cord damage. Steve called Dr Elkins.

He arrived late in the afternoon, took a brief look at me, and told Steve, Richard and Dad: "He's too sick for an exam now. Let him rest, and I'll check tomorrow." Dr. Elkins did check the following day, and gave me a thorough neurological examination the day after. He found certain involuntary reflexes to be absent, crosschecked his findings with the X-ray, the observations of the nurses and staff, and concluded that I had suffered a bruise of the spinal cord. To corroborate this diagnosis, he gave me another exam thirty days later and by evaluating the gradual improvement, confirmed what he had earlier found.

Again, it was not only the eminence of Dr. Elkins as a top expert in his field that made its impression, but the manner in which he explained why he believed that I had suffered a severe injury to my spinal cord that no layman could see. Juries are frequently forced to rely on expert opinion in litigation, but they are usually more responsive to one that is fully explained and detailed than to one which is hung naked before them without any supporting explanation. I remember Dr. Elkins' testimony in the first trial, and it seemed to me that he was infinitely more persuasive in this one, even though what he said did not change. It must have been persuasive to Corrigan at least, for the State in final argument conceded that I had been hurt.

With the testimony of Dr. Elkins, Bailey rested my case. It was Monday, November 14th. It was the beginning of the fourth week. The State offered rebuttal.

First to appear was Jerome Poelking, a lieutenant in the Cleveland police, who had dusted the bedroom for fingerprints. He pointed to the blood spot that Dr. Kirk had said came from someone other than Marilyn or myself, and said that he had brushed fingerprint powder over it in the course of his work. Bailey went to the bench to protest the evidence as irrelevant. He said: "The defense objects unless our opponents represent that the presence of fingerprint powder on dried blood might in some way affect grouping tests." This was a trap by Bailey and the prosecution bit. This is not to say that they hadn't such evidence in mind or Poelking never would have been called, but because of the commitment extracted from them by this objection there was no way to back down thereafter.

Next to be called was Dr. Roger Marsters. He was a blood expert who had contradicted Dr. Kirk in 1955, when our motion for new trial was heard, and Bailey had been waiting for him. He was to be used as the vehicle for two defense bombshells, although I am sure he didn't know it when he took the witness stand.

In a relaxed position, he outlined his qualifications, then gave opinions about the subgrouping of dried blood which suggested that Dr. Kirk could not have told the difference between Marilyn's blood and any other type O blood he might have found. This of course, had been the critical point in Dr. Kirk's testimony, because a stranger's blood on the door proved the presence of a third person in the room. Bailey stood to cross-examine, and the tell-tale smile told me that he had some aces tucked away somewhere.

"You have some substantial experience with grouping whole blood, Dr. Marsters, have you not?"

"Yes, I do," replied Marsters.

"And prior to your participation in this case in 1955, had you ever tried to group dried blood, Doctor?" Bailey shot out.

There was no answer for a moment. Then Marsters said, softly, "As a matter of fact, no." I saw this admission hit the jury, and hit hard. Dr. Marsters' inexperience with dried blood, whose typing and grouping problems are very different from those of whole blood, became the subject of the next ten minutes' inquisition.

Having settled that matter, Bailey turned to a question which the prosecution had omitted to see.

"Dr. Marsters, there has been evidence that the blood spots that Dr. Kirk grouped were at one time dusted with fingerprint powder. Do you have an opinion as to whether or not this might interfere with later attempts to group the blood?"

"Oh yes," replied Marsters, "I think it might substantially interfere or contaminate the blood." No doubt the judge, as well as the other lawyers in the courtroom, thought Bailey a fool for eliciting so damaging a statement when the prosecution had overlooked it entirely.

"You are firm in this opinion, Dr. Marsters?"

"Oh, yes, definitely."

Bailey reached into his outside coat pocket and produced a sheaf of papers which represented an article of some sort.

"Did you, Dr. Marsters, by chance write an article about the deterioration of dried blood?" I saw Corrigan and Spellacy look at each other quizzically, and with obvious concern.

Dr. Marsters slowly recalled that he had written such an article, and had published it in a scientific journal.

"And did you, Dr. Marsters, report in that writing some tests which you made, in depth, in order to determine whether the presence of fingerprint powder would contaminate dried blood?"

Dr. Marsters reacted with hesitation. "Yes, I think I did make tests like that."

"And did you not report, Dr. Marsters, that fingerprint powder does *not* contaminate dried blood?"

Dr. Marsters allowed as how he had reported that fact, based on the tests he had made. Again I saw the jury react.

This was a pretty telling contradiction, but Bailey was not through. He chose Dr. Marsters as the vehicle for exploding the prosecution's "spatter" theory as to my watch. Dr. Marsters had examined the watch for twenty-five minutes, he said, and had noted the spatter. He contradicted Mary Cowan by saying that he noted no smears of any kind on the watch; she had seen several. It was apparent to me that he was acquainted with the spatter theory, and was prepared to back it. Bailey asked that the transparency be projected again, as an aid to his cross-examination. He held the watch in one hand—the watch now clear of all blood—and walked to the screen, where the projection showed.

"Dr. Marsters," he began, "does this photograph fairly represent the watch as it was when you inspected it?"

Marsters said that it did.

"And do you observe that when this photo was taken, at the top of it, the flexible hand is folded back against the back of the watch?"

Dr. Marsters nodded, puzzled.

Bailey continued. He pointed to a couple of blood spots on the *inside* of the band that had not been pointed out before. "And Dr. Marsters, did you notice these spots which could only have hit the watch while the hand was folded as shown?" Dr. Marsters had not. But the bombshell had been turned around. As indicated by these spots, whatever spatter had hit this watch had not struck it when the watch was being worn on a wrist. That was the last we heard of the watch as being proof of my guilt.

On Tuesday, November 15th, we listened to several hours of oratory as Spellacy and Corrigan summed up for the prosecution and Russ Sherman and Lee Bailey delivered a resounding argument on my behalf. Bailey was at his best, as he tore into the State's charges, calling the evidence against me "ten pounds of hogwash in a five-pound bag."

But perhaps he summed it all up with a short anecdote:

"The State of Ohio in this case is just like the woman who was hunting around in the gutter underneath a street light. When a passer-by asked her what she was doing, she said, 'I'm looking for a dollar bill that I dropped in the gutter.'

"'Where did you drop it?' inquired the gentleman, offering to help.

"'Over there,' she said, pointing to a spot fifty feet down the street.

"'Then why aren't you looking over there?' he asked in astonishment.

"'Because,' she replied, 'the light is better over here.'"

The State of Ohio, Bailey told the jury, is just like that lady. Instead of trying honestly to find Marilyn's killer through investigation, they went after me as a matter of convenience. They looked in the one place no killer could be found.

29 &

At 10:45 a.m. on the morning of November 16th, a jury of seven men and five women left their seats and walked slowly and stoically to the stairway that led to the sanctity of the deliberation room. I knew we had proven our case, but I had long ago came to realize that nobody could figure a jury. I had a great deal of faith in this group, because of its innate intelligence, but admit I had no idea what fate this group of men and women had in store for me.

We left the courthouse and went directly to the dining room at the Hollenden House Hotel for lunch. No one ate heartily. Then we went to a sixth-floor hotel room to await a decision. It was a game I had played a dozen times over the past dozen years, but never in the plush surroundings of a modern hotel room. The jurors ate a box lunch in the deliberation room.

I felt slightly relieved when Bailey, who always seems to be on the telephone, received a call from a lawyer friend who said that bookies in Cleveland were quoting six-to-five odds for my acquittal and that the odds in Las Vegas were one hundred-to-five odds for my acquittal.

We spent several hours speculating on what was happening in the jury room. Every minute was a day. Each person in the room, lawyers and friends, had a different version of why it was taking the jury so long to reach a verdict. We went back to the court at 6 p.m. to be present when Judge Talty sent the jurors to a restaurant for dinner.

The jurors were grim as they walked down the steps of the court-house and though he said nothing to me, it was obvious that Lee Bailey was disturbed at what he saw. He conveyed this feeling to a friend after we returned to the hotel. Ariane, Russ Sherman, *New York World Journal* columnist Dick Schaap and I went directly to the restaurant for cocktails and dinner, where we could try to relax for at least an hour and a half, knowing there would be no word from the jury, good or bad. We sat in a corner booth, shielded from the curious by an bank of artificial roses.

By 7:30 p.m., the jurors were back at work, and shortly thereafter we were back in the hotel room to wait, wait, wait. Lee Bailey
went down to the hotel cocktail lounge to pursue his favorite jury-
waiting pastime, slowly sipping scotch for the nerves.

At 9:30 p.m., the telephone rang in the cocktail lounge and the
bartender summoned a nervous Bailey to take a call. Bailey left his
two companions, William Levy and Wallace Exman and strode
briskly to the bar. It was Judge Talty, and he informed Bailey that
the jury had not yet reached a verdict and he planned to send
seven men and five women to the Statler Hilton for the night. Bailey
hung up the phone, called his room and told Russ Sherman to have
me down in the lobby in ten minutes, for a quick trip to the courthouse. Then he turned and told his friends to sit tight, that he was
"putting the jury to bed," and that he'd be back in a few moments
to resume the conversation.

Russ Sherman drove Ariane, Lee Bailey and me to the courthouse.
Outside we were met by the usual crowd of newsmen, photographers, and newsreel cameramen. We walked quickly up the steps
into the courthouse and then up to the second floor to the courtroom.
Lee Bailey went into Judge Talty's chambers for a brief conference
with the judge. Talty shocked Bailey when he notified him that
while we were en route to the courthouse, the jury had sent word
that it had indeed reached a verdict. Lee walked out of the judge's
chambers, took me into the witness room, and told me that it
appeared the jury had a verdict.

"If it goes the wrong way, Sam we'll do whatever we have to do
to keep you from going back to the Ohio Penitentiary," Bailey said
solemnly. I gave him my identification bracelet, my wallet and other
personal effects because I feared that if I was found guilty Judge
Talty might pass sentence immediately. Then we proceeded to the
courtroom. I don't mind saying I was just plain scared because of
the horrible feeling that the verdict might not be favorable.

Judge Talty walked into the courtroom and took his seat at the
bench. The serious looks on the juror' faces as they filed into the
courtroom did not ease my apprehension. It was 10:20 p.m. I was
unaware at that moment that as the jurors took their seats, one of
the men in the back row of the jury box, smiled at Russ Sherman.
The boyish-faced, former football player leaned over and whispered
to Bailey: "Lee, we've got this thing wired." He said nothing to me,
although he was sure that the jury was bringing in a not guilty
verdict. He was sure, he told me later, but he just didn't want to

raise my hopes and then have them crushed because he misread a sign.

"You have caused the following note to be sent to the court," Talty said to the jury.

"We have a verdict," replied Ralph J. Vichell, the General Electric engineer who had been elected foreman of the panel.

"Do you have that verdict?"

Vichell handed the folded note to bailiff Laurence Patrick, who in turn passed it to Judge Talty. I held my breath as he unfolded the paper. Then I closed my eyes, clasped my hands and prayed. I heard Talty say:

"We find the defendnt *not* guilty."

I jumped to my feet and banged my hand on the table. "Sit down," Bailey said. I felt Russ Sherman's firm hand on my shoulder. I sank back into the chair and began to sob.

Two days later Lee gave me, as a souvenir, the gray ball point pen that the twelve jurors had used to sign the final ballot.